Y0-BXR-544

Ordering Anarchy

Ordering Anarchy

Armies and Leaders in
Tacitus' Histories

Rhiannon Ash

Ann Arbor

The University of Michigan Press

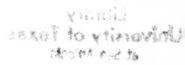

Copyright © 1999 by Rhiannon Ash
All rights reserved
Published in the United States of America by
The University of Michigan Press

2002 2001 2000 1999   4 3 2 1

Library of Congress Cataloging-in-Publication Data applied for

ISBN 0-472-11113-2

Printed in Great Britain

Contents

Preface

I make a prediction (and the omen does not deceive me) that your
Histories will be immortal. (*Epistle* 7.33.1)

So, in AD 107, an admiring Pliny the Younger began a letter to his friend
Tacitus, who was busily engaged in research for a major historical work,
which we now know as the *Histories*. Pliny's prediction, confident
though it was, proved to be only partially correct. Of the original twelve
or fourteen books of the *Histories*, only the first four and a quarter have
survived, thanks to a single eleventh-century manuscript. In these
books, Tacitus narrates the destructive civil wars which flared up in AD
68-9, when four successive claimants, Galba, Otho, Vitellius and
Vespasian, each aspired to become emperor: Nero's suicide, on 9 June
68 (Suetonius *Nero* 57.1), had released quite a storm.[1]

Tacitus' narrative of these events is unique in ancient historiography.
Although Tacitus wrote almost forty years after the civil wars and
originally covered the whole twenty-seven-year period between 69 and
96 (the death of Domitian) in the *Histories*, we know from the surviving
books that the historian devotes considerably more space to the year
and a half of the civil wars than to the twenty-five and a half years
which followed. Originally, perhaps as much as a third of the whole
work narrated a period of less than two years. Even the most extensive
accounts of individual years in Tacitus' final historical work, the *Annals*,
are not on this scale. The distinctive nature of Tacitus' *Histories* becomes even clearer when compared with the other main surviving
accounts for the period, namely (1) the imperial biographies of Suetonius, which were published at least a decade after the *Histories*, (2)
Plutarch's brief biographies, *Galba* and *Otho*, perhaps published before
the *Histories*, (3) a history of the Jewish war published by Josephus
between AD 75 and 79, and (4) Cassius Dio's history of Rome from its
foundation until AD 229 in eighty books, which unfortunately survives
only in epitome before 68 BC and after AD 46. Even though Tacitus'
chronological framework in the *Histories* has caused modern critics to
disagree with one another, the level of detail in the surviving books
remains unparalleled in ancient historiography.

Particularly in the last decade, Roman historiography has become
the focus of sustained critical re-evaluation by modern scholars. Kraus

and Woodman observe succinctly that 'the *form* of a text can contribute as much to its meaning as does its content'.[2] So, suggestive juxtaposition of episodes, pointed allusion to previous writers, selection or omission of material, the allocation of speeches to individual protagonists, and the starting and finishing points of a narrative, can all be used, subtly and cumulatively, to manipulate a reader's interpretations. Arguably, a 'fact' taken from an ancient historical work and divorced from its original context can be likened to a single piece from a shredded photograph: without looking at the rest of the photograph, an observer will naturally have difficulties in understanding the relationship between the fragment of image and the photograph as a whole. Yet even an observer who can see the whole photograph is only getting one possible version of events: if the photographer views the same subject matter from a different angle, the observer can be nudged towards a different interpretation. Lintott has argued that it is 'dangerous to think that matter and method can be easily separated in a historian, so that one can distrust the presentation without having doubts about the facts related'.[3] Thus, we can detect an increasing tendency amongst modern scholars to regard the work of ancient historical writers in a more integrated and literary way. Facts have become less of a focus for discussion than presentation, particularly since the publication of Woodman's *Rhetoric in Classical Historiography* in 1988.[4]

The aim of this book, then, is primarily (though not only) to elucidate Tacitus' techniques as a literary artist in the *Histories*. This work in its own right has generally received much less critical attention than the *Annals*: in recent years[5] the location of battles, the precise troop-movements and the detailed chronology of the civil war have all been reconstructed and evaluated using information drawn from Tacitus' narrative, but this scholarly debate has not enhanced our appreciation of the *Histories* as a literary creation. The reason for this phenomenon lies partly, I suggest, in the subject matter: in the *Histories* Tacitus presents complex portraits, not just of individual generals and emperors, but also of armies, whose collective identities develop distinctively as the narrative progresses. Yet these large groups, whose constituent members fluctuate and change allegiance, are even more challenging for a reader to appreciate than dominant individuals such as the enigmatic Tiberius or the flamboyant Nero from the *Annals*.

My approach is comparative in two senses. First, throughout the book, I draw on the parallel accounts of the 68-9 civil war to clarify what is distinctive about Tacitus' own narrative technique. Second, I open the discussion with three historiographical case studies which investigate the strategies adopted by other prose authors when tackling the characterisation of opposing armies in a civil war. With the ground thus prepared, I turn to analyse Tacitus' ground-breaking depiction of civil war armies in the *Histories*. Drawing on material from the Roman historiographical tradition and from Flavian epic, I explore how Tacitus evokes the ethnic identities of Rome's foreign enemies to characterise the civil war armies in a complex and distinctive way. Next, using a series of different analytical techniques, I investigate Tacitus' portraits of Galba, Otho, Vitellius and Vespasian, and of the Flavian general, Antonius Primus. Only the charismatic Primus possesses the necessary leadership skills to control the armies, but Tacitus shows us why there is no room for this talented general in the new Flavian regime after the war. In so doing, Tacitus raises disturbing questions about the victorious Vespasian's methods and reputation. Finally, throughout the book, I introduce a number of analogies from more recent wars: such parallels stem from an approach which is more historical than literary, but the fact that certain patterns and moral dilemmas in civil war recur over the centuries may clarify why this part of the *Histories*, at least, has fulfilled Pliny's enthusiastic prophecy of immortality and continues to be read today.

University College   Rhiannon Ash
London

Acknowledgements

So many different people have helped to make this book a reality. It was the prospect of having my undergraduate tutor, Chris Pelling, as a supervisor, which originally lured me away from Medieval Latin at the University of Toronto and back to Oxford to undertake research on Tacitus. Chris Pelling constantly provided cheerful support and advice, even when he was on research leave himself, and for that I offer him my fondest thanks. I am also extremely grateful for the help and support of Tony Woodman and Michael Winterbottom, who both read large sections of my thesis and made many helpful comments.

Most of my research was carried out at St Hugh's College, Oxford, where I was awarded a Centenary Scholarship. My thanks are also due to the Oxford University Craven Committee for awarding me a Derby Scholarship and to the Deutscher Akademischer Austauschdienst, who between them enabled me to spend a valuable term at the University of Tübingen. My D. Phil. thesis was examined by Miriam Griffin and Chris Kraus, who helped to shape my thoughts in all sorts of ways as the thesis became a book. This process was greatly enhanced by a British Academy Postdoctoral Fellowship held at St Hilda's College, Oxford from 1996-97. This college offered a wonderful environment in which to work, particularly since my Classical colleagues were Barbara Levick, who taught me as an undergraduate for the Tacitus and Tiberius special subject, and Doreen Innes. Since 1997 I have been lecturing at University College London, and I appreciate the kindness and generosity of all my new colleagues in London, who have made me feel so at home.

I am very grateful to Susanna Morton Braund, and to all at Duckworth, especially my editor Deborah Blake. Finally, I want to offer my warmest thanks to Peter Derow, Michael Comber, Paula Sage, Christiane Sourvinou-Inwood, Tom Tarver, Oliver Taplin, Roland Mayer, George and Pat Cawkwell, Tom Harrison, Bruce Gibson, Mark Pobjoy, Ben Tipping, Aletta Ritchie, Claudia Jessop, David Mackie, Andrew Mein, Llewelyn Morgan, Andrea Swinton, Neil Reynolds, Richard Steadman-Jones, Jon Hesk, Brenda Assael, Mike Senior, Gillian Hickman and Nancy Silver. Last but not least, I send out thanks for help and support to all of the Ashes and Joneses, especially Elanwy, David (Ash), Tom, Robin, David (Jones), Hazel, Jan, Irene and finally to Carl, who sadly is no longer here to read a book which I hope he would have enjoyed.

Introduction

The art of characterising any army in a meaningful way presented ancient writers with a challenge. It was less simple, perhaps even less necessary, to reconstruct the motives and desires of a group than to do the same for an individual. Even if the result of collective action was clear, the dynamics within a group which brought about this particular outcome could prove elusive for a historian. This problem was particularly acute if a work was being composed many years after an event, when the principal eye-witnesses were dead or difficult to track down. Conspicuous individuals, who left convenient memoirs, were so much more accessible for investigation than anonymous groups, who had long since dispersed. Certainly, ancient biography was very different from its modern counterpart,[1] but there is perhaps an even wider gulf between the works of writers such as Le Bon (the 'founding father of modern crowd psychology'),[2] who regarded collective behaviour as a subject worthy of separate analysis, and ancient writers, who tended to treat collective behaviour as a component of a broad historical narrative.

Of course, a distinction must be made between the notion of the 'crowd', often perceived as a disruptive group who assembled menacingly in times of political upheaval, and the 'army', which was (ideally) a more organised group, with its own rules and code of behaviour. Yet it also mattered *which* army a writer was examining. War tends to polarise moral categories sharply, particularly during the conflict itself: one's own soldiers are portrayed as heroes, fighting for a just cause, but the enemy is characterised as evil, and their individual personalities and concerns are masked behind a conveniently negative construction of their national character. One important theory of war (the 'just war' theory) sought to establish the rule that the good of the aims to be achieved by a war must outweigh the evils of destruction wrought in the conflict.[3] However, this concept of the 'just war' could easily be misappropriated, since negative images of the enemy help to add weight to one side of the equation: if the opponent is perceived to be sufficiently evil, then extreme measures become justified in ridding the world of the enemy's presence.

If anything, characterising civil war armies involved an even wider range of complex moral and artistic challenges. Civil war, by its very

nature, tends to force civilian onlookers to revise the assumption that
one side is good and the other evil, partly because such conflicts are
usually fought at home rather than abroad. Heroising either faction is
more difficult when the reality of slaughter is so tangible.[4] Soldiers of
the same nationality who fight on different sides can become hard to
differentiate in moral terms.[5] No longer can we resort to straightforward polarities, which develop the basic assumption that the domestic
side is good and the foreign side evil. This is not to say that ancient
narratives of foreign wars naively present heroes and villains along
national lines. Thus Virgil famously presents the conflict between
Trojans and Italians in the second half of the *Aeneid* in terms which
recall the later civil wars between Caesar and Pompey, and between
Octavian and Antony. Virgil provokes his readers to critical perplexity
about what (if anything) differentiates Aeneas and Turnus.[6] Likewise,
the Athenians are beginning to look distinctly barbarian at the end of
Herodotus' *Histories*, which leaves disorientated readers having to
modify their prejudices, rather than being reassured by the reinforce-
ment of national stereotypes.[7]

However, partisan writers could still try to demonise one side in a
civil conflict, much as in a foreign war,[8] and this phenomenon meant
that the historian had to exercise delicate judgment when sifting
through source material. The task of maintaining a neutral stance was
even more difficult when a writer confronted a society anxious not to
reopen old wounds. Those who had lost, but survived, were unlikely to
appreciate an attempt to reconstruct painful episodes, which could have
direct repercussions on their new lives; and the victors might not resist
the temptation to idealise their own cause, thereby suggesting
retrospectively that their success was inevitable. The historian's usual
teleological problem of knowing the winning side while attempting
balanced analysis was accentuated when the victors still needed to
legitimise their new regime. If the civil war had taken place recently, it
could be dangerous even to attempt to reconstruct the viewpoint of the
losers when the victors were still in power. If the civil war had happened
long ago, it was difficult to maintain a neutral stance under the cumulative weight of historical tradition.

Even if a writer successfully tackled these wider issues, there were
other pitfalls. In civil war, different groups on the same side often fight
for different reasons, so that a single cause can conceal a whole range
of disparate motives. Even the process of declaring war tends to be less
organised than in a foreign conflict, where an individual does not have
to choose sides (short of deserting to the enemy). Escalation, rather
than a deliberate declaration of war, typifies civil conflict, which makes
untangling the moral issues particularly challenging: thus, initiators of
a civil war may have different motives from later adherents. In the
context of a discussion on intervention, Walzer sums up the complexi-

ties of civil war: 'More often history presents a tangle of parties and factions, each claiming to speak for an entire community, fighting with one another, drawing outside powers into the struggle in secret, or at least unacknowledged ways.'[9] Writers who faced the task of presenting this anarchy in an orderly framework had to develop organisational strategies which would prevent a reader from getting lost in a kaleidoscopic narrative. Of course, Tacitus had to present, not two, but four civil war armies, some of which metamorphosed from earlier forces and contained the same soldiers fighting for a new imperial candidate. Even when the Galbians and Othonians were clashing in Rome, the Vitellian and Flavian movements were gradually gaining momentum in the provinces, so Tacitus could not afford to construct a narrative which was too compartmentalised.

The main purpose of this book will be to analyse how Tacitus in the *Histories* responds to such distinctive problems of narrating civil war, particularly in his characterisation of leaders and soldiers. However, as a prelude to this study, we will first examine some techniques of characterisation adopted by other ancient prose authors in depicting armies in the context of civil war. This initial survey will inevitably be selective, but the analysis should offer a yardstick against which to measure Tacitus' account of leaders and soldiers in the civil war in 68-9. The spotlight will fall on authors (both Greek and Roman) from different eras who had sharply contrasting perspectives and levels of experience, but who all narrate civil wars: studies of Julius Caesar (100–44 BC), Appian (c. AD 95–160s) and Cassius Dio (c. AD 164 – after 229) will explore the range of historiographical techniques used by these authors in characterising and constructing the identities of leaders and armies.

1

Images of Leaders and Armies in Civil War Narratives

Julius Caesar

Caesar's *Bellum Civile* narrates the events of the civil war between 49 and 48 BC, culminating in the battle of Pharsalus and Pompey's final defeat. According to some scholars, the work may originally have been written both to provide raw material for other historians and to preserve Caesar's own version of events for posterity, even if the narrative was never finished or was overtaken by events. Critics have disagreed about the extent to which the *BC* should be characterised as a work of propaganda. Thus, Hammond argues that 'Caesar's way of describing a civil war is not a uniquely self-interested distortion, but participates in a set of perceptions and political modes of interpretation common to his contemporaries', while Carter advises us to 'be aware of the bias in presentation which is apt to lie beneath the deceptively straightforward surface of the text'.[1] Certainly, the *Bellum Civile* is problematic and unique in extant civil war literature: Tacitus may have benefited from the Flavian dynasty in the years after the civil war, but at least he was not recording events in which he participated personally. My goal in the following survey is not so much to identify strands of propaganda in Caesar's account, but to establish the terms in which the author presented the relationship between himself, as supreme commander, and his own soldiers. Yet two such investigations are not necessarily mutually exclusive, so a focus on the second question may shed some light on the first. Finally, Caesar's characterisation of the enemy Pompeian soldiers will also be examined.

In the first century BC, the phenomenon of continuous military service created unprecedented bonds between generals and soldiers.[2] The remarkable relationship between Caesar and his men is indeed a crucial theme of the *BC*, even if some tense moments, such as the mutiny at Placentia, have been conveniently glossed over.[3] The extraordinary nature of the bond is first suggested when Caesar addresses his troops before setting out for Ariminum. Caesar not only exploits this rhetorical occasion to explain for a wider audience the wrongs which his enemies have done him, particularly in turning Pompey against him, but also articulates his healthy relationship with his troops. Caesar concludes with an exhortation 'to defend from his enemies the reputation and dignity of the commander under whose guidance they have administered the state with unfailing good fortune for nine years, fought many successful battles, and pacified the whole of Germany and Gaul' (*BC* 1.7.7).[4] The Thirteenth Legion responds by pledging to strike back after the wrongs done to their commander and the tribunes. This is an important moment, in that it programmatically establishes the flavour of the relationship between the supreme commander and his men. Caesar treats his soldiers, not as subordinates, but as intelligent individuals who will be able to digest information. We can and perhaps should contrast this moment with a subsequent scene where the Pompeian Domitius lies to his troops, who quickly spot the trick and accuse their general of abandoning them (*BC* 1.19-20). These Pompeians therefore share certain characteristics with the Caesarian troops, and it is their dishonest generals who are presented as being flawed. Moreover, the response of the thirteenth legion to Caesar's address is significant, in that the soldiers are characterised as a unified group, whose respect for their general dominates them all. This will be a pervasive feature of Caesar's narrative: when soldiers act or react, they tend to do so unanimously (cf. *BC* 1.86.2 'all the soldiers began to signal', *BC* 2.42.1 'all the soldiers were panic-stricken', *BC* 3.6.1 'all the soldiers raised a shout' and *BC* 3.74.2 'remorse seized the whole army'). Perhaps it should not surprise us that Caesar, wishing to cast himself in a good light, regularly elides any differences of opinion among his own soldiers. It may reveal more about the nature of collective characterisation of soldiers in previous Roman historiography that Caesar felt able to elide differences in this way without undermining his own credibility. Finally, Caesar does not differentiate between common soldiers and centurions when elucidating the reaction to his speech. Centurions will merit attention as the narrative progresses, but at this early stage, Caesar does not allow the presence of officers to detract from our appreciation of the healthy relationship which exists between himself, as the supreme commander, and his men.[5]

Nevertheless, Caesar does not idealise his soldiers completely, partly because the depiction of unruly behaviour enables him to emphasise his own leadership skills in controlling such a potentially destructive force. When the Pompeians send envoys to him explaining that they are prepared to hand over their commander Domitius and surrender the town of Corfinium, Caesar is worried that his own soldiers might take advantage of the darkness to plunder the place (*BC* 1.21). The danger is averted by surrounding Corfinium and waiting until dawn to orchestrate the surrender. Even so, Caesar still has to protect the inhabitants from the 'abuse and insults of the soldiers' (*BC* 1.23.3). Likewise, there are disturbing undercurrents when Caesar borrows money from the centurions and tribunes and distributes it amongst the soldiers, thus binding both officers and men to him (*BC* 1.39). This suggests that Caesar is not confident in the loyalty of his army and wants to establish a safety-net. Moreover, in a military context, Caesar highlights the tension between his own strategy, which involves blockading the enemy general Afranius, and the demands of his soldiers, who want a pitched battle (*BC* 1.82). Caesar prevails and the Afranians surrender. All these examples indicate that although the Caesarians are remarkably loyal to their supreme commander, they still have the capacity to disobey or to behave violently. In the hands of a lesser general, we must conclude, the military hierarchy might well have deteriorated, and thus Caesar is characterised as a sturdy buffer between order and chaos. This message is reinforced dramatically in the final chapter of book 1: even the defeated soldiers of Petreius and Afranius, on the point of mutiny because they have not been paid, are happy to turn the matter over to Caesar for investigation (*BC* 1.87.3; cf. *BC* 3.59.4). Once again, Caesar averts the spectre of collective violence, which is all the more impressive given that these are enemy troops.

Foucault coined the term 'agonism' to describe a relationship which is 'less of a face-to-face confrontation which paralyzes both sides than a permanent struggle'.[6] Caesar's narrative is punctuated by incidents which suggest that such an agonistic relationship exists between himself and his soldiers. At the same time, it is clear that Caesar is the dominant partner who almost invariably maintains the equilibrium, despite avoiding harsh techniques of military discipline. We do see Caesar on one occasion demoting some standard-bearers (*BC* 3.74.1), who let the army down during the campaign at Dyrrachium (*BC* 3.69.4), but the army is so full of remorse that 'each man imposed even heavier tasks on himself by way of penalty' (*BC* 3.74.2).[7] On the whole, the soldiers are presented as respecting Caesar and being proud to serve under him, so much so that order is maintained and a productive martial fervour is generated on his behalf (cf. *BC* 3.26).

Other commanders are not so successful in checking the impulses of their soldiers, notably Pompey, who decides to fight a pitched battle at Pharsalus 'with the encouragement of all his men' (*BC* 3.86.1). Likewise, Caesar's commander Curio undertakes a battle using remorseful soldiers who have encouraged him to test their valour (*BC* 2.33.1), and the result is disastrous.[8] In both cases, Caesar points to the risks run by a commander who is too influenced by his soldiers' enthusiasm. Certainly, Caesar is exposed to similar pressures, but imposes his own limitations on his ardent troops. So, when during the Ilerda campaign his men complain that the enemy is being allowed to slip from their hands, Caesar carefully selects only the strongest men from his army to cross the River Sicoris (*BC* 1.64.4-5). Thus, despite the universal enthusiasm, Caesar chooses only the troops who are most suited to the task in hand, and once his men catch up with the enemy, he does not allow them to fight immediately because they are tired (*BC* 1.65.2). In this way, Caesar presents himself as allowing his soldiers to express their zeal by action, but in such a manner that they will not come to any harm. He becomes a type of father figure, who is benign, indulgent, but above all, watchful.[9]

Although centurions and tribunes are less prominent in *BC* 1 and 2, perhaps because Caesar wished to establish his own dominance as a commander, the emphasis on high calibre intermediate officers in *BC* 3 is striking.[10] The first shining example is Quintus Fulginius, a principal centurion of the Fourteenth Legion, who is killed during the Ilerda campaign and who attained his post 'by his remarkable valour' (*BC* 1.46.4). We learn nothing from Caesar about his precise role in the battle, but the comment on Fulginius' bravery contrasts with the centurions on the other side, whose deaths are recorded without praise. Next, there are four brave but nameless centurions, who lose their eyes in battle, which suggests the lengths to which they were prepared to go on Caesar's behalf (*BC* 3.53.3. cf. Sallust *Histories* 1.88, L.D. Reynolds, and Plutarch *Sertorius* 4.3). In addition, Caesar highlights the famous Scaeva, whose shield had one hundred and twenty holes in it (*BC* 3.53.4). His selfless heroism, together with Caesar's praise, quickly ensured Scaeva a place in the *exempla* tradition.[11] Less well-known, but equally useful, is Titus Puleo,[12] who leads the fighting 'most bravely' (*BC* 3.67.5). Last but not least, there is Gaius Crastinus, 'a man of remarkable valour' (*BC* 3.91.1; cf. *BC* 3.99.2-3), whose courageous death at Pharsalus is made to cast a glorious light on Caesar.[13] Apart from this array of talented individuals, Caesar also records without embellishment the deaths of other centurions and tribunes: thus, thirty-two unnamed officers are killed at Dyrrachium (*BC* 3.71.1), while thirty 'brave centurions' are lost at Pharsalus (*BC* 3.99.1).[14]

What effect does Caesar gain by highlighting so many heroic officers? Of course, the bravery of these devoted men, who even sacrifice their own lives, suggests that Caesar's appeal as a military leader extends to the officer class as well as to the soldiers. Their selfless devotion offers a commentary on Caesar's calibre as a general, as well as showing that the military hierarchy is functioning excellently. We are meant to notice that Caesar has the respect of those who know the business of war best. Also, the collective character of these loyal centurions enhances the credibility of Caesar's cause in the civil war. If so many officers are prepared to support him to the death, then Caesar must be fighting for the right reasons. Finally, the absence of such figures on the other side must diminish Pompey's stature. Few Pompeian centurions and tribunes are mentioned specifically, and when they are, the context is rarely positive: the centurion Lucius Pupius deserts to Caesar (*BC* 1.13.4) and the tribune Lucius Septimius actually participates in Pompey's murder

(*BC* 3.104.2). We are forced to conclude that Pompey simply does not inspire the same passionate devotion as Caesar, which polarises the two supreme commanders. An ominous note is struck when Caesar generalises about the Pompeian leaders, who rashly presuppose their own victory at Pharsalus and squabble about honours and prizes before they have even won (*BC* 3.83). Such hybris is a marker of complacency and foreshadows a likely defeat. No wonder the Pompeian soldiers could get away with living in such a luxurious camp (*BC* 3.96.1-2; cf. Herodotus 9.80, the Persian camp after Plataea): we are meant to conclude that they were only following their selfish leaders.

What impression does Caesar give us of these common Pompeian soldiers? They are certainly not demons. We see the vulnerable Pompeians being lied to by Domitius, which prompts them to hold a well-organised meeting (*BC* 1.20), and we see them humanely reaching out to the Caesarians, with whom they are temporarily reconciled (*BC* 1.74). The reconciliation is only averted when their commander Petreius intervenes, and in fact many altruistic Pompeians risk their lives by smuggling Caesarian soldiers out of the camp (*BC* 1.76).[15] Caesar notes the discrepancy between the Pompeian soldiers and their war-mongering generals in a speech to Afranius: 'Thus the part played by all ranks has been based on compassion, but the leaders themselves have recoiled from peace' (*BC* 1.85.3; cf. *BC* 3.19.1). Caesar shrewdly casts the enemy soldiers as misguided rather than evil, pinning the blame for their conduct firmly on the Pompeian leaders and thus leaving the door open for the Pompeian rank-and-file to join the Caesarians. This they do at the surrender after Pharsalus, when Caesar goes out of his way to ensure that his own soldiers do not maltreat the Pompeians (*BC* 3.98). So, the Pompeians, as others had done before them, serve as a vehicle for Caesar's clemency.[16]

That said, the Pompeians still wreak havoc in the absence of a strong leader: so the Brundisians are described as being embittered at the wrongs inflicted on them by the Pompeian soldiers (*BC* 1.28.1). Moreover, there are disturbing components in the Pompeian army, namely gladiators (*BC* 1.14.4), as well as slaves and shepherds[17] (*BC* 1.24.2. Cf. *BC* 3.4.4, 3.21.4 and 3.103.1), and large numbers of foreign auxiliaries (*BC* 3.4 and 3.95.3). Pompey himself is said to enjoy a particularly strong reputation 'amongst foreign nations' (*BC* 3.43.3). It is also revealing that on several occasions the Pompeian soldiers are forced to follow their commanders in swearing an oath of loyalty to Pompey (*BC* 1.76.2-3 and 3.13.3). This suggests that their allegiance is precarious, particularly because the devotion of the Caesarians, who swear no such oaths, is unconditional. Only once does Caesar experience problems of loyalty, when two Gaulish knights desert to Pompey, but the incident reinforces the pervasive Roman construction of how foreigners tend to behave:[18] no *Romans* abandon Caesar! In any case, this setback provokes a stirring generalisation: 'For before that time no one, either infantry or cavalry, had changed sides from Caesar to Pompey, though men were deserting every day from Pompey to Caesar' (*BC* 3.61.2). So, in depicting desertion as a one-way street, Caesar reinforces the notion that Pompey's men are temporarily misguided, but have the capacity to choose the better cause in the end. Certainly, he sets up an antithesis between Caesarian and Pompeian, particularly by regularly calling the former 'our men (*nostri*)' and the latter 'Pompeians (*Pompeiani*)'[19] To call Roman troops participating in foreign wars *nostri* was fairly common from the time of Cassius Hemina onwards,[20] so Caesar's formulation may suggest that his own men were more 'Roman' than Pompey's. Yet this opposition between 'Roman' Caesarians and 'non-Roman' Pompeians is not necessarily permanent. According to Caesar, Pompeians can easily become Caesarian soldiers, with few qualms about abandoning their old cause. In any case, Caesar makes it easy for his readers to disapprove of the other side: those who support Pompey are men like Bibulus (surely a suggestive name),[21] who burns to death some sailors and captains (*BC* 3.8.3), and Otacilius Crassus, who treacherously massacres two hundred and twenty Caesarian rookies 'most cruelly and before his eyes' (*BC* 3.28.4) despite a pledge that they would come to no harm. The pleasure gained by Crassus as a spectator here triggers the image of the stereotypical tyrant. This brutality is in obvious contrast, as Carter notes, to Caesar's own humanity which was stressed at the end of the previous chapter.[22]

We can therefore conclude that in general Caesar presents the civil war armies collectively as undifferentiated groups, who have the capacity to do damage, but who are transformed for better or worse by the calibre of their supreme commanders. Yet the Pompeians can still be distinguished from the Caesarians, partly by the sinister presence of an undesirable element in their midst, particularly the gladiators and slaves. In addition, Caesar rarely uses internal focalisation[23] to reveal what different groups within any one army feel: all the soldiers tend to act and to express their feelings as a unit. Furthermore, Caesar's command structure is bolstered by a group of supremely loyal centurions and tribunes, who are prepared to fight to the death for their general, and who thereby offer a positive model of conduct to the Caesarian soldiers. Conversely, the Pompeian soldiers are not supported to the same extent by first-rate centurions and tribunes, and in fact, many Pompeian leaders are motivated by selfish concerns (e.g. *BC* 3.82-3), which cause them to be unreliable in a crisis. Above all, Caesar's dominant personality and shrewd leadership pervade the narrative and influence individual and collective characterisation at every level. Such is the idealised image presented by Caesar in his account, which tends to simplify the moral complexities of civil war outlined at the start of the chapter, masking the self-destructive element behind a palatable façade.

Appian

Appian has always been read with interest as a valuable source of information about a complicated period. So, William Shakespeare, while writing *Antony and Cleopatra* and *Julius Caesar*, consulted the first translation of Appian into English produced in 1578 by William Barker, and Karl Marx wrote in a letter to Engels that he used to read Appian on the Roman Civil Wars in Greek for relaxation.[24] Studies of Appian have recently been flourishing, and critics have expanded the range of questions and approaches being applied to his text.[25] The following discussion will concentrate primarily on Appian *Bella Civilia* 2 (= *Romaica* 14),[26] which covers the years 63-44 BC, and will address some of the same issues about civil war leaders and armies which have been raised in the previous section.

Appian's perspective as a writer dealing with the civil wars is different from Caesar's viewpoint in every respect. Not only was Appian (c. AD 95-160s) temporally removed from the subject-matter, rather than being a principal protagonist, but he also located his account of the civil wars within a larger framework, which outlined the interaction of Rome and particular ethnic groups, rather than constructing a self-contained narrative of the civil war, as Caesar did. Moreover, Appian's chronological scope is conspicuously much broader than Caesar's, moving from the Kings of Rome (*Romaica* 1) to Trajan's war in Arabia in his final book (*Romaica* 24). As far as we can tell, Appian was writing for a cultured Greek-speaking readership, who wanted to understand more about Roman history and institutions, rather than for a Latin-speaking readership whose reaction to the *BC* was politically significant as in the case of Caesar.[27] Hence, Appian offers explanations for potentially unfamiliar terms such as the Roman military eagle, 'the symbol held in highest regard by the Romans' (*BC* 2.62.256). Although Appian was writing when civil war between Romans was dormant, he had still experienced stasis at first hand in Alexandria, his birth-place, as is clear from the dramatic surviving fragment of his autobiography.[28] This background may have given him a special interest in examining the civil wars of the first century BC. Certainly, Appian allocates them a disproportionate amount of space compared with the other narratives in the project as a whole, especially given that his ostensible aim in writing was, as Carter summarises, 'to paint a clearer picture of the relationship of the Romans to the various nations whom they brought under their sway'.[29] This focus recalls the pragmatic historiography of Polybius (c. 200-118 BC), who in his *Histories* likewise seeks to explain the growth of Roman imperial power.[30]

A crucial passage for establishing Appian's general attitude to the relationship between leaders and armies is the following, which discusses the breakdown of military authority during the Perusine War (41-40 BC).

This occurred because the majority of the commanders were unelected, as happens in civil war, and their armies were recruited neither from the register according to ancestral custom, nor to meet any need of their country. Instead of serving the common interest, they served only the men who had enlisted them, and even so not under compulsion of the law, but by private inducements. Nor did they fight against enemies of the state, but against private enemies, nor against foreigners, but against Romans who were their equals in status. All these factors undermined their fear of military discipline. They felt they were not so much serving in the army as lending assistance from personal goodwill and by their own choice, and that their commanders were forced to rely on them to attain their private ends. Desertion, formerly an unpardonable offence for a Roman, was at that time actually rewarded by gifts, and it was practised by both armies *en masse* and by some prominent men, because they considered that changing like for like was not desertion. All parties were alike, and none had been officially condemned as public enemies. The common pretext of the generals, that they were all assisting the interests of their country, made men readier to change sides since they were assisting their country wherever they were. The generals understood this and tolerated it, knowing that they ruled, not by law but by bribes. (Appian *BC* 5.17.68-71, trans. J. Carter)

This biting passage shows the extent to which Appian is prepared to elide the differences between opposing leaders and armies. Self-interested generals all pretend that they are fighting in the interests of their country and thus cannot easily be distinguished from one another, while greedy soldiers are drawn to fight by financial inducements and happily change sides in search of the greatest rewards, displaying a potential mobility which makes the generals shy away from traditional techniques of military discipline. As we saw, Caesar presented the armies as fairly homogeneous groups, who were differentiated largely by the calibre of their leaders, but Appian suggests that the personality of the general was less significant in dictating behaviour than the level of bribes made available to the soldiers. Appian suggests an inversion of the usual military hierarchy, as commanders find themselves at the mercy of their soldiers, rather than *vice versa*.[31] Certainly, Appian is here analysing a period after Caesar's death, but his general assertion that military desertion was a two-way phenomenon contrasts with Caesar's own claim about 48 BC that only Pompey's soldiers changed sides (*BC* 3.61.2): previously, Appian does at least acknowledge that there were Caesarian 'deserters' (*BC* 2.61.252).

One of Appian's main themes is the readiness with which civil war leaders resort to buying off their troops to ensure loyalty: his portrait of Caesar is no exception. The book opens with the general observation that 'in pursuit of his ambition, Caesar was also prodigal beyond his means' (*BC* 2.1.3). The context is civic rather than martial, but plants an important idea in our minds. The text is punctuated by Caesar's distribution of money amongst his soldiers: so, Caesar awards each legionary the substantial sum of 250 drachmae (= 1,000 sestertii) (*BC* 2.29.115),[32] the mutinous soldiers at Placentia have been promised 500 denarii (= 2,000 sestertii) by Caesar as a donative (*BC* 2.47.191), Caesar promises his rebellious soldiers 1,000 drachmae (= 4,000 sestertii) in addition to an unspecified sum which he had pledged after Pharsalus, and after his triumphal procession in Rome 'to each soldier Caesar gave 5,000 denarii (= 20,000 sestertii), to each centurion double that amount, to each military tribune and prefect of cavalry double again' (*BC* 2.102.422). Suetonius puts this figure even higher (*Divus Iulius* 38.1). By such references, Appian modifies Caesar's picture of troops, who are inspired by their supreme commander's charisma.[33] Instead, each soldier is galvanised to fight 'because that is the soldier's code and because they had profited both from the ordinary spoils of war and from Caesar's additional generosity' (*BC* 2.30.117). If, according to Appian, soldiers during the Perusine War are motivated by financial incentives, Caesar's earlier practice of resorting to donatives has given the men a taste for profit.[34] Caesar might have been able to afford impressive grants of money after his profitable campaigns in Gaul, but the impact on military discipline was potentially unsettling.

Appian adds further disturbing notes to his collective portrayal of the Caesarian soldiers. On two occasions, Pompey calls Caesar's men 'beasts' (*BC* 2.61.252 and 2.75.312. cf. Cicero *Fam.* 8.17.2, Plutarch *Caesar* 39.2 and Suetonius *Divus Iulius* 68.2), because of their inhuman ability to endure hunger, but Caesar himself in his own account omits this label (*BC* 3.48), perhaps because it could suggest that his soldiers possess other bestial qualities too.[35] Certainly, Appian is focalising the Caesarians through an enemy, which might make us wary, but Pompey's assessment is corroborated by an authorial statement that Caesar's troops 'resembled wild beasts when it came to battle' (*BC* 2.151.632). In one scene the Caesarians show that they can also be violent outside battle. After their defeat at Dyrrachium, the Caesarians are full of remorse and want to redeem themselves. Caesar is anxious to restore their morale and leads them to Gomphi in Thessaly, which Appian pointedly describes as a 'small town' (*BC* 2.64.267; Cf. Dio 41.51.4). When the people of Gomphi refuse to open their gates, Caesar takes the city by storm and gives it to his army to plunder. The description which follows is provocative. Appian points out that the Caesarian troops 'stuffed themselves endlessly with everything and became disgracefully drunk' (*BC* 2.64.268), which left them vulnerable to a potential attack from Pompey. Both Dio (41.51.4) and Caesar (*BC* 3.80) omit to mention either the feasting or the risk of an enemy assault. Moreover, Appian explicitly refers to the intense sufferings experienced by the people of Gomphi, including the dramatic incident where twenty distinguished elders are discovered with goblets scattered around them. They are lying on the floor 'as if they had succumbed to drunkenness'

(*BC* 2.64.269), but in reality they have committed suicide by poison. The genuine inebriation of Caesar's callous soldiers is poignantly juxtaposed with the apparent drunkenness of these desperate citizens, who have killed themselves to avert a more horrific fate. Again, Dio and Caesar do not include this graphic scene, which perhaps originally appeared in the work of Asinius Pollio, who believed that Caesar 'was either disingenuous or forgetful in describing his own actions' (Suetonius *Divus Iulius* 56.4).[36] The earlier case of Caesar omitting the Placentia mutiny (see p. 5 above) suggests that Pollio may have had a point. Whatever source Appian used for events at Gomphi, the account still illustrates another important concern of the work, namely the ways in which civil war inflicted horrors on an innocent populace. As Gowing has observed of *BC* 5, 'Appian's narrative is not, like Dio's, built entirely around the individual protagonists. On the contrary, he seems equally, if not more interested in elucidating the sheer misery to which the Italian peninsula had been reduced.'[37]

The Caesarians can be particularly menacing, but there are also moments when Appian takes to its logical conclusion the notion that a civil war is an internal conflict between two groups, who share the same national identity. As Pompey and Caesar face each other at Pharsalus with their armies drawn up behind them, Appian makes both men ponder the horror of what is about to happen: 'They were sorry for the ordinary soldiers, for never previously had such large Italian forces met on a single field, and they felt pity for the courage of two armies of outstanding quality, particularly when they saw Italian lined up against Italian' (*BC* 2.77.321).[38] Yet these sentiments come, not from the soldiers themselves, but from the supreme commanders, who temporarily detach themselves from the imminent battle and contemplate the situation, as a narrator might do (cf. Lucan *Pharsalia* 7.385-459). Appian gives precedence to individual rather than collective sentiment in this instance. Dio creates a similar picture, but focalises the feelings of horror through the soldiers rather than through their leaders (41.58), while Plutarch makes some nameless onlookers reflect along these lines (*Pompey* 70.1). Neither Appian nor Dio nor Plutarch in their descriptions of Pharsalus speculate about the different feelings which might have gripped the soldiers, whether on the same or opposite sides. Perhaps this would have been to fragment the striking mirroring effect of this moment, which is more dramatic than detailed characterisation of separate groups would have been. A bird's eye view of the two armies inevitably leaves much out. These men may have looked identical and indeed had a shared history and experiences, but nevertheless below the surface lay divergences in personality, motivations and aspirations, even if such internal distinctions were difficult to retrieve after the event. For an attempt to peer more closely into such murky realms of collective character, we will have to wait until Tacitus' *Histories*.

This technique of eliding the differences between the two sides in a civil war had a long history in ancient literature. So Livy records the anxiety of the Romans when they have to fight against the Latins, 'who were like themselves in language, customs, type of arms, and above all in military institutions; soldiers had mingled with soldiers, tribunes with tribunes, as equals and colleagues in the same garrisons and often in the same maniples' (Livy 8.6.15).[39] Such similarities made unquestioning obedience to authority in a civil war far from automatic, particularly if the soldiers were not wholeheartedly dedicated to the cause. There are modern parallels for the notion of mirroring, but these tend to be generated in the context of *foreign* wars when surprised soldiers discover that their hated enemies are just like themselves. So, Emilio Lussu, an Italian soldier who fought the Austrians in World War I, spies on the enemy trenches and feels shocked:

Those strongly defended trenches, which we had attacked so many times without success had ended by seeming to us inanimate, like desolate buildings uninhabited by men, the refuge only of mysterious and terrible beings of whom we knew nothing. Now they were showing themselves to us as they really were, men and soldiers just like us, in uniform like us, moving about, talking, and drinking coffee, just as our own comrades behind us were doing at that moment.[40]

In order to rationalise the process of killing, soldiers frequently visualise the enemy as monsters, who must be eliminated.[41] Problems arise when this convenient image is shattered, as here, and a soldier finds himself unexpectedly empathising with his opposite number. There is an interesting sequence in Monsarrat's *The Cruel Sea*, where some German survivors are plucked from the sea: 'These were people from another and infinitely abhorrent world – not just Germans, but U-boat Germans, doubly revolting.'[42] Yet it becomes increasingly difficult for the British captain, Ericson, to maintain this viewpoint, and cracks begin to appear in his hostile image of the enemy as the German prisoners spend more time on board. This theme, whereby human qualities are identified in a hated foreign enemy, differs from the ancient notion of beloved friends and relatives being spotted on the other side in a civil war (cf. Lucan *Phar.* 4.169-79 and 7.460-9), but there is a connection. Both types of scene draw power from a moment of recognition followed by a moment of shock.

On the whole, Appian devotes less attention to characterising Pompey's soldiers, but there are still conclusions we can draw about them. Appian's Pharsalus sequence might lead us to believe that the Pompeians are no different from the Caesarians, but this is not strictly true. Where Caesar repeatedly offers money to his soldiers to galvanise their enthusiasm for his cause, Pompey's men are not presented as succumbing to such temptations, which is a distinctive point of contrast. Appian

omits Caesar's critical description of Pompey's luxurious camp after
Pharsalus (Caesar *BC* 3.96; cf. Plutarch *Pompey* 72.6), saying only that
'he himself dined on Pompey's food, his whole army on that of Pompey's
men' (*BC* 2.81.344). This collective dining perhaps triggers a recollection of the disturbing scene after the sack of Gomphi, where Caesar's
greedy soldiers ate and drank to excess (*BC* 2.64.268). Certainly, we
learn that Pompey's allies 'sacked and pillaged from their own fortifica-
tions whatever they could carry away with them in their flight' (*BC*
2.80.334), but this suggests not greed but desperation, as the allies
frantically try to salvage a means of survival after their disastrous
defeat.

In addition, Pompey's army seems better disciplined than the Caesarians.[43] There is nothing to parallel the dangerous Caesarian
mutinies at Placentia (*BC* 2.47.191-5) and in Campania (*BC* 2.92.386-
2.94.396), and in contrast Appian describes Pompey's army in Spain as
'large and well trained through long service' (*BC* 2.40.160). Another
scene which suggests the high calibre of Pompey's soldiers occurs
directly after the Placentia mutiny: 'when Pompey put his army into
training, he ran and rode with them and took the lead in endurance,
allowing for his age, so that he gained their good will without any
difficulty and they all flocked to see Pompey's practice as though it were
a show' (*BC* 2.49.200). The harmonious hierarchy within the Pompeian
command structure contrasts sharply with the anarchic disorder which
dominates the Caesarians. Indeed, if a Roman reader, who did not know
the outcome of Pharsalus, was called on to make a prediction about the
likely result, then the Pompeians would surely look the more promising
prospect. To counteract this impression, Appian introduces the notion
of 'heaven-sent madness' (*BC* 2.71.298 and 2.87.366) to explain Pompey's defeat:[44] if Pompey had not been gripped by such a force, which
prompted him to abandon his initial plan and to engage in battle too
soon, then Pompey and his well-trained soldiers might have beaten
Caesar. At the same time, Appian emphasises Caesar's 'famous good
luck' (*BC* 2.66.275) and the 'supernatural enthusiasm' (*BC* 2.66.274) of
the Caesarians, which also contribute to the victory.[45]

There is one crucial point of continuity between the accounts of
Caesar and Appian, which is relevant for the subsequent discussion of
Tacitus. In the depiction of a group of soldiers, whether Caesarian or
Pompeian, Appian tends not to use internal focalisation to suggest what
individual men within that larger group might be feeling. Thus he
suggests that in response to Caesar's speech at Placentia, 'A cry of
despair at once went up from the *entire* legion' (*BC* 2.47.195). Likewise,
the Pompeians and Caesarians respond identically to the speeches of
their commanders: 'When Pompey had finished, the *entire* army ...
cheered and told him to lead them wherever he liked' (*BC* 2.52.212), and
'The *whole* army shouted enthusiastically for Caesar to lead them on'

(*BC* 2.54.221). Appian may record fluctuations in behaviour within a larger group, as when Pompey's allies, unlike his legionaries, flee headlong at Pharsalus, but emotions of soldiers tend to be recorded in an undifferentiated way. So, when the Caesarians glimpse Pompey in the distance, 'they turned round and fled, each where he could, impervious to shame or instructions or rational thought' (*BC* 2.62.257). Appian therefore uses a similar technique to Caesar in depicting large groups of men: both writers generally avoid segmentation in presenting collective thoughts and emotions, even if they differentiate between the actions of separate units within a single army.

To conclude, Appian perceives that the armies of Caesar and Pompey are a powerful force in dictating leadership techniques and the course of events. Appian shows Caesar periodically buying off his men with money, and Pompey being forced to fight at Pharsalus by his enthusiastic soldiers, which means that both supreme commanders are being compromised in different ways. On the whole, Appian presents Caesar's soldiers as a more menacing presence than Pompey's men, who remain untainted by mutiny and by bribes. Moreover, Appian plays down the positive role of the centurions and tribunes, who made valuable contributions especially in Caesar *BC* 3. Certainly, Appian praises the exemplary Caesarian heroes Scaeva (*BC* 2.60.247-9) and Crassinius (*BC* 2.82.347), but these are isolated cases. Elsewhere, the intermediate commanders are characterised as a flawed group. So, Scipio's campaign on behalf of Pompey is said to have 'collapsed through the misjudgment of the commanders, who failed either to wear Caesar down until he ran short of supplies ... or to carry their first victory through to conclusion' (*BC* 2.97.405). Appian seems more concerned to elucidate the relationships between Caesar and Pompey and their respective armies than to focus on dominant personalities in other ranks of the military hierarchy. Finally, Appian naturally dispenses with Caesar's loaded terminology by which his own soldiers were 'our men' and the other side were 'Pompeians': instead, we have the neutral 'Pompey's army' (*BC* 2.38.152) or 'Caesar's army' (*BC* 2.34.134). This balanced nomenclature means that readers do not identify with one army more than another, but judge each group according to their conduct.

Cassius Dio

Dio's *Roman History* can be contrasted with the narratives of Caesar and Appian in a number of ways. The scale of the work is monumental, running from the period of the kings to his own retirement from public office in AD 229, and resulting in eighty books of history. Moreover, Dio differed from both Caesar and Appian in choosing the annalistic structure for his format, although naturally this did not prevent him from manipulating chronology and including digressions where he saw fit (e.g. 42.34-55). The civil wars from 49 BC to 31 BC seem to have held a special interest for Dio, who devotes more space to this chronologically distant period than to events of his own time.[46] The explanation may lie in the fact that the civil wars mark the transition between republic and principate, so Dio may have decided that a lengthy analysis was justified. Possibly, Dio's own experiences as a commander made him especially sensitive to the power of truculent armies: so the historian reflects that 'the soldiers indulge in such wantonness, licence and lack of discipline, that those in Mesopotamia even dared to murder their commander, Flavius Heracleo, and the Praetorians denounced me in the presence of Ulpianus because I controlled the soldiers in Pannonia strictly' (80.4). Given that it was imperative for a good leader to control disruptive soldiers, Dio may be prompting readers to contrast his own strictness with the disciplinary failures of other commanders.[47] However that may be, critics have certainly suggested that Dio filtered his narrative of the triumviral period through his own experiences of the civil wars of Septimius Severus.[48] Let us turn now to Dio *Roman History* 41, which narrates the events of 49-48 BC, and assess in more detail how he tackles the relationship between leaders and armies.

Although Dio thoroughly approves of the stability brought about by the principate, or 'monarchy' as he terms it (44.2)[49] he makes his moral position on civil war clear: 'for there is no doubt that in civil wars the state is injured by both sides' (41.14.2). If Dio ever read Lucan, it would have been interesting to learn the historian's reaction to the poet's ironic assertion that all the destruction of the civil wars was worthwhile because it led to the advent of Nero (*Phar.* 1.33-7). Certainly, Dio accepted that flawed emperors like Nero could come to prominence, but believed even so that the imperial system was still the most stable option (e.g. 44.2). Dio therefore probably had more tolerance for the principate as an institution than Lucan did, but considers civil war to be unacceptably damaging to the state. What form does Dio see this damage as taking?

At one point, Dio condemns the hypocrisy of both leaders: 'But Caesar and Pompey called their opponents enemies of their country and declared that they themselves were fighting for the public interests, whereas each alike was really ruining those interests and advancing merely his own private ends' (41.17). Here and elsewhere, Dio is sensitive to the misleading rhetoric of civil war, where selfish individual aims are dressed up as concern for the state. This idea can be traced back to Thucydides, whom Dio often imitates,[50] but it also reverses a prominent notion in Roman historiography whereby the individual is encouraged by example to subordinate his or her own interests to those of the state.[51] The hypocrisy of Caesar and Pompey culminates in the dramatic scene at Pharsalus, where Dio does not differentiate between the pre-battle harangues of the two leaders. Both come from the same state and call the other a tyrant and himself a liberator: 'They had nothing different to say on either side' (41.57). It is as if both leaders give their speeches in tandem, each man simultaneously articulating the other's arguments word for word. The scene becomes a synecdoche for the fundamental nature of civil war, where differences between the two sides are elided completely.

Dio is also sensitive to the psychological damage inflicted on the Roman national character by civil war. The opening of Book 41 eloquently reconstructs the climate of fear which gripped Rome in 49 BC after Caesar has invaded Italy (cf. Cicero *Att.* 7.12.1). Before Caesar's arrival, exaggerated reports reach Rome about the Caesarian soldiers (41.6 and 41.8), which prompt many civilians to leave: 'Anyone who saw them would have supposed that two peoples and two cities were being made from one, and that the one group was being driven out and was going into exile, while the other was being left to its fate and taken captive' (41.9).[52] Dio thus portrays the whole population as victims and encapsulates the impossible choice which faced all civilians in civil war. Yet, at the same time, although a reader must feel pity for the populace, the departure of such a large group before Caesar has even arrived suggests a degeneration in their collective spirit, which has been caused exclusively by the civil war. As Cicero says, the citizens would not have abandoned Rome if the Gauls had been invading (*Att.* 7.11.3). Walzer has observed that 'besieged cities are arenas for collective heroism', but not in this case (cf. Lucan *Phar.* 1.503-4).[53] The abandonment of Rome looks even more cowardly when juxtaposed with the defiant resistance of the Massilians in Gaul, who fend off Caesar's troops for some time (41.19). These Gauls are behaving more nobly than the people of Rome (cf. Florus *Epitome* 2.13.23-5). Thus, the damage to the Roman state is expressed in terms of the crippling effect on the morale of the citizens.

Futhermore, Dio condemns civil war because of the contamination inflicted on the Roman army. Thus, Pompey 'proposed to use against his country foreigners and the allies once enslaved by him' (41.13). As so often happens in such situations, this war does not remain exclusively civil for long: Dio's implicit message is that the Roman army should be conquering foreign nations, not inviting foreigners to fight fellow Romans.[54] A particularly ominous note is struck when Dio highlights Caesar's fears that the Gauls might be induced to revolt (41.18). In addition, Dio is sensitive towards the erosion of traditional standards of military discipline, which tends to occur in civil war. Soldiers find that identical behaviour on two separate occasions can provoke diametrically different reactions from their commanders: one Caesarian riot provokes Caesar to agree to his soldiers' demands for dismissal from service with lavish rewards (Dio 42.52-3), while a second disturbance prompts Caesar to seize one man with his own hands and send the soldier to be executed (43.24). Such inconsistency unsettles the military hierarchy and shatters the rigidly delineated world of these men.

A crucial scene for assessing the relationship between leaders and soldiers is Dio's narrative of the Placentia mutiny (41.26-35), a scene which is conspicuously absent from Caesar's account. Like their leaders, the Caesarian soldiers disguise their real motive (a desire to plunder the Italian countryside) behind a more respectable façade, whereby they claim exhaustion from such long service. These troops have already shown their true colours by stealing money from the treasury in Rome, despite opposition from the tribune, Lucius Metellus (41.17). Caesar did not intervene then, but now his authority is being challenged directly, so retaliation is essential. On the surface, his speech contains many sentiments which appear respectable, particularly if we note that there are links with Livy's well-known version of Scipio's address to his mutinous soldiers at Carthago Nova in Spain in 206 BC (Livy 28.27-9).[55] So, Caesar evokes the notion that the transgressions of a violent minority are tarnishing the reputation of the obedient majority (41.30.1; cf. Livy 28.27.6); compares his men to hordes of foreign invaders (41.30.2; cf. Livy 28.28.4); claims that the soldiers are in Italy to defend their country against oppressors (41.32.1); notes that the duty of soldiers is to obey their commanders without question (41.33.4); suggests that he would rather die than command such reprobates (41.34.4; cf. Livy 28.27.10); is at a loss about what to call his soldiers (41.35.4; cf. Livy 28.27.1-5); and calls their bluff by telling them that they are free to go (41.35.4). In this way, Caesar appeals to normal standards of military discipline and patriotism, although these have hardly been visible in the preceding narrative. Perhaps Dio is presenting us with a Caesar who has some heroic traits after all.

Yet if we look below the surface, Dio's characterisation of Caesar here is disturbing and provocative. Those echoes of Scipio's speech in Livy should prompt us to compare contexts: Scipio is in the process of fighting a war against foreigners in Spain, whereas Caesar has just returned from Spain where he has been fighting fellow Romans. Scipio and Caesar deploy similar arguments, but the Livian context is so much more appropriate for such sentiments than Dio's civil war framework, and we are surely meant to feel uncomfortable that Caesar's tough disciplinarian stance comes only when the soldiers are inconveniencing him personally. Furthermore, Dio's generalisation about the levels of hypocrisy at work in the civil war (41.17) should make us suspicious about the sincerity of Caesar's speech. As the narrative progresses, we will see Caesar raising some incredible points, considering preceding incidents like the Placentia mutiny. So the general addresses the senate in 46 BC and says: 'Do not fear the soldiers either, or regard them in any other light than as guardians of my empire, which is at the same time yours. That they should be supported is necessary, for many reasons, but they will be supported for your benefit, not against you' (43.18.1).[56] Such rhetoric seems misleading, since Dio has progressively characterised the soldiers as greedy, manipulative and selfish (cf. 42.52, 43.5, and 43.14). In any case, Caesar's hasty and unconvincing correction when he refers to 'my empire, which is at the same time yours' is disturbing: the slip reveals where real power lies. On one level, we can admire Caesar for his practical handling of the mutiny at Placentia, but at the same time we cannot condone his double standards. Often, Dio's speeches are categorised as detachable from the immediate context and unconcerned to characterise protagonists.[57] This may often be true, but Dio's version of Caesar's speech at Placentia can be productively reintegrated with the surrounding narrative: a reader can then ponder the gulf between words and deeds, and speculate about Caesar's manipulative character.[58]

On the whole, Dio characterises the armies of Caesar and of Pompey in a fairly uniform way. At Pharsalus, as we have seen, differences between the two sides are elided completely, so that Caesarians and Pompeians are presented as equally terrified: 'Sprung from the same country and from the same hearth, with almost identical weapons and similar formation, each side recoiled from beginning the battle, recoiled from killing anyone' (41.58). Elsewhere, at the battle of Munda, the two armies are said to be 'matched in determination ... and matched in physical strength' (43.38). The Pompeians only waver when their general Labienus leaves the battlefield, a characteristic which further likens them to the Caesarians, who were said to have been inspired above all 'by their leader's presence' (43.36). Dio presents the armies on both sides as having a uniform set of characteristics, and, like Caesar and Appian before him, avoids depicting their collective emotions in a fragmented way.

Conclusion

Civil war is a complex phenomenon, as is the process of producing a historical record of such self-destructive conflicts. Caesar, Appian and Dio all have distinctive historiographical approaches to the subject, but even so, some common patterns emerge, which will offer a constructive backdrop against which to set our investigation of Tacitus' *Histories*. All three authors tend to elide the differences between civil war armies, particularly in battle descriptions. Neither Caesar nor Appian nor Dio tries to reconstruct in any detail what individual soldiers, or groups of such men within a larger unit, might be thinking or feeling. Even collectively, the troops display a fairly narrow range of characteristics: fear, bravery, greed, and despair are the most common traits which are highlighted. Moreover, Appian and Dio have little interest in the role played within the military hierarchy by the centurions and tribunes in contributing to the smooth running of the army, and although Caesar accentuates these intermediate ranks, his purpose in so doing is to corroborate his own dominance: these loyal officers, like his soldiers, are prepared to make the ultimate sacrifice on Caesar's behalf, which enhances his standing in the narrative.

This discussion has also raised general questions about what motivates soldiers to fight in a civil war, where it is less easy to cast the other side in a demonic light. We have seen that financial incentives become crucial and that collective loyalty is often precarious, despite Caesar's emphasis in the *Bellum Civile*. In connection with this issue, generals face acute problems when it comes to discipline: excessive strictness becomes self-defeating when truculent soldiers have the option of changing sides on their own terms, and even when generals feel able to chastise their men, the patterns of discipline thereby established are erratic. Normal rules do not apply; or what is even worse, normal rules can apply, but sometimes they are ignored for the sake of short term expediency. Let us turn now to the *Histories* to see how Tacitus responds to such issues.

2

The Galbians and Othonians

Introduction

It will be the task of the next two chapters to investigate how Tacitus presents the collective identities of the four civil war armies, and to see what factors Tacitus sees as galvanising the soldiers to act. In Tacitus' *Histories* are soldiers always motivated by similar emotions, such as greed, fear, or respect? Is it possible to differentiate the separate groups within an army? There are naturally limitations imposed by genre in comparing Tacitus' version of events with parallel accounts of the civil war, but it will still be helpful to consider the alternative narratives of Plutarch, Dio and Suetonius. For example, Plutarch, in line with his general theory that nothing is more fearful than a military force gripped by 'rough and irrational impulses' (*Galba* 1.4), tends to elide the differences between the civil war armies.[1] He shows the Othonian and Vitellian forces mirroring one another, as the former accuse their commander Paulinus of cowardice at the same time as the latter stone their general Valens for excessive caution (*Otho* 7.5-9). Both groups show common behaviour patterns which transcend partisan loyalty to either Otho or Vitellius, or indeed to any of their generals. To achieve this effect, Plutarch has omitted Tacitus' detailed account of the Vitellian mutiny (*Histories* 2.27-30) which was sparked off by Valens' decision to move the troublesome Batavian troops to Gallia Narbonensis. Plutarch does not even mention the Batavians, but uses the two mutinies to illustrate common behaviour patterns on both sides and to highlight the problems faced by all commanders in a civil war. Even if Plutarch's notion that all armies in a civil war are gripped by irrational forces is palatable, it avoids some difficult questions. Where did this frenzy come from and how was it sustained? As will become clear, Tacitus was just as fascinated by the complex causes of the civil war as by the devastating effects, and his own distinctive collective characterisation of the soldiers in AD 69 particularly reflects this interest.

The Galbians

It might seem unpromising to begin an investigation into Tacitus' collective characterisation in the *Histories* with the Galbians. Since

Tacitus starts his narrative only when Galba is already emperor and quickly reaches the old man's death-scene, the identity of the troops who supported his challenge against Nero is comparatively nebulous. In history as well as in literature, former supporters of a dead emperor tended to disperse rapidly or to assimilate themselves quietly to the next ruler: yesterday's Galbian soon becomes tomorrow's Othonian. Even the convenient label 'Galbian' is misleading: Tacitus uses the umbrella term *Galbiani* for the first and last time after Galba's death (*Histories* 1.51.3). Rather than conjuring up a clearly delineated group of the emperor's supporters, the tag serves as an insult amongst the Gauls to describe those of their compatriots who supported Vindex. Perhaps of all four civil war armies in Tacitus' narrative, the Galbians are the least sharply defined. Nevertheless, it is illuminating to examine their portrayal because this is the starting-point for Tacitus' collective characterisation of the other civil war armies.

One common historical thread, which links the surviving accounts of Galba's downfall, is that the frugal emperor failed to produce the promised cash bonus for the soldiers, whose loyalty soon began to waver as a result (Tacitus *Histories* 1.5.2, Plutarch *Galba* 18.3, Suetonius *Galba* 16.1 and Cassius Dio 64.3.3). Even within this comparatively simple cause-and-effect analysis, Tacitus introduces some refinements which characterise both the emperor and the soldiers in important ways. Let us examine one particular Tacitean scene where the issue of the bonus is central, namely the adoption of Piso (1.17-8). Although Tacitus as narrator has already highlighted the issue of the bonus (1.5.2), he returns to the theme, which is suggestively embedded in his account of Galba's adoption of Piso. Galba and his supporters, deliberating between the speaker's platform in the forum, the senate or the military camp as the best location for the adoption, choose the military camp:[2] 'this would be a tribute to the soldiers, whose favour ought not to be sought by bribery or by corruption, but was not to be despised if won by honourable means' (*Histories* 1.17.2). Tacitus leaves open whether this is Galba's own viewpoint or the consensus of a wider group, but either way the stance reinforces our impression that Galba is an honourable but stubborn leader, who mistakenly thinks that the adoption in the military camp will flatter the troops. Thus, whereas Plutarch and Suetonius omit the logic behind the choice, Tacitus shows the vulnerable emperor walking a tightrope: the honourable Galba understands the fundamental importance of winning the soldiers' support, but like a good general, stubbornly rejects bribery, in practice the most effective means of gaining their favour. Galba may emerge from this episode as an idealist, but at the same time his decision to adopt Piso before the soldiers, rather than in the forum or the senate, reveals his dependency on them.

Tacitus focuses again on the issue of the bonus by noting that Galba does not conclude his speech by pandering to the troops or by bribing them (1.18.2). Such a tough stance provokes varied reactions from the men who are listening: 'the tribunes, centurions and front-ranks (*proximi militum*) responded with a gratifying cheer, but amongst the others there was gloomy silence (*maestitia ac silentium*)' (1.18.3).[3] This is a striking feature of the episode, namely that the army's reaction to Galba is not homogeneous, but depends on rank and on physical proximity to the emperor. Whether or not they are sincere, the officers come up with the appropriate response, but most of the common soldiers cannot feign enthusiasm, and their gloomy silence ominously foreshadows their passive disloyalty.

Finally, Tacitus concludes the episode (1.18.3) with a generalisation that it would have been possible to win over the soldiers even with a relatively small donative. His tone suggests frustration that the civil war was not averted in this way, rather than straightforward approval of such methods of leadership. Thus, Tacitus makes the bonus structurally central to this episode, and uses it as a device to characterise not just Galba but the soldiers too. Plutarch (*Galba* 23.4) and Suetonius (*Galba* 17) present the question of the bonus very much as a coda to the adoption scene: Plutarch's main concern is the ominous thunder and lightning which accompanied Galba's speech, while Suetonius is intrigued by the apparent spontaneity of the adoption.[4] In Tacitus' version, the bonus serves to emphasise the dangerous gulf between the old-fashioned general and his materialistic troops. To remind us of this, Tacitus returns to the topic through Galba's last words, including the version that 'he asked pleadingly why he deserved such a bad end, begging for just a few more days to pay off the donative' (1.41.2). Neither Plutarch (*Galba* 27.1) nor Dio (64.6.3) raises the subject of the donative at this powerful moment, though Suetonius includes a brief reference (*Galba* 20).

Tacitus' distinction between ranks as they respond to Galba's speech introduces an important theme. It is not just the relationship between undifferentiated armies and emperors, but also the role played by the intermediate officers which attracts his analytical eye. This differentiation between the silence of the Galbian soldiers and the enthusiasm of their centurions and tribunes during Galba's speech suggests that the two groups are motivated by different factors. As we shall see, the relationship between the Othonian troops and their superior officers is particularly tense. The Othonians actually refuse the centurions and tribunes access to Otho (1.36.1) and have their spirits broken when Otho leaves his soldiers in the hands of 'suspected generals' before the first battle of Bedriacum (2.33.3). The Othonians, unlike the Galbians, are seen at an early stage to embrace a peculiarly exclusive relationship with their emperor: all other intervening ranks are by-passed as 'they commended now the emperor to the soldiers, now the soldiers to the emperor' (1.36.2). In a normal and healthy relationship between an emperor and his soldiers, such camaraderie is certainly important, but the feelings are not usually so powerful that they short-circuit the military hierarchy.[5] Where the Othonians show extreme devotion to their emperor, the Galbians are latently hostile to theirs, but both groups are linked by feelings of detachment from their immediate commanding officers. We should note that Tacitus' sensitivity towards such rifts between soldiers and officers differentiates his account from those of Suetonius and Plutarch, who tend to talk more in terms of large, unstratified military groups.

It is important to note the form that the Galbians' dissatisfaction with their emperor's speech takes. Tacitus emphasises their silence and suggests a passive, rather than active, disaffection.[6] Although all the soldiers resent Galba's non-payment of the bonus, their transformation from hostile but obedient men to active rebels is not so instantaneous as Plutarch's theory of irrational forces suggests. A catalyst is needed to cause this change, but even then it will take time for the movement to gain momentum. Tacitus' fire imagery reflects this: 'Maevius Pudens, one of Tigellinus' associates, added torches to the soldiers' smouldering discontent' (1.24.1). Perhaps the soldiers would have unleashed their anger even without Pudens' intervention, but the imagery suggests that it would have taken longer for the fire to blaze.[7] Thus, in this initial analysis of the Galbian soldiers, several points have emerged about Tacitus' collective characterisation of the troops. First, he distinguishes between the behaviour of the common soldiers and of officers. Second, he suggests that these common soldiers are motivated by material concerns rather than by loyalty to their emperor. Third, he presents a model whereby in the early stages of trouble, most low-ranking soldiers allow their resentment to smoulder rather than to explode dramatically.

The Othonians

The way in which Tacitus' Galbian troops are gently coaxed into abandoning Galba and adopting Otho is remarkable. Not only is the conversion carried out by relatively few agents, but the resulting movement is extremely indecisive in its early stages. Tacitus stresses the sparse numbers who actually initiate and carry out these vast political changes: Maevius Pudens bribes the guard 100 sestertii per man every time Galba dines with Otho,[8] the freedman Onomastus is put in charge of the plot by Otho, and finally, there are the two men enlisted by Onomastus from the bodyguards, namely Barbius Proculus, a watchword officer, and Veturius, a centurion's deputy, who intensify their comrades' insecurities to ensure that resentment about the bonus does not fade (cf. Plutarch *Galba* 24.1-2). Neither man is named again elsewhere in the *Histories*. Tacitus employs some characteristic hyperbole to sum up the situation: 'two common soldiers undertook to hand over control of the Roman empire – and succeeded' (1.25.1).[9] In comparison, Suetonius suggests that Otho's plot rests on a broader base of support: five unnamed bodyguards select two others to make fifteen agents overall. Suetonius adds that even then a few others are enrolled, although not many, 'from a confident assurance that more would join when the undertaking was in progress' (*Otho* 5.2). The numbers are still small, but Suetonius avoids Tacitus' outraged formulation in which only two common soldiers have the empire in their gift.

Yet it is in the description of Otho's proclamation itself that Tacitus' distinctive analysis comes into its own. Tacitus explains that after Otho leaves the Palace to keep his rendezvous by the Golden Milestone in the Forum Romanum, the would-be emperor is appalled to find only 23 bodyguards there to salute him (*Histories* 1.27.2 and Plutarch *Galba* 25.1). The Golden Milestone, which listed distances from Rome to the principal cities of the empire, is indeed a symbolic meeting-point for an imperial pretender and his men, but the fact that such small numbers are involved creates bathos.[10] Until this point, the parallel accounts of Tacitus and Plutarch are fairly similar, but subsequently each author presents the material with a different emphasis. Plutarch says that, as Otho was carried through the forum, 'as many soldiers again met him, and still more approached by threes and fours. Then they all crowded around, saluting him as emperor and brandishing their drawn swords' (*Galba* 25.4). Despite the poor initial showing, there is a slow, steady climb in numbers until the soldiers unanimously salute Otho as emperor. Note Plutarch's ring-structure when Otho is acclaimed by the troops *twice*: once (25.1) when only 23 men are present, but then there is a second salutation (25.4) from a much larger group. Tacitus' version certainly presents an initial group joined by roughly the same number of men again, but the soldiers are not nearly so unified as Plutarch's troops, and there is no double acclamation.

Moreover, Tacitus uses internal focalisation to suggest the different motives which lead even this small group to act, and he notes the corresponding divergences in their behaviour: 'some knew about the plot, but most were surprised, some were shouting and brandishing swords, and some were silent, intending to suit their reaction to the outcome' (1.27.2). The fragmentation is striking: all the soldiers act together, but Tacitus allows his audience to see the diverging motives which lie behind this apparently unified collective movement. By contrast, Plutarch restricts himself to external focalisation, which draws a veil over the soldiers' different motives. Plutarch certainly concedes (*Galba* 25.6) that some soldiers know about the plot, but they are separate from this initial group. The similar visual focus on brandished swords in each narrative only serves to underline the contrasting techniques of biographer and historian: Plutarch suggests that all the soldiers wave their swords in unison, but Tacitus claims that only some do this.[11] This sword-waving motif highlights the fact that Tacitus characterises his group of soldiers as heterogeneous while Plutarch presents a unified company.

Even Plutarch's point that more soldiers joined the initial group 'by threes and fours' (*Galba* 25.4) suggests a slow, steady gathering of momentum. Tacitus omits this detail and creates the impression that the group assembled more erratically. We might even compare the smooth expansion of Plutarch's crowd during Otho's proclamation with the following simile. Silius Italicus, trying to capture the effect of the steadily increasing desire in Hannibal's army to invade Rome, uses the image of a pebble being thrown into a pool.

> So, when a pebble breaks the surface of a motionless pool, in its first movements, it forms tiny rings; and next, making the shimmering water shake under the growing force, it increases the number of circles on the round pond, until finally the extended circle reaches from bank to bank with its broad curve[12] (*Pun.* 13.24-9)

Plutarch's focus on the consistent increase in Othonian numbers, as well as his avoidance of Tacitus' internal focalisation of the soldiers, offers a collective characterisation, which is in the same vein as Silius' portrayal of Hannibal's army. Plutarch is not concerned to break the army into smaller constituent groups or to look below the surface of the 'pool'. Tacitus, on the other hand, certainly does not deny that the soldiers can function very dangerously as a unified force: the bloody climax of the Othonian coup illustrates this (1.41.3). Yet he traces the progression towards such moments rather more carefully than Plutarch. The army in Tacitus' account does not behave savagely at the very start, since the soldiers need to gain courage and momentum from one another.[13] Most soldiers are hesitant and relatively few are prepared to take decisive action. Piso, in his speech, stresses the small number actually involved: 'will less than thirty renegades and deserters … allocate imperial power?' (1.30.3). Galba's nominee is trying to sting his audience into action, but the irony is that he is absolutely right; less than thirty men *will* have the empire in their gift.

This does not mean that the indecisive majority amongst the soldiers is harmless. The collusion of such men plays an important role in the chaos, as Tacitus notes: 'such was their mood that a few men (*pauci*) dared to commit the worst crime, though more of them (*plures*) wanted to do so, and they all (*omnes*) allowed it to happen' (1.28). The dynamics are rather similar when Tacitus describes the general behaviour of a large unspecified group after Galba's death: 'in rivalry they showed their bloody hands – those who had done the killing, those who had witnessed it, and those who (truly or falsely) boasted about what they called a fine and memorable deed' (1.44.2). Here Tacitus breaks the composite group into genuine murderers and those who are just by-standers, implying that the actual killers are not many.[14] His methods of analysis move beyond Plutarch's model of soldiers gripped by irrational forces; instead, Tacitus emphasises collective apathy more than collective violence, at least during Otho's rise to power. There is a parallel in the behaviour of the mutinous soldiers of the French army following the Chemon des Dames offensive in the spring of 1917. One commentator has observed: 'The "good" soldierly majority was also a silent one that did nothing to stop the more effervescent minority. For many soldiers as well as officers, one of the most important forms of action was inaction'[15]

The Othonian soldiers may have been apathetic in the early stages, but once Otho is emperor, their passivity vanishes. Even if Otho's more geographically distant supporters are less enthusiastic (1.76.2), those in the immediate vicinity become increasingly zealous and fiercely suspicious of anything or anyone who threatens their emperor. The most extreme manifestation of this phenomenon is in the mutiny sequence (1.80-2).[16] The soldiers, whose spirited devotion to Otho rather than to their superior officers is already clear (1.36), become extremely alarmed upon finding a tribune preparing a transport of arms in the middle of the night:

> the troops raised a clamour and charged the tribunes and centurions with treason on the grounds that the household servants of the senators were being armed for Otho's murder. Some soldiers (*pars*) were ignorant and groggy with wine, every bad man (*pessimus quisque*) seized the chance to plunder, and the riff-raff (*vulgus*), as usual, was keen on any kind of new excitement; night had taken away the obedience of the better men (*meliorum*). (1.80.2)

It might initially look as if all the troops are concerned about Otho, but Tacitus suggests that less respectable explanations can be found for the trouble: drunkenness, greed and a desire for excitement drive separate groups of soldiers to act. Not all of them are motivated by such disreputable factors, but again Tacitus introduces sub-categories within the larger group and attributes a range of motives to the soldiers.

In other accounts the rebels are a much less fragmented group. Although Plutarch is uncertain (*Otho* 3.3) whether the soldiers are genuinely worried about the emperor or just want an excuse to plunder, he seems to suggest that they all act for the same reason; and Suetonius' condensed version of the riot (*Otho* 8.2) assumes that all the troops are motivated by genuine concern for the emperor. When Tacitus' Otho eventually chastises the men, he naturally prefers to portray the riot retrospectively as an instance of the soldiers' excessive enthusiasm for his safety, but his insistence at the opening of his speech that the trouble was *of course* not caused 'by greed or by hatred, which have driven many armies into disorder' (1.83.2) seems disingenuous. The emperor has, after all, spent time bonding with his men in the early stages of his challenge to Galba. Tacitus remarks that on the march from Spain Otho 'greeted some, asked after others, gave help with money or favours, often dropping complaints and double-edged remarks about Galba and other comments designed to disturb the mob' (1.23.1).[17] Unlike Galba, Otho is a product of his times and knows how to win over his soldiers by a variety of methods, including bribery.

Another striking aspect of Tacitus' description is that the mutineers directly accuse the tribunes and centurions of plotting against Otho with the help of the senators' household slaves. This suggests that although the Othonians clearly suspect the senators, above all they direct their mistrust against their own officers. Even when the soldiers burst into the palace at the height of the riot, they threaten 'now the centurions and tribunes, now the whole senate' (1.82.1). Suetonius says (*Otho* 8.2) that the soldiers actually kill several tribunes, but their real targets are the treacherous senators.[18] In Suetonius' version the troops are denouncing the *senators* as traitors rather than the tribunes: this moves the focus of the mutiny further away from the military sphere. Likewise, Plutarch says that the mutinous soldiers complain that 'the senate was trying to bring about a revolution' (*Otho* 3.4). Perhaps Tacitus' different emphasis on this small point is irrelevant. Yet in this way he reinforces a collective character trait of the military that was first broached when these soldiers were still Galbians. Though the relationship between common soldiers and their superior officers was always problematic, now the troops are confident enough to express this hostility through rioting. Unlike the Galbians, the Othonians are prepared to by-pass their superiors violently in favour of direct contact with their emperor: already, the command structure has broken down in a dangerous and perhaps irreversible way.

The manner in which discipline is restored does nothing to re-establish the traditional hierarchy and provides the soldiers with an ominous precedent. The trouble is only halted when Otho springs onto a couch and restrains the men 'by requests and by tears' (1.82.1), after which they grudgingly return to barracks.[19] On the next day the soldiers are addressed by Licinius Proculus and Plotius Firmus, the praetorian prefects who were selected (1.46.1) by the troops themselves soon after Galba's defeat.[20] The former uses a gentle tone, the latter (appropriately, given his name) a stern one, but the end result is that 'five thousand *sestertii* were paid to each soldier' (1.82.3). The stakes have clearly risen since the days when these praetorians were happy with a mere one hundred *sestertii*. Even though it is the next day and the immediate danger has dissipated, the praetorian prefects still resort to handing out money as the most practical solution to the problem. Just as Galba's stern words were undercut by his decision to adopt Piso in the military camp, so the prefects' hand-out effectively undermines many of the impressive sentiments which Otho goes on to express in his speech (1.83-4). It is commendable that the emperor requests a return to traditional standards of obedience and a restoration of the normal military hierarchy, but since the troops have just been given such a huge financial sweetener, they do not have to listen. After all, the soldiers have just learned the lesson that by resorting to violence and threats, they can successfully extort money from their superiors. Why on earth *should* they obey their generals without question, as Otho requests? By the end of *Histories* 1, the soldiers have discovered that their desire for money can be gratified by allowing their resentment to explode rather than to smoulder.

So far then, the collective identity of the Othonians has been typified by deep suspicion of their commanders, particular enthusiasm towards Otho, and a tendency to crave financial rewards in return for loyalty. These traits continue to manifest themselves as the troops travel north to confront the Vitellians at the first battle of Bedriacum. One of the earliest events of the campaign is an Othonian raid on the Maritime Alps which is a prelude to attacking Gallia Narbonensis. Even before the fighting has started, Tacitus makes it clear that the Othonian soldiers have not changed their ways just because they have left Rome. In fact, if anything, the liberty gained by being on campaign allows the soldiers greater opportunity to assert their power. Three commanders are in charge, namely Aemilius Pacensis, Antonius Novellus and Suedius Clemens.[21] However, the first officer is arrested by his troops, while the second is ignored by his men because he has no authority. Only Suedius Clemens has any power, but this is because he is 'hostile towards the moderating influence of discipline' (2.12.1).[22] Again the Othonian troops are effectively choosing their commanders, even if Otho has made official appointments which suggests imposition of control from above.

The violence of the ensuing campaign reflects this warped military hierarchy: the soldiers approach Italy 'as though it were foreign shores and enemy cities which they burned, devastated, plundered (*urere, vastare, rapere*)' (2.12.2).[23] It is not even true that their victims are dangerous or aggressively pro-Vitellian. Certainly, nearby Gallia Narbonensis is said to support the Vitellian cause simply because her stronger neighbours do so, and there is no reason to think that the placid Maritime Alps are any different (1.76.1). Tacitus carefully exaggerates the peaceful country atmosphere and the idyllic landscape dominated by Italian farmers: 'the fields were full, the farmhouses were open (*pleni agri, apertae domus*)' (2.12.2).[24] Similar rhetorical strategies had been used by others, as for example when Cicero in the *Verrines* had cast the Sicilians as typical farmers rather than typical Greeks.[25] Yet the civil war context makes the Othonians' savagery and senseless destruction especially shocking. The fact that their violence is directed against farmers is symbolic: men who normally raise crops and nurture the land are forced by the Othonian soldiers to abandon their work and to embrace civil war.[26] Such hardy farmer-types traditionally made good soldiers, especially if they lived in the mountains: thus, Caesar notes (*BC* 1.57) the competence of the mountain-dwelling Albici, who are almost as capable as Roman legionaries, and Sallust recounts the exploits of a tough Ligurian soldier in conquering a mountain fortress (*Jug.* 93-4). However, the Othonians are seen to overturn this model by winning a crushing victory against their opponents, who are pointedly described as 'mountain-dwellers (*montani*)' (2.12.3). Thus, Tacitus demonises the greedy and violent Othonians, aligning them with foreign invaders for dramatic and emotional effect.

Yet the violence of these soldiers does not damage the Othonian campaign. It may seem bizarre, but it is the troops' loyalty to their emperor which leads to defeat, even though this could have been a great strength. In the narrative of the earlier mutiny (1.80-2), it is not clear that the soldiers' protestations of loyalty to Otho are completely sincere: as we have seen, some men certainly have ulterior motives, and their successful extortion of a sizeable bonus immediately makes their assertions of devotion look disingenuous.[27] However, Tacitus reveals over the course of *Histories* 2 that the loyalty of the Othonians gradually deepens. A crucial yardstick is the Othonian mutiny at Placentia, which is sparked off because the soldiers think that 'Otho is being betrayed and Caecina has been summoned' (2.18.2). This explanation immediately recalls their earlier riot in Rome (1.80), and a reader may be entitled to expect a replay of that scene. Some themes are mirrored: for example, the soldiers seize the standards and abandon the camp, 'with centurions and tribunes scorned' (2.18.2). Yet there are some significant differences too. If the soldiers simply crave plunder, why bother to take their standards with them when they leave the camp? This may be a reflex action, but it does suggest that they intend to continue the campaign for Otho, albeit without their current commanders.

It is also suggestive that in this mutiny the soldiers are not drunk: Tacitus pointedly excludes Plutarch's detail that some drunken mutineers accosted Spurinna during the night to obtain travel funds (*Otho* 5.10). This omission immediately gives Tacitus' Othonians more credibility because they seem sober and rational, even if they are rioting. Moreover, Tacitus, unlike Plutarch, does not specify that night has fallen until after the soldiers have left Placentia and are building their new camp beside the river Po (2.19.1). Military riots which occur at night are always more sinister, partly because the darkness serves as a cover for violence and hides the identities of the wrongdoers.[28] Certainly, the fact that it is dark during the earlier mutiny aggravates the situation: 'the darkness even demolished the obedience of the better soldiers' (1.80.2). Elsewhere, even troublemakers find darkness too dangerous, as when Otho's agents want to initiate the proclamation, 'but feared ... the uncertainties of night-time' (1.26.1). If Tacitus had stressed that the Placentia mutiny happened at night, he could have made it more sinister, but he chooses to omit this detail. As a result, the riot seems less irrational and the mutineers seem more sincere. The incident contrasts with other typical mutiny scenes such as the Caesarian mutiny at Placentia, discussed in the previous chapter. Readers might well be prompted to think of this Caesarian mutiny, which also took place in Placentia.

This phenomenon of the Othonians' devotion to their emperor is reiterated at several points before the final battle. When the council of war disastrously decides to fight at Bedriacum without Otho being present, Tacitus notes that 'this was the first day to shatter the Othonian cause (*is primus dies Othonianas partes adflixit*)' (2.33.3). The language here echoes Virgil's description of the tragic encounter between Dido and Aeneas in the cave: 'that was the first day of death (*ille dies primus leti*)' (*Aeneid* 4.169).[29] Tacitus thus adds dramatic resonances to his narrative, partly by evoking a Virgilian formula from Dido's and Aeneas' moment of *peripeteia*. Tacitus' explanation is pivotal: 'those who remained lost heart, since the generals were regarded with suspicion and since Otho, who trusted no one but the troops and who was the only one they trusted, had left the chain of command in uncertainty' (2.33.3; cf. 2.39.2). Even if the Othonian troops were initially materialistic, their personal attachment to the emperor has evolved considerably, so that his absence from Bedriacum causes low morale and, ultimately, defeat.

Yet their obsessive loyalty to Otho does not on its own make the situation irretrievable. What proves deadly is the fact that it is combined with a deep hatred of their officers. This is a peculiarly Tacitean emphasis. Plutarch also focuses on Otho's potential for engendering respect and ambition amongst the troops and on the disastrous removal of the best soldiers for the emperor's bodyguard, but says nothing about the Othonians' suspicions towards their generals (*Otho* 10.1).[30] This omission is understandable, given Plutarch's self-imposed parameters as a biographer, but Tacitus' wider reaching explanation is helpful: if the hierarchy of command beneath Otho had been functional, then the emperor's absence would not have been so devastating. As it is, however, the Othonians devote more energy to fighting their immediate superiors than they do to confronting the Vitellians.

For example, after an unsuccessful skirmish against some Vitellians, a contingent of Othonian gladiators actually threaten their commander Martius Macer with death and wound him with a lance (2.36.1). Plutarch does not mention Macer's predicament in his account of this incident (*Otho* 10.2-5); and neither Suetonius nor Dio focus on the general at all. According to Tacitus, Macer is only saved by the hasty intervention of the tribunes and centurions, but even these Othonian officers are flawed: 'the tribunes and centurions were unreliable because the better types were rejected and the worst sort had power' (2.39.1).[31] When the battle commences, the defective Othonian generals understandably fear their own men more than they do the Vitellians: 'amongst the Othonians there were frightened generals and soldiers hostile to their leaders' (2.41.3. Cf. Pliny *Panegyricus* 18.3). This inverts the familiar theme that in battle a good soldier should fear his general's anger more than the enemy. So, the general Servilius Priscus executes a standard-bearer for hesitating to advance against the Faliscans, thus causing the other soldiers, 'thoroughly scared', to attack the enemy (Frontinus 2.8.8).[32] When these dynamics are reversed and the generals fear their own soldiers more than the enemy, this must foreshadow disaster.

Thus Tacitus does not trace the Othonians' devotion to their emperor in isolation. The other half of the formula is the troops' extreme hatred for the officers, which eventually leads to their defeat at Bedriacum. Their passion for Otho ultimately proves to be so self-destructive that some soldiers even copy the emperor's suicide:

> The praetorian cohorts carried the body amidst tributes and tears, kissing (*exosculantes*) his wound and hands. Some soldiers killed themselves by the funeral pyre, not because they were guilty or afraid, but because they loved their emperor and wished to share his glory. Afterwards, at Bedriacum, Placentia and other camps alike, this type of death was common. (2.49.4; cf. Suetonius *Otho* 12.2, Plutarch *Otho* 17.10 and Dio 64.15)

This supreme expression of solidarity with the emperor shows that the allegiance of these soldiers has deepened considerably since the days of the praetorian mutiny in Rome. Tacitus first uses the verb *exosculari* when the sycophantic senate and people kiss Otho's hand after he has become emperor (1.45.1), but ironically, an action which was insincere when Otho was still alive becomes a sign of genuine affection amongst the praetorians once he is dead.[33]

In addition it is striking that the suicides are not just restricted to the praetorians, with whom Otho had a special rapport. Soldiers outside this privileged inner circle also kill themselves. Certainly, it was an intrinsic part of the military oath that a soldier should value no life more than his emperor's,[34] but the spectacular scale on which the soldiers commit suicide is still surprising. Although groups of Romans are sometimes portrayed as enacting suicide collectively (e.g. Lucan *Phar.* 4.529-81), ancient authors often attribute this form of death to barbarians,[35] which may explain why Tacitus insists that the Othonians were not guilty or afraid when they killed themselves. Even so, there may be something alarming in the excessive, almost feminine grief of Otho's soldiers, who submerge their own identities in that of their emperor, and act like ideal wives who choose not to survive their husbands.[36] Some critics explain the suicides as a natural consequence of contagion.[37] Not even at Julius Caesar's funeral do the grieving soldiers kill themselves like this, but this is because their murdered general did not die by his own hand. The poignant wounds on Caesar's corpse still stir profound emotions amongst onlookers, but they desire revenge on others rather than suicide for themselves.[38] At any rate, whatever the psychological explanation for the collective Othonian suicides, Tacitus captures vividly the soldiers' passion for their dead emperor, which will have a lasting impact: amongst those who survive, affection for Otho develops into implacable hatred for Vitellius. These deep feelings ultimately benefit not Otho, but Vespasian, who will later exploit them during his own campaign.

Conclusion

In his portrayal of the Othonians, Tacitus offers a yardstick against which to measure the Vitellians and the Flavians, and raises an important paradox. If increasingly widespread personal popularity amongst the army cannot sustain an emperor's power, then what can? One answer is a strong and involved general, who can channel the collective feelings of the troops in a constructive way. The devastating effect of Otho's abandonment of his troops helps us to understand the need for a commander such as the charismatic Flavian, Antonius Primus. For Tacitus, much more than for the authors of the parallel accounts, the Othonians' rejection of their immediate commanders plays a crucial role in explaining their defeat. Tacitus' Othonians certainly show an initiative which sustains the campaign even after the officers have abandoned the struggle (2.43.2), but the Vitellian generals Caecina and Valens do not have their counterparts on the Othonian side, and this eventually proves telling. In other eras, the calibre of officers is presented as fundamental to the efficiency of the whole army: so, in World War I, attempts were made to stem the damage to morale caused by officers' deaths by making them wear the same uniforms as their men and by hiding their insignia of rank.[39] In contrast, the Othonian officers prove worse than useless in a crisis, and the common soldiers are left to fend for themselves. They succeed up to a point, but Otho's absence proves an insurmountable hurdle.

The Othonian soldiers certainly manifest dubious qualities, such as the violence which exploded in the Maritime Alps, but at least they develop genuine loyalty to their emperor.[40] Such devotion differentiates the Othonians from the fickle Galbians, although of course some of

Otho's soldiers, who previously served the old-fashioned disciplinarian Galba, may have done so under duress. Our examination of other civil war narratives in historiography has shown that elsewhere in the literary tradition, civil war soldiers are often characterised as being fickle. The conspicuous exception is the army of Julius Caesar: so, Suetonius considers it striking that Julius Caesar's soldiers preferred death to the alternative of serving with the Pompeians (*Divus Iulius* 68.1). The fact that the Othonian soldiers are presented as being faithful to their leader even in death therefore goes against the grain of the predominant literary tradition about civil war armies, and is perhaps particularly surprising given that they did not have anyone like Julius Caesar to write a flattering account on their behalf. Tacitus does not portray the Othonian troops in a static way: they show a worrying combination of both greed and loyalty, but in comparison with their successors, as we shall see, their behaviour is relatively respectable.

3

The Vitellians and Flavians

The Vitellians

Let us turn now in detail to Tacitus' portrait of the Vitellians, which begins at *Histories* 1.51.1. 'Once an easy and safe victory in a most lucrative war (*ditissimi belli*) had been the outcome, the army, fierce through loot and glory, chose campaign and battle, and prizes rather than pay.' Tacitus immediately stresses that those soldiers who rise up to support Vitellius are initially motivated only by desire for richer prizes than regular army pay can offer. Indeed, Vitellius himself is the catalyst more than the cause of the movement. In a striking and unparalleled phrase, Tacitus presents the war against Julius Vindex as having been 'most lucrative (*ditissimus*)', for the military. Elsewhere this superlative adjective is commonly coupled with fields or crops (Virgil *Georgics* 2.136), but here Tacitus uses it to describe a war, which is provocative, given that some critics have identified the campaign against Vindex primarily as a civil conflict. Perhaps it initially seemed to be a nationalist secession and thus an appropriate place for legionaries to gain booty, but Vindex, the son of a Roman senator, may well have intended to overthrow Nero.[1]

The way in which Tacitus introduces the Vitellians is therefore alarming. It was a literary commonplace that competent soldiers (and generals) should not allow themselves to be distracted by the temptation of plunder, at least not during the battle itself. So, Silius Italicus makes the general Marcellus stop his men from sacking Syracuse (*Punica* 14.683), although Livy reflects a different tradition that the city *was* plundered (25.30.12). Similarly, Suetonius Paulinus advises his men before battle with Boudicca not to think of plunder; the soldiers follow his advice and thus win a decisive victory (Tacitus *Annals* 14.36). Good commanders rarely succumb to such temptations: so, Pompey's restraint marks him out as a moderate general of the old school (Cicero *Imp. Pomp.* 14.40) and Caesar strictly forbids looting at Hadrumentum ([Caesar] *Bell. Afr.* 3.1; cf. *Bell. Afr.* 54). In contrast, Lucan shows Julius Caesar actively offering his soldiers the defeated Pompey's wealthy camp to plunder after the battle of Pharsalus (*Phar.* 7.740-6), whereas Caesar himself explicitly stops his troops from being distracted by this booty (*BC* 3.97.1). This sort of inducement was often constructed as

being typically barbarian, as when Hannibal offers his men Saguntum
to make them fight (Livy 21.11.4). Indeed, such offers will form a rich
theme in Tacitus' *Histories*: the Flavian leaders allegedly offer Cremona
to their men to make them fight harder (3.27-8), Civilis and Classicus
think of offering Colonia Agrippinensis to their men but decide against
it so as to acquire a reputation for clemency (4.63.1), and Petilius
Cerialis, fearing infamy, vetoes his men's request to plunder Colonia
Trevirorum (4.72).

In practical terms, excessive fondness for plunder rarely brought
success for any army, whether foreign or Roman. So, the Romans are
delayed in their pursuit of Hasdrubal by plundering his abandoned
camp: Hasdrubal's deliberate desertion of his affluent camp is compared with a cunning beaver who chews off his own testicles to save his
life (Silius Italicus *Punica* 15.481-7).[2] At best, this hunger for loot meant
the loss of strategic advantages and the tedious continuation of a
campaign which could have been nipped in the bud. So, German pursuit
of loot provides a crucial breathing space for Germanicus' men (Tacitus
Annals 1.65.6), and Julius Civilis tells his troops that their success in a
previous battle was damaged by the gathering of plunder (Tacitus
Histories 5.17.1). Similarly, the Romans live to fight another day because the Numidians cannot resist plundering the camp (Sallust *Jug.*
38.8). At worst, pursuit of booty meant considerable but entirely unnec-
essary loss of life, as when the foolhardy Sarmatians are so heavily
laden with spoils that they become an easy target for the legionaries
(Tacitus *Histories* 1.79.2). Likewise, Virgil's Euryalus plunders a splen-
did helmet from Messapus, but its gleam reveals his presence to the
enemy and the weight of his booty hampers his escape (*Aeneid* 9.359-66
and 371-85). Therefore, Tacitus' initial focus on Vitellian desire for booty
not only characterises the legionaries through a trait often associated
with flawed Romans or with barbarians, but it also foreshadows their
potential defeat.[3]

Yet there was something more sinister in collective Vitellian desires
than a simple yearning for material gain: 'they lapped up the idea of
storming cities, devastating countryside and plundering homes (*expugnationes urbium, populationes agrorum, raptus penatium hauserunt
animo*)' (1.51.4). It is not just material gain but the fantasy of destruction which attracts these greedy soldiers. Their lust to annihilate
embraces both the town and the countryside, even if the latter only
offers slim pickings. As the Othonians will discover in their raids, the
inhabitants of the countryside are poor people (2.13.1). Such a phenomenon corroborates a disturbing assertion made by Tacitus' Calgacus
(*Agricola* 30.4): according to this British chieftain, the Romans are the
only people to whom both riches and poverty are equally irresistible.
The Vitellians exemplify this notion since, as well as the poor country
people, they also target the cities of their wealthy allies, the Aedui and

the Sequani. The sacking of cities can be an honourable goal, but only if the victims are foreign enemies.[4] Thus, when Tacitus first characterises Vitellius' supporters as a group, they are not promising material. In fact, they seem just the sort of dubious characters who would support a man like Vitellius – or at least the dissolute Vitellius of Flavian propaganda.

This initial impression is bolstered by the description of the Vitellian troops as they march towards the Alps in two separate columns led by Fabius Valens and Alienus Caecina. Both groups display a grotesque love of violence for its own sake. The first instance occurs at Divodurum, the capital of the Mediomatrici, where Valens' soldiers suddenly panic: 'arms were seized suddenly to slaughter an innocent community, not for the sake of booty or through desire for robbery: the Vitellians were gripped by frenzy, madness (*furore et rabie*[5]) and motives which were unknown and thus harder to cure' (1.63.1). This gratuitous outbreak of brutality is only stopped by Valens' desperate pleading. It seems as if the soldiers are trying to enact at Divodurum their earlier gruesome fantasy of sacking cities, plundering fields and looting homes: almost 4,000 Mediomatrici lose their lives as a result and terror strikes the Gaulish provinces as the Roman column proceeds. This is a striking reversal of the traditional panic which was said to have gripped those through whose lands Brennus and his Gauls marched in 390/387 BC *en route* to Rome:[6] here we see *Roman* Vitellians terrifying *Gauls*. Tacitus will develop this theme once the Vitellians actually reach the capital, but even now Valens' men are behaving like foreign invaders. This literary technique had been used by others before Tacitus. Lucan makes the inhabitants of Ariminum lament as Julius Caesar's army advances, 'O these walls inauspiciously built next to the Gauls!' (*Phar.* 1.248). Lucan thus shockingly aligns a Roman army with Gaulish invaders.[7]

When Valens' column is unable to bully the local populace, the men begin to turn against each other instead. Tacitus describes how some initial brawling between the Roman legionaries and Batavian allied cohorts nearly explodes into a full-scale battle (1.64.2). Such a tendency to fight one another rather than the enemy is a trait more familiar in barbarians than in a Roman army, where regular recruits and foreign auxiliaries were supposed to fight side by side.[8] The brawl is particularly disturbing if one recalls the supremely Roman omen which marked the start of the expedition (1.62.2-3). The column began its march accompanied by an eagle, which seemed to be leading the expedition on its way.[9] Ever since Marius decided that a silver eagle should grace each legion's standard, this bird had had particularly strong military associations.[10] Yet the column which advances on Rome under Valens becomes progressively less disciplined as the march continues.

Caecina's contingent does little better. After the Twenty-First Legion has greedily stolen some money ear-marked as pay for a Helvetian garrison, Caecina lets his men loose on a local spa town and devastates the surrounding lands. His soldiers, just like Valens' column beforehand, are given the chance to indulge their earlier fantasies of destruction and devastation: 'fields were devastated, and a place which had developed into a town over a long period of peace, and which was bustling through the agreeable enjoyment of health-giving waters, was plundered (*vastati agri, direptus longa pace in modum municipii exstructus locus, amoeno salubrium aquarum usu frequens*)' (1.67.2). The target of their anger, the tranquil spa town of Aquae Helveticae, poses no threat and is characterised as an idyllic tourist spot.[11] The vindictiveness of the Vitellian soldiers seems inappropriate since the Helvetians have given them little reason for such a vendetta.[12] In addition, although this tribe had once been famous for its fighting talents (Caesar *BG* 1.1.4), the Helvetians had long since been 'Romanised', in the sense of Tacitus *Agricola* 21.1, where Roman comforts such as baths are seen as having a detrimental effect on traditional military skills. This left them totally helpless in the face of attack. Moreover, all the Helvetian leaders – Claudius Severus (1.68.1), Julius Alpinus (1.68.2) and Claudius Cossus (1.69) – have Roman or Romanised names. Not one of these characters appears again in the *Histories*. So, just as before, the Romans play violent marauders while the local Gallic community serves as the passive victim. This inversion becomes more pronounced, after the Vitellians successfully cross the Alps: Caecina marches into Italy wearing typically barbarian trousers and a multi-coloured cloak as he addresses men who wear the archetypal symbol of Romanness, the toga (2.20.1).[13] The contrast between invaders and invaded could not be stronger, although Tacitus adds an interesting twist to the dichotomy by focusing on the small-town bigotry in response to Caecina's unconventional clothing. If Caecina had been wearing a toga, then perhaps these people would have been happy to welcome the Vitellian invaders. They are right to be wary of the new arrivals, but not because of the general's clothes.[14]

It tallies with this narrative strategy that Tacitus emphasises the heterogeneous nature of Caecina's troops. Wherever possible he mentions the original nationality of any cohort sent to carry out a particular task. Thus a Thracian cohort is directed to dislodge those Helvetians hiding on Mount Vocetius, while German and Raetian troops complete the job (1.68.2). Certainly, Tacitus' insistence on highlighting the provenance of these Roman soldiers could simply be intended to display his thorough historical research. However, he also creates an eerie literary effect by suggesting that the Vitellian army is an eclectic barbarian band while the highly Romanised Helvetians are 'slaughtered throughout the woods in the very shadows' (1.68.2).[15] Similarly, when the Silian cavalry unit declares its support for Vitellius and hands over a number of important towns in the Transpadane region, Tacitus carefully breaks down the nationalities of those Vitellian troops Caecina sends as help: 'Cohorts of Gauls, Lusitanians and Britons, as well as some German battalions and the Petrian cavalry unit, were sent ahead' (1.70.3). Even if these are the ethnic titles of the regiments, which do not necessarily reflect the origins of the men who composed them, Tacitus thereby suggests that Vitellius' army is a strangely mixed force.[16] Certainly, he avoids using the convenient umbrella label 'Vitellians' to refer to these soldiers until 1.75.1. By that stage a reader understands more clearly what the term means. In the narrative which traces the origins of the Vitellian movement, his careful avoidance of the term 'Vitellians' in favour of a more detailed breakdown of the troops has two results. Not only does it suggest that the soldiers are distinctly composite and fragmented with no real sense of unity, but it also enables him to suggest a foreign origin for these civil war troops. Men who come from the outer edges of the empire are advancing towards the centre, Rome, to decide the future of the principate.[17] Such are the initial impressions which Tacitus creates in his treatment of the Vitellian forces under Caecina and Valens. This may simply reflect hostile Flavian propaganda against the Vitellians, but as we shall see, Tacitus' portrait of the Vitellians is not static.

This initial impression becomes more clearly defined as the narrative reaches the first battle of Bedriacum. In particular, the Vitellian fighting techniques serve as an important marker for their collective identity. When Valens hears that Gallia Narbonensis is being threatened by Otho's fleet, he despatches a mixed force consisting of two Tungrian cohorts, four squadrons of cavalry, and the whole Treviran regiment supported by a Ligurian cohort and 500 Pannonians.[18] This motley collection of northern auxiliaries fight in a slapdash manner perceived as typically barbarian. When the two sides clash, the Vitellian regiment shows little self-restraint as the soldiers 'charged the enemy recklessly (*obtulere se hosti incaute*)' (2.14.3). Their rowdy onslaught contrasts with the calm response by Otho's veterans whose victory follows when the fleet makes a surprise attack on the Treviran rear. This was surely a predictable move on the part of the Othonian fleet and the Vitellian side should have anticipated it. The Treviran force may have been enthusiastic but it lacked professionalism. It was a familiar *topos* in ancient literature that barbarians, and especially Gauls, were fierce in the first moments of a battle but then tended to fade away.[19] Sometimes, Roman fighting methods could become contaminated by such barbarian techniques, as when the Pompeians, after constant war with the Lusitanians, begin to fight like the natives, especially in their deployment of speedy, disorganised charges (Caesar *BC* 1.44). Classicus' Treviran force coalesces with this barbarian model and accordingly, the determined counter-attack of the more 'Roman' Othonian veterans easily deflates their onslaught.

The boisterous and barbarian nature of the Vitellian troops continues to manifest itself as they fight. Once Caecina has crossed the Po and
started to besiege Placentia, Tacitus says that the Vitellians 'approached the walls openly and recklessly, bursting with food and wine
(*aperti incautique muros subiere*,[20] *cibo vinoque praegraves*)' (2.21.1).
Their approach shows the same reckless daring as the earlier attack on
the Othonians: there they advanced rashly (*incaute*) while here they
proceed rashly again (*incauti*). They seem to bear out Livy's view of the
Gauls as capable in rowdy skirmishes but not so good at the more
technical exercise of siege warfare (21.25.6). Tacitus' account of the
siege of Placentia corroborates Livy's observation as the Vitellians are
cut to pieces by the huge millstones which the Othonians roll down from
the walls.

In addition, the fact that the Vitellian attack was preceded by hearty
eating and drinking highlights their typically barbarian nature and
distinguishes them from regular Roman recruits. Legionaries on campaign tended to drink 'sour wine (*acetum*)', which they would sometimes
mix with water to form 'diluted sour wine (*posca*)'.[21] Even if Roman
soldiers did sometimes indulge in excessive drinking, the popular con-
ception was that, unlike barbarians, they would never allow
drunkenness to interfere with their fighting ability or to make them
vulnerable. This suggests that double standards prevailed in the Roman literary tradition. So, when Caesar's troops capture the Thessalian
city, Gomphi, his men drink much wine and are cured of a lingering
illness (Plutarch *Caesar* 41.7). Appian notes that although all the
soldiers drink, the Germans are 'especially ridiculous' (*BC* 2.64.268). An
ability to regulate the effects of alcohol or at least to judge when
drunkenness might be appropriate is often used to distinguish between
the Roman legionary and the average barbarian warrior. Caecina's men
clearly expose themselves to danger by their drunken charge and they
are repulsed with much bloodshed. The implication is that the wine is
largely responsible for the reverse.[22]

Indeed, this barbarian fondness for wine was proverbial: Gaulish
barbarians could not resist it, and although the German barbarians
originally drank beer rather than wine, they soon acquired a taste for
the latter. Livy even claims that the Gauls were originally enticed over
the Alps by the sweetness of the wine (5.33.2; cf. Plutarch *Camillus*
15.3) and makes Camillus describe the Gaulish invaders after Allia as
'gorged on food and hastily guzzled wine' (5.44.6). In ethnographic
works too, barbarians were characterised as excessively fond of alcohol.
Tacitus, after describing the simple food which the Germans usually
ate, remarks that 'they did not show the same restraint when they were
thirsty' (*Germania* 23), which elaborates his earlier comment that 'to
continue drinking day and night is not considered anything disgraceful'
(*Germania* 22).[23]

Tacitus subsequently shows that this fondness for food and drink made barbarians especially vulnerable in battle: Julius Civilis' Batavians 'as soon as they had feasted, when each man was glowing with wine, surged forward into battle with futile boldness' and thus the Romans aimed blows at the conspicuous barbarian ranks' (4.29.1). The wine has made the Batavians so confident that the sober and efficient Roman troops can easily pick them off. Over-indulgence in food and wine did not always incapacitate barbarian fighters (Plutarch *Marius* 19.4), but exceptions to the rule are rare. Nevertheless, although *excessive* eating and drinking is considered detrimental, the idea that an efficient army should be adequately nourished before battle is a pervasive literary motif. The notion is as old as Homer: thus Odysseus insists that the Achaeans do not fight without having first eaten (*Iliad* 19.155-72). Likewise, Livy conveys a powerful lesson about the risks of undernourishing an army. Scipio fails to ensure that his men have eaten before battle, but the wily Hannibal has carefully fed his troops, so the hungry Romans suffer a humiliating rout at the River Trebia (21.54-5). Similarly, Tacitus explains that the Vitellians fail to eat before the second battle of Bedriacum, so their immediate attack results in an unsuccessful night-battle (3.22.1). The motif is given a new twist by Dio, who presents the tired Vitellians and Flavians sharing their food with one another during the battle (64.13.3-5), much as the World War I soldiers did in their spontaneous Christmas truce.[24] Yet this food-sharing only succeeds in giving the civil war combatants the strength to prolong the atrocious battle. Roman military handbooks generally recommend moderate eating: Onasander says that a commander must prevent soldiers from being hungry before battle, but even so they should eat 'moderately, so as not to put a huge load into their stomachs' (*Strat.* 12.2). In contrast, the average barbarian tends to binge heartily before battle. When the Othonians jeer at the Vitellians from the walls of the besieged Placentia, calling them 'foreigners' and 'aliens' (2.21.4), they reinforce a thought which has probably already occurred to Tacitus' readers after the typically barbarian Vitellian attack.

Tacitus makes Otho plant the seed for this idea in his soldiers' heads when the emperor derisively claims that most of Vitellius' supporters are Germans (1.84.3). This is a shrewd psychological ploy: to fight a civil war under the illusion that the enemy is foreign is so much more palatable.[25] Yet how far does Otho's rhetoric correspond with reality? Certainly, during the siege of Placentia, Tacitus refers vividly to the rashly advancing German cohorts, who, with wild battle-songs and bodies bared in traditional fashion, clashed their shields together with upraised arms' (2.22.1).[26] These Vitellians seem formidably alien. In contrast, the Othonians are said to fight with 'javelins (*pila*)', which immediately locates them in a distinctly Roman world of warfare. So, Lucan encapsulates the special horror of a Roman civil war by referring

to 'javelins threatening javelins (*pila minantia pilis*)' (*Phar.* 1.7).[27]
Thus, Tacitus uses evocative descriptions of weapons and fighting
techniques to polarise the Othonians and Vitellians. In this case, the
'Roman' Othonians, disciplined and well-versed in siege strategy, win
the day while the 'barbarian' Vitellians have to abandon Placentia.

These familiar ethnographical models momentarily suggest to a
reader that the Othonians will win the war. However, when the two
sides eventually meet at the decisive first battle of Bedriacum, it
quickly emerges that the military proficiency of the 'Roman' Othonians
is not deeply rooted. They advance to a point four miles from Bedriacum, but suffer from lack of water, although there are plenty of
rivers nearby (2.39.2). Absence of good drinking water understandably
tends to terrify soldiers on campaign (cf. [Caesar] *Bell. Alex.* 8.1).
Moreover, Othonian mobility is hampered by the excessive baggage and
numerous camp-followers in attendance (2.41.3), which is a motif often
associated with barbarian armies or with Roman armies in disarray.[28]
After advancing with difficulty, the soldiers find themselves on a narrow road with steep sides, which is too cramped for so many men,
especially since they need to manoeuvre to find their standards. As if
this is not enough, next the Othonians are duped by the rumour that
the Vitellian army has spontaneously abandoned its emperor (2.42.1),
just as Galba was deceived by the false report of Otho's death (1.34.2).
Tacitus offers two sources for this report: either some Vitellian scouts
or the Othonian soldiers themselves circulate the story. The first possibility shows the ingenuity of Vitellius' troops in adopting such a devious,
albeit un-Roman, ruse, but the second suggestion reveals how desperate the Othonian soldiers are to avoid a confrontation. It is less
important for a reader to decide between the two alternatives than to
acknowledge their status as a Tacitean device which enhances collective
characterisation.[29]

Such Othonian hesitation is hardly surprising. The terrain is
cramped and the soldiers need to move 'over an area hampered by trees
and by vines' (2.42.2). This is not the sort of region in which Roman
legionaries tend to do their best fighting, especially if they are already
frightened before the battle (cf. Livy 21.25.13 and Tacitus *Annals* 1.65.4
and 2.5.3). In fact, when the Othonian soldiers do at last get a chance
to confront the Vitellians in an open area, they begin to turn the tide.
Otho's First *Adiutrix* Legion manages to capture the eagle of Vitellius'
Twenty-First *Rapax* Legion, but overall their recovery is short-lived
because Caecina and Valens send in waves of reinforcements, who
overwhelm the Othonian soldiers by weight of numbers. This is a
familiar trait of a barbarian army, which frequently replaces technical
proficiency by deploying numerous warriors. Usually this ploy ends in
barbarian defeat, since, as Vegetius observes (*Mil.* 1.8.5), quality rather
than quantity of fighters often leads to victory.[30]

However, on this occasion, quantity rather than quality prevails. Once the battle is won and the victorious Vitellians approach the capital, Tacitus elaborates the categories of Roman and foreigner. Not only do the soldiers strip the fields bare 'as if they were enemy territory' (2.87.2), but also Vitellius' entourage points out that the emperor's entry into the city dressed as a general could suggest that he is treating Rome 'like a captured city' (2.89.1). Suetonius says that the new emperor entered the city 'wearing a general's cloak and girded with a sword' (*Vitellius* 11.1), but the Tacitean Vitellius changes into a toga instead (cf. Dio 75.1.3-5, where Severus changes into civilian attire before entering the city). This is revealing about the historian's narrative technique. Tacitus has Vitellius enter Rome wearing a toga, but takes special care to mention the abortive plan, because of the impact of such visual details.[31] Nonetheless, despite Vitellius' efforts to disguise himself as a true Roman, he cannot so easily control the impression conveyed by his words and makes a speech 'as if in front of the senate and people of another state' (2.90.1). By this sequence of references, Tacitus heightens the notion that Vitellius and his men resemble foreign invaders, although they are fighting a civil war.[32]

Tacitus sharpens the focus considerably after Vitellius' troops have reached Rome. They behave like tourists who have never visited the capital before as they headed chiefly for the forum, being eager to see the spot where Galba had fallen (*forum maxime petebant cupidine visendi locum, in quo Galba iacuisset*) (2.88.3). Barbarians are often cast in the role of wide-eyed tourists, as when the Frisian leaders Verritus and Malorix visit Pompey's theatre, which is 'amongst those attractions which are shown off to barbarians' (Tacitus *Annals* 13.54.3). If one contrasts examples where Romans play the part of tourists, it becomes clear that this amused tone is culturally determined: so, Germanicus' eastern tour is romantically motivated 'by a desire to get to know the famous old sites' (*Annals* 2.54.1).[33] However, there is something very significant about the place for which these Vitellians instantly head: the site of Galba's murder, near the Lacus Curtius (1.41.2), is a peculiarly macabre spot to visit and enhances our earlier impression that these men were fixated by violence.[34] Tacitus' description of the Vitellians reflects a motif amongst ancient authors that foreigners enjoyed sightseeing in Rome, but adds a sinister twist. There is also one suggestive literary antecedent which we must consider. Livy, describing the arrival of the Gauls in Rome after their victory at Allia, says that 'they head for the forum, gazing about them at the temples of the gods and at the Capitol (*in forum perveniunt, circumferentes oculos ad templa deum arcemque*)' (5.41.4). Both the Allia Gauls and the Vitellian newcomers share an initial fascination with the Roman forum. Yet both groups quickly lose interest in their new surroundings and start to wander aimlessly: Livy's Camillus describes the Allia Gauls as 'roaming (*vagi*)' (5.44.5), and Tacitus says that the Vitellian army is 'roaming over the whole city (*urbe tota vagus*)' (2.93.1). This detail further emphasises the Vitellians' foreign identity, since barbarians are often described in such nomadic terms (cf. Tacitus *Histories* 1.79.1, 3.48.1, *Annals* 2.52.1, Sallust *Jug.* 18.2, 19.5). It also suggests a degeneration of their military skills: certainly, it is often a bad sign, if Roman troops are described as wandering.[35] Moreover, Tacitus portrays the Vitellians as shaggy figures, who are unfamiliar with the big city and who collide with people 'through awkwardness' (2.88.3).[36] The visual effect is comic and quickly denotes them as outsiders: Tacitus, heightening the contrast between town and country, and between Roman and barbarian, aptly calls them a 'savage spectacle' (2.88.3).

The Vitellians, bristling with huge weapons and wearing animal skins, certainly *look* barbaric (2.88.3). Similarly, when the people of Clusium first see the Allia Gauls, these 'unfamiliar figures' and their 'novel weapons' prove terrifying (Livy 5.35.4).[37] In addition, the Vitellian soldiers even have a typically northern barbarian constitution. In the war council before Bedriacum, Suetonius Paulinus predicts that Vitellius' German troops will have serious health problems if the conflict extends into the summer: 'Even the Germans, the most fierce troops amongst the enemy, will not tolerate the change of latitude and climate, once the war is prolonged into the summer and their bodies start to languish' (2.32.1). A careful reader of Tacitus' narrative might remember Nero's German battalions, who fell ill at sea *en route* to Alexandria and took a long time to recover (1.31.3).[38] This precedent makes it alarming that Paulinus' advice is ignored, but his words are ultimately vindicated. Tacitus notes that these German Vitellians become seriously debilitated through swimming in the Tiber (2.93.1).[39] These soldiers have not always been so feeble: they performed competently when they swam across the Po and confronted some Othonian gladiators on an island in the middle of the river (2.35). The difference is that previously they were on campaign, whereas in Rome they swim for pleasure.[40] This is another instance of the *topos* whereby life in the city impairs a soldier's ability to fight (cf. Livy 27.3.2 and Silius Italicus *Pun.* 11.410-39). Northern barbarians were normally characterised by their toughness, but the new environment has weakened the Vitellians' constitutions.[41]

This is not the only problem which the Vitellians must face. They are also enervated through their 'intolerance to heat' (2.93.1), which explains why they jumped into the Tiber at all. The point is emphasised again when the army leaves Rome, 'intolerant to sun, dust and bad weather' (2.99.1). To make matters worse, the soldiers camp in the unhealthy Vatican district of the city and so there are frequent deaths (2.93.1). Vitellius' bibulous men would not even have derived much comfort from the local wine, which Martial claims was notoriously bad:

'If you drink Vatican wine, you drink poison' (6.92.3). Although Tacitus' observations about the Vitellians embrace the traditional ethnographical distinctions between northerners and southerners, his remarks may accurately reflect the pathological reality. It has been suggested that the Vatican district of Rome was probably malarial, as were several other areas including the Pomptine marshes to the south-east.[42] If so, then any soldiers from the north, who lacked the natural resistance of the local populace to the disease, would have been extremely vulnerable.[43] Indeed, Caesar's troops fall ill in southern Italy after living in 'the healthy districts of Gaul and Spain' (Caesar *BC* 3.2). Such susceptibility to disease remained a problem for many years: the Holy Roman Emperor Otto III died of malaria on 23 January 1002 after travelling from Germany to his beloved Rome.[44] Certainly, Tacitus is manipulating a familiar ethnographical stereotype in his portrait of the barbaric Vitellians, but below the surface may lie the historical reality of a large influx of men who had not been exposed to the endemic diseases of Rome. Such environmental determinism is certainly not a theme which appears in the accounts of Suetonius or Dio.

Again, the susceptibility of Tacitus' Vitellians to disease and to climate-changes recalls the Allia Gauls. Both Plutarch and Livy emphasise these Gaulish warriors' distress when they have to confront a nasty combination of plague and intolerance to heat in Rome.[45] Livy refers to pestilence and dusty air, and calls the Gauls a 'race accustomed to damp and cold, and distressed by the stifling heat' (5.48.3). Plutarch refers to a sickness and air thick with ashes, and describes the Gauls' movement 'from shady places which offer temperate refuge from the summer heat ... to a low-lying country with an unnatural climate towards autumn' (*Camillus* 28.2).[46] Since the Gaulish invaders have previously been accustomed to a damp, cold climate, they are left highly vulnerable to disease in their new surroundings. Certainly, the Allia Gauls are not unique in being unable to stand the extreme heat of the south. Germans often have the same problem: so, the Cimbri struggle desperately against the August heat during their battle against Marius and Catulus (Plutarch *Marius* 26.8).[47] However, Tacitus' emphasis on both disease *and* discomfort in the heat evokes the Allia Gauls. Even Livy's and Plutarch's dusty air is recalled by Tacitus (2.99.1). All this suggests that Tacitus wants his readers to see the second set of invaders in terms of the first.

Tacitus' correlation between Vitellius' soldiers in AD 69 and the infamous Allia Gauls is dramatic, since his audience was likely to have been receptive to such a parallel. Tacitus is only making more graphic the popular habit of pessimistically comparing the latest disaster with the original Gaulish attack on Rome after Allia. Thus Dio reports that, after the fire of Rome in AD 64, people compared the calamity with the damage inflicted by the Gauls after Allia (62.17), and Tacitus describes how people noted that both the Allia Gauls' burning of Rome and the AD

64 fire took place on 19 July (*Annals* 15.41.2).[48] Even a representation
of high-level senatorial debate can plausibly suggest public concern
with the Allia Gauls as a live issue: amongst the arguments against
Claudius' proposal to admit some Gaulish chieftains to senatorial rank
is the objection that their ancestors killed Roman citizens on the Capitol
in 390 BC (Tacitus *Annals* 11.23.4). An event in the present could easily
be influenced by distant historical incidents, as when Thrasea Paetus'
besieged soldiers recall the Caudine Forks (321 BC) and Numantia (137
BC) defeats to justify their surrender (Tacitus *Annals* 15.13.2). In the
Histories, Tacitus clearly reminds his readers of the humiliating Allia
nexus by noting the people's negative response in AD 69 to Vitellius'
ill-judged assumption of the office of High Priest on the anniversary of
the Allia defeat (2.91.1). This nugget of information surely serves as
another marker for the context in which to place the descriptions of the
sickness-ridden German and Gaulish Vitellians in Rome.[49] Tacitus'
intertextuality with Livy's description of the Gaulish invasion after
Allia sets up a provocative interplay between Roman and barbarian
identities in a civil war setting.

Yet many of the Vitellian invaders of AD 69 really *are* Gaulish
auxiliaries and eventually the Vitellian invasion *will* bring about the
destruction of the Capitoline temple, so the foreshadowing is not just
an elegant literary device. Traditionally, the Capitol was the one part of
Rome that even the ferocious Allia invaders could not devastate. Tacitus
laments the fact that the Romans themselves destroyed the temple
'which neither Porsenna ... nor the Gauls could desecrate when the city
was captured' (3.72.1).[50] Woodman coined the useful phrase 'substan-
tive imitation' to describe the technique of giving substance to a poorly
documented incident by imitating one which is much better documented.[51] According to Woodman, sometimes the literary antecedent is
particularly significant in the new context but sometimes it is simply a
neutral template to aid composition. Tacitus' description of the Vitellians in Rome falls into the first category, where the original context is
important, rather than the second. After Vitellius' death, Tacitus reminds us again of the Gaulish invasion of Rome, when he notes that the
Gauls themselves in AD 69 were already enthusiastically recalling the
earlier attack:

> Above all, the burning of the Capitol impelled people to believe that the
> end of the empire was at hand. They reflected that Rome had once been
> captured by the Gauls, but that the empire had endured since Jupiter's
> temple had survived intact. Now, however, the Druids, according to their
> idle superstition (*superstitione vana*), predicted that a sign of divine
> anger had been given through this fatal fire and that world dominion was
> indicated for the nations north of the Alps. (4.54.2)[52]

Tacitus may dismiss the Druids' prophecies as being the result of *vana superstitio*, but this is not to deny the emotional impact made on the Gauls by the perceived parallels between the two invasions of Rome. Tacitus' initial hints that the Vitellian invaders are to be identified with the Allia Gauls therefore take on a disturbing twist, as the burning of the Capitol strengthens support for Julius Civilis' Gallo-Germanic war against Rome. Once again we perceive the vulnerability of a nation gripped by civil war: Tacitus' identification of the Vitellians with foreign invaders in *Histories* 2 is more than just decorative.

Indeed, the distinctive barbarian identity of Vitellius' troops and the fact that his supporters come from the north will continue to be explored in *Histories* 4 and 5. Once Julius Civilis has openly revolted from Rome, Tacitus notes that the Vitellian soldiers who are now under the Flavian commanders, Hordeonius Flaccus and Dillius Vocula, 'even prefer foreign slavery (*externum servitium*) than to have Vespasian as emperor' (4.54.1). The tone here seems pejorative, but there is an ambiguity about Tacitus' language. Is he simply condemning the Vitellian soldiers, who even resort to serving foreigners, for this unpatriotic *volte face*? Or is he using the reference to foreign slavery to communicate the depth of their hatred for Vespasian? Certainly, the general Vocula denounces these troops as traitors, even if he forgets for a moment that Vitellian soldiers have already marched on Rome under Roman leaders: 'If Germans and Gauls lead you to the walls of Rome, will you bear arms against your fatherland?' (4.58.5).[53] Yet it may be wrong for us to condemn these soldiers so abruptly. Tacitus has made their stance here understandable after their collective characterisation as northerners in the preceding narrative. In fact, their total refusal to accept the eastern pretender Vespasian as their emperor even suggests consistency and an odd sort of integrity. Unlike their commanders, they are not prepared to switch sides so easily, and since most of these troops have never actually seen Vespasian before, their hesitation to back him makes sense. In the long term, it may be misguided and self-destructive to support a foreign power instead of Vespasian, but in the short term, it has a peculiar logic to it, especially for soldiers who have grown accustomed to Germans and Gauls from prolonged service in these areas (cf. 2.80.3). Certainly, their persistent dislike of Vespasian is clear enough when Hordeonius Flaccus tries to get his unwilling troops to swear an oath to the victorious new emperor: most mumble his name or pass over it in silence (4.31.2). Julius Classicus, who had been sent by Fabius Valens into Gallia Narbonensis (2.14.1), and Julius Tutor, who had been 'placed in command of the bank of the Rhine by Vitellius' (4.55.2), are at least familiar to them as local commanders, who have fought fiercely on Vitellius' behalf.

Moreover, the Vitellian soldiers were doubtless worried about possible recriminations from the Flavians. Arriving in the Praetorian camp after the Flavian victory, Mucianus separates the Vitellian prisoners into groups, depending on whether they come from Germany or Britain or elsewhere. The troops from Germany are particularly terrified 'as they imagined that they were being picked out for execution' (4.46.3). Precedents from history suggest that their fear is justified. After the capture of Praeneste in 82 BC, Sulla divides his prisoners into three ethnic groups, and, sparing the Romans with a reminder that they deserve death, he slaughters the Samnites and the Praenestians (Appian *BC* 1.94.437-8). The Vitellians' fear has already been triggered by the Flavian troops rampaging around Rome and killing people at random: 'whenever they glimpsed a man who was tall in appearance and young, they cut him down regardless of whether he was a soldier or a civilian' (4.1.1). Such indiscriminate murders often take place during war and suggest that the Flavian soldiers are in the grip of a collective hysteria.[54] Nevertheless, it is still disturbing that no Flavian commander even tries to intervene.

This bloodletting naturally threatens anyone whom the angry Flavian troops encounter, but their vendetta against tall, young men is suggestive. Perhaps the rampaging Flavians are not being quite so indiscriminate after all. As has been seen, German fighters are characterised by the literary tradition as being conspicuously tall: so there is the 'tall stature' (5.14.2), which differentiates Civilis' German troops from the Romans, and Tacitus says of Batavians that, 'most of their boys are tall' (4.14.1). Indeed, Oakley even claims that 'the Romans had a complex about their short stature when compared to the Celts or the Germans'.[55] If Vespasian's troops perceive these Vitellians as being foreign, then such men are easier targets than soldiers who looked Roman or Italian. There is an interesting parallel from the American civil war, where the southerners consistently claimed that the majority of Union troops were foreigners,[56] which was not only designed to suggest that their enemy's cause was not very popular, but also made the northerners easier to demonise.

There is a similar tone when Lucan's Caesar addresses his soldiers before the battle of Pharsalus:

> With not much bloodshed do you realise your hope of the world. There will be at hand young men gathered from Greek training-schools, enfeebled through their devotion to the wrestling-school and scarcely able to carry their weapons, or a mixed crowd of jabbering barbarians, not able to bear the trumpets or their own shouting when the troops advance. Few hands of yours will wage war against citizens; most of the fighting will relieve the world of these peoples and will annihilate the enemies of Rome. (*Phar.* 7.269-76)

Caesar presents the imminent battle as being against foreigners rather than fellow Romans, thus making the encounter more palatable. By depicting Pompey's troops as either Greeks or unspecified barbarians,

Caesar quickly dispels any misgivings that his soldiers might have about killing their compatriots. The only drawback is that when Lucan's Caesarians eventually encounter the Pompeians face to face (*Phar.* 7.460-9), they immediately realise their commander's dishonest ruse. It is not surprising that Caesar's own account abridges this problematic exhortation before Pharsalus (*BC* 3.90). In indirect speech, Caesar says to his soldiers that he has never wished to deprive the republic of either of its armies, but there is no mention of foreign Pompeians. In contrast, Appian embraces the ethnic theme: his Caesar tells the soldiers that although some Pompeians are Italian, their allies are Syrian, Phrygian and Lydian slaves, who are equally ready for flight or servitude. Once they have put the enemy to flight, he proposes, they should spare the Italians but slaughter the allies (*BC* 2.73.303-2.74.310).[57] Appian's Caesar makes it all sound so simple, but, as in Lucan's narrative, his soldiers lose much of their enthusiasm when confronted directly with the Pompeian army. The Flavians in Rome are not so sensitive: they aim to kill German Vitellians, but they are sufficiently ruthless to include Roman civilians in their killing spree.

Yet the collective identity of Tacitus' Vitellian troops is not static. Although initially these soldiers crave violent destruction, nevertheless they gradually develop unexpected moral fibre and show increasing sophistication in their capacity to make judgments for themselves. In *Histories* 3 a pattern begins to emerge whereby Tacitus commends the common Vitellian soldiers, but casts their officers in a much less flattering light: essentially, the lower the rank, the more loyalty to the Vitellian cause is shown. We have already seen how Tacitus carefully differentiates between ranks amongst the Galbian and Othonian armies, and the same is true here. As the common Vitellian soldiers become losers instead of winners, they start to develop dignity as well as loyalty towards their failed leader.

The first instance of this motif is when Caecina uses the desertion of Lucilius Bassus' fleet to Vespasian to set in motion his own change of allegiance (3.13-14). He announces his decision to defect at a small meeting of senior centurions held just when most troops are scattered throughout the camp on various duties. Nonetheless, the news soon spreads and the common soldiers return to discover Vitellius' portraits torn down in favour of those of Vespasian (3.13.2). The soldiers react in a formative way at this point: initially struck dumb, they soon begin to protest unanimously against the *fait accompli*. Not only do they judge it humiliating to surrender without a fight, but they also resent Bassus' and Caecina's attempt to steal the emperor from his soldiers: 'So *this* was Bassus' and Caecina's plan (*id Basso, id Caecinae visum*)[58] – after stealing palaces, villas, and money from the emperor, they actually intended to take the emperor away from his soldiers!' (3.13.3). Like the Othonians, the Vitellians appear to have developed loyalty to their

emperor, something which Tacitus had not suggested they possessed in
the earlier narrative. This Vitellian characteristic will subsequently
become even more pronounced: when Julius Civilis asks the Fifth
Alaudae Legion and the Fifteenth *Primigenia* Legion to swear an oath
to Vespasian, they refuse on the grounds that they already have an
emperor, Vitellius, to whom they will remain loyal until death (4.21.2)
and only succumb after being reduced to near starvation at the siege of
Vetera (4.60). It is startling, in view of their previous conduct, that
military pride and personal fidelity now motivate them as they defiantly replace Vitellius' standards and arrest the treacherous Caecina
(3.14). Even the victorious Flavian soldiers will eventually be disgusted
by Caecina's duplicity: during the surrender they taunt the turncoat
general for his treachery (3.31.4).[59]

This episode raises a number of issues. Under normal circumstances,
Roman troops were not supposed to make decisions or to think for
themselves. Instead they were expected to entrust such complexities to
their superiors and to follow orders without question. Lucan carries this
concept to its logical extreme in Laelius' pledge of loyalty to Caesar: 'If
you order me to plunge my sword into my brother's breast or my
parent's throat or the full womb of my wife, I will carry out the order,
even if my hand is unwilling' (*Phar.* 1.376-8).[60] Army training has
always encouraged soldiers to carry out their orders automatically,
without necessarily understanding the full picture.[61] In practice, many
soldiers in ancient literature question and even disobey orders, but such
men are usually portrayed as rebellious troublemakers. However, in the
case of the Vitellian soldiers Tacitus inverts the usual formula: the
'rabble' has clearly seized the moral highground while the unscrupulous
officers behave like rats deserting a sinking ship.[62]

Moreover, Dio narrates the same incident (64.10.2-4), but portrays
the Vitellians differently. Caecina, after resolving to betray his emperor,
assembles all the soldiers, addresses them together and successfully
persuades them to change sides. In fact, they even remove Vitellius'
portrait from their standards themselves and swear an oath to
Vespasian. However, after returning to their tents, they change their
minds and hail Vitellius as emperor once more. Dio makes the soldiers
behave indecisively and erratically. The reader simply has to condemn
them as being typically unreliable and inconsistent, and they are left
with none of the independence and moral credibility of Tacitus' version.
Likewise, Josephus describes how the Vitellians change their mind
again in fear of Vitellius' potential victory (*BJ* 4.639-41).

The moral stature of the common Vitellian soldiers escalates when,
forced to fight the second battle of Bedriacum without adequate leadership, they face defeat.[63] Their few leaders begin to crumble in fear for
their own safety: 'The higher the rank, the more readily a man yielded
to the inevitable' (3.31.1), but 'the common soldier stood firm' (3.31.2).[64]

Finally, there is a successful replay of the earlier attempt to take down Vitellius' portraits, but again it is the 'leaders of the camp' (3.31.2) who carry this out. Eventually, the Vitellian troops must accept their defeat as reality and join their commanders in surrendering to the victorious Flavians.[65] We hear that the Vitellian leader Caecina is treated scathingly by the Flavians (even though he has helped them) because of his arrogance, savagery and treachery (3.31.3). As the standing of the common soldiers in Vitellius' army increases, that of their leader decreases and Caecina is dwarfed by his more admirable soldiers.

Two further surrender scenes serve as markers of the increasingly noble behaviour of Vitellius' common soldiers. When the emperor hears that his army has been defeated at Bedriacum, he divides his remaining legionaries into two groups: one, led by Julius Priscus and Alfenus Varus, is sent to hold the Appennines, while the second, led by Lucius Vitellius, remains behind to protect Rome (3.55) and to mop up trouble in Campania (3.58). Tacitus records the capitulation of both contingents. The first surrender occurs after Fabius Valens' severed head has been brandished at the Vitellian soldiers in their camp at Mevania at the foot of the Appennines (3.63). Such a ploy was used successfully elsewhere to demoralise defiant onlookers, as when the young Pompey's severed head was displayed to the people of Hispalis ([Caesar] *Bell. Hisp.* 39.3). The whole scene at Mevania mirrors the capitulation of Caecina and his men after the second battle of Bedriacum. Once again the officers desert first: it is only after Julius Priscus and Alfenus Varus have given themselves up that the common soldiers surrender. Moreover, Tacitus records these two officers' capitulation (3.61.3) *before* the dramatic display of Valens' severed head (3.62.1), after which the common soldiers give up. Thus the officers even desert their men before the final demoralising blow, which Tacitus must have recalled when describing Julius Priscus' suicide, 'less from compulsion than a sense of shame', while Alfenus Varus 'survived his cowardice and disgrace' (4.11.3). This is the scene where the Vitellian soldiers surrender.

> Since hope had collapsed everywhere, the Vitellian soldiers decided to go over to the enemy. Even this they achieved with dignity, as they marched down to the low-lying fields of Narnia with banners and standards held high. The Flavian army, alert and dressed as if for battle, stood to attention in tightly-packed ranks on either side of the road. The Vitellians were received in their midst, and Antonius Primus addressed the surrounded soldiers in kindly tones. (3.63.1)

Not only do the Vitellian soldiers retain their banners and standards, but the Flavian troops have learned to respect their defeated enemy. There are no taunts and jostles, as in the first surrender (3.31.3), and the Vitellians are welcomed as equals rather than as prisoners of war. This Flavian strategy is practical, in that if the ex-Vitellians are not publicly humiliated, they might be more receptive to the new regime. In addition, humane treatment of ex-Vitellians could encourage others to surrender. Certainly, Onasander recommends treating defeated cities humanely since 'nothing makes men so brave as fear of the atrocities they will suffer if they surrender' (*Strat.* 38.3). On a practical level, Caesar contrasts his sack of the stubbornly pro-Pompeian town Gomphi with his humane treatment of the wavering Metropolis, which leads other towns in the area to submit to his authority (*BC* 3.81.2). Thucydides has Diodotus argue that Mytilene's destruction would set a bad precedent to other rebel cities (3.46.2). Yet there is something more than tactical thinking for the future at work during the surrender at Mevania. Tacitus suggests that the Flavian soldiers react spontaneously to the tenacious loyalty of the Vitellians to their leader. If they wished to humiliate the Vitellians, then they could (and would) have done so. Another unusual aspect of the surrender is that the Flavian soldiers restrain themselves without any intervention from their commander (3.63.1). This can be contrasted with the scene where Julius Caesar has to commend the surrendering Pompeians to his own soldiers to prevent injury or looting (*BC* 3.98).

The next surrender takes place at Bovillae when the other contingent, led by the emperor's brother, Lucius Vitellius, has to give itself up at his instigation.

> Vitellius did not hesitate to entrust himself and his cohorts to the victor's judgment. The soldiers threw down their luckless weapons as much in disgust as in fear. A long line of prisoners (*longus deditorum ordo*) surrounded by armed guards marched through the city: nobody had a submissive expression, but, gloomy and resentful, they unflinchingly faced the clapping and insults of the jeering mob. The escorts restrained the few who tried to escape. The rest were taken into custody. Nobody said anything discreditable, and although the situation was intolerable, their reputation for honour was preserved intact. Lucius Vitellius was then executed.(4.2.2-3)

The speed of Lucius Vitellius' capitulation contrasts with his defiant soldiers' disgust at his decision to surrender. Again Tacitus emphasises the nobility of the common soldiers, who retain their dignity under difficult circumstances, unlike their craven commanders. The stalwart Vitellian soldiers, anxious not to look like suppliants, appear especially impressive against the backdrop of bloody carnage described only in the previous chapter. Tacitus does not deny their fear but instead stresses their ability to control their emotions. In this, the soldiers resemble Aeneas, who famously 'dissembles hope on his face and buries his despair deep in his heart' (Virgil *Aeneid* 1.209). This stoic suppression of terror marks them out as highly 'Roman', which is especially ironic since the 'long line of prisoners' recalls a Roman triumph or the familiar procession of the defeated in a captured city.[66] In fact, Tacitus' use of the formula 'long line', *longus ordo*, is especially pointed. It recalls Virgil's description of the conquered nations filing past Augustus on the shield, 'the conquered nations process in a long line (*longo ordine*)' (*Aeneid* 8.722), and his depiction of Troy's capture where 'the children and terrified mothers stand around in a long line (*longo ordine*)' (*Aeneid* 2.766-7; cf. Curtius Rufus 8.9.29). The noble Vitellian soldiers resemble the downtrodden foreign warriors of a triumph, except that they manage to keep their dignity intact.

What conclusions can we draw from this analysis of Tacitus' collective characterisation of the Vitellians? It is especially significant that their portrayal is not static. When Tacitus introduces the Vitellian soldiers, they are greedy and violent, but gradually this portrait is refined. The moral stature of the common Vitellian soldiers grows as their fickle commanders abandon Vitellius with few qualms, even though (or possibly because) they had had more direct contact with the emperor than the average common soldier. Tacitus does not deny that the initial participation of these Vitellian troops in the civil war is for all the wrong reasons, but they eventually redeem themselves in ways which did not look possible in *Histories* 1. This evolution of the Vitellians as a group in Tacitus' narrative provisionally suggests that the simple mirroring technique favoured by Appian and Dio will not suffice as a model for the characterisation of the Flavians and Vitellians in the *Histories*. The two sides may share certain traits at particular moments, but each army has a distinct identity with its own complexities: the Vitellians and Flavians are not straightforward mirror images of one another.

The Flavians

Josephus' characterisation of the Flavian soldiers contrasts sharply with Tacitus' portrait of the same men: before examining the latter, we should consider briefly the Jewish historian's account. A crucial aspect of pro-Flavian versions of the civil war involves the convenient idea that Vespasian was acclaimed emperor by a spontaneous movement of patriotic soldiers. Not only does this convey the notion of widespread support for the imperial challenger, but it also limits his personal responsibility for the more unpleasant incidents which took place during his rise to power. The most prominent expression of this idea can be found in Josephus:

Such were the remarks passed by the knots of soldiers, who then joined forces and, urging each other on, declared Vespasian emperor and called on him to save the tottering Empire. He had indeed long been anxious about the common good, but had never sought office for himself... But

> when he turned down their invitation the officers became more insistent,
> and the rank and file surrounded him sword in hand, and threatened to
> kill him if he refused the life that was his due. After earnestly impressing
> on them his many reasons for declining office, in the end, as he could not
> convince them, he accepted their nomination. (*BJ* 4.601-4)

The dramatic turning-point comes when the troops menacingly sur-
round Vespasian with drawn swords (*BJ* 4.603).[67] This incident might
at first seem to coalesce with Plutarch's model in the *Galba* and *Otho*,
where violent troops gripped by irrational forces will do anything to get
their own way. However Josephus carefully stresses that these soldiers
are motivated by a clear sense of right and wrong. The climactic scene
with the drawn swords is preceded by a measured exposition of current
thinking amongst the troops on the relative merits of Vitellius and
Vespasian as leaders (*BJ* 4.592-600). They set Vitellius' debauchery
against Vespasian's moderation, and suggest that neither the senate
nor people of Rome could possibly prefer a savage tyrant to a good
general. They also balance Vitellius' childlessness against Vespasian's
status as a father, and compare the luxurious life of the former's soldiers
in Rome with their own hard service abroad.[68] Their arguments display
a crude polarity, but the passage is clearly designed to characterise
these soldiers as having a sense of integrity and an ability to make
moral judgments. Their altruism and concern for the welfare of the
empire distances them from stereotypical soldiers, as violence becomes
a means to an end rather than an end in itself.[69]

How does the parallel scene in Tacitus' narrative compare with the
Josephan account? Certainly Tacitus subverts the notion of spontaneity
by observing that the various soldiers and commanders are approached
before the scene of acclamation: 'the tribunes, centurions and the common soldiery were brought over (*adsciscebantur*) by playing upon their
industry and licence, and upon their virtues and vices, depending on
each man's character' (2.5.2). Such careful methods of infiltration would
inevitably require time. The use of a verb in the imperfect (the only
example of *adscisco* in the imperfect in Tacitus' extant works), which is
emphatically placed last in the chapter, also suggests a gradual process.
In fact, the description may even strike a reader as reminiscent of
Otho's methods in preparing for his own challenge (1.23), which is not
a comforting parallel. Even at this early stage in the narrative, Tacitus
introduces a disturbing note to the collective identity of the Flavian
military at all levels. Although the passive verb 'they were brought over'
(2.5.2) ensures that the identity of the recruiting agents remains a
mystery, their methods of winning over the soldiers are revealing.
During the mutiny in Upper Germany before Vitellius' rise to power, the
legionaries bound themselves together 'by a secret bond' and then 'the
auxiliary soldiers were brought over (*adsciscitur*)' (1.54.3). The verbal

link does the Flavians no credit. What sort of men are these Flavians if so many support the movement because they are tempted by the prospect of licence and pleasures? Perhaps we should conclude that they are behaving like typical soldiers, whose character will change for the better once they are exposed to the leadership of the stern disciplinarian Vespasian. For the moment, let us just emphasise that Tacitus' Flavians are a far cry from Josephus' public-spirited troops, who feel compelled to act because they consider that Vitellius is too depraved to make a decent emperor.

This initial note of alarm is magnified by Tacitus in the next chapter:

> Soon, when it was widely rumoured that Otho and Vitellius were going to violate the Roman state with impious warfare, the troops feared that the prizes of empire would be in the hands of others, while only inevitable slavery would be theirs. So they began to grumble (*fremere*[70]) and to assess their own strength. (2.6.2)

Far from being concerned about the welfare of the empire, the soldiers are desperate not to miss out on the spoils of civil war. It is revealing that Tacitus, in attributing motives to the Flavian troops, has them equate failure in the civil war with servitude and success with financial rewards. The most natural contrast would have been between slavery and liberty (cf. *Annals* 4.24.1 and 12.34), but this polarity is conspicuous by its absence and makes their greedy focus on prizes even more striking.

Tacitus strengthens a reader's initial perceptions about the nature of the Flavian military:

> The best men were motivated by patriotism, but the enticement of booty attracted many (*multos dulcedo praedarum*[71] *stimulabat*[72]), while financial problems at home stimulated others. Thus there were good and bad men, who had their different motives, but they all longed for war with the same enthusiasm. (2.7.2)

Tacitus concedes that some Flavians are motivated by laudable factors, such as patriotism, but suggests that these men are outnumbered by the greedy and by the bankrupt. The fragmentation is striking: they all desire war, but for different reasons. The heterogeneous nature of these Flavians echoes Tacitus' description of the earlier Othonian proclamation (1.27) and suggests a general truth about the varied motives of troops in the earliest stages of an imperial challenge, regardless of allegiance. Their behaviour seems united, but their incentives and characters are not.

How far does the later narrative vindicate these early warning signs? In the initial fervour of Vespasian's rise to power, it seems as if the would-be emperor is not going to pander to his greedy men. Vespasian's

firm stand strikes a happy medium between Galba's total refusal to
bribe his soldiers (1.5, 1.18.3, 1.25.2, 1.37.5, 1.41.2) and Otho's
liberal use of money to smooth his path to the principate (1.23.1,
1.25.1, 1.30.3):

> At the first parade Mucianus had only presented a moderate bounty to
> the troops, and even Vespasian offered no more in a civil war than others
> had in peacetime. His firm stand against bribing the soldiers was excel-
> lent and created a better army. (2.82.2)

Yet just because Vespasian refuses to win his men over by a large
donative, their desire for financial reward in the long term does not
disappear. If the Flavian soldiers cannot enrich themselves by persuading their leaders to hand over a hefty sweetener, then other routes are
still open to them.

A seed of doubt about the calibre of Flavian support is planted a few
chapters later when Tacitus relates an incident involving the Seventh
and Eighth *Claudianae* Legions in Moesia (2.85). After hearing of
Otho's defeat, these soldiers tear Vitellius' name from the standards
and steal the camp funds which they then divide amongst themselves.
After the initial euphoria has worn off, they begin to fear the conse-
quences of their actions and therefore decide to offer their services to
Vespasian as a safety-net. Certainly, there is no doubt about their
natural hatred of Vitellius, but their loyalty towards Vespasian seems
extremely fragile. One particular divergence between Suetonius' and
Tacitus' accounts of this episode is revealing. Suetonius claims that
'they marked Vespasian's name on all the banners without delay'
(*Vespasian* 6.3), while Tacitus accentuates the negative: 'all banners
which bore Vitellius' name were torn to pieces' (2.85.1).[73] Tacitus' fledg-
ling Flavians rebel for opportunistic rather than premeditated reasons,
and the whole affair illustrates Vespasian's worried generalisation that
'soldiers' loyalty is precarious in troubled times' (2.75). Tacitus has
significantly chosen to separate the Moesian incident (2.85) from his
central account of Vespasian's acclamation in Alexandria (2.79) and in
Judaea (2.80). This may be because the episode is emblematic of the
factors which motivate the new Flavian troops (or at least some of them)
and therefore it serves as an illuminating precursor to 2.86. Here,
Tacitus introduces the rogue commanders, Antonius Primus and Cornelius Fuscus, who will have such impact on the Flavian cause. If the
Moesian troops are in any way representative of Vespasian's supporters, then they are more likely to favour the unconventional Antonius
Primus and the reckless Cornelius Fuscus as leaders than the exemplary Vespasian.

However, only in Book 3 does the conduct of the Flavian soldiers start
to deteriorate significantly. The men receive a strong signal from their

leaders when Minucius Justus, the camp commander of the Seventh *Galbiana* Legion,[74] is relieved of his command and sent to Vespasian for his own safety, 'because he tended to command too strictly for a civil war (*quia adductius quam civili bello imperitabat*)' (3.7.1). Tacitus chooses the intransitive and frequentative form of the verb, 'I (keep on) commanding (*imperito*)', which 'retains an archaic and grandiloquent tone'[75] and therefore may accentuate the mismatch between Justus' leadership and the civil war. Moreover, the metaphor 'to draw in the reins tightly (*habenas adducere*)',[76] is from horse riding. Such imagery is often used metaphorically to symbolise command, both on an empire-wide scale and in a less grandiose sense.[77] Certainly, it is not always true that keeping troops on a tight rein produces the best results. So, Julius Caesar often turned a blind eye to his soldiers' misdemeanours (Suetonius *Divus Julius* 67.1), and even the model commander Agricola 'knew everything that went on, but did not always punish misdemeanours' (Tacitus *Agricola* 19.3; cf. Pliny *Pan.* 70.3 and 80.3). Yet there is a difference between a commander who allows his troops a little leeway and one who has to quit his post altogether in fear for his life. Although Julius Caesar is indulgent, nevertheless he is still 'a most rigorous investigator and punisher of deserters and rebels' (Suetonius *Divus Julius* 67.1). Minucius Justus' dismissal suggests that well-disciplined soldiers are not a major prerequisite for the Flavian leaders, at least not for Antonius Primus, who faces the challenge of galvanising the movement at ground level. In fact, the Seventh *Galbiana* is Primus' own legion, so he himself may have precipitated Justus' dismissal. Vespasian may be a strict disciplinarian, but his distance from the military action allows him the luxury of adopting such a stance. In any case, as Tacitus notes, many steps are taken without Vespasian's knowledge or even against his instructions (3.8.2).

The unlucky Minucius Justus only appears once in the *Histories*, and not at all in either Suetonius' or Dio's narratives. This suggests that Tacitus considered his dismissal an important detail. Perhaps this should not be pushed too far, but it is apt that the removal of a man called 'Justus' precedes the many scenes of Flavian injustice and violence which punctuate *Histories* 3. Tacitus is often sensitive to the nuances of a name, as in the case of the aptly-named German puppet prince Italicus, who is 'trained to fight and to ride both in the manner of his forefathers and in our style' (*Annals* 11.16.1).[78] At any rate, Pliny describes Justus as an 'excellent man' (*Epistle* 7.11.4), which suggests that his personality lived up to his name. After Justus' departure, there is a striking dearth of adherents to strict standards of discipline. The one exception is the Flavian general Vipstanus Messalla, '... who was the only man to bring honourable conduct (*artes bonas*) to that war'[79] (3.9.4). Since Messalla is a source for the *Histories* (cf. 3.25 and 3.28), such commendation is striking: Tacitus, anxious not to seem naively

trusting of his sources, must have had good reason to cast Messalla in
a favourable light.

So far, the violent streak of the Flavian soldiers has remained largely
dormant. Tacitus has allowed glimpses of their collective character
without depicting any serious explosion of violence. All this changes
when the troops realise their potential on two occasions (3.10-11). The
first incident occurs when, as the Seventh *Galbiana* Legion builds a
rampart around Verona, the Flavians spot some cavalry in the distance
and wrongly identify them as Vitellians. Quickly the soldiers confront
their commander Tampius Flavianus, a relative of Vitellius, whom they
target as a likely traitor. Flavianus, 'with torn clothes, heaving chest
and lips quivering with sobs' (3.10.2), barely escapes with his life. The
incident raises some interesting points, not least the practical question
of how to identify the enemy from a distance in a civil war.[80] Yet the
central point of the Verona incident is that the soldiers (and Tacitus'
readers) begin to appreciate how deceptive appearances can be. Cavalry
in the distance who look Vitellian are actually Flavian, but Tampius
Flavianus, whose name seems so evocative of Vespasian's family, turns
out to be a relative of Vitellius.[81]

The second incident involves Aponius Saturninus, who commands
the forces from Moesia and is threatened by his troops, who think that
he has treacherously corresponded with Vitellius (3.11). Matters are
complicated in this case because the soldiers' suspicions initially seem
accurate: Saturninus did indeed send a letter to Vitellius announcing
the defection of the Third Legion. However, the general contacted
Vitellius 'before he too joined Vespasian's side' (2.96.1). These well-in-
tentioned but misguided soldiers are angry with Saturninus because of
some out-of-date correspondence. Nevertheless, their commander's
suitability for military command is still questionable. Not only does
Saturninus send a centurion to murder his personal enemy Julius
Tettianus, disguising the murder-attempt as an effort to help the
Flavian cause (2.85.2), but also the soldiers have to go and find their
commander in a residence described as 'gardens (*horti*)', namely a house
with its own grounds (3.11.2).[82] This sounds more like the locale for a
pleasant weekend in the country than the appropriate accommodation
for an active commander on campaign. So, in the final analysis the
Flavian troops may have had a case, but that does not make their
spontaneous mutiny acceptable. No matter how ambiguous Saturninus
is as a leader, the soldiers should still obey him, which is why Tacitus
remarks with disdain, 'although once Roman soldiers had competed in
courage and moderation, now the rivalry was in insolence (*procacita-
tis*[83]) and insubordination' (3.11.2). Saturninus' removal may ultimately
help the Flavian cause, but the soldiers' actions are not stimulated by
strategy or tactics: Tacitus presents love of violence and disorder as
their main motives.

This movement against Saturninus (3.11), which involves both the Moesian and Pannonian legions, is on a grander scale than the initial rebellion against Flavianus (3.10). By the time the insurrection against Saturninus occurs, the Flavian troops are said to have been 'infected, as it were, by plague (*velut tabe infectae*)' (3.11.1). The disease imagery is expressive, since it implies that no Flavian soldier is immune, not even a good one. It also recalls an earlier passage where Tacitus traces the emerging trouble amongst the budding Othonian legionaries: 'That plague infected (*Infecit ea tabes*) the legionaries and auxiliaries, whose minds were already disturbed' (1.26.1). Again Tacitus uses disease imagery, and the verbal echo hints at parallel forces at work on the soldiers in each case.[84] The historian gives us mirroring here, but in an unexpected way, given the likely prevalence of Flavian propaganda in Tacitus' sources: the eventual victors, the Flavians, are afflicted by the same rot which struck the unsuccessful Othonians.

Moreover, just before this metaphorical plague strikes the Othonians, Tacitus says that the common legionaries are stirred up 'by anger (*ira*) and despair at the repeated postponement of the bounty (*donativum*)' (1.25.2). Likewise, before the plague breaks out amongst the Flavians, the 'anger (*ira*) of the soldiers' focuses on Tampius Flavianus as an 'ambusher of the bounty (*interceptor donativi*)' (3.10.2), which is a unique phrase in Tacitus' works. It recalls Livy's greedy and cruel military tribune Marcus Postumius Regillensis, 'ambusher of booty (*praedae interceptor*)' (4.50.1), who crushes some of his own soldiers to death with stones and is called a 'beast' by the tribune of the people. Tacitus' ineffectual Tampius Flavianus pales into insignificance beside Livy's bloodthirsty general, which makes the vindictive Flavian troops seem rather irrational. At any rate, Tacitus traces a similar pattern in the collective behaviour of the Othonian and Flavian troops: initial anger arises when the soldiers demand bounty, but trouble soon spreads like a plague and rebellion begins to look increasingly attractive for its own sake. This common configuration is reflected in the narrative by the repetition of key words from 1.25-6 at 3.10-11, namely 'anger (*ira*)', 'bounty (*donativum*)', and 'plague (*tabes*)'.

Tacitus' characterisation of the Flavian soldiers continues to diverge from their morally upright counterparts in Josephus. Tacitus' narrative of the second battle of Bedriacum is especially striking in this respect. Pro-Flavian historians seized the opportunity to present this decisive encounter in polarised terms. For instance, the Vitellian general Caecina allegedly gives up without a fight as soon as he sees the size and discipline of the Flavian forces (Josephus *BJ* 4.635). Tacitus' account is different. Before the battle, Antonius Primus notoriously sends out his auxiliary cohorts into Cremonese territory, 'so that the soldiers, ostensibly foraging, would acquire a taste for plundering citizens (*civili praeda ... imbueretur*)[85]' (3.15.2). Vegetius proposes that there were practical and strategic reasons for procuring supplies before battle (*Mil.* 3.3), but Tacitus assigns shocking motives to Primus as he sends out his soldiers. The emphasis makes the eventual sack of Cremona seem like an inevitable consequence of the early collusion between Primus and his men. The adjective *civilis* is especially pointed because plunder ideally comes from foreign victims rather than Roman citizens: the unusual phrase sticks in the memory and is recalled when this section of the narrative culminates in the sack of Cremona.

When the Vitellian forces arrive for the battle, the Flavian army's response is rather chaotic. Antonius Primus may have been anticipating this onslaught like a good commander (3.16.2), but few others are adequately prepared: Arrius Varus is terrified after his hasty and misguided counter-attack, after which he plays no further part in the battle, and the eager foragers have to be recalled by a trumpet blast from plundering to fighting. This is hardly ideal since, however fast the auxiliaries drop their spoils, they will arrive in a state of disorder. The result is a dangerous Flavian rout, which almost sacrifices victory before battle has started. In fact, the entire opening sequence bolsters Onasander's warning on why generals should be cautious when sending their men to forage: 'Often the enemy, attacking scattered and disordered men who are searching for booty, kill many … thanks to this disarray and to the fact that they are heavily-laden while they retreat' (*Strat.* 10.7). Events could so easily have followed such a course, but the lucky Flavians are saved both by Primus' leadership and by the physical nature of the battle-field. A crucial narrowing of the road, as well as a demolished bridge over a river, make escape almost impossible for the fleeing Flavians. It is ignominious that the rout is only halted because the soldiers can run no further.[86]

Even when the tide turns against the Vitellians, the Flavians cannot resist the temptation of booty: ideally, their minds should have been on the immediate military objectives (cf. Homer *Iliad* 6.67-71), even if, on this occasion, their plundering does not lead to disaster. Note the gulf between the commander Antonius Primus and his men: 'Primus harassed the dispirited enemy and scattered those before him; at the same time, the others, according to each man's character, plundered the fallen, took prisoners and grabbed weapons and horses' (3.17.2). The general (to his credit) is maintaining pressure by killing Vitellians, while his selfish soldiers gather spoils from the dead. The Flavians' total disregard for the example being set by their commander is shocking, even if it does tally with their earlier behaviour. In addition, the phrase 'according to each man's character (*ut cuiquam ingenium*)', recalls Tacitus' language when agents recruit potential Flavians 'by playing upon their industry and licence, and upon their virtues and vices, according to each man's character (*ut cuiquam ingenium*)', (2.5.2).[87] There is little trace of such virtuous recruits left by the second battle of Bedriacum: the only way in which individual Flavians express their different characters is through the particular form which their plundering takes. Some choose to despoil the fallen (*spoliare*), others prefer to take prisoners (*capere*[88]), and others again decide to seize weapons and horses (*abripere*).

Their desire for spoils seems chillingly mechanical. After successfully routing the Vitellians, the Flavian army marches towards Cremona in hope of plunder, unemotionally trampling heaps of corpses (3.19.1).[89] Ancient writers often present such callousness as typifying barbarians rather than Romans: so, the German leader Civilis reminds his troops that they are 'trampling the bones and ashes of legionaries' (5.17.1) and Virgil's Turnus rides over dead bodies in his bloody chariot (*Aeneid* 12.337-40). Any Roman who does trample a corpse is usually characterised as diverging sharply from the Roman national character, as when Tullia rides her chariot over her father's body (Livy 1.48.7) or is acting under mitigating circumstances (Sallust *Jug.* 94.6).[90] The conduct of the Flavians at the second battle of Bedriacum becomes especially macabre, if one compares as an intertext Silius Italicus *Punica* 1.453-5, where Hannibal points the way to Saguntum and promises the city to his men as booty.

> The raging Hannibal pointed the way over actual piles of corpses and heaps of the dead, calling all his soldiers by name and boldly offering them the city as booty, though it still stood.

> perque ipsos *caedis cumulos* stragemque iacentum
> monstrabat furibundus iter cunctosque ciebat
> nomine et in praedas stantem dabat improbus urbem

Tacitus could easily have read and been influenced by the *Punica*, particularly since Silius himself was a participant in the civil war and therefore relevant to the action (3.65.2).[91] Like Hannibal, the Flavian generals offer their troops a city to spur them on (3.27.3). Like the Carthaginians, the Flavian troops ruthlessly march over dead comrades in the hope of enriching themselves by the sack of a city (3.19.1). Even if a reader did not recall this particular intertext, it was a common Roman construction of Carthaginian national character that they ruthlessly trampled dead bodies: Hannibal's sinister bridge of Roman corpses over the River Vergellus after Cannae is especially notorious (Valerius Maximus 9.2 *Ext.* 2, Florus 1.22.18 and Silius Italicus *Pun.* 8.668; cf. *Pun.* 8.660-2 and 12.471-2). Certainly, legionaries could not afford to be disturbed by corpses on the battlefield, but usually, burying the dead at the earliest opportunity was a priority. Those who failed to do so risked forfeiting their claim to be truly Roman: so, during the Frisian revolt Tacitus bitterly describes the commander Apronius by periphrasis as 'Roman general' (*Annals* 4.73.3) precisely when he is not burying the dead.

In this respect, the Flavians fail to behave like real Romans. Evening is falling and the fighting is over, but the Flavians remain more interested in pursuing plunder than in burying their dead comrades.[92] Onasander, in a relevant discussion of burial, recommends: 'Let the general take thought for the burial of the dead, offering as an excuse neither occasion, nor time, nor place, nor fear; he should do this whether he happens to be victorious or defeated' (*Strat.* 36.1). Onasander argues that burial serves both as a mark of reverence towards the dead, and also as a sign to the living that proper care will be taken with their own corpses: failure to bury the dead results in demoralisation and disgust amongst the living soldiers. Thus, Alexander buries his dead after the battle of the Granicus 'to console the others' (Justin *Epitome* 11.6.13; cf. Diodorus Siculus 17.21.6) and Euripides' Theseus argues that not burying the dead is a bad precedent because it will make all Greeks unwilling to fight (*Supplices* 536-41). However, burial of the dead is not a priority for the Flavians at any point during the second battle of Bedriacum. Tacitus records only one exception, Vipstanus Messalla's symbolic story of a son who kills his father (3.25). Julius Mansuetus from Spain enlists in the Vitellian Twenty-First *Rapax* Legion, but his son joins the Flavian Seventh *Gemina* Legion; at Cremona the inevitable happens and the son unwittingly kills his father.[93] Once he realises his terrible deed, the son prays that his father's spirit will not hate him as a parricide,[94] at which point 'he lifted the body, dug a grave, and performed the last duty for his father' (3.25.3). No other corpse in the whole narrative of the battle receives burial, but the make-shift funeral is still tinged with special horror. The only reason the burial happens is because family ties prevail over military ones. The interlude ends with a striking Tacitean inversion. The soldiers closest to hand realise what has happened and begin to curse this most savage war. Thus, Tacitus momentarily evokes the theme of civil war opponents, in a poignant moment of shared humanity, denouncing the futile conflict (cf. Tacitus *Histories* 2.37.1 and Dio 65.13). Yet the historian diverges from this model with an even more shocking idea: 'this did not stop them killing and plundering kinsmen, relatives and brothers: they denounced the deed as a crime and then did it themselves (*nec eo segnius propinquos adfinis fratres trucidant spoliant: factum esse scelus loquuntur faciuntque)*' (3.25.3).[95] The Flavian soldiers may have expressed horror, but in reality they are too busy despoiling the corpses of their own relatives to be upset for long.

Certainly, once the battle and the sack of Cremona are complete, the brief reference to the 'ground polluted with gore' (3.35.1) suggests that no burials took place even in the aftermath of the destruction. This is not just unpleasant but dangerous, since unburied corpses could spread disease, which often proved more lethal than an enemy.[96] Even the notorious Hannibal takes time to bury the dead after battle, and the victorious general's gracious burial of a dead enemy is a familiar literary motif.[97] By contrast, the Flavians' callous disregard for the dead provocatively links them with Vitellius, who supposedly attended gladiatorial games at Cremona, 'as if the mass of men who had died in the fighting and were even then lying unburied was not enough' (Dio 65.1.3). There is also his alleged aphorism after the first battle of Bedriacum: 'Only one thing smells better than a dead enemy, and that's a dead citizen' (Suetonius *Vitellius* 10.3).[98] Tacitus explains how, even forty days after the battle, there are 'mutilated corpses, severed limbs, rotting corpses of men and horses, and the ground polluted with gore' (2.70.1). This is a grim picture indeed. The continuity between Flavian and Vitellian treatment of the dead after their respective battles at Bedriacum is highlighted by verbal echoing here: the Flavian 'ground polluted with gore (*noxia tabo humus*)' (3.35.1) recalls the Vitellian 'ground polluted with gore (*infecta tabo humus*)' (2.70.1).[99] In other authors, especially in Lucan, failure to bury the dead or (worse) brutal maltreatment of corpses symbolises the warped morality of civil warfare.[100] Likewise, Tacitus' interest in this theme in the *Histories* links the Flavians and the Vitellians with each other at their moment of victory, even if the conduct of the Vitellians improves when they themselves face defeat. It is especially disturbing that the Flavians, who were characterised by Josephus as the morally upright inaugurators of the glorious new regime, conduct themselves so disreputably.[101]

Yet our estimation of the Flavian soldiers is already sinking even before the sack of Cremona, partly because Tacitus uses internal focalisation to reveal the Flavians' secret desires as they march over the corpses on the battlefield (3.19.1-2). They ostensibly want to attack the town immediately in order to enforce an enemy surrender, but in truth they think that a city sacked in darkness will offer a greater licence to plunder.[102] Tacitus exploits the contrast between appearance and reality, just as he did with his supposition about the Flavian auxiliaries apparently collecting supplies, but actually acquiring a taste for plundering fellow citizens (3.15.2). Antonius Primus' gambit seems to have worked because when the troops finally reach Cremona, any fear of death is outweighed 'by their eagerness for plunder' (3.26.3. Cf. Justin *Epitome* 11.5.9). Self-preservation now means little to the greedy Flavians.

The most pronounced criticism of the Flavian army comes when the commanders point to Cremona as a prize for victory to encourage their tired soldiers (3.27.2). The ploy works and the tide of the battle turns. It is ominous that the Flavian troops are motivated not by desire for glory but by the wealth of the many merchants, who are currently in Cremona to trade, 'an allurement to the assailants because of their wealth' (3.30.1). Tacitus analyses why the Flavian soldiers should feel such a deep-seated malevolence against Cremona, and the structure of this chapter (3.32) is illuminating. Certainly, their long-standing hatred for the local populace as Vitellian supporters is a consideration, but perhaps even more important is the fact that there is a market in progress, which fills an already opulent city with more wealth (3.32.2). This item is placed emphatically last in the list of motivating influences and adds weight to the passing comment with which Tacitus opened the discussion ('quite apart from their natural desire for plundering' 3.32.1). The analysis thus opens and closes with powerful references to the Flavian soldiers' natural avarice and the wealthy city of Cremona's potential for satiating this greed. Dio, who may have accepted at face value a pro-Flavian source, conveniently claims that the *Vitellians* do most damage in Cremona, even though the Cremonese were Vitellian supporters (64.15.1). Dio's Vitellians thus seem brutal and treacherous, as their prior knowledge of Cremona quickly enables them to find the richest houses. Instead, Tacitus points the finger of blame at the Flavians.

If the frustrated Flavians had sacked Cremona exclusively as revenge for supporting the Vitellians or even simply because they wanted money, then the devastation would at least have been understandable. As it is, the city falls victim to the frenzied desires of the soldiers not just for plunder but also for destruction *per se*. This is a quality which both the Othonians and Vitellians have already displayed at their worst moments and the continuity between the Flavian soldiers and their predecessors is thus most striking. Yet the Flavian excesses at Cremona are far more depraved than anything that the Othonians did at Albintimilium (2.13) or the Vitellians carried out at Divodurum (1.63.1), which are the most conspicuous blots on their respective records. The malicious Flavian destruction of Cremona plumbs new depths of violence, and while this does not excuse the earlier Othonian and Vitellian conduct, it certainly tarnishes the reputation of the Flavian troops. Tacitus observes: 'neither people's rank nor age prevented indiscriminate rape and slaughter. The soldiers dragged off for fun venerable old men and frail old women, who were valueless as booty (*non dignitas, non aetas protegebat, quo minus stupra caedibus, caedes stupris miscerentur. grandaevos*[103] *senes, exacta aetate feminas, viles ad praedam, in ludibrium trahebant*)' (3.33.1). This observation may surprise us after Tacitus' insistence about Flavian obsession with plunder. It would be logical to assume that the soldiers will not waste their time on old men and women, who are worth almost nothing as plunder, but they are still raped and murdered along with the younger inhabitants.

It is an open question how far such conduct usually characterised the sack of a city.[104] Sallust lists the rhetorical themes in the traditional description of such an assault, but says nothing about the fate of the elderly:

> Girls and boys are ravished, children are torn from their parents' arms, mothers are subjected to the lusts of conquerors, temples and homes are pillaged, there are fires and slaughter, and finally, weapons, corpses, blood and lamentation are everywhere. (*Cat.* 51.9)

Neither does Livy's Locrian ambassador, complaining to the Senate about the conduct of the Roman army, refer to the elderly: 'They rape respectable women, virgins, and free-born boys, who have been torn from their parents' embrace' (29.17.15). Perhaps, then, rape and murder of the elderly is perceived as a speciality of foreign rather than Roman armies. Certainly, Livy, narrating Hannibal's sack of Saguntum, notes that 'amidst the slaughter, rage made hardly any distinction because of age' (21.15.1). Likewise, Pyrrhus' cold-hearted murder of the elderly Priam during the sack of Troy serves as a graphic marker of an acute degeneration of morals (Virgil *Aeneid* 2.550-8).[105] Another example is the Macedonian sack of Thebes, during which old people are subjected to extreme violence (Justin *Epitome* 11.4.3; cf. Arrian *Anabasis* 1.8.8 and Diodorus Siculus 17.13.6). At the very least, ancient writers find it easier to revel in the horrors of such incidents if the perpetrators are foreign rather than Roman. If so, then Tacitus' decision to include rape of the elderly in his summary of Cremona's destruction is a damning reflection on the collective character of the Flavian army. Once again those who 'save' the Roman empire from Vitellius' frightening Germans are behaving with distressing barbarity.

One aspect of Tacitus' description of the sack of Cremona is particularly suggestive: 'since the army, which included citizens, allies and foreigners, was varied in language and in customs (*utque exercitu vario linguis moribus*), there was a spectrum of desires; each man had a different idea about what was right, and nothing was forbidden' (3.33.2). It seems that this Flavian army is just as hybrid as the previous civil war armies in AD 68-9. This diversity in their languages triggers various associations. Within the *Histories*, the Othonians and Vitellians themselves are described as 'armies different in language and in customs (*exercitus linguis moribus dissoni*)' (2.37.2), as Tacitus rejects the notion that the two armies considered selecting a new emperor between them. It is unclear whether this phrase means that the Othonian and Vitellian armies were different *from one another* (the former being predominantly Roman and the latter being predominantly German?) or whether it means that *each army* was mixed (or indeed whether it means both), but Tacitus' later phrasing (3.33.2) conspicuously echoes the earlier passage (2.37.2). In this way, the Flavian soldiers are again linked with earlier civil war armies.

Moreover, in describing the assorted languages spoken by the Flavian troops, Tacitus evokes a wider literary theme, which adds resonances to his characterisation. Armies which either originate or spend time in the east are frequently said to speak a startling variety of languages. So, Homer's Iris says of the Trojan army that 'the different men, who come from widespread places, speak different languages' (*Iliad* 2.804) and Homer as narrator describes the Trojans: 'there was no speech nor language common to them all, but their talk was mixed, since they had been summoned from many places' (*Iliad* 4.437-8). Such a cacophony of languages marks the Trojan army out as substantially different from the homogeneous Greek forces, all linked by their common tongue.[106] Language was naturally a crucial element in defining whether *any* nation was barbarian, whatever its origin. Homer's description of the Trojan army, with his emphasis on the mixed languages amongst the various contingents, marks the beginning of a literary theme. Likewise, Polybius says of Hannibal's army: 'he had Libyans, Iberians, Ligurians, Celts, Phoenicians, Italians, Greeks, who naturally had nothing in common with each other, neither laws, nor customs, nor language.' (11.19.4). For Polybius it is a credit to Hannibal's dynamic leadership that this linguistically heterogeneous army does not fall apart at the seams. The stereotype still prevailed in the twelfth century. So, Walter of Châtillon describes Darius' Persian soldiers, who are 'as varied in dress as in language and customs (*tam cultu variae quam lingua et moribus*)' (*Alexandreis* 2.108). His inspiration may have been Virgil's portrait of Cleopatra's defeated supporters, who are 'as varied in their manner of dress and weapons as in their language (*quam variae linguis, habitu tam vestis et armis*)' (*Aeneid* 8.723). The linguistic heterogeneity of eastern armies was clearly an enduring literary motif.

Another interesting twist is that such mixed armies often lose, whereas the Flavians win.[107] Perhaps familiarity with this idea should encourage us to speculate that if the Flavians had faced a better opponent, then they might have lost, like the mixed Trojan and Carthaginian armies. Tacitus often stresses that the Vitellians *lose* the war rather than that the Flavians win it. *Histories* 3 is punctuated with reminders of what flawed opponents the Vitellians are in practical terms, even if their moral stature progressively improves: so, if Fabius Valens had hurried, he could still have prevented Caecina's defection (3.40.1), and if Vitellius had crossed the Appennines, he could have made a surprise attack on the Flavians (3.56.3).[108] Any army which is too linguistically heterogeneous usually proves vulnerable and inefficient in the end. Lucan uses this same idea in characterising the Pompeians, particularly in the epic catalogue of Pompey's troops in the east: 'there never came together races so varied in their dress, nor a multitude whose languages sounded so different (*coiere nec umquam / tam variae cultu gentes, tam dissona volgi / ora*' (*Phar.* 3.288-90). The concept is reflected in the Pompeian demand for battle at Pharsalus: 'the crowded camp buzzed with mixed muttering (*mixto murmure*) ... and demanded the signal for battle' (7.45-6; cf. Appian *BC* 2.75.314). Once again an army from the east, which speaks a mixture of languages, is about to meet with disaster.

I have already suggested that a link between Tacitus' Flavians and the Carthaginian army is created by intertextuality with Silius Italicus. Perhaps the theme of linguistic heterogeneity suggests a further Carthaginian resonance. Certainly, individuals in poetry can be associated with Carthage for a variety of reasons. Thus Virgil compares Turnus with a wounded lion in the fields of Carthage (*Aeneid* 12.4-9), perhaps linking him with Dido and thereby evoking pathos, whereas Lucan in the *Pharsalia* progressively presents Caesar as a reincarnation of Hannibal, thus suggesting that the victorious Roman general is the agent of Carthaginian vengeance.[109] In the *Histories*, the hints of a link between the Flavians and Carthaginians makes Vespasian's army seem even further removed from the morally upright troops of Josephus' account. Of course, Tacitus may have been inspired, not directly by Polybius, but by Livy, who recasts the Polybian passage and says that Hannibal campaigned:

> having an army not made up of his own citizens, but mixed together from the dregs of all nations, who shared no law, no custom, no language (*non lex, non mos, non lingua communis*),[110], and who differed from one another in bearing, in clothing, in weapons, in rituals, in sacred observances, and, one might almost say, in their gods. (28.12.3; cf. Silius Italicus *Pun*. 3.220-1 and 16.19-22)

However, in spite of such a diverse army, Hannibal still manages to maintain discipline: there is no mutiny and none of the unspeakable acts like those committed by both Carthaginian commanders and soldiers in the first Punic war. Livy suggests that this state of affairs is very much to Hannibal's credit. The Livian intertext presents a successful working relationship between Hannibal and his army, which contrasts sharply with the association between Flavian leaders and soldiers at Cremona. The Carthaginian army obeys Hannibal because of his dynamic leadership, which transcends language and succeeds in keeping the soldiers in check. Not even the charismatic Antonius Primus can achieve this. So, Tacitus' echoing of Livy may underline that the Flavian soldiers are even more destructive than the Carthaginians. Certainly, the Flavians will do more than their fair share to devastate the Capitoline Temple once they reach Rome, thereby surpassing even Hannibal (cf. Silius Italicus *Pun*. 10.335-6). Tacitus' account of this incident (3.71) rather unusually leaves open the question of who actually set fire to the Temple, the Flavians or the Vitellians. Josephus (*BJ* 4.649), Suetonius (*Vitellius* 15.3) and Dio (64.17) all lay the blame firmly at the Vitellians' door.[111] Suetonius even presents Vitellius himself setting fire to the Capitol, just like some pantomime villain. The verbs are emphatically cast in the singular: 'Vitellius drove (*compulit*) Sabinus and the other Flavians into the Capitol ... and destroyed (*oppressit*) them by setting fire to the Temple of Jupiter the Best and Greatest' (Vitellius 15.3). By contrast, Tacitus acknowledges the difficulties of firmly blaming one side over another. He perceives that the question of who actually threw the first torch is irrelevant: the Temple would never have burned down if the two sides had not clashed on the Capitol in the first place. So it is that in destroying the Temple between them, Tacitus' Vitellians manage to surpass the Allia Gauls, while the Flavians outdo the Carthaginians.

Tacitus' obituary for the Temple (3.72) virtually personifies the building, which increases the pathos and heightens our awareness of the Romans' capacity for self-destruction. Even outside the context of civil war, a Roman's attitude to the Capitoline Temple could be used to measure his loyalty to the state. When Blossius claims that he will do whatever his friend Tiberius Gracchus wants, Cicero objects: 'Would you do so even if he asked you to set fire to the Capitol?' 'He would never want that, but if he did, I would obey' (*De Amicitia* 11.37; cf. Valerius Maximus 4.7.1). In weighing loyalty to an individual friend against loyalty to the state, Cicero deems setting fire to the Capitol as the ultimate test. Blossius tries to remove himself from the horns of a dilemma by formulating his answer in an evasive way, but Cicero has proved his point. Tacitus' Flavians and Vitellians in the *Histories* do not stop to think: their status as Romans only makes their thoughtless act of destruction all the more culpable.

Conclusion

The Vitellian and Flavian soldiers in Tacitus' narrative have distinctive collective identities. Each group may *at times* share qualities previously manifested by the other, such as a love of plunder, but there is no single convenient template of characteristics which will fit all the soldiers in the narrative. Each group retains a discrete identity which can develop and change in subtle ways. Collingwood criticised Tacitus for making no allowance for 'the way in which character itself may be moulded by the forces to which man is subjected by his environment',[112] but Tacitus' characterisation of the Vitellians and the Flavians as they respond to the fluctuating rhythms of the war is an interesting counter-example. The motif of two armies on the brink of battle looking at one another and simply seeing themselves could easily have misfired after Tacitus' careful portraits of each side. It is not surprising that he rejected the idea, but other authors included such a scene. Dio, perhaps remembering his own description of Pharsalus, includes a symbolic mirrored conversation between a Flavian and a Vitellian soldier before the combat: ' "Comrade, fellow-citizen, what are we doing? Why are we fighting? Come over here to my side." "No indeed! You come over here to my side" ' (65.13). The exchange hinges on the notion that the soldiers are interchangeable and thus it ceases to matter which legionary crosses no man's land first to join the other side.

There is also an important distinction to be drawn between Tacitus' and Plutarch's collective characterisation of the troops. Plutarch's focus had been on soldiers gripped from the very start by frightening 'irrational forces' (*Galba* 1.4), which gave them a pathological love of violence and civil war. Tacitus' soldiers are certainly not devoid of such qualities, as a glance at the Vitellian destruction at Divodurum shows (1.63.1). However, Tacitus offers his readers a model whereby the soldiers get progressively worse: it takes time for the irrational forces to take full effect. The Vitellian troops show a greater love of mindless destruction than the Othonians, but the Flavians surpass even the Vitellians. This gradual deterioration means that the troops who perhaps bear the closest resemblance to the Plutarchan model of men gripped by 'irrational forces' are the Flavians, the eventual victors. This shocking portrayal must have gone against the grain of many pro-Flavian sources who exploited a polarised contrast between evil Vitellians and virtuous Flavians. Even if subsequent propaganda did sometimes suggest that the Flavian soldiers were gripped by violent tendencies, these forces were portrayed as creative rather than destructive. After all, the end result *was* the creation of the new emperor Vespasian, which Flavian propagandists would naturally have deemed a desirable climax to the troubles.

Tacitus does not deny that there is a contrast between the two armies, but it is not a polarity between good and evil on which he dwells. Instead, he uses echoes of two ethnic groups to cast the two sides in differing lights. Where the Vitellians gradually began to resemble one traditional enemy of Rome, the Allia Gauls from the north, Tacitus makes the Flavians resemble another, Hannibal's Carthaginians; at the very least, Tacitus' Flavian soldiers have much in common with a succession of eastern armies. These literary models are appropriate in many ways because they reflect the polarised geographical origins of the Vitellian and Flavian movements. The Vitellians may have come from one side of the empire and the Flavians from the other, but they were both heading for the centre, Rome, and like the Gauls and the Carthaginians before them, they inflicted much damage along the way. Civil war might often start for the most patriotic motives, but eventually the result is always the same: self-destruction on a huge scale and devastation which even one's worst enemies might not have succeeded in inflicting. Thus, it is highly symbolic that the Romans themselves manage to destroy the Capitoline Temple 'although there was no foreign enemy' (3.72.1).[113] The conduct of both the Vitellians *and* the Flavians was far from patriotic, even though some authors had tried to brush aside this unpleasant truth when discussing the victors. Tacitus' evocation of Rome's most frightening foreign enemies as a model for his characterisation of the Vitellians and the Flavians is therefore both eloquent and creative. Differences between the two sides are *not* elided for dramatic effect. Subtle collective characterisation was not an easy task, especially when it was the individual emperors who tended to attract the attention of commentators, but Tacitus has risen admirably to the challenge in his portraits of the Vitellian and Flavian armies.

4

Galba and Otho

Introduction

Tacitus' appreciation of the discrete collective identities of the armies enriches his narrative, but he does not analyse the soldiers in isolation. Each emperor in whose name these troops fight also receives careful attention, as Tacitus focuses especially on how particular character traits could affect the relationship between an emperor and his soldiers. Thus, for instance, although both Suetonius and Tacitus cast Galba as a strict disciplinarian, they use different narrative techniques. Suetonius says that while Galba was governor in Spain, he was 'even excessive in punishing crime' (*Galba* 9.1) and illustrates this with a gory anecdote about Galba ordering a dishonest money-changer's hands to be amputated and nailed to the table where he carried out his crooked business.[1] Tacitus simply mentions Galba's 'strictness' (1.5.2) and allows this characteristic to emerge from his narrative in a less dramatic way, largely in connection with the emperor's treatment of his soldiers. This will be typical: Tacitus is interested in the different personalities of the four emperors, but analyses them in close connection with the collective identities of the soldiers.

Before we examine Tacitus' characterisation of Galba and Otho, it is important to consider two broad historical factors which influenced the representation of the personalities and events of AD 68-9. Firstly, during the war itself, every emperor, however short-lived, tried to manipulate public opinion and to galvanise support amongst the military in the hope of improving his own chances and blackening his opponents. Secondly, the final Flavian victory meant that Tacitus' historical sources risked over-simplifying their narratives or self-consciously shifting their emphasis to please the new dynasty. So, Tacitus criticises the writers who explain the treachery of the turncoat Vitellians, Alienus Caecina and Lucilius Bassus, in terms of 'concern for peace' and 'patriotism' (2.101).[2] Tacitus therefore faced *two* distorting lenses through which to view his subject matter: one resulted from the propaganda of AD 68-9 itself and the other was symptomatic of historiography in the decades after Vespasian's victory.[3]

When considering each emperor, we must both assess the images which Tacitus was likely to have encountered in his sources, and examine how far his own historical portraits were shaped by the dominant literary tradition. Although Tacitus' sources themselves have not survived, examining the parallel accounts of Plutarch, Suetonius, and Dio will be extremely useful in carrying out this task. Within this broad scheme, we will use various techniques to analyse Tacitus' narrative. In the first section of the chapter, we will consider Tacitean intertextuality, which will enable us to examine Galba's murder in the light of various suggestive historical and literary antecedents. In the second section, we will examine Tacitus' deployment of internal and external focalisation and consider the role of Flavian propaganda, which will reinstate the historian's portrait of Otho as a complex but coherent character. Tacitus' Galba and Otho play different roles within the narrative, so a flexible methodology offers the most productive means of appreciating both characterisation and historiography.

Galba

There is one approach which Tacitus could have used to portray Galba, but avoided. In his bid for power, Galba repeatedly exploited the fruitful contrast between polarised images of republican liberty and imperial tyranny: he himself symbolised the former, while Nero embodied the latter. This is a fairly obvious stratagem for a pretender to adopt, but Galba seized upon it enthusiastically and with some success. On his coinage, for example, the word for freedom, *libertas*, is common,[4] and Vespasian's coinage later employed many of the same symbols and messages[5] with which Galba had originally condemned Nero.[5] So, Vespasian's self-conferred accolade, 'restorer of public liberty (*adsertor libertatis publicae*)', which appeared on a *sestertius* issued at Rome in AD 71, reflects Vindex's original request that Galba become a 'liberator (*adsertor*)', and 'general (*dux*)' for the human race (*Galba* 9.2; cf. Plutarch *Galba* 4.5), while Pliny the Elder describes Vindex himself, Nero's original military challenger, as a 'restorer of liberty (*adsertor libertatis*)' (*HN* 20.57.160).[6]

Galba was not the first to exploit the emotive term *adsertor*. Originally, it meant the prosecutor of a person who was wrongfully holding a free man as a slave, but this stirring word had great potential for metaphorical use.[7] Suetonius claims that the Roman people, exasperated by Caesar, demanded *adsertores* to rescue them, thus neatly suggesting their collective status as slaves (*Divus Iulius* 80.1). Even the Boian rebel Mariccus represents himself as 'restorer of Gaulish liberty (*adsertor Galliarum*)'), thereby deliberately recalling Vindex's propaganda (Tacitus *Histories* 2.61).[8] This was a term above all associated with the year of Nero's death, AD 68, which was characterised as 'sacred, since the freedom of the world had been restored (*adserto ... sacer orbe fuit*)' (Martial *Epigram* 7.63.10). The survival of the expression probably reflects successive attempts to appropriate it, both during and after the war. Certainly, Galba swiftly entered into the spirit of Vindex's invitation to become a restorer of liberty for the human race. When the would-be emperor initially challenged Nero's authority, he deliberately made his proclamation coincide with a day when he was manumitting slaves. Both Suetonius (*Galba* 10.1) and Plutarch (*Galba* 5.1) focus on this as a powerful and suggestive moment.

Galba reinforced his identity as a liberator on one coin in particular. The obverse shows Liberty, who is personified and named, and the reverse displays a *pilleus*, the cap worn by a freed slave, with two daggers on either side of it; the legend is continued on the reverse, 'the restored republic (*P.R restituta*)'.[9] The design further indicates Galba's interest in the motif of liberty, particularly because it evokes another famous coin, a *denarius* of Brutus, which was struck after Caesar's murder. This coin also shows two daggers and a *pilleus*, and bears the slogan 'the Ides of March (*Eid[ibus] Mar[tiis]*)'. Howgego talks in terms of a 'dialogue between coin types' and in this context comments on the symbolism of Galba's decision to march against Nero with a dagger hanging around his neck (Suetonius *Galba* 11).[10] Galba thereby draws upon images with an emotive history, both on coins and in real life. For instance, one of Julius Caesar's assassins, after the murder, placed a *pilleus* on the end of a spear to symbolise freedom, which reflects the people's earlier plea for rescue by *adsertores* (Appian *BC* 2.119.499). In 100 BC Saturninus raised a *pilleus* aloft in front of slaves as a banner to call them to arms (Valerius Maximus 8.6.2). In addition in 201 BC when Scipio Africanus returned to Rome after successfully defeating Hannibal, the grateful Quintus Terentius Culleo, a senator who had been captured by the Carthaginians and then released, followed Scipio's triumphal procession 'with a liberty cap on his head (*pilleo capiti inposito*)' (Livy 30.45.5). Galba understood the associations of putting a *pilleus* on his coinage and the image he would thereby project.[11]

In contrast, even when Tacitus reflects on events before his official January 1st starting-point in the narrative, he does not characterise Galba as an *adsertor*. Shochat argues that dividing the historical narrative into an introductory survey, followed by a detailed account of events from 1 January AD 69, 'serves Tacitus' purpose of improving Galba's image' (202).[12] Yet the omission of earlier episodes surely emphasises Galba's identity as an elderly and outmoded disciplinarian rather than as a liberator. This strategy is striking, especially since elsewhere Tacitus often contrasts slavery and freedom to add stirring moral resonances to his narrative. So, he suggestively juxtaposes oppressed slaves in Italy who rebel for freedom's sake (*Annals* 4.27), and the chilling Vibius Serenus, a Roman citizen who prosecutes his own father (*Annals* 4.28).[13] One might have thought that the Galba-freedom / Nero-tyranny antithesis was potentially irresistible for Tacitus, particularly in view of Nero's characterisation as a tyrant in the literary tradition.[14] However, Tacitus downplays the Roman people's jubilant reaction to Galba's succession, which features in other accounts. The epitome of Dio explains that when Galba became emperor, some people even wore liberty caps on the grounds that they had become free (63.29.1; cf. Suetonius *Nero* 57.1).[15] Such scenes had great dramatic potential, which Tacitus chooses to avoid.

Surviving coinage and other literary accounts therefore suggest that one possible strategy for portraying Galba was to shift the focus from idealistic liberator to vulnerable old man butchered by frenzied troops. Yet Tacitus omits the first half of this formula and begins his narrative only when Galba's fortunes are already on the decline. Perhaps that sort of theatrical *peripeteia* would have over-emphasised Galba's importance as an individual in the broad scheme of events.[16] Although Tacitus acknowledges that Nero's death is initially greeted 'by a surge of happiness' (1.4.2), there are no people running through the streets with liberty caps. In fact, Tacitus, with characteristic sensitivity to collective identity, shows that different social ranks react in different ways: while the lower social ranks are 'sad and eager for rumours' (1.4.3), the senators and equestrians are happy at news of Nero's death. The only freedom in evidence is an exploitative sort, as the senators 'immediately take the liberty of dealing more freely with an inexperienced and absent emperor' (1.4.3). There is a hint here that Galba's presence will soon put an end to this holiday atmosphere.

Instead, Tacitus consistently foregrounds another characteristic, namely Galba's fondness for old-fashioned discipline. Galba prided himself on his strictness, despite the fact that his old age tended to diminish the respect that people had for him. His pithy aphorism that he chose, rather than bought, his soldiers features in all the accounts: his severity is a pervasive theme.[17] Perhaps Galba thought that a tough persona was just as instrumental in winning support as his stance as a liberator. By stressing his rigorous methods of military leadership, the new emperor indicates publicly that he will not be another Nero.[18] According to Suetonius, Galba assumes the title of *imperator* on the same occasion that he is acting as 'legate of the senate and Roman people', which pointedly distances him from Nero, who had appointed him *imperial* legate in the province of Tarraconensis (*Galba* 10.1).[19] Plutarch notes that initially Galba is hailed as emperor, but modestly accepts the title of general instead (*Galba* 5.2). Suetonius and Plutarch both cast the acclamation positively, but Tacitus is less interested in the formalities of Galba's accession, and more concerned about how people perceive him. So Tacitus stresses the disastrous mismatch between Galba's severity and the popular mood at the time: 'his military reputation had once been praised and commended everywhere, but his strictness vexed those who rejected the discipline of the past and who, in the course of fourteen years under Nero, had come to love the vices of their emperors no less than they had once feared their virtues' (1.5.2). Tacitus suggests that Galba is certainly different from Nero, but perhaps too much so.

Tacitus characterises the elderly Galba, not as a liberator, but as a man whose excessive severity masks any positive qualities. His march to Rome is notoriously 'slow' (as befits his age) and 'bloody' (1.6.1). Tacitus leaves open the extent of Galba's direct involvement in the murders of Cingonius Varro, the consul-designate, and Petronius Turpilianus, the ex-consul, by using an ablative absolute,[20] but the implication is that Galba's lieutenants Titus Vinius and Cornelius Laco are the agents for the murders, even if the emperor must bear the ultimate responsibility. The brutality does not stop there. Tacitus characterises Galba's entry into Rome as ill-omened, 'with thousands of unarmed troops having been massacred (*trucidatis tot milibus inermium militum*)' (1.6.2), although again the ablative absolute leaves open the question of responsibility. The description of these soldiers as 'unarmed' not only makes their deaths seem pitiful,[21] but also makes the perpetrators seem cowardly, just as when Tacitus questions the bravery of the Roman troops who assault some unarmed and half-asleep Germans (*Annals* 1.51.1). Suetonius also casts Galba's entry into Rome as savage by noting that the emperor 'decimated (*decimavit*)' some soldiers, who had been rowers until Nero promoted them: Galba himself is made the agent of the decimation (*Galba* 12.2). Plutarch makes Galba seem less savage since he only orders his cavalry to charge after the soldiers had drawn their swords, and there is no mention of decimation (*Galba* 15.7). It is also revealing that Tacitus does not identify the murdered soldiers as the marines who had been conscripted by Nero (cf. 1.6.2): Plutarch and Suetonius both make Galba's victims sound more motley by highlighting this detail. Finally, Tacitus' assertion that thousands of men were killed may be an exaggeration: Dio certainly claims that seven thousand were killed (64.3), but the other accounts say nothing about such huge numbers. These differences suggest that Tacitus wants his audience to feel some pity for these soldiers, as well as to note the eerie atmosphere created by their deaths, which Galba seems powerless to prevent.

When Otho denounces Galba's brutality before his soldiers, Tacitus puts emotive language into his mouth. Otho calls the murdered troops 'utterly innocent (*innocentissimi*)' (1.37.2), using an unusual superlative form, which only appears on one other occasion in Tacitus' extant works, again in a speech (cf. 4.7.2).[22] Otho explicitly says that Galba himself ordered the decimation of the soldiers, even though they had put themselves into the emperor's care and were begging for mercy. Tacitus' previous description does not vindicate this version, but Otho eloquently suggests that Galba is a monster and stirs up hatred amongst his listeners.[23] This is particularly effective: Plutarch says that after Galba's arrival in Rome, people who previously despised him as a weak old man regard him as 'horrible' and 'terrifying' (*Galba* 15.9), but Tacitus claims instead that although the emperor is 'hated' (1.7.2), people find his old age ridiculous: 'even Galba's old-age seemed laughable (*inrisui*) and loathsome.'[24] This must leave Galba vulnerable, since he is despised, but not feared personally. Fear was traditionally perceived as a protective device for rulers. Seneca makes Oedipus observe to Creon that 'fear preserves kingdoms' (*Oedipus* 704), and of course there is the famous and frequently quoted line from Accius' *Atreus*, 'let them hate me, as long as they fear me (*oderint dum metuant*)'.[25] People may fear Galba's lieutenants and their crimes, but the elderly emperor himself prompts scorn rather than terror. Certainly, Aristotle concludes that the two most dangerous factors for a monarch are hatred and contempt (*Politics* 1312b17).

Accordingly, Tacitus omits details which might undermine Galba's identity as a frail old man. For instance, in AD 39 Galba was fighting against the German tribes when the emperor Caligula was present (Suetonius *Galba* 6.3. Cf. *Caligula* 44.1). At this point, Galba allegedly ran beside the emperor's chariot for twenty miles, while directing a 'field manoeuvre (*decursio*)', shield in hand. This was no mean feat: a *decursio* was a gruelling exercise intended to accustom soldiers to long marches in full armour.[26] Suetonius' anecdote succinctly conveys Galba's stamina and tenacity, and it may also recall the heroes of old: so, Euripides describes how Achilles kept pace with a four-horsed chariot despite wearing full armour (*Iphigenia at Aulis* 206-15). It is understandable that Tacitus, as a historian, usually avoids such biographical anecdotes, but he is prepared to include retrospective material about Otho (1.13.3-4). However, for Tacitus, public scoffing at Galba's frailty is far more meaningful than a story of physical endurance which was thirty years out of date.[27]

Tacitus characterises Galba as weak and elderly, but the emperor still understands that there are problems with his public image because he is old. His solution is to adopt Piso, thinking misguidedly that once people hear about the adoption, he will no longer seem like an old man, 'the only slur that is currently being cast against me' (1.16.3).[28] Certainly, this is one of the accusations being made against him – in this much he is right – but there are other complaints. Tacitus' readers have already noted the hostile rumours about the emperor's 'feeble old-age (*senium*) and avarice' (1.5.2), a pairing which may even call to mind stereotypical greedy old men from Roman comedy. The complaint suggests that if Galba had been the right *kind* of old man, then he might have survived. It is the fact that the public and the soldiers consider him not just old but greedy which precipitates his downfall. Galba has disastrously misjudged those around him, which gives Otho the perfect opening. Otho mocks Galba's choice of successor because the old man had brought back from exile 'the man whose gloominess and avarice he judged most like his own' (1.38.1). Certainly, Otho is biased, but he strikes a chord amongst the soldiers, who rush into the forum and initiate the killings which end Galba's regime. Galba's naive assertion that people only criticise him because he is an old man exemplifies his failure as emperor to respond adequately to public opinion.

We can usefully compare Tacitus' description of Galba's downfall with some famous death-scenes from other authors and genres. As the false news spreads that Otho has been killed, the people are said to rush enthusiastically towards the palace: 'Galba yielded to the consensus of error. When he had put on his breastplate (*sumpto thorace*),[29] he was lifted in a chair, for he was too old and infirm to stand up to the crowds that kept flocking in' (1.35.1). Galba's vulnerability is already poignant, but it becomes more so if we see parallels with the death of Priam in Virgil's *Aeneid*.[30] The murder of a weak old man is a scene which featured elsewhere in epic, as when Lucan's Scaevola is killed before the altar of Vesta, mirroring Priam in his death (*Phar*. 2.126-9).[31] Tacitus' audience would therefore probably have been receptive to echoes of this particular Virgilian scene. Tacitus, like Virgil, focuses on the doors of the palace being broken down (1.35.1; cf. *Aeneid* 2.507-8 and *Aeneid* 2.492-3)[32], while Suetonius, Plutarch and Dio do not. In each case a building which should have provided security is violently breached. Moreover, in both Tacitus and Virgil a helpless old man (Priam / Galba), confronted in his palace by a surging crowd, responds by ineffectually putting on his armour (1.35.1. Cf. *Aeneid* 2.509-11). Virgil describes Priam's arming scene in this way:[33] 'the elderly Priam (*senior*) vainly drew onto his shoulders trembling with age his long unused corselet, and girded at his side an ineffectual sword. He rushed into the thick of the enemy, seeking death' (*Aeneid* 2.509-11). At least Virgil's Priam, frail though he is, has enough strength to confront the enemy. Tacitus' Galba is helplessly carried forth in a sedan chair, which immediately suggests his frailty and old age. The sedan chair appears again at Galba's death: 'Galba was catapulted from the chair and flung to the ground' (1.41.2). This is highly degrading, especially in comparison with the murder scenes of other famous old men. Priam arms himself and throws an ineffectual spear at Neoptolemus, and Cicero salvages some dignity by bravely thrusting his head from his litter for decapitation (Plutarch *Cicero* 48.5 and Livy *Per*. 120), but Galba can do nothing. Although Galba has put on a corselet, Tacitus notes that the Othonian soldiers are about to kill 'an unarmed old man (*inermis et senex*)' (1.40.1).[34] Tacitus' Galba is unable to defend himself, just like the unarmed soldiers who were killed when the emperor entered Rome (1.6.2).

In comparison, Suetonius changes the dynamics of this scene altogether by making the emperor himself observe wryly that his linen corselet will offer him little protection against so many swords (*Galba* 19.1). This ability to visualise death is lacking in Tacitus' account, where Galba is simply swept up by the incoming crowd.[35] These differences influence a reader's perception of Galba in each case. Suetonius' Galba is resigned to his own future, even picturing the precise moment of his death, and possesses a certain grandeur by making such a fatalistic observation (cf. Tacitus *Histories* 2.48.3 on Otho). Tacitus' Galba, by contrast, is unceremoniously lifted up by force, unable to resist the crowd because he is a weak old man. There is no feisty aphorism: even his final words are in indirect speech (1.41.2), which is further muted by Tacitus' observation that the killers were oblivious to his words. Even Priam utters a short but defiant speech before his death (*Aeneid* 2.535-43). All these factors further reinforce Tacitus' presentation of Galba as a particularly helpless old man.

We can also compare historical figures with Tacitus' narration of Galba's death. Livy's Servius Tullius, the sixth king of Rome, whose murder by Lucius Tarquinius is 'an example of tragic guilt' (1.46.3), offers an interesting point of comparison. The murderer (like Otho) is young and hot-headed (1.46.2), while the victim (like Galba) is old and weak (1.48.3). Servius Tullius' body (like Galba's) is publicly desecrated. Yet where Livy focuses on dominant individuals, Tacitus' protagonists are dwarfed by those around them. Tarquinius 'surrounded himself with a body of armed men and burst into the forum (*in forum inrupit*)' (1.47.8), whereas the Othonians, 'savage and armed, burst into the forum (*in forum inrumpunt*)' (1.40.2). Otho himself is nowhere to be seen. Livy's Tarquinius seats himself on the throne in front of the senate house (1.47.8), whereas a passive Otho is placed by his soldiers on the platform in the military camp (1.36.1). Furthermore, Livy's helpless old Tullius and his arrogant young Tarquinius are clearly polarised in moral terms. Tullius' political integrity is reflected in a fragment of Accius' *Brutus*, referring to 'Tullius, who had strengthened liberty (*libertas*) for the citizens' (Cicero *Pro Sestio* 58.123). Tacitus could have matched Galba much more closely with Tullius in this respect, but prefers to link the two characters through their old age.

Tacitus, in portraying Galba, also evokes the figure of Pompey, particularly through his distinctive description of the emperor's corpse: 'the others foully mutilated his arms and legs (his breast was protected) and with bestial savagery many wounds were inflicted on the already headless corpse (*trunco iam corpori*)' (1.41.3). Decapitation was a tried and tested way of degrading the dead, but perhaps the most famous case from a civil war involves Pompey.[36] One tradition, which is preserved by Plutarch, Appian, Juvenal and Lucan, is that Pompey's decapitated body was left on a shore. This motif probably originated in the *Histories* of Asinius Pollio, to which Tacitus may have alluded through his description of Galba's death. Pollio's account was certainly

well-known, and Virgil alluded to it for the treatment of Priam's corpse
(*Aeneid* 2.557-8).[37] There are several parallels between the fate of
Tacitus' Galba and the most extensive 'Pollian' description of Pompey's
death (Lucan *Phar.* 8.589-822).[38] Where Lucan suggests (8.612) that
Pompey's murder is a collective effort (a group inflicts multiple stab-
wounds in an 'Orient-express' style killing), Tacitus similarly describes
how a *group* of men hacked at Galba's legs and arms (1.41.3), despite
speculation on who inflicted the death-blow. Where Lucan singles out
Septimius, one of Pompey's own soldiers, for special criticism (*Phar.*
8.597; cf. Appian *BC* 2.85.359 and Plutarch *Pomp.* 79.4), Tacitus trumps
this by noting that all Galba's killers are the emperor's own soldiers.
Furthermore, Lucan refers to Pompey's headless corpse (*Phar.* 1.685
and 8.753: *truncus*), while Tacitus describes Galba in similar terms
(1.41.3: *truncum corpus*). Tacitus certainly uses this phrase elsewhere
of Flavius Sabinus (3.74.2: *truncum corpus*), but there are cumulative
details about Galba's corpse which make us recall Pompey. In Tacitus,
Galba's old retainer Argius buries his master's headless body at night
in a shallow grave (1.49.1). Likewise, Lucan describes how Cordus does
the same to Pompey's body (*Phar.* 8.789). The parallels between the
accounts of Lucan and Tacitus become clearer if one compares other
versions of Galba's death. Suetonius refers to Galba's *truncus* but says
nothing about the dramatic burial (*Galba* 20.2), while Plutarch claims
that Helvidius Priscus took the body away with Otho's permission
(*Galba* 28.4). Even Tacitus' detail about Galba's burial in the gardens of
his villa on the Aurelian way (1.49.1; cf. Suetonius *Galba* 20.2) evokes
Pompey. Plutarch claims (*Pomp.* 80.10) that Pompey's remains were
eventually brought to Cornelia, who reburied them at her husband's
Alban villa. Lucan also alludes obliquely to this tradition (*Phar.* 8.767-
70).[39] Thus, the Pompeian undertones of Galba's burial appear only in
Tacitus' account.

Moreover, Tacitus' audience was likely to have been receptive to such
echoes since Pompey's improvised burial retained its fame long after his
death. So when Hadrian visited Egypt in AD 130, he sacrificed to
Pompey's spirit and commented on the lack of tomb (Dio 69.11.1; cf.
Martial 5.74.1-2). Suggestive parallels between Galba and Pompey also
inform Silius Italicus' description of Galba (ancestor of the emperor) as
'Galba of glorious name (*magno nomine Galba*)' (*Pun.* 8.469), which
recalls Lucan's famous description of Pompey: 'he stands, the mere
shadow of a great name (*stat magni nominis umbra*' (*Phar.* 1.135).[40]
Pompey was clearly a pervasive reference point.

Yet why should Tacitus have bothered to link Galba with Pompey,
Servius Tullius and Priam at the moment of their deaths? A reader can
respond to the intertextuality in a number of ways. Tacitus' encouragement that his readers should see Galba through the Virgilian filter of
Priam momentarily simplifies the moralism of the episode, because the

elderly Trojan's murder was so clearly callous and wrong. Much the same can be said of the evocation of Tullius, the rightful ruler murdered at the hands of an arrogant young usurper. In addition, Tacitus' recollection of Pompey immediately lends the elderly emperor an air of dramatic vulnerability by identifying him with a historical 'loser'. So, Caesar implies that Pompey was a born loser after the battle of Dyrrachium, which he says the Pompeians could have won, if they had been led by a 'winner'.[41]

However, Tacitus' allusions also create deeper resonances, which do not necessarily all pull in the same direction.[42] Just because Pompey lost the civil war and his life, Tacitus does not automatically favour him. Tacitus, like Sallust before him, feels ambiguous about Pompey, who is 'more secretive, but no better [than Marius and Sulla]' (2.38.1) and 'a cure worse than the disease' (*Annals* 3.28.1). Tacitus stresses the depressing continuity between the past and present, suggesting that in each case 'the same divine anger, the same human frenzy' (2.38.2) drove men to conflict.[43] This suggests that Tacitus perceives civil war as a cyclical phenomenon, into which the Roman nation is inextricably locked. That we, as readers, are particularly meant to take note of Tacitus' analysis here is suggested by the fact that this is his one major authorial intervention in the *Histories*.[44] Yet this authorial viewpoint differs from that attributed to the internal audience in AD 68-9, who prefer to criticise their present leaders by glorifying those of the past. Tacitus recreates popular opinion at Rome along these lines:

> The world was nearly turned upside down even when the contest for power was between good men. Yet the empire had survived the victories of Julius Caesar and Augustus, just as the Republic would have survived under Pompey and Brutus. But were they now to visit the temples and pray for Otho or for Vitellius? To pray for either would be impious. It would be wicked to offer vows for the success of either in a war where the only thing you could be sure of was that the winner would turn out the worse. (1.50.2)

There is a related scene in Plutarch before the first battle of Bedriacum, but the biographer himself proposes that Otho and Vitellius are worse than previous leaders, rather than making a group within the text come to this conclusion (*Otho* 9.5). In so doing, Plutarch is buying into the familiar notion amongst Roman writers that decline is inevitable.[45] Tacitus' technique is different: he does not always idealise the past (except when it suits him to do so), but he can still use echoes of familiar historical figures to elaborate a less well-known character like Galba.

Various strands of thought are therefore triggered by Tacitus' intertextual reference to Pompey in particular. Either Galba is straightforwardly inferior to Pompey, as the Roman public is presented as thinking, or there is continuity between the past and present, as

Tacitus the narrator suggests.[46] Whichever view we adhere to, Galba emerges as a flawed character, but as readers, we still ponder the brutality of the emperor's murder. Pompey's death was perceived as a tragic reversal of personal fortune, but Galba's end can be cast in a similar (perhaps even more tragic) light. Galba was murdered by his legionaries in Rome at the Lacus Curtius, where the Republican hero Curtius had once sacrificed himself for the good of the state.[47] Pompey was killed by a predominantly Egyptian group (despite Septimius) outside Rome. What is more, the fleeing Pompey, having been defeated at Pharsalus, was allegedly planning to enlist the help of Rome's arch-enemies, the Parthians (Lucan *Phar.* 8.209-38 and Plutarch *Pomp.* 76.6), which may mute his status as a tragic hero. According to this view, had Pompey lived, the destruction within the empire could have escalated hugely in a war that was 'both civil and foreign' (Dio 42.9). In contrast, Galba's death ensured that the civil war, which had momentarily lost its momentum, continued. For Tacitus, Galba's death was more important than his life, as the starting-point of the *Histories* suggests. The historian's intertextual references to Pompey, Servius Tullius and Priam provoke an audience to measure Galba at the moment of his death against better-known historical and literary figures. The brutal killing of this elderly emperor will pave the way for worse atrocities and set a terrifying precedent. So, Tacitus exploits intertextuality and forces his readers to turn their collective gaze on the moment of Galba's death, which will serve as a yardstick for future murders, real (3.85) or imagined (2.75).

Otho

The characterisation of Otho in many authors is riddled with tensions and inconsistencies.[48] Tacitus' formulation encapsulates the paradox: 'by two acts, one most criminal and the other heroic, he earned in equal measure the praise and disapproval of posterity' (2.50.1). Otho may have instigated Galba's murder, but he also selflessly committed suicide to save the state. Murison refers to 'an almost audible shifting of the critical gears' in many accounts and suggests that Tacitus' version offers the most pronounced contrast between Otho's life and death.[49] What *is* the connection (if any) between the Otho who greedily gazes at Piso's severed head (1.44.1) and the Otho who dies with such dignity (2.49)?

Perhaps the two sides of Otho's character are simply irreconcilable. Such is the worry of Shochat: 'Was it possible that such a degenerate, corrupt, rotten and wretched person should be capable of displaying loftiness of spirit and sacrificing his life to prevent a blood-bath and to spare the state the havoc of a civil war?'.[50] Tacitus does nothing to hide the inconsistencies by noting Otho's desire for a speedy burial after his suicide 'in case his head was cut off and subjected to derision' (2.49.3).

This concern accentuates the inconsistent characterisation by triggering a recollection of Otho's past crimes even at his most glorious moment. After all, Otho knows all about such degradation from witnessing what happened to Galba's and Piso's severed heads. Galba's fate was infamous, as we have seen. So Juvenal describes his portrait mask as 'lacking ears and a nose' (8.5), which perpetuates the mutilation of the emperor's corpse.[51] Tacitus' Otho is naturally keen to avoid such degradation after his death and wants to be buried intact. His concern with burial recalls the final moments of epic heroes such as Hector (Homer *Iliad* 22.338-343) or Turnus (Virgil *Aeneid* 12.934-6), although Otho's request is not of course made directly to his enemy. The association with Nero, who also wanted to be cremated 'in one piece' (Suetonius *Nero* 49.4), is less propitious at what is supposed to be Otho's most glorious moment.

Of course, ancient writers generally relished such contradictions. The rogue who redeems himself (or herself) in death is a familiar figure in historiography: so, for Keitel, Otho's incompatible qualities recall Sallust's portrait of Catiline.[52] Another marriage of opposites is the stereotype of the efficient, but decadent, soldier: Alcibiades, Alexander the Great, Sulla, Caesar and, above all, Antony were characterised in this way.[53] Tacitus subsequently describes Otho in Lusitania as 'wanton in his spare time, but more moderate when wielding power' (*Annals* 13.46.3). However, in the *Histories*, Otho may be decadent, but he lacks martial skills, so the louche soldier stereotype does not really fit, nor explain away the incongruities within Otho's character. Perhaps Tacitus is more concerned to drive home a moral than to offer a consistent picture of Otho's personality (cf. Tacitus *Annals* 3.65).[54] Yet, as I shall argue, first impressions can be deceptive and Tacitus' Otho may actually cohere better than some critics have suggested.

Such an apparently extreme transformation from monster to hero in Tacitus' Otho should surprise us. Nonetheless although as a historian Tacitus often plays down sensational details, he does depict Otho leering at Piso's severed head (1.44.1). Even if this is not so shocking as the behaviour of Aquilius Regulus, who allegedly bit Piso's severed head (4.42.2; cf. Statius *Thebaid* 8.753), Tacitus' depiction of the emperor still seems more reminiscent of Suetonius' lurid narrative technique. In fact, Suetonius tones down this same scene, and Piso's severed head is not even mentioned (*Galba* 20.2). Perhaps Suetonius' family history may have led him to omit some damning incidents. After all, his own father had served under Otho (*Otho* 10.1), which might have led the biographer to modify his usual technique. Suetonius' *Otho* is certainly one of his shortest biographies, which may reveal some uneasiness about the subject matter.

Nevertheless Tacitus, like other authors, can certainly deploy the motif of someone leering at an enemy's severed head to symbolise deep depravity, particularly in connection with Nero.[55] So Nero's wife Poppaea inspects the young Octavia's head which has been brought to Rome (*Annals* 14.64), and after Cornelius Sulla's death, Nero 'mocked his head on the grounds that it was ugly through premature greyness' (*Annals* 14.57.4). The emperor's ghoulish scrutiny is made more sinister by his flippant comment. In the same vein, Nero looked at Rubellius Plautus' severed head and joked, 'I didn't know he had such a big nose' (Dio 62.14.1).[56] The dramatist of the pseudo-Senecan play, the *Octavia*, relishes such moments, as Nero's brutal opening words show: 'Carry out my orders. Send someone to fetch the severed heads of the murdered Sulla and Plautus' (*Octavia* 437). Perhaps Tacitus suggests a link between Nero and Otho through this motif of gazing at severed heads: Otho's behaviour is not so extreme or as regular as Nero's, but Tacitus still notes Otho's delight at seeing Piso's severed head (1.44.1; cf. 2.9.2[57] and 2.16.3).

Otho's apparent transformation for the better may also surprise us because Tacitus often tends to focus on deterioration of imperial behaviour rather than on its improvement. According to Tacitus, Vespasian 'was the only emperor of all his predecessors who changed for the better' (1.50.4).[58] How can this generalisation be reconciled with the Tacitean Otho, who also changes for the better, albeit in a final moment of glory? Of course, one can overemphasise Otho's sudden reversal of character. Although his final suicide is commendable, this single glorious deed is not a sustained improvement in his behaviour. It may therefore be wrong to put Tacitus' characterisation of Otho in the same category as Vespasian's prolonged upward progression. Martial underlines this point in his epigram about Otho's suicide: 'Cato in life may be greater even than Caesar: was he in death greater than Otho?' (6.32.5-6). Otho traditionally remains the antithesis of Cato the Younger until the moment of his death, which inverts his dubious past and aligns him with the Stoic hero.[59] So, Plutarch links the two suicides through parallel details.[60] Both men sleep soundly, both show altruistic concern for others, and both commit suicide immediately after the departure of a single person. Neither slits the veins in his arms, but both opt for a stab wound.

Tacitus therefore appears to have deviated from his usual narrative technique in portraying Otho by means of sensational detail and by this change from heroism to selflessness. Why? There are a number of possible explanations. One suggestion is that Tacitus deliberately blackens Otho until the moment of his suicide in order to offer a dramatic antithesis to both Galba and Piso.[61] Such foiling techniques were amongst the most basic literary tools of ancient writers, and could sometimes cause an author to distort characters or facts in order to draw stronger contrasts or parallels between two individuals. So Tacitus records Arminius' death in AD 19 instead of AD 22 to draw a parallel with Germanicus (*Annals* 2.88).[62] Tacitus certainly invests Galba and Otho with contrasting traits. Unlike Galba, Otho, for example, is realistic about the dangers of old-fashioned discipline; and Tacitus uses internal focalisation to show Otho 'thinking that a principate won by crime could not be retained by suddenly introducing discipline and old-fashioned strictness' (1.83.1). Nevertheless, as we shall see, Tacitus' Otho is a more complex character than simply a convenient foil to enhance the portraits of other protagonists.[63]

There is another possible explanation for Tacitus' contradictory representation of Otho, which is rooted in the discordant images of the historical emperor that emerged during the civil war itself. The 'real' Otho was undoubtedly the focus of conflicting propaganda messages at different stages, as the second distorting lens (post AD 69) reworked the effects of the first (AD 69). These contrasts were probably exaggerated by the fact that Otho's principate was so brief. Otho's image served different purposes at different times, and many literary portraits of him reflect this. At first glimpse, Tacitus may appear to echo this inconsistent propaganda uncritically, but as we shall see, he recasts these fragmented perceptions about Otho to create a more coherent character.

The first important propaganda strand stressed Otho's similarity to Nero, which served to discredit him amongst the higher social ranks. Suetonius suggests that Nero and Otho were birds of a feather and preserves a rumour about their 'habitual debauchery with one another' (*Otho* 2.2). Such denigration could have originated with Galba, but even if the elderly emperor did perceive Otho as a Nero-clone, as Tacitus suggests (1.13.2), there was little time for him to activate such propaganda. Perhaps Vespasian and his supporters had most time in which to vilify previous rulers. Even if, as Ferrill has argued, Nero superseded Otho as a target for denigration after the war, Otho's reputation may still have suffered because of the perceived closeness between the two men.[64] So, Nero's courtiers are said to favour Otho because the two are so similar (1.13.4), and the people and the soldiers salute the emperor as Nero Otho, which he ignores, 'afraid to forbid them or ashamed to acknowledge them' (1.78.2). There were clearly divergences in how Nero was perceived: popular amongst the *plebs* and hated by the senate, Nero was an ambiguous figure.[65] An association with Nero could easily backfire. So Plutarch says that Otho abandoned the practice of adding the surname Nero to his own name on certain diplomas when 'the leading citizens who were most powerful' became irritated (*Otho* 3.2). Sometimes Otho influenced public opinion more successfully, as when he forced Nero's old associate Ofonius Tigellinus to commit suicide (Tacitus *Histories* 1.72 and Plutarch *Otho* 2). Tacitus sees this as an inspired move, because it simultaneously delighted those who hated Nero (since Tigellinus had been a decadent Neronian courtier *par excellence*) and those who loved him (since Tigellinus had ultimately betrayed Nero). Yet it was not always possible to strike such a successful balance. Posterity ultimately condemned Otho for being too similar to Nero: such condemnation by association is pervasive in the literary tradition.[66]

However, a second important propaganda strand about Otho pulls in the opposite direction. In AD 69, Vespasian and his supporters appear to have accentuated heroic elements in Otho's death, not only to denigrate Vitellius, but also to win over Otho's former soldiers. Whether or not Otho's suicide was genuinely courageous and altruistic, it served Vespasian's interests to exaggerate these characteristics and to establish himself as Otho's avenger. Vespasian could thereby partially re-enact Octavian's role of avenger after Julius Caesar's murder[67] and thus cast the civil war as a more respectable enterprise than it really was. As Cicero observed, 'no war can rightly be undertaken save for vengeance or defence' (*De Re Publica* 3.23.35). Suetonius refers to the 'copy of a letter (possibly forged) in which the dead Otho in a final request instructed Vespasian to take vengeance and hoped that he would come to the aid of the empire' (*Vespasian* 6.4). This convenient voice from beyond the grave was a shrewd device. Dramatic descriptions of Otho's heroic death could stir up the soldiers' emotions and galvanise them to support Vespasian in his role as self-proclaimed avenger. Residual loyalty to Otho amongst the troops endured; Vespasian would have been foolish to ignore such a valuable resource.[68]

The representation of Otho's death was subsequently influenced by another powerful factor. The first century AD saw a sustained interest in *exitus* literature, that is vignettes of death scenes amongst the rich and famous. Pliny, whose letter collection itself is peppered with such descriptions, says that Titinius Capito wrote about 'the deaths of famous men' (*Epistle* 8.12.4), and Gaius Fannius about 'the deaths of those killed or exiled by Nero' (*Epistle* 5.5.3). Thus, the reality of Otho's suicide was ripe for distortion by writers (and an audience) who were steeped in this particular literary genre. Tacitus was right when he summarised, 'rumour is always more pernicious on the subject of rulers' deaths' (*Annals* 4.11.2); later, he pledges to record each noble death separately for posterity (*Annals* 16.16.2).[69] The conventions of the genre could result in stylisation and exaggeration: so, certain details were perceived as ennobling a suicide, such as a concern for others right to the end. In general, suicides were polarised into the 'good' and the 'bad', although some interesting twists were still possible within these opposite extremes. Tacitus' description of Petronius' suicide (*Annals* 16.18-19) is a case in point: his stylish death parodies the ritualisation of suicide, but still defies Nero and is thus praiseworthy.[70]

For an unambiguously 'bad' suicide, one can turn to the death of Tigellinus: 'having received the order to kill himself at the Sinuessa Spa, amidst orgies with his prostitutes, kisses, and discreditable delays, he cut his throat with a razor (*novacula*) and blackened his notorious life by a dishonourable death, which came too late' (1.72.3; cf. Plutarch *Otho* 2). For a start, Tigellinus is in the wrong place. Most respectable suicides take place privately at home where one can spend time putting affairs in order. The focus on Tigellinus' final worldly pleasures needs little elaboration, except to say that it contrasts with the peaceful spiritual contemplation which often marks a decent suicide. So, Seneca dictates his final thoughts to his secretaries (*Annals* 15.63.3), and Otho spends time 'pondering (*volutans*) final concerns in his heart' (2.49.1).[71] By contrast, Tacitus' observation that Tigellinus' death came 'too late' contradicts the Stoic notion that death should be engineered at the right time (cf. Seneca *Ad Marciam* 20.4). It is also striking that Tigellinus kills himself with a *novacula*, some sort of cut-throat razor. The word appears nowhere else in Tacitus' extant works and it seems a sordid instrument with which to do the deed. Martial refers to the *novacula* as being the kind of thing one might see in a disreputable street-fight (*Epigram* 7.61.7), and Suetonius indignantly notes the occasion when Caligula compels his father-in-law Marcus Silanus to cut his throat with a *novacula* (*Caligula* 23.3). Enforced suicide was bad enough, but making the victim use a razor was a further degradation.[72] The fact that Tigellinus voluntarily picks a *novacula* as his suicide weapon is thus meant to suggest a morally unsound individual.

Otho, by contrast, kills himself with a 'dagger (*pugio*)' (2.49.2), which is a symbolic weapon for his suicide, because it was worn by emperors to denote their power of life and death.[73] Likewise, Nero tests the points of two *pugiones* before his suicide, but then, unlike Otho, throws them away in fear (Suetonius *Nero* 49.2). Such hesitation is generally considered unseemly, as is clear from Tacitus' scathing reference to Tigellinus' 'discreditable delays' (1.72.3). Similarly, when Claudius' disgraced wife Messalina tries to commit suicide, she cannot do so and is killed by the tribune (*Annals* 11.38.1). In Tacitus' narratives, the morally corrupt often vacillate before killing themselves, which neatly suggests their excessive fondness for life. In general, efficiency and ingenuity are frequently markers of a 'good' suicide, even if the perpetrator has been a lowly figure in life: so, a German gladiator creatively commits suicide by choking himself to death with a toilet brush (Seneca *Epistle* 70.20). This may have been an undignified method, but in Seneca's eyes, the gladiator's inventiveness in the face of adversity is commendable. Likewise, Cato tells his worried slaves, who have confiscated his dagger, that this will not stop his suicide: strangling himself with his clothing, dashing his head against a wall or holding his breath are all options (Appian *BC* 2.98.409, Dio 43.11 and [Caesar] *Bell. Afr.* 88). Nevertheless Cato still goes to some trouble to retrieve his dagger, which suggests that he considered this the most impressive weapon to use.

Any description of Otho's suicide, therefore, was coloured not only by

Flavian propaganda, but also by the powerful heritage of *exitus* literature. Perhaps inconsistent characterisation within a single work is
inevitable when a figure has been exposed to such a strong combination
of historical and literary influences. To what extent is Tacitus uncritically following the prevailing tradition about Otho? One way to answer
this question is to examine whether the positive and negative sides of
Tacitus' Otho are really so contradictory as some critics maintain.
Although Tacitus' early narrative certainly criticises Otho, such comments are often focalised through other characters in the narrative.
Tacitus acknowledges hostile reactions to Otho, but does not necessarily
endorse these views himself. The description of Otho gazing with relish
on Piso's severed head, for example, is introduced by 'it is said' (1.44.1),
which qualifies the remark. Likewise, 'against everyone's expectation'
(1.71.1), Otho did not sink into a lethargic mood of idle hedonism. Or
there is the observation that 'Otho was considered (*ducebatur*) more
deadly for the state because of his debauchery, savagery and reckless-
ness' (2.31.1). At the very least, Tacitus leaves room for these hostile
points of view to be proved incorrect.

Some critics see such comments as symptomatic of Tacitus' under-
hand historical methods, in which criticisms surreptitiously infiltrate a
fundamentally biased narrative, and the technique has been likened to
the rhetorical device of 'passing by (*praeteritio*)' or 'hiding (*occultatio*)'.[74]
However, there is another possibility: Tacitus may have wanted to
reconstruct the malicious atmosphere of the times, and to highlight how
important public image was during a civil war, whatever Otho's character was like in reality. It was indeed difficult for a historian who was
writing about such a shifting and unstable world to establish any firm
ground for judging the short-lived Otho, but Tacitus' language did need
to reflect what contemporaries may have thought about their emperor.
Tacitus' characterisation of Otho may seem less fragmented if we
remember that Otho was the focus for both negative and positive
evaluations, and that Tacitus does not necessarily straightforwardly
endorse every hostile comment which appears in his narrative. Besides,
if Tacitus had really found Otho so objectionable, then why write such
a moving description of his suicide?[75] This approach offers us a constructive way to reconcile Tacitus' apparently contradictory portrait: Otho's
reputation for decadence was pervasive in AD 69 and beyond, but this
may not accurately reflect the full complexity of his character. So, when
Tacitus describes Otho as 'quite unlike his reputation (*famaeque dis-
similis*)' (2.11.3), marching from Rome at the head of his troops and
wearing an iron breastplate, this does not have to be read as a straightforwardly vindictive comment. Tacitus carefully plays off Otho's bad
reputation against his more positive actions, thereby encouraging his
readers to contemplate the gulf between image and reality. The inter-
weaving of these positive and negative elements can be seen as

something more than Tacitus' indulgence of an implacable hatred of a short-lived emperor.

Tacitus' characterisation of Otho is usually called inconsistent because the emperor's noble suicide seems too sudden a reversal of his previous personality. Yet from an early point, Tacitus foreshadows Otho's glorious death. When Otho ponders making a bid for power, he brings his reflections to a close with the idea that 'death is the natural end for all alike, and the only difference is between fame and oblivion in the eyes of posterity. Moreover, if the same end awaits guilty and innocent alike, then a spirited man should die for a reason' (1.21.2). In this way, Tacitus characterises Otho more fully than Plutarch, who only notes that at Piso's adoption, the pretender is 'not without fear for the future' and 'full of many passions' (*Galba* 23.6). In contrast, Tacitus' Otho irrationally fears Galba and Piso, and grimly dwells on the possibility of his own murder. His thoughts move smoothly from the particular to the general. Tacitus' artistic reconstruction of Otho's thoughts presents a well-rounded character, whose noble suicide is not a bolt from the blue. Such foreshadowing at almost Otho's first appearance must challenge the proposal that Tacitus' characterisation is wildly inconsistent.

Furthermore, qualities which Otho displayed during his rise to power recur in a more positive context during his dramatic death.[76] One such skill is a talent for managing people. Otho uses his affability effectively whilst angling for the support of the troops: 'calling each of the oldest soldiers by name and addressing them as "comrades" when he mentioned their service together under Nero; he renewed acquaintance with some, asked after others and helped them with money or favours' (1.23.1). Plutarch notes how Otho during his rise to power arranges promotions and gives a gold piece to Galba's cohort whenever the emperor dines at his house (*Galba* 20.6-7), but money rather than affability is the chief weapon in this account. Tacitus' readers may have been shocked that Otho's talents are being misdirected towards such selfish ends, but it will not always be so. Tacitus eventually shows Otho using the same affability more commendably, as the emperor comforts the soldiers and staff who are distraught at his impending suicide:

> After some such speech, Otho addressed each one courteously (*comiter*[77]) according to age and rank. He urged them to leave quickly and not provoke the victor's anger by lingering; he stirred the young men by his authority and the old men by his pleas. His face was calm, his speech was firm, as he checked the untimely (*intempestivas*) tears of his people. (2.48.1)

Otho's calmness pointedly contrasts with everyone else's despair. In particular, his ability to think practically about what might happen after his death is poignant. The nuances of the adjective 'untimely (*intempestivae*)', suggest that Otho can envisage the moment after his death when tears *will* be appropriate. Moreover, like Antony, who in his final speech advises Cleopatra to think of her own safety (Plutarch *Ant.* 77.7), Otho is selflessly worried about what will happen to his friends after his own death. We see how sensitively he modifies his words depending on the addressee: this worked with the soldiers in his rise to power and is just as effective now, although the circumstances are sadder. This time Otho's motives are altruistic, whereas previously he had just wanted to win the troops over to his cause. The methods are similar in each instance, but the reasons for his coaxing rhetoric have changed. Perhaps Tacitus' Otho does not fall quite as securely into two separate halves as was initially supposed.[78]

Another factor differentiates Tacitus' subtle portrait of Otho from other versions of the emperor. Tacitus shows far less interest than most in the lurid details of Otho's private life for their own sake. Perhaps this was partly symptomatic of the genre of history, although elsewhere Tacitus certainly includes lurid elements when it suits him, as in his description of Tigellinus' banquet and Nero's 'marriage' to Pythagoras (*Annals* 15.37). Therefore, Tacitus was not entirely prevented from presenting risqué material by generic considerations. A good example of Tacitus' more muted narrative voice in the *Histories* is his account of the Poppaea scandal (1.13): while Nero is trying to eliminate his wife Octavia, he entrusts his mistress Poppaea to Otho, but, suspecting that his friend has fallen in love with her, Nero removes Otho to Lusitania. This simple act of collusion pales into insignificance beside the version in the *Annals* (13.46): Otho, after seducing and marrying Poppaea (who already has a husband and a son), praises his new wife's charms before an eager Nero, who starts a relationship with Poppaea and sends his rival to Lusitania (cf. Macro, Ennia and Caligula at *Annals* 6.45.3). This need not be a case of the *Annals* report 'correcting' the earlier passage, as some have supposed.[79] The incident in the *Histories* is designed to emphasise similarities and tensions between Nero and Otho, whereas the *Annals* passage is more concerned to provide a thorough introduction to Nero's future wife Poppaea. Whether or not Tacitus deliberately suppressed the more sensational details of the Poppaea story in the *Histories* narrative, other writers could not resist the temptation to provide lurid titbits about Otho. Even though Suetonius was relatively favourable towards his father's one-time commanding officer, the biographer still records the rumour of Otho's and Nero's 'habitual debauchery with one another' (*Otho* 2.2), and notes that Otho was 'almost as fastidious about appearances as a woman' (*Otho* 12.1). Perhaps Juvenal *Satire* 2.99-109 illustrates the popular tradition about Otho's effeminacy most graphically:[80]

> That one clutches a mirror, the heroic trophy of Auruncian Actor, the
> accoutrement of the fag (*pathicus*) Otho, before which the armour-clad
> emperor used to preen himself, when he ordered the standards to be
> raised. Material fit to be mentioned in the new annals and recent history
> (*novis annalibus atque recenti historia*)! A civil war where a mirror was
> part of the fighting kit! Certainly, it is the mark of the greatest general
> both to kill Galba *and* to look after his complexion, and it is the bravery
> of the greatest citizen both to strive after the Palatine throne on the fields
> of Bedriacum and to apply a face-pack with his fingers. Not even Semi-
> ramis armed with a quiver in Assyria, nor Cleopatra on her unlucky boat
> at Actium did this.

Juvenal describes Otho as a *pathicus*,[81] a passive homosexual, and sets
up a sustained parody of the emperor as the antithesis of the military
hero. Plutarch had already likened Otho to the archetypal effeminate
warrior Paris (*Galba* 19.2),[82] but Juvenal goes much further. Otho
carries, not a shield, but a mirror in which to admire himself (cf.
Suetonius *Caligula* 50.1), which suggests both effeminacy and complacency. Moreover, the incongruity between the flawed Otho and the ideal
emperor is further underlined by direct quotation from Virgil (Juvenal
Satire 2.100 *Actoris Aurunci spolium* = *Aeneid* 12.94).[83] It is pointed
that Virgil uses this phrase to describe the mighty spear of Turnus, who
is preparing to kill Aeneas. Turnus hopes 'to defile in the dust his hair
crimped with the hot iron and drenched in myrrh' (*Aeneid* 12.99-100).[84]
Therefore Juvenal echoes Turnus' aggressively masculine sentiments in
a dissonant new context, which further underlines Otho's effeminate
persona. Incongruity is the keynote of Juvenal's technique, as we are
forced to conclude that even real women such as Cleopatra and Semi-
ramis are not so feminine as Otho.

If Juvenal's comically exaggerated satirical portrait reflects the prevailing perception of Otho after his death, Tacitus' toned-down version
of the emperor may go against the grain of popular opinion.[85] As we have
seen, even Martial, who admired Otho, calls him 'soft (*mollis*)' (*Epigram*
6.32.2), and plays with the paradox that such a dissolute man could die
honourably. Such labels can be linked to traditions of Roman invective
whereby high profile politicians were accused of effeminacy in dress,
adornment and gait in an attempt to undermine them. So Cicero saw
the fact that Julius Caesar used to scratch his head with one finger as
indicating that he was not a threat (Plutarch *Caesar* 4.9).[86] Experts in
physiognomy were often asked to work out if someone was a homosexual, even if the alleged 'signs' were not immediately obvious. An
involuntary reflex like sneezing was considered useful in this respect
(cf. Diogenes Laertius 7.173). Otho's outward appearance was apparently not so difficult to pigeonhole, but the assumptions that were then
made about his character could be misleading. Tacitus highlights the
dangers of complacent responses to a man's appearance: 'Otho's mind

was not soft (*mollis*) like his body' (1.22.1). Tacitus acknowledges how
the incongruity between Otho's body and mind causes people to under-
estimate him as a threat. Piso's speech to the troops certainly pours
scorn on Otho's effeminate ways, and his vitriolic words help to put into
context the emperor's eventual delight at seeing Piso's severed head:
'Should he deserve the empire because of his appearance and gait or
because of his effeminate costume? ... In his mind (*animo*), he now longs
for debauchery, revels and cavortings with women' (1.30.1).[87] Piso so
easily equates Otho's outer appearance and inner character, but such
prejudice can backfire: Piso becomes vulnerable because he underestimates not only Otho, but also Otho's soldiers, whose values do not
necessarily mirror his own. Yet as we have seen, Otho will stir such
loyalty amongst his troops that intermediate commanders will have
enormous trouble asserting their authority (1.36.2, 1.80.2, 2.18.2, 2.33.3
and 2.55.1). One of the disturbing lessons of the civil war is that the
soldiers often consider a dissolute commander to be more palatable
than a strait-laced general. Subsequently, when Domitian dies, the
soldiers are said to be distraught, although the emperor possessed few
of the traditional qualities of the upright military leader: this suggests
that the troops could still feel genuine affection for leaders who did not
cohere with the ideal (Suetonius *Domitian* 23.1). So, Piso is playing a
dangerous game by denouncing Otho's immoral habits before the army.
Thus, Tacitus' treatment of Otho's effeminacy rejects sensationalism for
its own sake and instead uses the contrast between outward appearance and character to illuminate other characters in the text, especially
Piso and the soldiers. Tacitus shows how swiftly misconceptions such
as Piso's could be overtaken by a more complex reality. Piso and the
soldiers may even share the same view of Otho's character generated by
his appearance, but the newly adopted leader and his men are not
linked by the same system of values.

Conclusion

Although Tacitus has shown himself to be acutely aware of the polarised
tradition that existed about Otho, his portrayal of the emperor sets out
to do far more than simply label him as good or bad.[88] Tacitus, writing
when the dominant political assessment of Otho no longer had to be so
black-and-white, moves away from presenting issues in such clear-cut
terms and embraces moral ambiguity in his account of the civil war.
Tacitus quickly establishes that Otho had spent a dubious youth and
gained a reputation as Nero's constant companion, but the new emperor
does not really live up to his decadent image. Challenging Galba as a
result of his own insecurity and financial problems, Otho soon finds that
he has set in motion a movement which he cannot efficiently control.
The brutal murder of Galba is naturally laid at his door, creating a mood

of apprehension and fear, but in fact Otho is progressively dwarfed by events which move beyond the sphere of his personal influence until he dramatically reasserts control by suicide. Tacitus plays creatively with the contrast between Otho's reputation as a decadent murderer and the reality of a bewildered usurper who struggles to exert authority but finds himself powerless. The brilliant and moving narrative of the suicide should perhaps be seen as a development of this second, more bewildered Otho and not of the first. Thus Tacitus' characterisation of Otho is complex and challenging, and raises questions about the nature of power, but it is not intrinsically inconsistent or contradictory, as has commonly been supposed. It is certainly time to move away from the pervasive notion that Tacitus had a pathological hatred of Otho, which led him to blacken the emperor whenever possible, and that Tacitus somehow saw the noble suicide as an isolated event that was inexplicable in the light of Otho's past conduct.

5

Vitellius

Introduction

Vitellius was the last in a succession of losers in the civil war, and his portrayal was therefore the most susceptible of all the short-lived emperors of AD 68-9 to sustained denigration. Galba may have acquired a reputation for stinginess and Otho for depravity, but Vespasian had not been fighting directly against these two imperial candidates. Once the fighting was over, Vitellius' image was ripe for distortion by partisan writers, since the more flawed Vitellius appeared to be, the more justified Vespasian's action became in challenging him. The impetus for such exaggeration did not necessarily have to come from Vespasian himself, although official documents like the *Lex de Imperio Vespasiani* (probably part of the senatorial decree passed when Vespasian was first recognised at Rome in December AD 69) gave a clear lead in showing who was initially beyond the pale after the war: Caligula, Nero, Galba, Otho and Vitellius are conspicuously not mentioned as precedents.[1] Galvanised by such official signals, opportunistic authors could themselves take the initiative in providing the Flavian dynasty with a palatable version of recent history.

This chapter is divided into two sections. The first part seeks to establish ways in which Vitellius was blackened in the literary tradition which developed after the civil war and draws parallels with what happened to Antony after his defeat by Octavian. Image is just as influential as reality (if that can ever be retrieved) in driving events, and moreover the dominant impression of a historical figure tends to be compounded in literary sources over time. The second part examines how Tacitus responded to this negative literary heritage in his own characterisation of Vitellius to create a narrative which takes into account many more factors than just the personality of the short-lived emperor. As is appropriate for a historian, Tacitus chooses a broader focus than other writers, setting Vitellius' passive and listless character in the context of the collective identity of the military. Vitellius, just like Otho before him, is disengaged from the conflict at a decisive moment, thus leaving his weakened army vulnerable to the challenge of the Flavians, led by the charismatic general Antonius Primus.

The negative characterisation of Vitellius in the literary and historical tradition

There were many hostile caricatures from the rich culture of Roman political invective and elsewhere on which pro-Flavian writers could have drawn to mobilise public opinion against Vitellius, but the stereotype of the tyrant possessed a particularly serviceable range of unpleasant characteristics which could be exploited.[2] To manipulate the portrayal of Vitellius was relatively easy because he ruled for less than a year and because his death meant that incongruities between negative character sketches and reality were less visible. Effective denigration of some historical figures was difficult because their character traits were too well known. Cato the Younger falls into this category, although Caesar still tried to blacken him in his *Anticato*.[3] Otho was also vulnerable to such negative treatment, particularly because of his close connection with Nero, but his heroic suicide and popularity amongst the troops even after his death meant few advantages in attacking him posthumously. Vitellius was an easy and productive target by contrast.

The stereotypical tyrant possessed standard traits, such as greed, cruelty, impiety, sexual voracity and an appetite for luxurious food and particularly drink, some or all of which could be activated by a writer to rouse hostility against an individual. This last attribute, the tendency for conspicuous consumption of food and drink, is one which we must explore further in connection with the portrayal of Vitellius in the literary tradition. Roman audiences were particularly ready to conjure up this motif, as is illustrated by Velleius Paterculus' comparison of Julius Caesar and Alexander the Great:

> [Caesar] was the most excellent of all citizens in his appearance, most acute in his intellectual vitality, most lavish in his generosity, and in his spirit, he excelled both what was natural and what was credible for a man; in the grandeur of his ambitions, in the speed of his military operations, and in the endurance of dangers, he was just like Alexander the Great, but only when Alexander was sober and free from anger. In short, Caesar always made use of food and sleep to stay alive and not to satisfy his desires.[4] (2.41)

Velleius Paterculus draws the analogy, but then caps it by suggesting that Caesar is even better than Alexander. Unlike the Macedonian, Caesar eats and sleeps simply for survival. Notice how Velleius plays Caesar's trump by shifting his emphasis from Alexander's *drunkenness* to Caesar's modest consumption of *food*. His sensitivity reveals how receptive a Roman audience could be to the typical warning signs of a tyrannical nature. Certain traits, such as fondness for alcohol, had become such a familiar signpost for a despotic character that Velleius not only negates Alexander's fondness for drink in portraying Caesar, but replaces it entirely with an attribute from the ideal general stereotype.[5]

However, it was not just excessive gratification of the appetite which marked someone out as having a tyrannical personality. The indulgence had to be enacted in a context where the tyrant could play grim power games with those around him.[6] Pliny inversely highlights many traits of the stereotypical tyrant by clarifying what Trajan, the ideal emperor, does *not* do.

> For you do not gorge yourself on a solitary meal before midday and you do not loom over your guests as a spectator who notes down everything they do; when they are hungry and empty, you do not belch from a full stomach and present or rather throw at them the food which you yourself disdain to touch; and you do not, after managing with difficulty to endure this arrogant pretence of a banquet, take yourself off to secret gluttony and private debauchery.[7] (*Pan.* 49.6)

Pliny finds it intolerable that the tyrannical Domitian gorges himself in private, which enables him to use the public banquet to abuse his guests. Certainly, other emperors failed to observe regular mealtimes. Augustus frequently dined alone and touched nothing at dinner parties (Suetonius *Augustus* 76.2), but this is presented as the commendable routine of an industrious emperor who eats when necessary, without neglecting his duty to interact with the nobility. Likewise, the main purpose of Hadrian's communal meal was to engage in civilised discussion with his guests (Dio 69.7.3). In contrast, Pliny's Domitian transgresses his guests' expectation of imperial hospitality, and eats alone for self-gratification. Such a portrait can be set against the backdrop of the wider debate about the differences between Greek and Roman identities. So, Cicero concludes from the etymology of the Roman 'social feast (*convivium*)', and the Greek 'drinking party (*sumposion*)', that Romans valued the shared company of a banquet, while Greeks prioritised drinking (*Fam.* 9.24.3 and *Sen.* 13.45). Thus, by rejecting the proper social element of the communal banquet, Pliny's Domitian behaves in a thoroughly un-Roman manner.[8]

Dio gives us a particularly eerie account of an imperial feast (67.9). One night, Domitian summons the foremost senators and knights to a macabre banquet. The venue is a black room, with place-names in the shape of gravestones, black plates and attendants who are painted black. For food, there is the meal which is habitually served to the spirits of the dead. An awareness of one's own mortality traditionally added a frisson of excitement to the pleasures of the banquet, but it was easy to transgress boundaries — Vatinius even provoked outrage for wearing a black toga at a banquet (Cicero *In Vatinium* 12.30). Domitian goes much further. Throughout the feast, the emperor speaks vividly about death and slaughter, and inevitably, every guest concludes that the proceedings are a ghoulish prelude to widespread executions.[9] Yet Domitian eventually sends his guests home safely with the paraphernalia from the banquet: the black objects are in fact made from silver or from other valuable materials.[10] The entire meal is an elaborate hoax designed to demonstrate Domitian's power to the terrified guests. By sparing them, the emperor is confirming his place at the top of the power structure.[11]

Domitian is clearly an extreme case of an emperor who is made to coalesce suggestively with the literary stereotype of the tyrant. The negative portraits of Vitellius are not exaggerated to quite the same extent, but nevertheless we can see that writers often deploy the motif of food and drink to condemn the character of the emperor, albeit as a more passive individual than the stereotypical tyrant. Thus, Josephus describes Vitellius' final moments:

> Then Vitellius came out of the palace: he was drunk and gorged on a banquet that was more lavish and profligate than ever, as if it was his last meal. After being dragged through the mob and subjected to indignities of every sort, he was slaughtered at the heart of Rome, having ruled for eight months and five days. If he had chanced to live for longer, I don't suppose that even the empire itself would have been enough to satisfy his lusts. (*BJ* 4.651)

This is an extremely succinct and forceful description.[12] After all, Josephus was not writing a history of events at Rome, so the short digressions and character sketches had to be memorable. Josephus' assertion that Vitellius had been indulging in a *grande bouffe* so spectacular that it could have been his last meal is richly ironic: of course, the privileged reader (unlike the complacent emperor) knows that this *is* Vitellius' last meal. Moreover, the suggestion that Vitellius' banquet was even more lavish than usual neatly encapsulates the emperor's lifestyle before his downfall. It is particularly alarming that Vitellius' drunkenness and feasting have made him incapable of responding properly when the crisis does come. Drinking and statesmanship do not mix, as Plato argues (*Leges* 674a-c). The speed with which Josephus' text moves from Vitellius leaving the palace to his being dragged through the mob mirrors the rapidity of the drunken emperor's fall from power. Finally, Josephus' speculation that Vitellius' appetite could potentially outstrip even the limits of the Roman empire is shocking. The infinite variety of produce available in Rome usually reflects the patriotic notion that the city was at the heart of a global empire. So, Pliny calls the Tiber 'the most peaceful merchant of the whole world's produce' (*HN* 3.5.54). Josephus perverts this idea to indicate the magnitude of Vitellius' greed.

Plutarch makes a comment along similar lines which perhaps foreshadows the emperor's portrait in the lost *Vitellius*. When Fabius Valens approaches Vitellius' camp with many horsemen and salutes him as emperor, Plutarch observes:

> Previously, Vitellius seemed to decline and avoid the principate, fearing its magnitude, but on this occasion, so they say, being full of wine and a midday meal, he came out to the soldiers and accepted the title of Germanicus which they conferred upon him, though he rejected the name of Caesar. (*Galba* 22.11)

Plutarch specifies that Vitellius has washed down his midday meal with a great deal of wine, which gives him the courage to accept the soldiers' support. Besides casting doubt on Vitellius' motives, such indulgence too early in the day was generally a litmus test of a dissolute character in the literary tradition. So Cicero observes disapprovingly of Antony: 'From the third hour there was drinking, gambling, and vomiting' (*Phil.* 2.41.104).[13] Plutarch's reference to Vitellius' leisurely lunchbreak is not so explicit, but the reference does point to a strong divergence between his lifestyle and that of the ideal emperor and general.

There is some variation between authors about which vice dominated Vitellius to the greater extent, gluttony or drunkenness. Cassius Dio highlights Vitellius' passion for food.

> Then, when he was established in a position of such great authority, he became even more riotous and he squandered money most of the day and the night; he stuffed himself insatiably and he was continually vomiting everything up so that he was nourished by the mere passage of the food. This was the only way that he was able to hold out, even though his fellow diners went off in a terrible state. (65.2)

This is a novel way to express the scale of the emperor's eating: to obtain sufficient nourishment simply by meals passing up and down his throat must have required much food. Elsewhere, Sidonius describes the parasite's unsettled stomach as 'the hold for overflowing dinners' (*Epistulae* 3.13.6), which is a variation on this same theme. Dio's Vitellius probably struck readers as offensive not because he threw up, but because he wasted so much food. Modern sensibilities are more delicate than ancient attitudes in this area, since vomiting to renew the appetite was not something the Romans considered offensive.[14] Even so, it was not a technique to be used too often. Celsus records Asclepiades' disapproval of those who 'by throwing up every day achieve a capacity for gormandising' (*De Medicina* 1.3.17). Celsus' own view (*De Medicina* 1.3.21) is that vomiting should not be practised for the sake of luxury on a daily basis: otherwise the patient will not live to a ripe old age. Dio's Vitellius therefore is courting death by his constant over-indulgence, and his behaviour is not only wasteful but self-destructive.

Dio preserves (65.3) another salient detail about Vitellius' gormandising habits. One of the emperor's dishes allegedly cost 1 million *sestertii* and consisted of a mixture of exotic foods, which were all blended together and cooked in one huge dish. Suetonius is more specific about the ingredients for this recipe, which became known as Minerva's Shield:

> The most notorious feast in the series was a welcoming dinner given to him by his brother in which two thousand choice fish and seven thousand birds are said to have been served. Vitellius himself surpassed even this by the dedication of a dish, which, because of its tremendous size, he kept on calling the Shield of Minerva, Protectress of the city. In this recipe Vitellius mixed together wrasse livers, pheasant brains, peacock brains, flamingo tongues and lamprey guts. These items were collected all the way from Parthia to the Spanish Straits by senior captains and triremes. (*Vitellius* 13.2)

In this striking passage Suetonius launches a two-fold attack on Vitellius. Both feasts are monumental, but the first banquet is remarkable for the quantity of food served, while Minerva's Shield is both huge and infinitely varied in its ingredients. Even the notion that Minerva's Shield is a dedication suggests size, since buildings or temples were normally consecrated, not dishes.[15] In addition, Suetonius has fixed the boundaries over which Vitellius' appetite extended much more specifically than Josephus. Now the delicacies are collected all the way from Parthia to the Spanish Straits. These are rather unusual eastern and western markers of the world to choose, since the familiar limits were the Pillars of Hercules or Gades in the west and the Ganges in the east.[16] In fact, Parthia is such a distinctive choice for the eastern limit that some editors have wanted to emend the text. Yet Suetonius' deviation from the familiar formula is suggestive. A good Roman emperor should have been fighting Parthia, not using it as a source of delicacies: elsewhere, Seneca uses the same idea more explicitly when he notes that the Romans need to punish the Parthians rather than importing exotic birds from them (*Helv.* 10.3). Likewise, although there may be virtually no geographical difference between Gades and the Spanish Straits as boundary markers, Suetonius' reminder that Vitellius had access to the produce of the sea is fitting, given that a fish, the wrasse, features in the recipe. We might also compare the fishy feast served up when Lentulus was ordained priest of Mars, which caused similar outrage (Macrobius *Sat.* 3.13.11-12). Moreover, Suetonius specifies that the triremes are commanded, not by the usual captains (*trierarchs*), but by senior officers (*navarchs*), who surely should be engaged in more pressing matters than collecting provisions.[17] In short, Vitellius' acquisition of exotic food from all around the empire was an abuse of the emperor's privileged position as ruler of the world, *orbis terrarum.*

Elsewhere, such centripetal consumption was almost always an indication of a tyrannical personality.[18]

Why precisely would 'Minerva's Shield' have struck a Roman reader as being so distasteful? There is some helpful supplementary material from one of Seneca's letters. Here, Seneca colourfully recreates the words of a glutton, who suggests that the best way to serve food is to mix all the ingredients together, but the philosopher responds with a devastating interjection of his own.

> [Glutton] 'Let food that is usually served separately arrive together, drenched in one sauce. Let there be no difference. Let oysters, sea-urchins, shell-fish, and mullets be mixed together and cooked in the same dish.'
> [Seneca] 'Not even vomited food could be more jumbled up.' (*Epistle* 95.28)

Seneca's disgusted imagery here is especially appropriate: what happens to the food on the dinner table surpasses even what will happen if the extravagant diner vomits. Not only is there ostentatious waste because Vitellius accumulates such varied and luxurious ingredients from all over the world, but the process of blending such rich food together is also dangerous. The problem, as Seneca perceives it, is that the peculiar combination of food will disturb the natural balance of the body (*Epistle* 95.16-18). This concern is reflected elsewhere in ancient literature, as when Disarius and Eustathius argue about whether a simple or a complex diet is more desirable. Disarius suggests that 'a diet which consists of a number of dishes is a cause of diseases' (Macrobius *Sat.* 7.4.30). The Roman medical writer Celsus gives a comprehensive classification of foodstuffs into weak, middling and strong nutrients, and advises moderation in consuming items from this last category (*De Medicina* 2.18.13). Therefore, to mix a variety of rich food together as Vitellius does was not just wasteful but self-destructive.[19] For a Roman emperor to be so careless of his own life was disastrous because unlike Seneca's glutton, his life was not his own to do with as he pleased. It is hardly surprising therefore that Minerva's Shield was stigmatized by Mucianus in AD 70 in a speech which attacked Vitellius' memory for his 'great swamp-like dishes (*patinarum paludes*)' (Pliny *HN* 35.46.163). One can see how Mucianus' swamp imagery, with its focus on size and mixture, was developed later in the tradition, particularly in discussions of Minerva's Shield.[20]

Suetonius' description of Vitellius mirrors Seneca's account of the glutton's physical condition in two respects. Both authors mention not only the distinctive complexion but also the pot-belly. Suetonius says that Vitellius had a 'flushed face at most times because of his drinking' and a 'huge paunch' (*Vitellius* 17.2; cf. Dio 65.20), while Seneca highlights the glutton's 'distended stomach' and 'discoloured face' (*Epistle*

95.16). The features emphasised by Suetonius thus ensure that Vitellius' physical traits can be associated with the glutton. The biographer thereby hints that the emperor would have soon destroyed himself through over-indulgence, even if Vespasian's men had not intervened. As Corbeill has observed: 'Physical traits or affectations of a person not only reveal past involvement in an immoderate feast, but also presage future affiliation with a convivial setting'.[21] In addition, it is significant that pot-bellies were often associated with tyrannical rulers. Domitian and Nero each had one (Suetonius *Domitian* 18.1 and *Nero* 51), and Ptolemy VIII, who was nicknamed 'Pot-Bellied' (Diodorus Siculus 33.22.1), was renowned for his cruelty, as when he killed and mutilated his own son in order to send the corpse to his estranged wife for her birthday (Diodorus Siculus 34.14). In comparison, Titus, who was boisterous as a young man but then calmed down, had a small residual pot-belly (Suetonius *Titus* 3.1). Pot-bellied men were also considered physically lethargic: Vegetius specifically says that pot-bellied men should not be recruited as soldiers (*Mil.* 1.6.4). Virgil even makes a 'broad paunch' (*Georgics* 4.94) one of the physical characteristics of the slothful bee.

The third-century AD writer Philostratus prefers to focus on Vitellius' drinking habits. Philostratus' Vespasian explains to the holy-man Apollonius why his bid for power was essential. Vespasian claims that Vitellius was just like Nero, that Vitellius frequently suffered from hangovers, and that Vitellius' constant bouts of drinking had made him mad (*Vita Apollonii* 5.29). This suggests that Vitellius had not been diluting his wine with water, since elsewhere ancient writers perceived a link between drinking unmixed wine and madness.[22] As a further insult, Vespasian adds the colourful detail that his rival used more perfume in his bath than he himself used water, and surmises that if someone stabbed Vitellius, more perfume would flood out than blood. This may further hint at Vitellius' drinking habits because perfume was sometimes added to wine as a sweetener (Aelian *VH* 12.31). Philostratus' Vespasian does not have to be expansive to evoke the audience's prejudices, although claiming to be too bashful to mention Vitellius' worst excesses before the venerable Neo-Pythagorean sage Apollonius gives added bite. This allows the audience to supply further lurid details from their own imaginations.

To denigrate someone as a drunkard was a very efficient way to rally opinion against a public figure.[23] Above all, Cicero vilifies Antony in this way, as when the orator fulminates: 'You guzzled so much wine at Hippias' wedding that on the next day in full view of the Roman people, you had to vomit' (*Phil.* 2.26.63). To emphasise that this spectacle was caused by over-indulgence and not illness, Cicero provides nauseous details, explaining how Antony 'vomited and filled his own lap and the whole platform with scraps of food which reeked of wine'. This dramatic scene remained popular long after Cicero and Antony were dead (cf. Seneca the Elder *Suasoriae* 6.3). Plutarch adds the detail that Antony vomited into a toga thoughtfully held out for him by a friend (*Ant.* 9.6). Cicero's rhetoric was clearly effective, but there were some who tried to turn the tables on the orator. In one speech Calenus claimed that the apparently respectable orator brought up his son amidst such debauchery that the boy was never sober (Dio 46.18), and Pseudo-Sallust mentions Cicero's 'weak tongue, very greedy hands, huge appetite, cowardly feet' (*In Ciceronem* 3.5).

However, Antony rather than Cicero was ultimately disparaged most successfully by this line of invective.[24] Seneca, writing to Lucilius about drunkenness, uses Antony as the climactic example, since the competent general was ruined by his twin passions for alcohol and for Cleopatra.

> Antony was a great man of noble character. What else destroyed him and drove him into foreign ways and non-Roman vices but drunkenness and love of Cleopatra (which equalled his passion for wine)? These influences made him a public enemy, but one who could not confront his own foes. These influences made Antony cruel, when the severed heads of the leading men of the state were brought to him as he dined, when, amidst the most sumptuous banquets and regal luxuries, he recognised the faces and hands of those who had been proscribed, and when he still thirsted for blood, though he was full of wine. (*Epistle* 83.25)

Seneca has taken the hostile invective against Antony to a new level, associating him with the bloodthirsty tyrant (cf. Aelian *VH* 2.41 on tyrants and drink). His gleeful gazing at severed heads over dinner is even more extreme than Appian's comment that Antony looked at Cicero's head at meals (*BC* 4.20.81; cf. Plutarch *Ant.* 20.4). Seneca, writing in a different genre, has taken the liberty of exaggerating the number of heads and adding the detail that Antony was drunk. Perhaps the gruesome image was kept alive and embellished over the years by the rhetorical schools. Seneca may have been inspired by his father's description of Antony: 'he himself, reeling with wine and sleep, raises drooping eyes to the heads of those he proscribed' (*Suasoriae* 6.7). Historiography, as well as the declamation schools, offers other historical characters in similar voyeuristic poses: at a climactic moment Tacitus makes Tiberius 'almost gaze at the homes deluged in blood' (*Annals* 6.39.2). One might also compare the gory images which decorated the dining-room grotto by the sea-shore at Spelunca and which were perhaps gazed at by Tiberius: when real carnage was unavailable, grisly pictures were a good substitute.[25]

Seneca exploits a flexible metaphor in characterising Antony as equally thirsty for blood and for wine.[26] This motif appears in other writers such as Suetonius, who preserves a popular slur against

Tiberius: 'He shrinks from wine, because he thirsts for blood now: he drinks this as eagerly as he used to drink wine' (*Tiberius* 59.1). The fact that passion for wine is often linked with bloodthirstiness by ancient writers is another advantage of portraying Vitellius as a drunkard: it was an economical way to hint at the emperor's ferocity. In Vitellius' case, the metaphor is given a different twist when both Tacitus and Suetonius preserve the emperor's aphorism about 'feasting his eyes' on a death (*Histories* 3.39.1 and *Vitellius* 14.2; cf. Cicero *Verr.* 5.26.65 and *Phil.* 11.3.8, and Dio 75.6-7). This choice of metaphor in the Latin authors may suggest that they were more interested in Vitellius' gluttony than in his drunkenness as an expression of his savagery.

Attributes such as these suggested to writers and readers alike that there were parallels between Vitellius and Nero. Nor was this connection purely literary, since the historical Vitellius himself tried to cash in on Nero's popularity by identifying with him (Suetonius *Vitellius* 11.2, Dio 65.7 and Tacitus *Histories* 2.71, 2.95.1). Nevertheless, the tone of most writers is highly critical. Dio describes Vitellius' dissatisfaction with Nero's notorious Golden House as a residence:

> I will add that not even Nero's Golden House could satisfy Vitellius. For although he admired and praised Nero's name, life and habits, nevertheless he criticised him for living in such a wretched house so scantily and poorly equipped ... His wife Galeria ridiculed the small amount of decoration that was found in the royal apartments. (65.4)

After Vespasian chose not to live in the Golden House, preferring instead the Gardens of Sallust (Dio 66.10.4-5), the building was targeted by writers as an emblem of Nero's despotism.[27] For Dio's Vitellius to belittle it so flippantly shows the emperor's potential to surpass Nero, even if he did not live to do so. It is an ingenious touch that Vitellius' wife, Galeria, mirrors her husband's dissatisfaction with the luxurious house and thus serves as the female extension of Vitellius' grasping and greedy nature. Dio presents Vitellius and Galeria as the antithesis of the perfect imperial marriage, embodied for example in the idealised public image of Augustus and Livia. Certainly, Galeria is characterised as a far more virtuous woman by Tacitus (*Histories* 2.64.2).

Suetonius also casts the relationship between Nero and Vitellius in a pejorative light, claiming that the latter was 'contaminated by every kind of vice' (*Vitellius* 4), particularly by his role as president at the Neronian contests. In this capacity Vitellius provides a special service to the theatrical emperor by asking him on the people's behalf to participate in the cithara-playing contest. This connection is hardly the most damning example of a courtier's collaboration with an autocratic imperial regime.[28] Yet the fact that Suetonius highlights this relatively innocuous detail suggests that the biographer was anxious to establish a thematic link between Vitellius and Nero in the *Vitellius*. Suetonius describes Nero's performances on the cithara elsewhere, but Cluvius Rufus rather than Vitellius is the collaborator (*Nero* 21.2). Suetonius reinforces this initial connection by noting that Vitellius sacrifices to Nero's spirit and asks a musician to play one of Nero's tunes (*Vitellius* 11.2. Cf. Dio 65.7.3 and Tacitus *Histories* 2.95.1). His enthusiasm for Nero's singing talents appears especially distasteful in comparison with Vespasian's indifference. When Nero began to sing, Vespasian would either leave or defiantly fall fast asleep.[29] Finally, even while the Capitol itself burns as Flavians and Vitellians clash in the final struggle, Vitellius is said to gaze at the fire whilst banqueting in Tiberius' mansion (*Vitellius* 15.3). The soldiers taunt the emperor as a 'fire-starter' (*Vitellius* 17.2), the same slur which had been used of Nero (Tacitus *Annals* 15.67.2). Suetonius does not draw the parallel explicitly, but this is surely a new twist on the old theme of Nero fiddling while Rome burned.[30]

This notion of an alignment between Vitellius and Nero is deeply entrenched in later writers. Thus, Philostratus' Euphrates refers to Vitellius simply as Nero's image (*Vita Apollonii* 7.33), and the author of the *Historia Augusta* links Vitellius securely with both Nero and Caligula in the list of archetypal tyrannical emperors, claiming that he would never have embarked on the biography of such a disreputable ruler as Elagabalus, 'unless men like Caligula, Nero and Vitellius had held power before this' (*Elagabalus* 1.1). Likewise, the author of the *Historia Augusta* observes that there were many more evil emperors than good ones, citing Vitellius, Caligula and Nero as the worst (*Divus Aurelianus* 42.6). This infamous trio recurs when the emperor Verus is said to rival Caligula, Nero and Vitellius because, like them, he roams incognito through taverns and brothels and gets into fights (*Lucius Verus* 4.6). Thus, the author of the *Historia Augusta* considers Vitellius the perfect figure to link with the more familiar evil emperors Caligula and Nero: three names were rhetorically more effective than two and Vitellius, with his dubious reputation, admirably filled the gap.

Tacitus' response to the literary tradition about Vitellius

Vitellius' paradoxical rise to power

When Tacitus began the *Histories*, it must have been difficult to find sources which did not incorporate elements of this exaggerated Vitellius. The task of sifting this material and creating a balanced historical portrait of the emperor, rather than a stereotype, was surely challenging. According to some modern critics, such as Engel, although there is evidence from literary sources and coins that the emperor was a competent general who did not covet imperial power, Tacitus deliberately chose to create a hostile picture of Vitellius.[31] Engel argues that there are traces of a pro-Vitellian source in the *Histories*, which can be recovered despite Tacitus' malevolent presentation. However, I will argue that there are more constructive ways of reading Vitellius in the *Histories* than to see him as a figure generated by Tacitus' hostility or inability to use his sources critically.

There is one technique which Tacitus exploits forcefully. By presupposing that most readers were familiar with Vitellius' conventional image as a power-hungry usurper, the historian gradually balances this audience expectation against a different reality, and focuses instead on Vitellius' lack of personal ambition and on his acquisition of power through the intervention of other men. This literary technique differs from Tacitus' shifting use of internal and external focalisation to characterise Otho and to question how far a reader should share the viewpoint of critics within the narrative. Some of the criticisms commonly levelled against Vitellius may even have been true, but there were grander destructive forces at work, for which we cannot hold the emperor responsible quite so easily.

Tacitus allocates his Vitellius a surprisingly low profile before *Histories* 1.50. The emperor is only mentioned when necessary (1.1.3, 1.9.1, 1.14.1 and 1.44.2.), and the main dash of colour comes when Vitellius is said to have executed all those who petitioned Otho for rewards after Galba's death (1.44.2). By itself, this detail does little to counteract expectations of a bloodthirsty Vitellius, particularly since Tacitus says that the executions were not done 'out of respect for Galba' (1.44.1). There is certainly no separate character-sketch of Vitellius.[32] Thus, Tacitus creates suspense and mounting curiosity in his audience before Vitellius even appears. However, once Otho is emperor and Galba is dead, the introduction can be delayed no longer. Even so Tacitus defers Vitellius' direct appearance in favour of an outline of public opinion at Rome (1.50). The overall mood is gloomy and fearful as the internal audience pessimistically compare the two contenders for the principate and conclude that they are faced with 'the two most notorious men in the world because of their immorality, laziness and extravagance, who were appointed by Fate, as it were, to destroy the empire' (1.50.1). Tacitus' personification of the terrified city and his focus on the fearful mood in Rome is a clever touch. Given the predominant reputation of Vitellius in the literary tradition, such details must nudge a reader to anticipate a menacing Vitellius. So even at this early stage, we are invited to consider Vitellius' reputation and its capacity to influence onlookers.[33]

Nevertheless the reaction in Rome needs to be put into context. Vitellius' reputation for immorality, laziness and extravagance is alarming, but this image hardly tallies with the reality of the man who commands the troops in Lower Germany. Even when Tacitus promises to outline the origin and causes of the Vitellian movement (1.51.1), the historian still avoids a direct character-sketch of Vitellius himself, even though Otho (1.13), Piso (1.14) and Mucianus (1.10) are all introduced with one. This subtly diminishes Vitellius' stature as a leader and underlines that the impetus for the movement came from elsewhere. Tacitus makes it clear that a desire for civil war already existed amongst the soldiers who, having defeated Vindex, had acquired a taste for rewards which were only available on campaign. Vitellius' arrival provides a convenient figurehead for these troops, but Tacitus implies that Vitellius himself galvanises the disaffection only in that he happened to get the appointment. In contrast, Suetonius suggests a direct causal link between Vitellius' personality and the movement in Germany: not only do we hear about his affable treatment of the soldiers on the march to Germany (*Vitellius* 7.3), but Suetonius also refers to Vitellius' poverty, which gives him a conventional motive for seizing the principate (*Vitellius* 7.2). Certainly, Tacitus also informs his readers about Vitellius' money problems (2.59.2), but only retrospectively, which thus diminishes the sense that Vitellius' poverty drove him to seize power. In addition, the Tacitean phrase 'Vitellian movement (*motus Vitellianus*)' (1.51.1), raises pertinent questions. How much personal involvement on Vitellius' part does this formulation suggest? Is Vitellius central or merely a figurehead? The wording is unusual, in that Tacitus does not refer elsewhere to an 'Othonian movement (*motus Othonianus*)', and it contrasts with the phrase, the 'war started by Vespasian (*motum a Vespasiano bellum*)' (2.67.1), which certainly suggests strong personal involvement on Vespasian's part.

The sense of bathos is heightened when Vitellius eventually appears in person in Lower Germany. The future emperor's actions seem prudent, but not indicative of an excessively ambitious or dangerous personality. Vitellius reinstates a number of men who had been dismissed by Fonteius Capito and reduces sentences (1.52.1), but Tacitus suggests his actions are dictated both by 'a desire for popularity (*ambitio*)', and by 'sound judgment (*iudicium*)'. These factors point to a commander anxious for a quiet life, rather than to the monster of the historical tradition. Indeed, Tacitus implies that Vitellius' passive nature may have led to his appointment to the governorship of Lower Germany in the first place. We are reminded of Vitellius' 'sluggish personality (*segne ingenium*)' (1.52.4) and Tacitus' Galba at any rate makes the appointment because of Vitellius' father's successful career: 'That seemed sufficient' (1.9.1) is the succinct phrase which questions the wisdom of such complacent allocation of posts. Tacitus subsequently develops this theme by making Valens observe that Vitellius should feel frightened because of his father's illustrious background (1.52.4). This further accentuates the idea that Tacitus' Vitellius is ineffectual in comparison with his father. Suetonius' Galba much more luridly appoints Vitellius on the grounds that 'no men are to be feared less than those who think about food alone' (*Vitellius* 7.1), which suggests a passivity that sits rather oddly with later chapters about his tyrannical cruelty (*Vitellius* 13-14).

Even when Tacitus' Vitellius spends money and makes gifts 'without limit, without judgment' (1.52.2), there is no indication that his objective is the principate. In fact, his imperial aspirations are effectively mapped on to him by others. Tacitus obscures Vitellius' own motives with a passive verb, which describes only how his actions were received and not why he took them: 'All Vitellius' actions were judged (*accipiebantur*) not as those of a consular governor, but as something more significant' (1.52.2). Also, Tacitus suggests a discrepancy between Vitellius' faults and the positive way in which wilful onlookers regarded them: 'At the same time, they regarded even his faults as good qualities, since they were so eager for power (*simul* [*aviditate imperandi*[34]] *vitia pro virtutibus interpretabantur*)' (1.52.2). This phrase echoes Sallust's assessment of Marius: 'Any ill-considered action on his part was regarded as a good quality (*Omnia non bene consulta in virtutem trahebantur*)' (*Jug.* 92.2). Yet Marius has just made a lightning attack on Capsa and successfully initiated his campaign against Jugurtha, so has at least done something to deserve such adulation. Tacitus' Vitellius is a pale shadow in comparison, and his own desires at this stage of the narrative are overshadowed by the ambitions of other men. In addition, Tacitus avoids any parallels with *Histories* 1.21, where internal focalisation was used to suggest Otho's personal motives for seeking power.

Vitellius' weak personality is overshadowed still further by the introduction of Alienus Caecina and Fabius Valens, a pair who are 'extravagantly greedy and notoriously reckless' (1.52.3). These two men possess many of the sinister qualities which a well-informed reader might more naturally have expected to have found in Vitellius. Both Caecina and Valens are ambitious men with special personal grudges against Galba, who will do anything to improve their own positions. Between them, they practically manufacture the Vitellian challenge out of thin air, and act as the catalysts for a movement which might otherwise have petered out. The two men make a perfect team: while Valens points out the 'enthusiasm of the troops' (1.52.4), Caecina conveniently 'had elicited support from the troops (*studia militum inlexerat*)' (1.53.1). This is just what Otho had done when angling for the principate: 'he had solicited ... support from the troops (*studia militum ... adfectaverat*)' (1.23.1). It is striking that the general Caecina rather than the pretender Vitellius performs this crucial task.

Tacitus highlights the combined action of Caecina and Valens (neither of whom Suetonius even mentions) as the decisive galvanising factor in Vitellius' rise to power. Suetonius is not interested in the complex origins of the movement which brought Vitellius to power, preferring instead to see his meteoric rise as the result of a natural rapport between Vitellius and the troops. This in turn allows Suetonius to amplify the coarser side of Vitellius' character as a device to explain why he was so popular: his chummy habit of belching loudly after asking his men whether they had enjoyed a good breakfast is unique to Suetonius and economically characterises Vitellius as the soldier's soldier (*Vitellius* 7.3). The presence of Caecina and Valens as mediators would have diverted attention away from Vitellius by blurring his direct camaraderie with the soldiers. Likewise, although Plutarch includes Caecina and Valens, they are noticeably absent from the description of Vitellius' rise to power (*Galba* 22). An unnamed soldier urges his comrades to choose Vitellius as emperor, and although Valens appears in the camp on the following day, he does not manipulate Vitellius directly (cf. Dio 64.4, where Caecina and Valens are conspicuously absent). In contrast, Tacitus puts the limits of the personal power into perspective and illustrates the future emperor's vulnerability to other men's intervention. Vitellius' hopes and ambitions are marginalised to an incredible degree, and paradoxically, the movement which bore his name gained momentum with minimal contribution from its figurehead. In this context, it is suggestive that Flavian propaganda relied so heavily on the idea that Vespasian had been unwillingly forced to become emperor by eager troops (Josephus *BJ* 4.601-4).[35] Tacitus' narrative inverts this notion, and instead *Vitellius* is saluted as emperor on a surge of enthusiasm from the common soldiers, who are prepared to make huge personal sacrifices on his behalf (1.57). MacMullen has observed that 'Power depends in part on the appearance of it, on perceptions, on symbols and gestures'.[36] Vitellius might initially look powerful because of the collective support of the soldiers, but his real influence has still not been tested: the momentum for the imperial challenge comes from below rather than from above.

Tacitus' introduction of Vitellius into the narrative therefore plays with traditional images of the emperor and challenges audience assumptions about his menacing presence. One might have expected such a colourful and notorious figure to have dominated the story from the start, but he does not. Yet Tacitus still perceives Vitellius' passivity and propensity to self-indulge as instrumental in his rise to power: the imperial challenger is a weak man with an impressive family background, which might have suggested a more robust personality than he actually displayed. After all, his father Lucius Vitellius had been consul three times (*Annals* 14.56.1), and ruled the province of Syria 'with old-fashioned integrity' (*Annals* 6.32.4). His uncle, Publius Vitellius, had commanded legions under Germanicus, as well as being active in Piso's prosecution.[37] Tacitus will remind us in the emperor's obituary that Vitellius earned his position amongst the ruling classes 'through no efforts of his own ... but through his father's eminence' and that he was popular with the army 'because he had done nothing (*per ig-naviam*)' (3.86.1).[38] Tacitus casts Vitellius' malleable personality as ripe for manipulation by opportunists such as Caecina and Valens. Yet if they had not targeted Vitellius, they might easily have latched onto the feckless governor of Upper Germany, Hordeonius Flaccus, who is 'slug-gish and cowardly' (1.56.1). Vitellius and Flaccus mirror one another in lethargy and passivity: the former happens to contend for the princi-pate, but his personal campaign shows no energy or enthusiasm for the task. Even Vitellius' message to the troops asking them to nominate an emperor is remarkably languid:

> Messengers were dispatched by Vitellius to the legions and legates to announce that the army of Upper Germany had revolted from Galba: so they must either make war on the rebels or, if they preferred unity and peace, they had to make someone emperor; and an emperor who was taken up (*sumi*) rather than searched for (*quaeri*) would be safer. (1.56.3)

This is hardly the aggressive tone of a man desperate for power. It is conspicuous again that Tacitus uses passive verb forms (*sumi* and *quaeri*), which suggest that the emperor will be created by the soldiers rather than galvanising matters himself. Vitellius does not even name himself directly as a possible candidate, and cautiously leaves the choice in the hands of the soldiers. Of course, civil wars are unpre-dictable, and wariness is a good survival technique, but Vitellius' cau-tion is extreme. If Valens had not marched into Colonia Agrippinensis and instigated Vitellius' successful acclamation, then the soldiers might have gone elsewhere for their new emperor.

From the beginning, Tacitus shows that the new emperor has mini-mal control over his soldiers. Far from curtailing his men, Vitellius 'concedes the soldiers' savage demands for one execution after another' (1.58.1). Pompeius Propinquus, the procurator in Belgica, is killed almost immediately, but perhaps even more alarmingly, Vitellius allows his men to unleash their brutality against their centurions. Slaughter-ing officers in this way often marks the beginning of a mutiny[39] and is a sinister sign at the start of a principate. One centurion, Crispinus, who had participated in the execution of Fonteius Capito, the former governor of Lower Germany, is given to the troops as a 'propitiation (*piaculum*)' (1.58.2), and four centurions, who tried to restore order during the initial outbreak of trouble, are executed 'on a charge of loyalty (*fidei crimine*)' (1.59.1).[40] Vitellius' laxity lets the soldiers believe that they have complete freedom, which triggers their appalling con-duct on the marches headed by Valens (1.62-66) and Caecina (1.67-70). Not only does an inexplicable panic amongst Valens' troops cause the deaths of almost 4,000 civilians at Divodurum (1.63), but also Caecina's

Twenty-First Legion steal some Helvetian money intended for the upkeep of a fortress, which sparks off a battle in which many thousands of Helvetians die (1.67). Greed is the trait which links both commanders and their respective armies. Valens' soldiers use their collective strength to intimidate the people of Vienna until their commander offers them a bonus in return for not attacking, while Valens himself threatened to set fire to Lucus 'until he was appeased with money' (1.66.3). If anything, Caecina is worse than Valens: 'Caecina swallowed more booty and blood (*Plus praedae ac sanguinis Caecina hausit*)' (1.67.1). Tacitus' reference to Caecina's bloodthirstiness recalls the metaphorical language of thirst often used to epitomise a tyrannical nature, but the surprise is that Caecina and not Vitellius is described in this way.[41]

So far then, Vitellius has been upstaged by the genuinely monstrous behaviour of his two generals, who have done most damage as agents of senseless destruction. Even if Vitellius is at fault for condoning their actions, Tacitus puts his behaviour into context. Certainly, Vitellius may have been described as 'drunk and stuffed through overeating in the middle of the day' (1.62.2), but this is different from directly initiating the senseless killing of thousands of civilians. Tacitus encourages a reader to cast a critical eye not just at Vitellius, but at his soldiers and generals. One scene in particular puts Vitellius' sphere of influence into perspective. Caecina and his men have been conducting a vicious campaign against the once warlike Gallic tribe, the Helvetii, who are left with no option but surrender. When the Helvetian envoys come to confront Vitellius and his troops, the balance of power is made clear by the following suggestive Tacitean juxtaposition:

> It is hard to say whether the Helvetian envoys found Vitellius or the soldiers the more implacable. The soldiers clamoured for the destruction of the town, and brandished their weapons and fists in the envoys' faces. Even Vitellius indulged in threatening language, but Claudius Cossus, one of the envoys, a noted speaker, who was more persuasive because he hid his eloquence under a well-judged display of nervousness, softened the hearts of the soldiers. (1.69.1)

The army calls the shots, and although Vitellius blusters and threatens as well, the emperor is marginal: his empty words are contrasted graphically with the physical reality of the soldiers' weapons. Claudius Cossus' performance is said to soften the hearts of the *troops*, whose change of feeling saves the Helvetians from seeing their home town Aventicum obliterated. Vitellius may have felt pity too, but the power to spare the Helvetians is not in his hands. His impotence contrasts with Caesar's problematic clemency in the previous civil wars, which is often characterised as a thinly disguised assertion of absolute power.[42]

Vitellius as Princeps

So far, then, Tacitus' Vitellius has not corroborated the tyrannical figure of the literary tradition: passivity has been the emperor's most prominent feature. Tacitus has even set up a mismatch between the fear in Rome and the unimpressive leadership of Vitellius in Lower Germany, which modifies our reaction to the new emperor: tyrants are supposed to be not just greedy, but frightening as well. However, once Caecina and Valens have defeated Otho at Bedriacum, there is a significant shift in Tacitus' presentation of Vitellius. Actions which were relatively harmless when Vitellius was a private citizen do much more damage once he is emperor. So, Vitellius initially refuses his soldiers' request to make the freedman Asiaticus a knight, but then, 'with characteristic instability (*mobilitate ingenii*)' (2.57), reverses his earlier determined stand. Vitellius thereby undermines his own authority at the one moment when he could have sent a clear message to his soldiers that the beginning of a new regime called for improved conduct. Suetonius, elaborating Asiaticus' role as Vitellius' lover, also mentions the emperor's change of heart in making the boy a knight, but is not so explicit that the impetus came from the soldiers (*Vitellius* 12). In Suetonius, the story adds spicy biographical details about Vitellius, but in Tacitus, Asiaticus' rise is used to emphasise the emperor's willingness to do the will of his troops. This is ominous and conflicts with the image of the ideal commander. As Dio said of Octavian, 'he thought that a commander should never do anything contrary to his own judgment under pressure from his soldiers' (49.13.4). Octavian's conviction here is meant to seem particularly impressive because his soldiers are threatening him, but Vitellius concedes without any particular pressure being exerted on him.

There is added horror in Vitellius' inconsistency because of the troops' recent behaviour in Italy after their victory at the first battle of Bedriacum. If anything, the soldiers, rather than Vitellius, begin to display alarming avarice and violence as the ineffectual emperor is dwarfed by his terrifying men. Their greed manifests itself in a far more active way than Vitellius' passive voracity (cf. Tacitus *Histories* 1.62.1, where the soldiers' behaviour has not yet deteriorated). In a passage which appropriately echoes Sallust's description of Sulla's corrupt army in Asia (*Cat.* 11.5.6), Tacitus gives a graphic picture of the Vitellians' behaviour in Italy:

> The Vitellians scattered throughout the towns and colonies, indulging in plunder, violence and rape; greedy and open to bribes, they cared nothing for right or wrong and did not hold back from anything, whether sacred or wicked.

dispersi per municipia et colonias Vitelliani spoliare rapere, vi et stupris
polluere; in omne fas nefasque avidi aut venales non sacro, non profano
abstinebant. (2.56.1)

Perhaps the people in Rome were right to be afraid after all. Vitellius'
earlier indulgence of his soldiers was bad enough, but conducting
himself in the same way as emperor is dangerously irresponsible.
Flatterers initially called his obliging treatment of his troops 'affability
(*comitas*)', or 'kindness (*bonitas*)' (1.52.2),[43] but Vitellius' leniency has
serious repercussions. His malleability, together with his self-indulgent
lifestyle, means that the troops develop contempt for their leader, and
hence his ability to control his men is undermined. In any case, Vitellius'
peripheral role is highlighted by what follows in Tacitus' description of
the rampaging soldiers: 'Meanwhile Vitellius, unaware of his victory ...'
(2.57.1). The new emperor does not even know that his soldiers have
won, and the arrangement of the narrative points to a gulf between the
aggressive troops and their impotent leader.

Although Tacitus acknowledges that Vitellius progressively abuses
his position to indulge his desires, the historian is primarily concerned
to explore the detrimental effect of such leadership on the soldiers.
Tacitus does not simply provide a shocking exposé of Vitellius' gluttonous behaviour without considering firstly how such a weak-willed
person could win power, and secondly what repercussions his actions
would have on his soldiers. Despite their later deterioration Vitellius'
troops had initially been able to compensate for the absence of decent
leadership: 'the zeal and energy of the soldiers made them carry out the
duties of the commander as well as their own, just as if he was present
to encourage the alert or frighten the cowards' (1.62.2). At the beginning, the Vitellian soldiers distinguish themselves as an efficient force
endowed with considerable moral fibre, who rise above Vitellius' influence 'with his idle pleasures and sumptuous banquets' (1.62.2). Such
self-sufficiency is commendable up to a point, and there are precedents
for impressive leaderless armies, such as the Fabii at Cremera. Yet
although these Fabii fight well at first, they still meet a dreadful fate in
the absence of good leaders (Ovid *Fasti* 2.227-36). Likewise, Vitellius'
flawed leadership will eventually have an impact, particularly at the
second battle of Bedriacum (3.18.1, 3.22.1 and 3.25.1). One is reminded
of Chabrias' aphorism that an army of deer commanded by a lion is more
terrifying than an army of lions commanded by a deer (Plutarch *Moralia* 187D). Tacitus, perceiving Vitellius' bad leadership as gradually
seeping down and damaging the lower ranks, proposes a general rule:
officers tend to emulate their supreme commander, and ordinary soldiers in turn imitate their officers (2.68). Therefore, Vitellius'
increasingly prodigal lifestyle gradually wears down traditional standards of discipline at the lower levels of the military hierarchy.

Vitellius' faults are mirrored with increasing clarity by his men. Even in the aftermath of the first battle of Bedriacum, the Vitellian troops prove themselves 'greedy and open to bribes' (2.56.1), but this need not have continued. It was after all fairly common for victorious soldiers to be allowed to go on the rampage for a limited period. When Vitellius orders the whole army to parade before his infant son at Lugdunum (2.59), the new emperor *could* have taken a firm stand and addressed his men, but his silence in the Tacitean narrative is conspicuous.[44] Vitellius is not only apathetic, but increasingly serves as a negative role model for his men. One passage is revealing about Tacitus' concerns:

> Indeed, if Vitellius had restricted his luxurious lifestyle, you would not have feared his greed. It was his foul and insatiable appetite for banquets. Dainties to tickle his palate were brought from Rome and Italy, and from shore to shore, the roads were buzzing with traffic. The leading provincials were ruined by having to provide for his feasts, and the towns were devastated. The soldiers were beginning to lose their diligence and courage, as they became accustomed to pleasures and resented their leader. (2.62.1)

At first, this passage looks as if it is simply reworking the familiar literary motif of Vitellius' self-destructive and gluttonous nature, but Tacitus adds a unique touch. He begins with Vitellius, but finally focuses on the soldiers and on their growing disdain for the emperor. This deterioration in the collective behaviour of the Vitellian military as they move closer to Rome is a theme which will become increasingly important in Tacitus' narrative. It provides a graphic backdrop for the characterisation of Vitellius himself and becomes an important explanatory thread in Tacitus' exploration of the Vitellian failure to retain power. Chilver suggests that Tacitus uncritically draws on Flavian propaganda in his portrayal of the Vitellian army,[45] but the historian is surely trying to anticipate why these troops will lose against the Flavians. Suetonius briefly refers to the deterioration of the Vitellian forces (*Vitellius* 10.2), but says nothing about their contempt for their emperor; the emphasis instead is on the partnership in villainy and the rapport which flourished between the leader and his men.

There is one startling incident where the Vitellian troops graphically mirror the self-destructive behaviour of their emperor, as a confrontation which begins playfully ends in catastrophe.

> So, two soldiers, one belonging to the Fifth Legion, the other to the Gallic auxiliaries, were playfully provoked into a wrestling match. After the legionary had fallen down, the Gaul jeered at him (*insultante Gallo*) and the onlookers took sides; the legionaries lashed out against the auxiliaries and two cohorts were killed. (2.68.2)

Even on its own, the incident is highly symbolic of the widespread discord amongst troops who are supposedly fighting for the same side. Yet the clash becomes more significant, if one considers that it may evoke the famous encounter between Manlius Torquatus and the Gaul, which was narrated both by Claudius Quadrigarius (Aulus Gellius *NA* 9.13) and by Livy (7.9.6-10.14). Historiography certainly offers many instances of single combat,[46] but several elements of Tacitus' account have particular resonances with the story of Torquatus and the Gaul. The fact that Tacitus' Gaulish auxiliary mocks his opponent recalls the way in which the Gaul in Claudius Quadrigarius and Livy provocatively sticks his tongue out and mocks the Romans until Torquatus steps forward to preserve Roman honour: Tacitus' verb *insulto* may recall the extremely unusual Livian verb *praesulto*,[47] both of which describe the insulting behaviour of the Gaul. Moreover, although Torquatus and the Gaul fight in front of an audience, their duel is completed entirely without the intervention of any of the onlookers. This contrasts totally with the episode in Tacitus where the spectators participate in the fighting, with disastrous results. Finally, the encounter between Torquatus and the Gaul is presented as a shining example of Roman valour triumphing over barbarity as represented by the huge Gaul. The moralism is reassuringly simple and the whole soothing tale presents good triumphing over evil through the vindication of Roman honour. In Tacitus' narrative, Roman confronts Gaul once again, except this time they are both supposed to be on the same side. If indeed the fight between Torquatus and the Gaul is in the background at this point, then Tacitus has inverted the happy outcome of the story. In this case it is the Gaul who triumphs, and although the Roman eventually reasserts control, this only happens through the collective intervention of the legionaries, which further undermines the grandeur and the nobility of the single combat. If the Gaulish auxiliary had been a real enemy, then it would have been acceptable (albeit unimpressive) to enlist the help of the Roman legionaries who were watching. Yet the Gaul is not a real enemy, and the echoes serve to emphasise even further the self-destructive nature of Vitellius' troops. Even the fact that Tacitus' combatants are wrestling as opposed to fighting with swords marks a deterioration: wrestling was regarded as a pastime of decadent nations (Silius Italicus *Pun.* 14.136 and Lucan *Phar.* 7.271) and it was certainly a view held by some that good soldiers should not wrestle (Plutarch *Philopoemen* 3.3-5).[48] Nor is this clash between legionaries and auxiliaries an isolated incident, since Tacitus notes that hostility between the two groups still festered (2.88). When some citizens playfully cut off the legionaries' belts without their knowledge and then keep asking them where their equipment is, the soldiers respond by killing the practical jokers. This pair of playful incidents which turn nasty significantly straddle the digression about Vespasian's proclamation as emperor (2.74-86).

Vitellius' response, both to the wrestling incident and to the demand made by these same soldiers for Verginius Rufus' head (2.68), is bizarre. The emperor goes into the camp and praises all the soldiers for their dutiful conduct, which deeply offends the Gaulish auxiliaries:

> On the next day Vitellius granted an audience to the senatorial delega-
> tion, which he had ordered to wait for him at Ticinum. Then he entered
> the camp and spontaneously praised the soldiers for their dutiful conduct
> (*pietatem militum conlaudavit*), though the auxiliaries noisily protested
> at the extensive impunity and arrogance enjoyed by the legionaries.
> (2.69.1)

The moral outrage of the Gaulish auxiliaries at Vitellius' indiscriminate approval is understandable. The emperor responds rashly, since prais-ing all the soldiers, regardless of the bad behaviour of some, must surely exacerbate existing tensions between the men and cause further divi-sions. We can compare this dubious moment with a scene from Livy, where Publius Scipio praises his soldiers after their arduous but suc-cessful assault on *Carthago Nova*: 'then he praised the soldiers' valour (*militum deinde virtutem conlaudavit*)'[49] (26.48.4). Publius Scipio com-mends his exhausted soldiers after an impressive victory, whereas the most recent act of Vitellius' unruly troops has been to demand the execution of their former general Verginius Rufus. Naturally, the more that Vitellius praises his men inappropriately, the less value his ap-proval will have. Soldiers were unlikely to strive for their supreme commander's praise if they found they had access to it so easily. Vitellius is unwise to praise his supporters so indiscriminately: he commends the soldiers (2.57.2, 2.69.1, 3.36.2), Caecina and Valens (2.59.3), and even himself (2.90.1). It was a familiar motif that the good commander praised the brave and rebuked the cowardly, thus giving clear responses to different groups within the army as a whole.[50] This could be produc-tive outside the immediate context of a battle, as when Julius Caesar judiciously praises his men for their swift ship building before the second invasion of Britain (*BG* 5.2.3).[51] A counter-example is Caligula's inappropriate commendation of his men for having overcome great hardships, although all they had done was to cross from Bauli to Puteoli on the emperor's bridge (Dio 59.17.8). Vitellius clearly has more in common with Caligula than with Caesar.

However, the troops respond ominously, not to his praise, but to his decadent lifestyle so that, 'their energy was being dissipated by luxury, which was totally at variance with old-fashioned discipline and the habits of our ancestors' (2.69.2). The soldiers begin to destroy them-selves just as their supreme commander does. Tacitus is not denying that Vitellius abused his position to indulge himself, but uniquely offers a broader perspective on the simultaneous deterioration of the troops, which accelerates the closer they get to Rome (cf. 3.49, the degeneration of Antonius Primus and his men as they approach Rome). In Tacitus' account, the emperor leads the way, but he is followed by 60,000 armed men, 'ruined by loose discipline' (2.87.1). Certainly, Tacitus has used elements from the literary tradition about Vitellius to trace the evolution of his self-indulgent gluttony, but his decline is not analysed in isolation. Rome is a magnet, which corrupts and debilitates at all levels:[52]

> the soldiers ... did not know where to parade, did not observe sentry-duty, did not keep themselves in training. Thanks to the attractions of the city and its unspeakable vices, they ruined their physique by idleness and their morals by debauchery. (2.93.1)

This is a blow from which they never recover. By the time that the troops must leave Rome to confront the Flavian challenge, they are completely demoralised and weakened by their exposure to urban pleasures (2.99). Even the morale of their two dynamic commanders has been sapped: Valens is ill and Caecina has been overwhelmed by 'newly acquired apathy (*torpor recens*)' (2.99.2), which aligns him closely with Vitellius (cf. 'Vitellius was apathetic (*torpebat Vitellius*)' 1.62.2 and Vitellius' 'apathy (*torpor*)' 2.77.3). The corrupting influence both of the emperor and of the city have combined in undermining the capacity of the Vitellian side to respond to the Flavians. If Vitellius himself succumbs to temptation, so too do his officers and soldiers. This is the real cause of the emperor's problems.

Alien qualities pervade both Vitellius and his men as they leave Rome. How different their squalid departure is from their ebullient arrival! Preceded by eagles and standards on entering the city, the soldiers proudly displayed their medals, and the officers were all dressed in white (2.89). This may have been a façade, but at least the Vitellians had bothered to make the effort. Tacitus' readers would have found it especially galling that the transformation had taken place in Rome. It was normally a spell in the east which was supposed to precipitate such moral degeneration. So, Livy proposes that if Alexander the Great had attacked Italy after his eastern conquests, he would have led 'an army forgetful of Macedonia and already degenerating into Persian ways' (9.18.3). Likewise, Sulla's army falls victim to Asia's temptations:

> What is more, Sulla had sought to secure the loyalty of the army he commanded in Asia by treating it too generously and by indulging it in luxury against ancestral customs. The attractive places, pleasantly beguiling during leisure-time, softened the soldiers' fierce spirits. There for the first time, the Roman people's army grew accustomed to lovemaking, drinking, admiring statues, paintings and embossed dishes, which they stole from private and public buildings, plundering temples and desecrating everything, whether sacred or wicked.

Huc adcedebat quod L. Sulla exercitum quem in Asia ductaverat, quo sibi fidum faceret, contra morem maiorum luxuriose nimisque liberaliter habuerat. Loca amoena, voluptaria facile in otio ferocis militum animos molliverant: ibi primum insuevit exercitus populi Romani amare potare, signa tabulas pictas vasa caelata mirari, ea privatim et publice rapere, delubra spoliare, sacra profanaque omnia polluere. (Sallust *Cat.* 11.5-6)

This Sallustian intertext suggests that Tacitus has creatively reversed a traditional theme. Under the Republic, exposure to foreign (particularly eastern) temptations, ideally unavailable in Italy, led Romans to decadence, but imperial Rome, at the heart of a huge empire, has drawn all enticements to the centre, so that Romans no longer need to leave the city to indulge themselves.[53] Lucan plays with this same idea in his wholesome ethnographical description of Libya, whose cedar trees are felled to provide tables for banquets at Rome (*Phar.* 9.429-30).[54] Thus, Tacitus develops the stereotypical Vitellius of the sources by relating the excesses of his character to the collective deterioration of the Vitellian soldiers.

The decline of Vitellius

Vitellius' capacity to terrorise may have temporarily soared following his arrival in Rome, but after dispatching Caecina to confront the Flavians, the emperor simultaneously becomes less frightening and more terrified. Certainly, Otho too had been frightened, but nevertheless people were still afraid of him (1.81.1). Thus Tacitus' Otho corroborates Laberius' opinion that 'if many people fear a man, then he must fear many people' (Macrobius *Sat.* 2.7.4-5). However, the ineffectual Vitellius is increasingly regarded almost with pity, especially in *Histories* 3, and Tacitus thereby distances him from the negative stereotype of the literary tradition.[55] It is striking that Tacitus follows his narrative of the final Flavian victory at Cremona (3.1-3.35) with Vitellius' personal story before the defeat (3.36-48), which is resumed from 2.101, but chronologically the second section (3.36-48) comes *before* the first section (3.1-3.35). Thus, the audience's knowledge that the Vitellian cause will collapse dramatically underscores their response to Tacitus' account of Vitellius' own futile preparations for the confrontation. The suggestive narrative arrangement intensifies the atmosphere of doom and hopelessness surrounding the emperor.

Vitellius, although sensitive towards the impending danger, takes no positive action, but 'begins to mask his cares in debauchery' (3.36.1). It was a literary theme that leaders often had to seek shelter from their worries by various means, but it was rarely through debauchery that they found solace: work or war were the respectable distractions. So, Hannibal tolerates separation from his wife by concentrating on war (Silius Italicus *Pun.* 3.158), Agricola consoles himself for his lost son

through battle (Tacitus *Agricola* 29.1), and the bereaved Tiberius comforts himself by attending the senate (Tacitus *Annals* 4.8.2). All three
try to carry on with their lives as best they can. Yet the distressed
Vitellius removes himself from the public eye, and is now hidden in his
villa like some animal. The emperor is not even in Rome, but has
withdrawn to the forests near Aricia on the Via Appia, as Tacitus
emphasises (3.36.2). These woods contain the famous Temple of Diana
Nemorensis, whose presiding priest, the 'king of the grove', was a
runaway slave who acquired office by killing his predecessor, which
seems a suggestive analogy in a civil war.[56] In addition, Diana was
associated with asylum (Dionysius of Halicarnassus *Ant. Rom.* 4.26.3),
which the beleaguered Vitellius desperately needs to claim. Tacitus has
already told the story of a real runaway slave Geta, who impersonated
Scribonianus and made an abortive bid for power (2.72).[57] It is in the
forests of Aricia that Vitellius receives news of the treachery of Bassus
and Caecina, and his reaction to this disclosure shows his utter failure
to adapt to his role as emperor. There is something desperate about his
enthusiastic gratitude as 'at a crowded meeting he piled praises on the
troops' dutiful conduct (*frequenti contione pietatem militum laudibus
cumulat*)' (3.36.2). By a verbal echo, Tacitus encourages his readers to
compare this ambivalent moment with the emperor's conduct during
the aftermath of the Vitellian victory at Bedriacum. The first thing that
jubilant Vitellius did after being informed of the victory is exactly the
same: 'having summoned a meeting, he piled praises on the troops'
valour (*vocata contione virtutem militum laudibus cumulat*)' (2.57.2). In
the first instance Vitellius' response is appropriate, while in the second
it is a mark of desperation. The echo conveys the emperor's vulnerability: Vitellius' inflexible leadership techniques fail to take account of the
wider picture.

In the narrative of Vitellius' decline and defeat, Tacitus often stresses
how disengaged the helpless emperor is from the realities of the situation. His indecision about how best to deal with his so-called enemy,
Junius Blaesus, is a good example.[58] Vitellius' own brother, Lucius,
wants to eliminate Blaesus for personal reasons, but, callously playing
on the emperor's insecurities, encourages him not to worry about the
distant Vespasian when such a dangerous traitor as Blaesus threatens
him in Rome (3.38). Lucius disingenuously claims that 'his prayers and
tears were for his brother and for his brother's children' (3.38.3).[59]
Vitellius is taken in by this act, and instead of addressing the real
problem, the Flavian invasion, wastes his energy on eliminating a man
whose distinguishing characteristic is 'unshakeable loyalty (*obstinata
fides*)' (3.39.2). We certainly pity Vitellius for being duped by his manipulative brother, particularly given the bad timing of the attack on
the loyal Blaesus after Caecina's recent treachery. Vitellius needs as
many loyal supporters as possible, but the elimination of Blaesus sends

out a powerful message that loyalty does not pay. With friends like Vitellius, who needs enemies?

Even after Vitellius hears firm news of the military defeat (3.54), his response is still inadequate. Instead of publicly acknowledging the crisis, the emperor simply pretends that nothing has happened. As Tacitus stresses, this proves the decisive factor in Vitellius' downfall, because despite the loss of his two generals, Caecina and Valens, in such short succession, 'prospects and resources still existed' (3.54.1). Only the suicide of a loyal centurion, Julius Agrestis, who recently inspected the battlefield at Bedriacum, shakes Vitellius from his lethargy. There is a similar story about an Othonian soldier, who commits suicide after bringing news of the Othonian defeat at Bedriacum (Suetonius *Otho* 10.1 and Dio 63.11). Tacitus may have transferred the story from an Othonian to a Vitellian context, or at least chose to anchor a floating anecdote here. However, even when Vitellius realises the danger and finally tries to do something useful, he proves incompetent. Tacitus lists two bad omens concerning a flock of birds and an escaped bull, but the 'chief portent' is said to be Vitellius himself:

> Ignorant of soldiering, incapable of planning, clueless about the marching order, the procedure for scouting, or how far operations should be pressed forward or held back, he was always asking others. With every piece of news, his expression and movement showed panic. Afterwards he would get drunk. (3.56.2)

This picture of Vitellius in the final crisis is critical and shocking: even the stereotypical rogue general chooses his moment for drinking, but thereafter copes efficiently with the basic military duties about which Vitellius is ignorant. By this stage the emperor's drinking, so clearly a retreat from reality, may even begin to elicit our sympathy as well as our disapproval. Whatever our reaction, the internal audience of the text do not condemn the emperor. The depressed Vitellius is revived 'by the enthusiastic shouts of the soldiers and the people calling for arms' (3.58.1). People feel sorry for him as he began 'by his looks, voice and tears, to rouse pity' (3.58.3; cf. 3.68.1). Whatever Vitellius' faults, on-lookers could still sympathise with his reversal of fortune, just as some do when the harsh Armenian king Mithridates is treacherously captured (*Annals* 12.47.4).

Our compassion is intensified by Vitellius' naive response to the offers of amnesty from the enemy generals, Antonius Primus and Arrius Varus. Rather than acknowledging that even considering such proposals is futile, Vitellius begins to ponder practicalities (3.63.2): how many slaves should he take with him? Which will be the best seaside resort for his retirement? His innocence is distressing.[60] The way that Vitellius *should* have viewed this offer of amnesty is suggested when Tacitus uses internal focalisation to recreate the thoughts of his most loyal followers: 'It was clear that Primus, Fuscus and that typical Flavian, Mucianus, would have no alternative but to kill Vitellius' (3.66.3). Such harsh realism so soon after Vitellius' naive response to the offer should make a reader feel pity for the emperor. The guileless Vitellius increasingly plays the role of victim, who is entirely at the mercy of the developing situation around him.

However, in one striking instance the emperor does try to reassert control by abdicating. The scene is visually striking, as Vitellius leaves the palace, dressed in black and accompanied by 'his little son who is carried on a tiny litter, as if to his funeral (*ferebatur lecticula parvulus filius velut in funebrem pompam*)' (3.67.2). According to Dio, the boy was six years old and could therefore walk on his own, but the litter enhances the tragic air (65.1.2a). The diminutive, *lecticula*, appears only here in Tacitus' works; it is poignantly followed by a second example, *parvulus*, which intensifies the pathos of the spectacle.[61] All Vitellius' frantic carousing, so self-destructive as to recall the 'eat, drink, and be merry' motif of sympotic poetry,[62] has taken a rather literal turn: he is conducting his abdication like a funeral, which is appropriate, since his death will follow in three days' time and his son will also be executed by the victors (4.80.1). Yet on this occasion the emperor, emotional and on the point of tears, is not drunk. Calling a meeting, Vitellius announces his abdication and appeals to the audience to look after his boy. There was certainly a long tradition in courtroom scenes of children being strategically deployed to manipulate an audience's emotions (cf. Cicero *Pro Sulla* 31.89 and Quintilian 6.1.30), and in historiography too, the presence of children could have a dramatic effect. During the mutiny in Germany, Agrippina leaves the camp with Caligula, 'clutching her little son to her breast', which causes the rebellious soldiers to have a change of heart (Tacitus *Annals* 1.40.3-4), and after the death of Germanicus, in an emotional scene Agrippina disembarks at Brundisium 'clutching the funeral urn, with her two children' (*Annals* 3.1.4).[63] Likewise, Vitellius' devious brother deploys the familiar courtroom trick when he 'clutches the boy to his breast' (3.38.2) in the prelude to Blaesus' murder. Tacitus *could* have hinted that Vitellius was self-consciously using his son to further his own plans (cf. Dio 65.16.5), but there is no suggestion of a hidden agenda. Any impact that the boy's presence has works against Vitellius, who is forced to retain power against his will. It is the collective forces around the emperor who control the situation and not the emperor himself. In a symbolic gesture, Vitellius tries to hand his dagger to the consul, Caecilius Simplex, who (despite earlier kind treatment at the emperor's hands: 2.60.4) refuses to take it. Tension rises in the crowd and eventually Vitellius finds his way blocked so that his only option is to return to the palace. It is astonishing but his abdication fails and his sole attempt to assert control over the situation backfires dramatically. What is more, the focus on his little son mirrors the earlier triumphant scene at Lugdunum (2.59.3), when the troops filed past the boy after the Vitellian victory. Our memory of this earlier scene must provoke an acute sense of dramatic reversal.[64] Vitellius' reign has been so short that his young son, now only a few months older, symbolises a dynasty that might have been, as well as reminding us that Vespasian conveniently has two adult sons waiting in the wings.

In addition, the attempt of Tacitus' Vitellius to abdicate can be compared with the way in which some tyrants pretended to resign power in order to strengthen their position. So, Gelon voluntarily 'gave up' autocratic power in Syracuse, insisting that the Syracusans were his superiors, whereupon the people in turn played benefactor and handed Gelon what he most desired, lifelong autocratic power (Diodorus Siculus 11.26.5-6). Likewise, the governor of Miletus, Aristagoras, resigned his position in favour of a democratic government, but Herodotus characterises him as power-hungry (5.37.2). Augustus' constitutional settlements can also be considered in this light. To 'give up' power ostentatiously could paradoxically be a means of strengthening a ruler's hold on the state, which placed emperors in a difficult position if they genuinely wanted to relinquish control or play a less central role in government. When Tiberius wants to move away from Rome into semi-retirement in AD 26, Tacitus claims that the emperor left the city under the pretext of dedicating temples and did not indicate that his absence would be permanent (*Annals* 4.57.1): presumably this decision reflects the original difficulties which Tiberius faced in trying to reject imperial power during the senatorial debate after Augustus' death (*Annals* 1.11-12 and 1.13.5). Tacitus famously questions Tiberius' sincerity in refusing the principate: Vitellius' desire to abdicate seems to be genuine, but despite his wishes he is not allowed to relinquish his power.

The misery and helplessness which engulf the Tacitean Vitellius as he is forced to retain imperial power against his will contrast sharply with Suetonius' account. There, although Vitellius claims to be laying aside a position 'which he had taken up against his will' (*Vitellius* 15.2), the soldiers force him to postpone his abdication overnight, so on the next day the emperor makes a second attempt, but 'when the soldiers and people interrupted again, encouraging him not to lose heart and vying in promising him all their help, he plucked up spirit (*animum resumpsit*)' (*Vitellius* 15.3). The crowd therefore brings about a genuine change in the emperor's state of mind. Vitellius' abdication attempt is presented as a momentary loss of confidence, rather than an expression of deep and irreversible despair. Where Tacitus' Vitellius is impotent, in Suetonius' version he is indecisive. Dio too presents the emperor as an irresolute figure, whose attempts to abdicate are insincere (Dio 65.16).

Certainly, previous emperors had occasionally tried to abdicate, but
nobody had been successful: Nero made frequent histrionic threats
to abdicate (Suetonius *Nero* 34.1 and 47.2) and Claudius resigned
office in the senate, although nothing came of this gesture (Suetonius
Claudius 36).

Thus Tacitus' Vitellius cannot even abdicate despite his wishes.
Nevertheless, Flavius Sabinus, trapped on the Capitoline hill and
indignant that Vitellius has not resigned his position, as he had previously promised, sends a centurion to protest against the emperor's
'pretence and sham of laying aside the principate' (3.70.1). Sabinus
thereby credits Vitellius with far more cunning than Tacitus has presented the emperor as possessing. A sensitive reader begins to see how
easily the gulf between image and reality can develop. Sabinus' assumption that the fiasco of the abdication was all deviously planned in
advance clashes dramatically with the recent narrative of the event,
where Vitellius was sincere, but impotent. The only defence which the
frightened emperor can offer is to blame the uncontrollable ardour of
his soldiers. It sounds like the feeble excuse of a man who was desperate
to retain power, but nothing could have been further from the truth.

By now, the forlorn picture of a helpless man for whom the audience
must feel increasing sympathy has been superimposed on the traditional image of a gluttonous and cruel Vitellius. The emperor cannot
even intervene successfully to save the indignant Sabinus after his
capture. He hesitantly plans to appeal to the better judgment of the
crowd, but 'Sabinus was stabbed and mutilated; once his head was cut
off, they dragged (*trahunt*[65]) his headless body to the Gemonian steps'
(3.74.2). Vitellius himself is not a bloodthirsty maniac, but it does not
really matter because the crowd butchers Sabinus in any case: the
emperor's wishes carry little weight, but the blame for Sabinus' death
is still laid at his door. As Tacitus has pointed out, Vitellius is 'no longer
an emperor, only an excuse for war' (3.70.4). To have responsibility
without power is an unenviable predicament, but the office of emperor
should have made this impossible. When Vitellius sends some Vestal
Virgins to ask Antonius Primus for a day's grace before the final conflict,
the reply is that Sabinus' murder and the burning of the Capitol have
made 'war deals (*belli commercia*)', impossible (3.81.2). The phrase
momentarily evokes the shocking scene where the Latin warrior Magus
begs Aeneas for his life, but is told that Turnus' killing of Pallas has
made all *belli commercia* out of the question (Virgil *Aeneid* 10.532). It
is hardly Magus' fault that Pallas is dead, but Aeneas will kill him
anyway, just as the Flavian soldiers will slay Vitellius. Likewise, although the emperor himself did not kill Sabinus or burn the Capitol,
Tacitus' Antonius Primus holds him personally responsible in each case.
If we read Josephus' account (*BJ* 4.647), a bloodthirsty Vitellius himself
initiates the attack on the Capitol and has a personal vendetta against

Sabinus, which simplifies the process of allocating blame. According to Tacitus however, Vitellius is 'incapable either of issuing orders or prohibitions' (3.70.4). Through direct comment and a Virgilian echo, Tacitus highlights the inadequacy of making one individual, Vitellius, totally accountable for all the actions carried out in his name.

This escalating sense of injustice becomes more acute in Tacitus' description of Vitellius' murder.[66] Once the city has been captured, the terrified emperor is carried in a 'litter (*sellula*)' (3.84.4) to his wife's house. The unusual diminutive may even recall the *lecticula* on which his son was carried during the attempted abdication (3.67.2), thus momentarily linking the father and son. If so, the association increases our perception of the emperor as a helpless victim.[67] Ominous too is the fact that Tacitus' Galba was swept off to his death on a 'litter (*sella*)' (1.35.1 and 1.41.2), which may align Vitellius with his elderly predecessor. Certainly, before his death, Vitellius is forced by the soldiers to look at the exact spot where Galba died, as if to suggest that he is about to meet the same fate. The fifty-seven-year-old Vitellius, on the brink of his final crisis, is simultaneously associated with a young boy and an old man, neither of whom are strong figures. Thus the incidental detail about the *sellula* adds to the sense of foreboding because of these associations with previous scenes.

After Vitellius reaches his wife's house on the litter, there is no reunion: even the admirable Galeria has disappeared, which denies him some final comforting moments. At least Pompey was able to embrace Cornelia after the Pharsalus defeat (Lucan *Phar.* 8.66-70), but the unlucky Vitellius is completely alone. So, 'with characteristic instability (*mobilitate ingenii*)' (3.84.4), the emperor decides to return to the empty palace. The verbal echo of the scene where, *mobilitate ingenii*[68] (2.57), he made the freedman Asiaticus a knight despite an initial veto, is poignant. It is appropriate that this inability to make a firm decision, which was a dominant character trait even when Vitellius was at his most successful, recurs during his final ruin. The climax comes when Vitellius is driven by the angry soldiers to the Gemonian steps 'where Flavius Sabinus' body had lain' (3.85). Neither Suetonius (*Vitellius* 17)[69] nor Dio (65.20-1) mention Sabinus' body in their descriptions of Vitellius' murder, which suggests that Tacitus included such a specific reminder for a reason. This was the murder for which Antonius Primus had blamed Vitellius, although it could perhaps have been prevented if the emperor had acted decisively. However, rather than offering a sense of Vitellius finally suffering retribution for this and other atrocities, the reference to Sabinus only reminds us how much *both* men were victims of collective violence. Yet Vitellius was condemned by posterity as a monster, while Sabinus became a Flavian martyr. Such polarised fates caught Tacitus' eye. They are highlighted again when Tacitus notes that Domitian cancels the consulships awarded by Vitellius and awards

Sabinus a state funeral,[70] which are 'great proofs of the fickleness of fortune, mixing prosperity with catastrophe' (4.47).

Conclusion

By exploiting audience familiarity with the emperor's traditional character traits, Tacitus suggests a mismatch between Vitellius' grotesque reputation and the rather less impressive commander of the troops in Lower Germany. By introducing this dissonant note, Tacitus suggests how unsatisfactory and simplistic it was to blame Vitellius alone for the momentous events of the civil war. There is emphasis on collective, as well as on individual guilt. In particular, Tacitus acknowledges how far the opportunistic Alienus Caecina and Fabius Valens played a critical role in galvanising the Vitellian challenge: deftly he contrasts the energy of this pair with the lethargy of the would-be emperor.

Certainly, Tacitus knew posterity's evaluation of Vitellius, but while acknowledging that the emperor developed or already possessed undesirable character traits, he puts the man into context and focuses on how inadequate his personality was for dealing with the crisis of civil war. Tacitus unusually puts less weight than most writers on the lurid and sensational details of Vitellius' gluttonous lifestyle and concentrates instead on the corrosive effect that this sort of personality had on his troops. The gradual decline of these soldiers' fighting ability and their increasing contempt for Vitellius as a leader play a crucial role in their eventual defeat at the second battle of Bedriacum. Tacitus' analysis of Vitellius' personality against the backdrop of the collective identity of the Vitellian troops is incisive and innovative. By forcing a reader to put Vitellius into context and by gradually suggesting how impotent he was (despite his imperial powers), Tacitus adds meaning and depth to a character, who could so easily have remained a shallow stereotype.

6

Vespasian, Domitian and Titus

Introduction

Tacitus only owed his career to the Flavians (1.1.3), (whereas Josephus owed them his life: *BJ* 3.396-7 and 5.541), but this still left him vulnerable to possible charges of partisanship in his historical analysis.[1] Other authors found themselves plagued by anxieties about their credibility in the wake of the Flavian victory. So, Pliny the Elder did not want his (now lost) historical work to be published during his own lifetime, in case critics accused him of pro-Flavian bias (*HN Praef.* 20).[2] Tacitus deflects attention from his own potential flaws by expressing dissatisfaction with the unnamed historians, who wrote under the Flavian dynasty: by implication, his own work is truthful in comparison.[3] Of course, all historians promised, implicitly or explicitly, to tell the truth, and this was such a well-known historiographical motif that Seneca was able to parody it (*Apocolocyntosis* 1.1).[4] Even so, Tacitus' apparently formulaic assertions of honesty take on a special relevance in the aftermath of the civil wars. Tacitus' dissatisfaction is especially acute when criticising writers who misleadingly describe the treachery of Caecina and Bassus as 'concern for peace' and 'love of the state' (2.101). Vitellius may have been a flawed emperor, but Tacitus can still condemn both the traitors and the historians who present such treachery so positively. Tacitus' interest in denouncing those with shifting loyalty punctuates the first three books of the *Histories*: offenders include Alienus Caecina (1.53.1 and 2.101), Antonius Primus (2.86.2), Valerius Festus (2.98.1), some unnamed Vitellian officers (3.61.1), and those who desert both Galba and Vitellius (3.86.2). Conversely, the few who maintain their integrity by staying loyal, such as Junius Blaesus (3.39.2), win praise from Tacitus. The historian's concern with this topic transcends individual emperors and embraces the whole narrative of the civil war period.

However sensitive Tacitus was to such pitfalls, a balanced assessment of Vespasian's rise to power was still difficult to achieve. The victorious new emperor and his family had so much more time than the losers to preserve for posterity their own version of events. Even if they themselves grew progressively less concerned to orchestrate an 'official' account of the civil war, many writers would still have tried hard to forestall imperial desires through their own enthusiastic historical narratives. Flavian propaganda must have taken on a new momentum once it became clear that there were no more challengers waiting in the wings to usurp Vespasian's power. In addition, those who had fought on the wrong side may not have wanted (or been able) to produce their own version of events. Plutarch, relating how his friend and patron Mestrius Florus, the ex-consul, gave him a tour of the battlefield after the first battle of Bedriacum, adds that Florus was 'one of those who was with Otho at that time by coercion, not of his own free will' (*Otho* 14.2). This special pleading probably derives from Plutarch rather than from Florus, but reveals intense discomfort about the fact that the ex-consul fought on the wrong side in the civil war.[5] Florus survived despite this 'mistake', and seems to have established a reasonably good relationship with Vespasian, if we believe Suetonius' anecdote (*Vespasian* 22). Others, particularly those who supported Vitellius, had tense relationships with the new regime and were perhaps less forthcoming about their experiences in the civil war as a result. Alienus Caecina's treacherous abandonment of Vitellius must have made reminiscence a particularly unattractive prospect for him. A change of allegiance did not always rule out writing memoirs or history, as the cases of Quintus Dellius and Valerius Messalla in the triumviral period show, but Caecina's execution in AD 79 (on Titus' orders, but before Vespasian's death) for conspiring with Eprius Marcellus suggests that rhetorical fanfares about his concern for peace in reality masked a tense relationship with the new Flavian regime.[6] Nor was the market dominated by the memoirs of Flavian generals: Licinius Mucianus evasively wrote about natural curiosities and edited ancient documents (Tacitus *Dialogus* 37.2 and Pliny *HN passim*). Even for the victors, writing about the conflict was problematic because they had won a *civil* war.

This chapter will explore some of the questions raised by Tacitus about the moral standing of the Flavian dynasty in its rise to power and suggest that there was actually a disturbing continuity between the way in which Vespasian and his predecessors gained control. Vespasian happened to be the ultimate victor, but if *fortuna* had conspired differently, then historians might have had to write about a Vitellian rather than a Flavian dynasty, and the roles of Vitellius and Vespasian could have been reversed.[7] During the civil war between Octavian and Antony, one famous entrepreneur flattered Octavian by producing a trained crow which could say: 'Hail Caesar, victorious commander!' This proved a great hit until the embarrassing discovery that the man owned a second crow, which could say: 'Hail Antony, victorious commander!' (Macrobius *Sat.* 2.4.29). Antony may have been a more competent contender for power than Vitellius, but Tacitus had to recreate in his narrative the time when the conflict between Vespasian and Vitellius still hung in the balance: as he observes, 'We came to believe in the mysteries of fate and in an empire predestined for Vespasian and his children by portents and oracles only after his victory (*post fortunam*)' (1.10.3). Although this does not necessarily mean that Tacitus was a religious sceptic, the statement does show his perceptiveness about human nature and his sensitivity towards the difficulties of shaping a balanced historical narrative after the Flavian victory.

Omens and prodigies

Tacitus' introduction of Vespasian as a model general at first seems reassuring. Vespasian, 'scarcely different from a common soldier in his appearance and dress' (2.5.1), displays a wholesome intimacy with his men which contrasts with Galba's excessive severity or Otho's dangerously sporadic shifts between comrade and commander. Likewise, Pliny uses this notion to praise Trajan's skills as a general and to emphasise the affection which the army felt for him (*Panegyricus* 19.3-4). Even the fact that Vespasian is the antithesis of the devious and eloquent Mucianus (2.5.2) initially seems encouraging. Ideal commanders were often portrayed as candid and gruff.[8] Perhaps Vespasian will prove a worthy focus for his supporters after all: his straightforward personality looks refreshing, even if it may also be unsuited to tackling the murky political complexities of an imperial challenge.

Despite this reassuring first impression, Tacitus' Vespasian proves more problematic than the initial character sketch would suggest. Tacitus has already noted that 'there was doubtful talk about Vespasian, and he was the only one of all the emperors to change for the better' (1.50.4). Whatever the precise nature of this change, Tacitus suggests that people had their doubts about Vespasian's suitability as a candidate for the principate, perhaps because he had neither the lineage nor the achievements that one might expect of an emperor. During Vespasian's rise to power, Tacitus explores one troubling characteristic of the would-be emperor, which is intimately connected with his straightforward military persona. After Mucianus' speech to encourage the wavering Vespasian to challenge Vitellius, Tacitus says that 'the others all stood around him more confidently, offering their encouragement and citing the answers of the soothsayers and the movements of the stars. Vespasian was not immune to such superstition (*nec erat intactus tali superstitione*[9])' (2.78.1). Tacitus therefore suggests a surprising vulnerability in the would-be emperor. It was more usual for the common soldier rather than the supreme commander to be presented as susceptible to superstition, which Cicero defines as a 'groundless fear of the gods' (*De Natura Deorum* 1.42.117). Thus, Thucydides implies that Nicias, who refused to move his troops for twenty-seven days after a lunar eclipse, should have been more immune to such credulity than his men (7.50).[10] Certainly, Pericles does not allow an eclipse to distract

him (Plutarch *Pericles* 35.2) and Dion has a much more scientific
attitude to this natural phenomenon than his soldiers do (Plutarch *Dion*
24.1). Tacitus projects a similar message about the differing attitudes
of commanders and soldiers during the Pannonian mutiny. The soldiers, terrified by a lunar eclipse, link their own chances of success to
the fluctuating appearance of the moon, but the astute general Drusus
exploits the collective vulnerability of his men to break the back of the
mutiny (*Annals* 1.28.1-3). The superstitious soldiers are thus contrasted with the sceptical commanding officer.[11] The moralism of such
stories is not always straightforward. When Silius Italicus makes
Flaminius criticise his superstitious troops before the battle at Lake
Trasimene, the general protests that 'groundless superstition is degrading for an army' (*Pun.* 5.125-6). On this particular occasion the soldiers
happen to be right: generals who scoff at naive faith in signs were not
always vindicated, as when Thrasea Paetus crosses the Taurus mountain range despite bad omens (*Annals* 15.8.1). Tacitus elsewhere
condemns uncritical belief in omens, as when the historian calls
Vespasian's men 'ignorant' (*Histories* 4.26.2) for believing that the water
shortage on the Rhine was a bad sign. However, despite authorial
disapproval, such omens could still play a role in the narrative as
markers of impending disaster. Tacitus frequently uses prodigies to
reflect an unsettled society and to indicate collective vulnerability.[12]

Such examples shed an interesting light on Vespasian's character. As
a general, Vespasian should not have been unduly influenced by superstition, but by fraternising with his soldiers as a good commander
should, it seems as if he has taken on aspects of their mentality. This
contrasts greatly with Titus, who mixes with the soldiers 'without
compromising his dignity as a general' (5.1.1). Excessive superstition
can be not only degrading for a general, but also dangerous. In the
sickroom of Germanicus (another fraterniser), human remains, spells,
curses and lead tablets were discovered in the walls and floors (*Annals*
2.69.3), which may even suggest that his death was accelerated by his
superstitious nature. Furthermore, Vespasian's tendency towards superstition in the *Histories* contrasts with other portraits of the emperor,
which suggest a practical man, who would not have been influenced by
such beliefs. So, the emperor cracks some famous jokes about his
impending death and the prodigies which foreshadowed it. Upon seeing
a long-tailed comet, the bald Vespasian joked that it could only presage
the death of the long-haired King of Parthia (Suetonius *Vespasian* 23.4
and Dio 66.17.3). The emperor's over-literal interpretation thus dissi-
pates the frightening impact of the omen.

What effects does Tacitus create by presenting Vespasian as a credu-
lous character? Above all, he suggests that Vespasian, like his
predecessors, was vulnerable to the unscrupulous men who could exploit him in order to further their own careers. Tacitus is not concerned

with omens and prodigies so much for their own sake, but as a way of charting Vespasian's relationships with his subordinates. The scene where Vespasian is encouraged by supporters eagerly citing soothsayers' predictions and the movements of the stars (2.78.1) contains disturbing resonances of Otho's rise to power. Charlatan astrologers, 'who declared by their observation of the stars new developments and a glorious year for Otho' (1.22.1), had likewise pressurised the future emperor to seize power. Yet Otho died and these glorious predictions were never realised. Tacitus viewed such men, who inevitably materialised whenever power changed hands, as 'treacherous to the powerful and deceptive to the hopeful' (1.22.1).[13] The parallel scenes suggest continuity in that Otho and Vespasian were equally susceptible to such manipulation. Perhaps surprisingly, it was Vitellius who took a no-nonsense attitude towards such astrologers (Tacitus *Histories* 2.62.2 and Suetonius *Vitellius* 14.4), which suggests a rational personality.

Tacitus *could* have used these portents to present an optimistic Vespasian, who was assured of victory by the overwhelming torrent of prodigies which presaged his principate. Suetonius says that Vespasian 'began to hope for power, a hope which he had long since conceived because of the following portents' (*Vespasian* 5.1), whereupon the biographer lists eleven omens. Such emphasis is perhaps natural from a writer who appears to have been a superstitious man himself and had once written to Pliny for comfort after being terrified by a dream (*Epistle* 1.18).[14] Suetonius portrays a confident Vespasian, who is buoyed up by his long-standing faith in portents, which is a motif that also appears elsewhere in his imperial biographies (cf. *Tiberius* 14.1 and *Augustus* 92.1). Yet although Tacitus' Vespasian likewise has faith in omens, it still takes the intervention of Mucianus and others to stir him to action. Vespasian, encouraged by the opportunists who talk of omens and prodigies, begins to reminisce about 'early omens' (2.78.2), which now seem to take on a new significance. In particular, the would-be emperor recalls the tall cypress tree which withered, but then sprang up again the next day more sturdy than ever (cf. Suetonius *Vespasian* 5.4 and Dio 66.1). The growth or decline of trees was often associated with the rise or fall of a dynasty.[15] Yet the cypress tree incident is somehow a peculiar portent for Tacitus to make Vespasian conjure up, since it was hardly the most spectacular. Much more startling is the stray dog who picks up a severed human hand and drops it under the table where Vespasian is eating, or the ox who throws off its yoke, bursts into Vespasian's dining room and prostrates itself at the future emperor's feet (cf. Dio 66.1 and Suetonius *Vespasian* 5.4). In comparison with these dramatic prodigies, the cypress tree omen is relatively bland, and Chilver calls it a 'curiously insignificant' omen to select.[16] Nevertheless, Tacitus had good reasons for his choice. His specific reference to a cypress implicitly casts a sombre shadow on Vespasian's exultant mood and perhaps points to the future: as Pliny notes (*HN* 16.60.139), the tree was sacred to Pluto and used at funerals.[17] We know about the next downfall of this same tree, which coincided with the overthrow of Domitian in AD 96 (Suetonius *Domitian* 15.2). Tacitus probably had this later incident in mind when choosing to highlight Vespasian's interest in the cypress tree omen at the start of the Flavian dynasty; surely the historian would have referred to this second portent when narrating Domitian's death in the lost section of the *Histories*. Omens, like dreams, often came in linked pairs which were separated by a period of time (cf. Herodotus 1.108 and 1.208). Thus, Tacitus probably foreshadows the eventual collapse of the ruling dynasty at its very inception.[18] In addition, Tacitus' focus on the cypress tree incident may reveal more about Vespasian's psychology than about the power of omens. His simple pursuit of appropriate portents seems innocent (or at any rate less practical) in comparison with Mucianus' manipulation of the troops in the theatre at Antioch (2.80) or the inflammatory letters sent out around the empire by Antonius Primus and Cornelius Fuscus (2.86). All these men are actively pursuing the goal of empire on Vespasian's behalf in highly practical ways. At the same time, Vespasian the 'ideal general' is pursuing omens. The contrast is pointed and becomes more so as the narrative proceeds.

Interesting in this respect is Vespasian's visit to the oracle at Carmel. The priest Basilides' pronouncement is phrased in a disturbing way.

> ' "Whatever it is which you have in mind, Vespasian," he said, "whether it is to build a house or to enlarge your estate or to increase the number of your slaves, there is granted to you a great mansion, vast boundaries and a multitude of men." '

> ' "quidquid est" inquit "Vespasiane, quod paras, seu domum exstruere seu prolatare agros sive ampliare servitia, datur tibi magna sedes, ingentes termini, multum hominum." ' (2.78.3)

On one level Basilides' prediction has a straightforward significance for Vespasian's management of his personal affairs as a private citizen, but at the same time the portent offers wider resonances in the context of Vespasian's ascent to the principate. His manipulative associates, quickly spotting the ambiguities, discuss the omen enthusiastically in front of him. Basilides' reference to the construction of a *domus* gains added weight if a reader extends the meaning metaphorically and applies it to the creation of a dynasty. Particularly striking is Basilides' suggestion that Vespasian might be planning to expand the number of slaves he owned. Given the subsequent Flavian claim that taking the empire from Vitellius was an act of liberation from slavery, Tacitus' imagery is unsettling. The undercurrent of tyranny in Basilides' words seems to be absent from the parallel version in Suetonius, which is also less vivid because it is not in direct speech:

> In Judaea, when Vespasian consulted the oracle of the God of Carmel, the lots were so assuring as to promise him that whatever he was thinking or turning over in his mind, however great it might be, would come to pass.

> Apud Iudaeam Carmeli dei oraculum consulentem ita confirmavere sortes, ut quidquid cogitaret volveretque animo quamlibet magnum, id esse proventurum pollicerentur. (*Vespasian* 5.6)

In comparison with Suetonius' prophecy, Tacitus sets up a more explicit interplay between the apparent and real meaning of this omen. Furthermore, Morgan proposes that Tacitus' version implies a time-lag between Vespasian's visit to Mount Carmel and a full appreciation of the answer, which explains why Tacitus can still describe the future emperor's hopes of power as 'secret' (2.78.2).[19] Such an emphasis places Vespasian's designs upon the principate disturbingly early and counteracts the Flavian claims that the challenge to Vitellius was spontaneous. Suetonius' positive version of the prophecy is not so riddled with double-meanings, but it is strangely evocative of a scene in Sallust where a soothsayer encourages another general, Marius, in his long-term desires:

> Accordingly, if he had any projects in mind, he could undertake them with full confidence in the will of heaven; and he should seize every opportunity as frequently as possible. Everything would turn out prosperously.

> proinde quae animo agitabat fretus dis ageret, fortunam quam saepissume experiretur; cuncta prospere eventura. (*Jug.* 63.1; cf. Plutarch *Marius* 8.6)

Marius' ambition is a consulship while Vespasian's is the principate, but both men are driven by a political desire which will gradually override their respective identities as simple military men.[20] Marius will eventually march on Rome with an armed force, while Flavian troops under Antonius Primus will do the same thing on Vespasian's behalf. It seems unlikely that Suetonius himself would have wanted us to make such unflattering comparisons since his portrait of Vespasian is on the whole fairly positive, but the Sallust passage does offer us a productive intertext.

Such fascination with omens and portents dominates another member of the Flavian dynasty. Vespasian's encounter with Basilides mirrors an earlier scene where Titus, journeying to Syria, stops at Cyprus to visit the Temple of Venus at Paphos (2.2-4). The young man is ostensibly enquiring about his voyage, but also wants to ask about his own future, which he does 'in veiled language' (2.4.1). Tacitus takes the trouble to name the priest, Sostratus, whereas Suetonius leaves him unspecified (*Titus* 5.1). In addition, Tacitus includes a digression in each case about the distinctive religious rituals of Venus (2.2.2-2.3) and Carmel (2.78.3). Venus at Paphos has an altar in the open air and 'an image of the goddess with a statue that is not in human form (*simulacrum deae non effigie humana*)' (2.3.2), while for the god Carmel 'there is no image or temple: ... only an altar where they worship (*nec simulacrum deo aut templum: ... ara tantum et reverentia*)' (2.78.3). Tacitus' focus on the unusual representation of each divinity encourages a reader to compare the two consultations. It is important to see that the responses of Titus and Vespasian to the respective oracles link the personalities of father and son. Titus, after his visit to Paphos, returns to Vespasian in high spirits, which improves the general mood in the provinces and the armies (2.4.2). Vespasian, after his visit to Carmel, sets off for Caesarea in a determined mood (2.79.1). Mucianus' speech had done much to counter Vespasian's panic, but the visit to Carmel played a crucial part in boosting his confidence.[21] In each case, Tacitus suggests that at a critical moment, these omens bolster the superstitious natures of father and son, who both pursue power with a greater tenacity as a result. Elsewhere, Tacitus acknowledges that it was politically astute for an emperor to have the right attitude towards portents, because this was what people expected. Vespasian's and Titus' attitude contrasts pointedly with Vitellius, who was 'so ignorant of all human and divine law' (2.91.1) as to assume the office of High Priest on the anniversary of the Allia defeat.

Vespasian subsequently makes another religious trip, this time to the Temple of Serapis in Egypt (4.82-4), which Tacitus links with Titus' earlier visit to Paphos. Just as Titus was struck by a 'desire to go (*cupido ... adeundi*) and see the temple of Venus at Paphus' (2.2.2), Vespasian felt a 'desire to visit (*cupido adeundi*) the holy place' (4.82.1). This identical enthusiasm strengthens the impression of resemblance between father and son. In addition, the desire to see things can be linked with Tacitus' subsequent portrait of the idealistic Germanicus, who showed 'a desire (*cupido*) to get to know the famous ancient sites' (*Annals* 2.54), which also prompted him to visit the oracle of Apollo at Clarus.[22] Titus and Vespasian both use similar cloak-and-dagger methods: the son asks about the future 'in veiled language' (2.4.1), while the father gives orders that nobody should enter the temple with him (4.82.1). Both omens are thus rather difficult to corroborate because there is only one witness, but in each case Tacitus is interested in these portents not only as reflections of the Flavian propaganda, which strengthened the idea that Vespasian's principate was divinely sanctioned, but also as devices of characterisation.

The context of the miraculous appearance of Basilides in the Temple of Serapis is especially interesting.[23] As Vespasian waits in Alexandria for the right weather to cross over into Italy, 'many miraculous events occurred, which showed celestial support and a certain favour of the divinities towards Vespasian' (4.81.1). The magical land of Egypt is certainly an appropriate place for extraordinary events to occur, and the 'populace inclined to superstitious beliefs' (4.81.1) mirrors Vespasian's own personality.[24] The first *miraculum* involves a blind man, who begs to be cured with Vespasian's spit.[25] This plea may have been intended to take advantage of Vespasian as the human instrument of the god Serapis, who once restored Demetrius of Phaleron's sight in Alexandria (Diogenes Laertius 5.76).[26] At the same time, Vespasian is confronted by a man who wants the future emperor to heal him by standing on his maimed hand (cf. Suetonius *Vespasian* 7.2 and Dio 66.8.1).[27] Vespasian is initially sceptical, but after being urged on by flatterers, he decides to consult some doctors who convince him that if the cure works, he will gain all the glory, while if it fails, any ridicule will fall on the two disabled men. This assurance gives him the confidence to proceed and he executes the cure, wearing a serene smile on his face.[28] Although Tacitus closes the scene with corroboration of the miracle from eye-witnesses, who do not have any financial incentive to lie any more, we are left with the impression that Vespasian has been cajoled into this spectacular healing by those around him. This emphasis could plausibly derive from pro-Flavian sources, who were reluctant to suggest that Vespasian had divine aspirations, but Tacitus' insistence that he acted 'because of the cries of flatterers (*vocibus adulantium*)' (4.81.2) does Vespasian less credit than Suetonius' statement that he acted 'because of the encouragement of his friends (*hortantibus amicis*)' (*Vespasian* 7.3). Tacitus' general reference may suggest a wider and more anonymous group of people who intervene than Suetonius does. Whatever the truth about these spectacular cures, Vespasian was happy to play to the crowd and the audience in Alexandria was certainly happy to be beguiled.[29]

When Vespasian decides to visit the Temple of Serapis, the way in which Tacitus narrates the miraculous appearance of Basilides reveals something else about the future emperor's personality. It is as if Vespasian is playing at private detective: 'he asked the priests ... he asked everyone he met (*percunctatur sacerdotes ... percunctatur obvios*)' (4.82.2). The choice of verb, together with the anaphora, implies a thorough and methodical investigation, as does the fact that Vespasian sends horsemen on a long journey to ascertain that Basilides was eighty miles away on the day in question. The culmination of all this is that Vespasian triumphantly interprets the omen for himself: he concludes that the vision was divine and that its relevance lay in the meaning of the name *Basilides*, or 'king's son' (4.82.2). Yet Vespasian's own father was a tax collector in Asia (Suetonius *Vespasian* 1.2), which hardly corroborates this interpretation and which is a point to which I will return. This rather nebulous conclusion, together with the thoroughness of the investigation into the miracle, may increase our sense that Vespasian is strangely detached from the real action. Vespasian's involvement with omens and miracle cures in Alexandria may be important for propaganda purposes, but the real business of winning the empire is being enacted elsewhere by men like Antonius Primus. There is a suggestive parallel for such detachment in Tiberius' response to the domestic drama of the praetor Plautius Silvanus 'accidentally' throwing his wife from the bedroom window (*Annals* 4.22). The emperor rushes off to the scene of the crime, but Tiberius' careful investigations seem misdirected in the light of Sejanus' insidious attacks on the imperial family. In Suetonius (*Vespasian* 7.1), Vespasian's sojourn in Alexandria seems much less idle than in Tacitus' account. The Basilides miracle is preceded by an explanation of Vespasian's strategic reasons for staying in Egypt, and is followed by the announcement of Vitellius' defeat. The vision thus takes on a significance which is lacking in Tacitus' narrative, where Vespasian already knows about his victory (3.48.3).

Vespasian and his sons

By now it should be clear that Tacitus had considerable scope to enrich his literary characterisation of Vespasian by putting him into a family context. The historical Vespasian certainly seems to have drawn much good publicity from the notion that there were two grown up sons at his side, who together could support their father in running the empire. Titus and Domitian were useful assets, as is clear from Josephus' account of the Flavian trio reunited in Rome in AD 70 at the triumph to celebrate the fall of Jerusalem (*BJ* 7.120). This focus continues to feature in Flavian ideology of the AD 70s: 'Vespasian Augustus, the greatest guide of the whole age, coming to the aid of sluggish affairs (*fessis rebus subveniens*),[30] proceeds, together with his children' (Pliny the Elder *HN* 2.5.18). Likewise, the so-called Frieze B of the Cancelleria Reliefs shows that such images of a united dynasty continued to have useful resonances, even after the Flavians were established in power.[31] Even the lucky coincidence that Vespasian was able to rely on *two* adult sons, not just one, surpasses the dynastic security offered by any previous emperor and recalls the precedent of Augustus, who repeatedly singled out dynastic pairs to help run the principate.[32]

Vespasian's immediate predecessors had not been so fortunate. Galba was a childless old man, who had felt obliged to adopt Piso and thereby aroused Otho's jealousy. Although Otho was a younger man, the libertine bachelor had not succeeded in producing a son, although there was his devoted nephew, the unfortunate Salvius Cocceianus, later executed by Domitian for celebrating his dead uncle's birthday (Suetonius *Domitian* 10.3). Vitellius had at least produced three children, two of whom were even male, but his son from his first marriage had died before the civil war, while his second boy was only about six years old.[33] Dressing the child up in a general's cloak (2.59.3) and showing him to the army, as if to cast him as a second Caligula, was no substitute for having the adult Titus and Domitian available as assistants. Moreover, Caligula had won the devotion of the troops because he was brought up with them (Suetonius *Caligula* 9 and Tacitus *Annals* 1.41.2 and 1.69.4) and this sort of affection could not be artificially engineered on the spur of the moment. Certainly, Vitellius tried to exploit images of his children on his coinage, particularly on an *aureus* with his own head pictured on the obverse, and busts of his son and daughter facing one another on the reverse,[34] but such propaganda had a limited impact.

In any case, Suetonius preserves some suggestive details about Vitellius' children. Vitellius' first son is described as being 'damaged in one eye (*captus altero oculo*)' (*Vitellius* 6), while the second boy is supposed to have had a particularly bad stammer. The affliction of the first boy recalls a dubious predecessor, Hannibal, who is also 'damaged in one eye (*altero oculo capitur*)' (Livy 22.2.11).[35] The stammer evokes the physically flawed emperor, Claudius (Suetonius *Claudius* 30), as well as Battos the stammerer (Herodotus 4.155-8).[36] Vitellius' boys may even have suffered from these problems, but their disabilities could still have been usefully emphasised by Flavian propagandists. Both Vitellius' sons had been stricken with a physical impairment, despite being born to different mothers, which probably suggested to Roman observers that the father, the common link, was responsible for the genetic problems.[37] Genetic transmission was a powerful concept, which could easily have an impact on an individual's political reputation. Augustus' acute embarrassment over his grand-nephew Claudius in a letter to Livia is a case in point: 'Men must not be given the opportunity to make fun both of him and of us' (Suetonius *Claudius* 4.2).[38] Augustus, anxious that people should not think that his family might be flawed in any way, decides to minimise Claudius' public appearances.

If Vitellius' two sons both had disabilities while Vespasian's sons were healthy, the public was probably already receptive to the message behind such contrasts, even before the propagandists got to work. Perhaps Vespasian thought along these lines when he agreed to try to cure the lame man and the blind man in Alexandria, although there is no explicit link made in the sources: Vitellius produced a blind son, while Vespasian not only creates healthy offspring, but even transfers his vitality to the blind man through the application of his own spittle to the man's eyes (4.81). However Tacitus ultimately considered such shallow distinctions between a tainted Vitellius and a thriving

Vespasian to be unsatisfactory. Titus and Domitian may indeed have been fine physical specimens, but this did not disguise the fact that below the harmonious surface of the dynasty lay potential rifts and tensions, which could easily have prolonged the civil war.

One particularly disturbing flaw in the dynasty is Tacitus' contrast between the innocent Titus and Vespasian on the one hand, and the scheming Domitian on the other. Titus' basic faith in human nature is stressed when, early in January AD 70, Vespasian hears both about Vitellius' death and about rumours that Domitian has been abusing his position as the emperor's son in Rome (4.51; cf. 4.2.1 and 4.39.2). Other authors use Domitian's transgression as the peg on which to hang an instance of Vespasianic humour: so, the emperor jokes about being thankful not to have been dismissed from office by his upstart son (Suetonius *Domitian* 1.3 and Dio 66.2.3). In contrast, Tacitus complicates the scene by omitting the joke and by focusing instead on Titus' relationship with his father and brother. The benign Titus intervenes on his brother's behalf, suggesting to his father that:

> Neither legions nor fleets are such sturdy defences of the empire as a number of children. Time, chance, and often too, ambition and mistakes weaken, alienate or extinguish friendship: a man's own blood is inseparable from him, especially in the case of emperors, whose good fortunes others enjoy, but whose misfortunes concern only his nearest kin.

> non legiones, non classes proinde firma imperi munimenta quam numerum liberorum; nam amicos tempore fortuna, cupidinibus aliquando aut erroribus imminui transferri desinere: suum cuique sanguinem indiscretum, sed maxime principibus, quorum prosperis et alii fruantur, adversa ad iunctissimos pertineant. (4.52.1)

This short discussion throws the three Flavians into sharp relief at a strategic moment in the narrative.[39] That Titus' view is woefully misjudged is suggested partly by the response of Vespasian, who appreciates Titus' loyalty without abandoning his suspicions of Domitian (4.52.2). However, more suggestive still is Tacitus' allusion to Sallust. The elderly king Micipsa, in a death-bed speech, tries to ensure future harmony between his adoptive son Jugurtha and his two real sons:

> Neither armies nor hoards of treasure can protect a throne, but only friends – and friends one cannot make by force of arms or buy with money: they must be won with devoted service and loyalty. And who can be a closer friend than a brother to a brother?

> Non exercitus neque thesauri praesidia regni sunt, verum amici, quos neque armis cogere neque auro parare queas: officio et fide pariuntur. Quis autem amicior quam frater fratri? (*Jug.* 10.4-5)[40]

Tacitus has therefore sharpened Sallust's message by modifying the practicality of relying on friends and by emphasising the infallibility of family ties over friendship. Yet the context of the Sallustian passage undercuts the plausibility of Titus' sentiments. After Micipsa's death, Jugurtha treacherously kills one of his 'brothers' in a night-time raid and defeats the other in battle. Jugurtha's rampant hostility to Micipsa's real sons makes nonsense of the elderly king's death-bed generalisations about friendly fraternal feelings; the fact that Tacitus alludes to this sequence of events in Titus' speech to Vespasian must surely question the practicality of the young prince's words.

In any case, Tacitus' readers already knew that family ties were no guarantee of loyalty in imperial politics, and that often the expectation of family allegiance just deepened the pain of betrayal. Vitellius discovered this when his brother Lucius Vitellius exploited him to indulge his personal hatred of Blaesus, thereby distracting the emperor from the looming Flavian invasion (3.38). Tacitus calls Lucius Vitellius at his execution 'as flawed as his brother' (4.2.3), but his cavalier attitude to the emperor's best interests makes him seem perhaps more despicable than his brother. Even the relationship between Vespasian and his brother, Flavius Sabinus, is called into question by Tacitus: though the two were openly friendly, there were suspicions of secret hostility (3.65.1). It was certainly a pervasive literary motif that civil war fragmented traditional family allegiances,[41] and if this happened in peacetime, it was a marker of a degenerate society (cf. Tacitus *Annals* 4.28 and 13.17). Likewise, Plutarch discusses the tendency of powerful dynasties to self-destruct as rulers killed their brothers to secure their own safety (*Demetrius* 3.3-5).[42] Tacitus' Vespasian is portrayed as more of a realist than Titus, but he does not address the problem of Domitian adequately simply by pledging to keep an eye on the imperial household.

Even on their own Titus' arguments seem naive, but his assertions appear especially vulnerable given what we learn at the end of Book 4. Tacitus records the rumour that Domitian secretly contacted Petilius Cerialis and tried to persuade the commander to hand over his army and authority: 'It was uncertain whether Domitian's plan was to stir up war against his father or to acquire power and support against his brother' (4.86.1). Vespasian had been grudgingly tolerant of Domitian, but the youngest Flavian is not so patient about his own family. Tacitus offers two alternative explanations for Domitian's conduct, which were allegedly circulating at the time, but both possibilities are alarming. Cerealis may treat Domitian as if he is a day-dreaming boy, but like Vespasian and Titus, the commander has fallen into the trap of underestimating the youngest Flavian's dangerous personality.[43] Suetonius refers to this same incident without mentioning Cerialis by name, and suggests only that Domitian is motivated by petty fraternal jealousy

(*Domitian* 2.1). It is also striking that Tacitus creates mounting tension by closing Books 3 and 4 with a spotlight on Domitian. So, Tacitus could have ended Book 3 neatly with Vitellius' obituary (3.86.1-2), but the historian adds a telling *coda*: armed Flavian soldiers hail Domitian as Caesar and take him off to the family home (3.86.3), although the young man rapidly moves into the imperial palace on the Palatine (4.2.1).[44] The military theme here is echoed at the end of the next book, as Domitian tries to acquire his own army (4.86.1). The sense of escalation is clear: one can only speculate as to how Tacitus chose to end *Histories* 5, but perhaps once again his focus was on Domitian. Tacitean book-endings often signpost important themes or characters in the future, as when the historian announces the marriage of the younger Agrippina to Cn. Domitius Ahenobarbus, which will produce the emperor Nero (*Annals* 4.75).[45]

Tacitus accentuates our unease by evoking Sallust's portrait of Sulla in his character sketch of Domitian.[46] While Domitian is 'burying himself deeply behind an innocent and modest appearance and feigning literary tastes and a love of poetry (*simplicitatis ac modestiae imagine in altitudinem conditus studiumque litterarum et amorem carminum simulans*)' (4.86.2), Sulla is 'equally skilled in Greek and Latin literature (*litteris Graecis atque Latinis iuxta eruditus*)' and has 'incredible depth of intelligence for feigning things (*ad simulanda negotia altitudo ingeni incredibilis*)' (*Jug.* 95.3). This link between Sulla and Domitian artfully suggests the direction in which the Flavian dynasty could so easily have gone. The smouldering antagonism between Marius and Sulla notoriously flared up into civil war, until the latter eventually became dictator of Rome. Plutarch dates the incurable hatred between the two men to the original quarrel over which of them deserved credit for subduing Jugurtha (*Marius* 10.7.9). Sallust appropriately foreshadows Rome's future troubles in his *Jugurtha*, and Levene comments that when Marius and Sulla are each introduced Sallust concludes their character sketches with a sinister reference to their future actions (63.6 and 95.4).[47] Levene also observes that Sallust ends the *Jugurtha* with an implicit contrast between Marius' role in the present, when the state pins all her hopes on him, and in the future, when the state will almost be destroyed by this former hero. Tacitus' character-sketch of Domitian, suggestively and unexpectedly placed at the end of Book 4, likewise offers a contrast between Domitian's present and future career. The young Domitian, upon whom the senate had conferred the praetorship with the powers of a consul (4.3.4; cf. Suetonius *Domitian* 1.3), must have attracted attention after his adventurous escape from the besieged Capitol.[48] However, Tacitus, by evoking Sallust's portrait of Sulla, lays the foundations of the tyrannical emperor in his characterisation of Domitian as a young man. Elsewhere, Tacitus uses Sulla for similar reasons, as when Tiberius predicts that Caligula will have all of Sulla's faults and none of his virtues (Tacitus *Annals* 6.46.4; cf. Suetonius *Tiberius* 59.2).

These Sallustian echoes artfully reinforce the sense of a potential divide between Vespasian and Domitian, and Tacitus probably continued to introduce Sullan characteristics into his portrait of Domitian in the lost portion of the *Histories*. The association between Domitian and Sulla has already been triggered by Tacitus' physical description of Domitian addressing the senate: 'as his character was still unknown, his repeated blushes were taken as a sign of modesty' (4.40.1).[49] Tacitus does not usually dwell on bodily features to the same extent as Suetonius, which suggests that his description of Domitian's blushing face serves a special narrative purpose. Seneca, noting that it was not just good people who tended to blush, backs up his general observation with an example: 'Sulla was at his most violent at the moment when blood infused his face' (*Epistle* 11.3).[50] Passion rather than modesty generates Sulla's red face, but this was probably the explanation for the same physical phenomenon in Tacitus' Domitian: it was just that onlookers read the signs inaccurately. Seneca's description offers a different emphasis from Plutarch, who suggests that Sulla's complexion was permanently covered in red blotches and who preserves the joke of a heckler that Sulla resembled a mulberry sprinkled with flour (*Sulla* 2.2).[51] Still, whether one visualises a flushed or a blotchy Sulla, the colour red clearly had associations for the ancients with violence and anger, as well as with modesty. Plutarch in his vision of the underworld looks at this notion from the inside out: suggestively, the soul of a man whose leading traits in life were cruelty and savagery was 'bloody and fiery' (*Moralia* 565C).[52] The red colour in the young Domitian's face is perhaps meant to reflect his tyrannical soul. Even if the link with Sulla is unclear, Tacitus still injects his portrait of the young Domitian with foreshadowing of the future, when nobody could misinterpret such blushes. Readers who had experienced Domitian as emperor must have found the assumptions of the onlookers in AD 70 particularly ironic.

The contrast between naive father and devious son is heightened because Tacitus places the notice about Domitian's sinister plans against his father or brother (4.86) *after* Vespasian's innocent vision of Basilides in the Temple of Serapis (4.82). The benign Vespasian has been playing games with oracles while Domitian contemplates backstabbing members of his family. Thus, Vespasian's interpretation of his vision in the Temple of Serapis acquires another meaning in retrospect: although his assumption is that the significance of the word *Basilides* refers to himself, equally 'king's son' (the meaning of *Basilides* given in the Suda) serves as a warning about his own son, Domitian. Certainly, when Tacitus outlines King Ptolemy's foundation of the Serapis cult, the historian focuses on three visions, which seem with increasing urgency to warn rather than to advise. The first vision, a benign young man, advises Ptolemy to fetch his image from Pontus and thereby make the kingdom prosper (4.83.1). The second vision threatens Ptolemy with death unless the orders are carried out (4.83.3). The third threatening vision appears to Scydrothemis, King of Sinope, urging him not to delay the divine plan any longer (4.84.2). Does Tacitus' version of these three Serapian visions therefore undermine Vespasian's supposedly auspicious vision in the Temple? When Plutarch relates the story about Ptolemy (*Moralia* 361F-362B), there is only one vision, which focuses on a talking statue, instead of Tacitus' three dreams. Nor is Plutarch's version so marked by *enargeia* ('vividness'; cf. Quintilian 6.2.31) as the triple sequence in Tacitus:[53] so, in Plutarch the statue just talks, whereas in Tacitus the young man 'appeared to ascend into heaven in a sheet of flame' (4.83.1).

It is also unsettling that Serapis plays a pivotal role in the death of Vespasian's hero, Alexander the Great.[54] As Alexander lies racked with fever in Babylon, some of the king's closest friends spend the night in Serapis' Temple to ask the god whether they should move Alexander to the Temple (Plutarch *Alex.* 76.9 and Arrian *Anabasis* 7.26.2). Serapis, god of healing and oracular dreams, bluntly suggests that they should leave the king where he is: presumably the prophetic god knows that Alexander is doomed, so moving him would be pointless. At any rate, the Macedonian dies on the following day. Thus, at one dramatic moment Serapis, a god who was associated with the underworld (Diodorus Siculus 1.25.2), withholds his powers of healing and involves himself in a famous king's death. Against this background, Vespasian's optimistic response to the Basilides vision is complacently uncritical.[55] At the very least, the connotations of the word *Basilides* remain ambiguous, especially when compared with other 'propitious names' omens. So, Augustus was reassured by a meeting with a peasant called *Eutychus* ('Lucky') and his donkey *Nicon* ('Winner') on the eve of Actium (Suetonius *Augustus* 96.2). Vespasian clearly valued auspicious names, as when he used soldiers who had 'names of good omen' in the ceremony for the rebuilding of the Capitoline Temple (4.53.2: cf. Cicero *De Divinatione* 1.45.102 and Pliny *HN* 28.5.22). Yet Vespasian's optimistic response to the Basilides omen is surely misplaced; and the nuances of Tacitus' narrative hint at this.

It should be emphasised at this point that in Tacitus' eyes, *both* Vespasian's sons were potential threats to Flavian unity. Domitian is the obvious fly in the ointment, but Tacitus also acknowledges that the popular Titus could easily have challenged Vitellius in his own right, had he been willing to do so. Thus, Tacitus destabilises the audience's perceptions about the prelude to Vespasian's principate: Titus, rather than his father, could have been the first Flavian emperor. Even before Vespasian is formally introduced, we hear how popular gossip was already speculating that Galba had summoned Titus for adoption

(2.1.1).[56] Where Domitian is placed prominently at the end of books, Titus (rather than Vespasian) is prominent in two opening chapters, 'Titus Vespasianus ...' (2.1.1) and 'Caesar Titus ...' (5.1.1). Of course, the story about Titus' possible adoption may reflect retroactive flattery of the prince after the civil war. If so, it was an ingenious strategy: as Vespasian's son, Titus had a hereditary claim to the principate, but was also the kind of man whom Galba might have chosen for adoption as his own successor regardless of his father. Titus thus wins on two counts. Tacitus makes Galba observe that 'adoption will always find the best man' (1.16.2), and although the elderly emperor's own choice of Piso casts doubts on the truth of this generalisation, the rumour about Titus as a possible successor suggests that the young man had a higher profile than his father. Although Tacitus acknowledges that people appreciate Titus even more in the light of his father's successes, Vespasian is simply not the focus of the popular gaze in the same way (2.1.2). In fact, the historian reminds us that even the valuable Mucianus was 'more supportive of Titus' (2.74.1). The future emperor Vespasian is initially dwarfed by his own son, who stayed loyal but could have exploited his popularity.

Titus is generally portrayed as a romantic figure, who has nothing but kind things to say about those around him. His cordiality and good looks win him friends and supporters everywhere, and Titus particularly wins over the soldiers, 'calling forth devotion by his affable conversation and regularly mingling with the common soldiers at their duties or on the march without compromising his dignity as a general' (5.1.1). In this respect, Titus foreshadows Germanicus in the *Annals*, where the dour Tiberius suffers by comparison. The soldiers are even prepared to offer Germanicus the principate (*Annals* 1.35.3). Likewise, after the final assault on Jerusalem, the troops hail Titus as their commander and try to prevent him from leaving the province, which led to suspicions 'that he was trying to revolt from his father and to claim for himself sovereignty in the East' (Suetonius *Titus* 5.3). It would have been fascinating to have seen how Tacitus handled this incident in the lost part of the *Histories*. Both Titus and Germanicus may have been extremely loyal, but they were still dangerously powerful because of their popularity with the soldiers.

Yet although affability is presented as being Titus' main quality, Tacitus also hints at a less respectable side. So, when the prince is busily engaged in the assault on Jerusalem, Tacitus uses internal focalisation to suggest that Titus sees images of 'Rome and wealth and pleasures' (5.11.2). His desire to satisfy these daydreams makes him agree to his greedy soldiers' demands for an immediate attack, and such malleability contradicts our expectations of the appropriate behaviour for a good general. Perhaps Titus can be forgiven as a young commander, who is behaving according to type.[57] In historiography, young generals who are not impetuous, such as Scipio Africanus (Polybius 10.40.6 and 15.4.11), tended to attract comment, and in any case, young commanders did not always inspire confidence.[58] Nevertheless, in Titus' case there is a disturbing tension between the young man's idealised image, 'famous for his soldiering' (5.1.1), and his materialistic concerns which manifest themselves in Jerusalem. Levene aptly comments that 'Tacitus sets the war with the "foreign" Jews against a reminder of the moral problems arising from the Flavians' conquest of their compatriots'.[59] Perhaps Titus is not quite so wholesome as some observers would like to think.

This discordant note about Titus' greed in the military sphere coheres with Tacitus' earlier comment about the young man's passion for Queen Berenice in a private context. Titus' relationship with Berenice (daughter of Agrippa I, King of the Jews) seems to have begun at some point after his arrival in Judaea with his father, and may have flourished during the three weeks spent at Agrippa's palace at Caesarea Philippi in the summer of AD 67 (Josephus *BJ* 3.444).[60] According to popular gossip, Titus, who was missing his lover Queen Berenice, failed to complete his mission to congratulate Galba. Tacitus remains sceptical about this analysis of Titus' motives for returning, but acknowledges as a general rule that 'Titus spent a happy youth indulging in pleasures, and was more restrained in his own reign than in his father's' (2.2.1). Vespasian, both in his public and private life, is portrayed as being less extravagant than his son, but as a result, the future emperor is perhaps less attractive to the soldiers as a leader, despite his 'ideal general' qualities. Tacitus has invested father and son with opposing traits, which suggest the traditional polarity between younger and older commanders. However, the former type of leader is likely to seem more attractive to soldiers than the latter, which heightens our awareness of Vespasian's vulnerability.

Queen Berenice provides Tacitus with a useful marker for one difference between the personalities of Vespasian and Titus. The historian assesses Titus' passion for Berenice in a nicely understated way: 'nor did his youthful spirit recoil from Berenice' (2.2.1). Certainly, Vespasian also finds the Queen attractive, but for a different reason: 'blossoming in age and beauty, her magnificent gifts won the old man's heart too' (2.81.2). The son's lust is balanced by the father's greed. Despite Berenice's beauty, Vespasian proves unflappable and only finds her money attractive (cf. 2.5.1 on the emperor's avarice). The sexual restraint of great generals is a motif in ancient literature, particularly in the case of Alexander the Great (Curtius Rufus 3.12.21-23 and Plutarch *Alex.* 21.5), but Vespasian is tempted by the money rather than by the woman. Tacitus' account is thrown into sharp relief by other writers, who suggest that the emperor generally found women alluring. So, there is discussion of Vespasian's attraction for the freedwoman Caenis

(Suetonius *Vespasian* 3 and Dio 66.14), as well as for some unnamed concubines (Suetonius *Vespasian* 21).[61] Tacitus, whose interest in the power-structure within an imperial household is clear from the *Annals*, probably developed this theme in the missing portion of the *Histories*. However, in the early stages Tacitus' Berenice serves as a focus for a contrast between the personalities of father and son. Vespasian's ubiquitous concern with money looks tedious in comparison with the colourful Titus, even if his long-term association with Berenice will cause problems after the Flavian victory.[62] So, in AD 75 Diogenes the Cynic and Heras denounce Titus and Berenice before a packed theatre in Rome: the outburst is punished by a flogging and a beheading, which suggests that the protestors had hit a raw nerve (Dio 66.15.3-5). Yet during the civil war itself, when Titus looked such a promising leader, people may have been prepared to turn a blind eye to his youthful indiscretion. In any case, Berenice was useful to the Flavians because of her financial resources, which must have made her tolerable in Vespasian's eyes.

Conclusion: Vespasian, Titus and the soldiers

An interesting pattern begins to suggest itself. A striking aspect of Tacitus' portrait of Vitellius is how enthusiastically the common soldiers react to the ineffectual emperor, particularly in the final stages of his principate. Vitellian officers quickly switch their allegiance to support Vespasian, but the troops only follow when all else is lost (cf. 3.61.3). Tacitus suggests that we should see the more sober Vespasian as the sort of commander whose primary appeal was amongst the officers rather than the lower ranks. This is despite (or even because of?) the character-sketch which presents him as 'equal to the generals of old' (2.5.1). The question arises as to whether most soldiers really wanted to be led by a commander like Vespasian, as opposed to a Titus or an Antonius Primus, who indulged their desires and allowed them more freedom. Without Titus' participation, Vespasian could have met the same fate as his predecessor Galba, whose tendency towards greed the Flavian shares (1.5.2, 1.37.4, 1.38.1 and 1.49.3). Galba had also tried to model himself on the traditional general but this had backfired because contemporary tastes had changed: 'His severity, once admired and set high in soldiers' estimation, only annoyed troops whose contempt for the old methods of discipline had been fostered by fourteen years of service under Nero' (1.5.2). The precedent of Galba further complicates Tacitus' initial character-sketch of Vespasian, which is much less positive than it initially seems, once the context has been explored.

Certainly, Vespasian needed Titus at the same time as Titus needed Vespasian, and each man enhanced the credibility of the other. At the same time, this was a precarious equilibrium, especially for Vespasian. Where Josephus in his *BJ* had presented the two men's leadership styles as being complementary (an older experienced Vespasian blends with a younger dashing Titus), Tacitus suggests a tension. Instead of working with one another, the two men could easily have pulled (or been pulled) in opposite directions. Tacitus' characterisation of Vespasian as a somewhat innocent, superstitious man, who fails to provide the dynamic but disreputable leadership which could have been offered by his son, Titus, suggests the fragility of the Flavian triumph. Vespasian could so easily have been overtaken by other events and personalities even though, in the event, *Fortuna* was on his side: the end of the civil war happened to coincide with his victory, but Tacitus draws our attention to the fact that this need not have been the final outcome.

7

Antonius Primus

Antonius Primus, the unfortunate but invaluable whipping-boy of the
Flavian cause, plays a complex role in Tacitus' narrative.[1] Although this
unscrupulous but talented general from Gallia Narbonensis had once
supported Galba, he changed his allegiance to Vespasian in AD 69 and
went on to lead the successful Flavian invasion of Italy, bringing the
civil war to a close. Under his generalship the Flavians not only secured
victory over the Vitellians at the second battle of Bedriacum but also
captured Rome. Such efficiency certainly seems to threaten Vespasian's
status as ideal general (2.5), particularly since he remains detached
from the military action throughout, but then again some of the destructive tasks carried out by Antonius Primus would have done the new
emperor little credit if he had perpetrated them himself. Vespasian may
be an experienced general, but the ugly responsibility of winning the
civil war is conveniently left to Antonius Primus. Not even the influential Mucianus, whose character-sketch is twice interwoven with
Vespasian's portrait (1.10 and 2.5), seems to possess the necessary
military skills to finish the war.[2] Antonius Primus, therefore, as self-
proclaimed general of the Flavian cause, is filling a gap in the leadership structure and doing an unpopular but necessary job. Tacitus
underlines his importance by a delayed entrance (2.86), which suggestively follows the account of the first Flavian moves in the east to
challenge Vitellius. One critic, Meulder, observes that the way in which
Tacitus presents Antonius Primus is particularly rich,[3] but does not
elaborate his comment with extended discussion. It will be the task of
this chapter to analyse Tacitus' portrayal of Antonius Primus, setting
the general's leadership methods against the collective characterisation
of the Flavian soldiers as investigated in Chapter 3.

Perhaps the emergence of such an unscrupulous but practical general was inevitable as the soldiers became increasingly frustrated with
leaders who constantly procrastinated. Tacitus describes Primus as 'the
worst man in peace, but not someone to be scorned in war (*pace
pessimus, bello non spernendus*)' (2.86.2), which evokes Velleius Paterculus' description of Marius, 'as excellent in war as he was the worst
man in peace (*quantum bello optimus, tantum pace pessimus*)' (2.11.1;
cf. Plutarch *Marius* 2.1). Tacitus concedes that Primus is morally

flawed, but perhaps a 'plunderer (*raptor*)' and a 'briber (*largitor*)'
(2.86.2) is just the sort of leader who might appeal to the frustrated
soldiers. At the highest level, they faced emperors, who dressed up as
generals as if the uniform would give them power,[4] while lower down in
the command structure, there were commanders unwilling to commit
themselves fully to their emperor's cause.[5] This particular combination of
stagnant leadership and enthusiastic troops led to a dangerous build-up of
pressure from below and prepared the way perfectly for Primus.

There is one reason why it is crucial to analyse Tacitus' subtle
      Tacitus' narrative suggests that Antonius Primus was not as
straightforward detrimental to the state as he might have seemed
immediately after the Flavian victory. At least his intervention finished
the war, even if his leadership techniques embarrassed the new regime
in retrospect.[6] Sallust makes Metellus's envoys observe: 'Every war can
be started easily, but stopped only with great difficulty' (*Jug.* 83.1).[7] The
new Flavian regime may have been distinctly uncomfortable about its
debt to Antonius Primus. This is perhaps reflected when Martial depicts
Antonius Primus as an old man proudly surveying his life, but pointedly
omits any direct mention of his military exploits. Nevertheless, there
may be a hidden defence of Primus' contribution to the civil war in
Martial's insistence that: 'there is no day which is displeasing or bur-
densome for him to remember; there was no day which he would not
wish to recall' (10.23.5-6). This is hardly a forthright denunciation of
Primus' critics, but the fact that Martial felt the need for such a
diplomatic tone so long after the civil war indicates that Flavian resentment towards the general to whom they owed so much had not
decreased.[8] Tacitus explores more complex questions than whether
Primus was the hero or villain in AD 69. Tacitus offers us a disturbing
portrayal of a man who possesses the practical flair associated with the
ideal general, but whose moral code allows him to use sinister methods
for the sake of short-term expediency.

      There is one reason why it is crucial to analyse Tacitus' subtle
characterisation of Primus more sensitively. Some critics have categori-
cally condemned Tacitus by arguing that fluctuations in his portrayal
of the rogue general indicate an incompetent historian, who cannot
reconcile conflicts within his source material to create a coherent presentation. So, Chilver proposes that Tacitus used a hostile source,
possibly Pliny, when creating his character-sketch of Antonius Primus
(2.86), but that in Book 3, which offers a relatively favourable account
of the general's actions, the historian must have drawn on a more
friendly source, primarily Vipstanus Messala.[9] Yet this seems too sche-
matic. In recent years, styles of reading have developed, so that we as
critics are less prone to assume incompetence in the ancient author
than to look for layers of meaning in a text. Paradoxes and troublesome
details, which at first do not seem to fit, are often deeply thought-provoking when analysed more closely.[10] Tacitus' Antonius Primus is a

pertinent figure to consider in this respect. As we shall see, the damning observations in the character-sketch (2.86) are not irreconcilible with the more positive emphasis in Book 3. There is logical coherence in casting Primus as a competent but disreputable soldier (2.86), whose valuable contribution to the Flavian campaign in Book 3 vindicates Tacitus' earlier generalisation. So too Tacitus' exploration of Primus' problematic role in Book 4 after the Flavian victory will develop the point that the general was 'the worst man in peace' (2.86.2). Primus is the right man to tackle the aberrations of civil war, but once peace is restored, the general's disreputable skills are no longer required by the new dynasty. Tacitus' apparently contradictory portrait of Primus is therefore an eloquent marker of a society in flux. Political *circumstances* may change, but Primus does not, and herein lies the problem. It is no longer adequate to use Primus uncritically to dismiss Tacitus' competence as a historian.

The contrast between cautious and dynamic commanders had long been a familiar motif in Greek and Roman historiography. Thucydides portrays Nicias and Alcibiades along these lines (6.8-24). Likewise, Livy famously contrasts the cautious Fabius Maximus and the energetic Scipio Africanus (28.40-4), but similar pairs are replicated throughout his work, such as Camillus and Furius (Livy 6.22.5-26 and 8.33.15-16), and Decius Mus and Fabius Rullianus (Livy 10.28 and Diodorus Siculus 21.6.2.).[11] The cautious partner is usually unpopular but correct, while the impetuous leader tends to be popular but wrong.[12] This theme can be traced back to Homer's *Iliad*, where the wise Poulydamas offers advice to Hektor, who spurns his prudent words of caution (*Iliad* 12.210-29 and 18.249-83). However, caution and audacity do not always pull in opposite directions: sometimes two colleagues are made to complement one another through their different leadership techniques, such as the careful Vespasian and the spirited Titus in Josephus' *Bellum Judaicum*.

In the *Histories*, Tacitus explores the question of caution as opposed to speed on a number of levels, ranging from the individual skirmish to the strategy of a whole campaign. So, Tacitus describes a fracas before the second battle of Bedriacum (3.16-17), which contrasts Primus' commendable caution with Varus' foolish haste, and which may be modelled on Livy's Camillus and Furius (6.22.5-26).[13] On a strategic level, it is Tacitus' Vespasian above all who advocates caution, despite his initial characterisation as a dynamic general, while Primus advocates speed, for which he is later criticised (3.53.3). Tacitus emphasises Vespasian's scheme to starve the Vitellians into submission before any confrontation on the battlefield: 'since Egypt, the key to the corn supply, and the revenues of the richest provinces were in his control, Vitellius' army could be reduced to submission through lack of pay and food' (3.8.2). Dio inverts this notion by suggesting that a benign Vespasian actually collected grain in Egypt because he wanted to send it to Rome (65.9). There is no sign of this in Tacitus. Even when Vespasian hears that the Vitellians have been defeated at Bedriacum, the new emperor hurries to Alexandria 'to oppress with famine Vitellius' broken troops and Rome, which needed imports. For he was preparing to invade the adjacent province of Africa by land and sea, intending to sow famine and dissension among the enemy by cutting off the corn supply' (3.48.3).[14] The new emperor is thus portrayed as planning to use the blockade to mop up any final Vitellian resistance. Vespasian's scheme is helped by the bad weather, which delays the corn-ships and enables some loyal Vitellian survivors to heighten rumours that the African coast was being blockaded (4.38.2). When the ships eventually reach Rome in February AD 70, there is only enough corn left to last for ten more days (4.52.2).[15] Tacitus' focus on Vespasian's relatively passive plan for a corn embargo both before and after the Flavian victory at Bedriacum contrasts with the more active methods of the dynamic Primus.

One aspect of Vespasian's alleged plan to blockade the corn-supply needs further investigation. When Vespasian explains his strategy, his lieutenant Mucianus is supposed to have written several letters giving the same advice, 'under the pretext that the victory would be bloodless and without grief and so on' (3.8.3).[16] Tacitus highlights Mucianus' insincerity here, and the theory that a blockade of the food-supply was safer than a destructive military campaign can certainly be challenged. Tacitus' original readers would probably have found Mucianus' assertion problematic because of their knowledge of historical precedents. Severing the corn-supply was a move which had suggested itself to Pompey at the outbreak of the civil war in 49 BC, but this met with criticism (Cicero *Att.* 9.9.2). Also, when Sextus Pompey seized Sicily in 40 BC and severed the corn-supply, the result was popular rioting against Octavian and Antony, who were held responsible for the crisis (Appian *BC* 5.67.280-5.68.289). Indeed, the situation became so desperate that Octavian and Antony had to agree to the Treaty of Misenum with Sextus Pompey in 39 BC.[17] The correlation between food-shortages and outbursts of popular violence was a fact of life, even if the destruction caused by such outbursts in Rome was considered unacceptable compared with 'legitimate' military devastation abroad.[18] Yet the notion that a blockade was a peaceful method of warfare was still used. In the summer of 49 BC in Spain, Caesar hopes that, 'having cut off his enemies from their food supply, he would be able to finish the business without exposing his men to fighting or bloodshed' (*BC* 1.72). Caesar casts himself as so concerned for his soldiers' safety that he even deems battle too much of an imposition, but conveniently declines to elaborate the effects of a food-blockade on his enemy. This contrast between violent battle and peaceful embargo is artificial, but might seem plausible to a reader who had not seen the worst horrors resulting from a prolonged food-blockade.[19] So Josephus offers an extensive description of the effects of starvation on human conduct during the siege of Jerusalem, including the murder of children who were clinging onto scraps of food (*BJ* 5.433): there may be rhetorical embellishment at work here, but even so, the passage allows us to question Mucianus' stance that cutting off the food supply does not result in bloodshed and grief. Moreover, as we know from the situation in Iraq, a blockade targets civilians, as well as the military, and is more likely to destroy the poor and the weak, as opposed to their leaders.[20]

In AD 69, Vespasian adopted the same stance as Caesar, namely that he was a cautious and caring strategist, who was anxious to spare his soldiers from destructive battles. Nevertheless, it is unlikely that such a strategy would have been acceptable to the soldiers themselves. Action rather than inertia always seems to hold the most appeal for soldiers.[21] So, Titus' soldiers ponder their strategy in Jerusalem: 'It seemed undignified to sit and wait for the enemy to starve' (5.11.2). The notion of a corn-blockade might have won public approval once the war was finished (particularly if Rome had not suffered the miseries of a prolonged embargo), but at the time, Vespasian risked alienating his troops by preventing them from fighting. There is a suggestive parallel in Calvia Crispinilla, who went to Africa to instigate Clodius Macer to revolt, 'openly contriving famine against the Roman people' (1.73).[22] The fact that a similar corn-blockade had recently been concocted by a woman would not have enhanced Vespasian's plan in the eyes of his troops.

This discussion has a bearing on the way in which posterity viewed Antonius Primus. The general took a course of action which inevitably caused destruction, but it may paradoxically have ended the civil war faster and with less harm to civilians than Vespasian's corn-blockade would have done (particularly in combination with Mucianus' military advance). This is not in any sense to suggest that Tacitus is skirting around Primus' harmful role in a devastating war. After all, the general is traditionally blamed for trouble in Moesia (which was prompted by the removal of legionaries for the invasion of Italy), the sack of Cremona, the burning of the Capitol, and Civilis' rebellion on the Rhine.[23] Tacitus addresses all these issues, but also allows for the possibility that if Primus had not intervened, then the devastation could have been more extensive. Primus, advocating prompt action, expresses open concern before his troops that 'Germany, the source of their strength, is not far away, Britain is only separated by the Channel, Gaul and Spain are close at hand, and from both places they can get men, horses and tribute' (3.2.2). This anxious tone is not just some rhetorical device to scare the troops into action, but a legitimate fear which is confirmed by the preceding narrative. Tacitus' audience has already seen that the Vitellian war machine has started to grind into action, albeit slowly. So,

Vitellius has summoned auxiliaries 'from Germany, Britain and the Spanish provinces' (2.97.1). Even if the governors here are initially unresponsive, these places still remain a dangerous source of troops and supplies, as Primus acknowledges. His concern is subsequently vindicated by Tacitus' authorial comment: 'Vitellius had summoned auxiliaries from Britain, Gaul, and Spain, and the calamity of war would have been huge (*immensam belli luem*), if Primus had not seized the victory in a lightning battle because he feared this very thing' (3.15.1). In Tacitus' eyes, Antonius Primus' action is justifiable, given the possibility of escalation: the phrase *immensa belli lues* graphically reflects the potentially massive destruction which could have resulted from delay.[24]

Let us examine in more detail Primus' programmatic speech to the assembled Flavians at Poetovio (3.2). This address, the first in a succession of Primus' interactions with the troops, continues to explore the relative merits of speed and delay. We have already seen how this same antithesis has dominated two earlier discussions. In the debate about whether or not Galba should leave the palace to confront Otho (1.32-3), the advocates of a speedy exit prevail and Galba 'delaying no longer' (1.34.1) is dead by the end of that same day. In the debate about whether the Othonians should fight the Vitellians immediately or wait, the advocates of speed again triumph and the Othonians lose the battle (2.32-3). These two precedents certainly question the wisdom of hasty action, as does a reader's familiarity with the historiographical theme whereby speed often proves more hazardous than delay.[25] Before the general speaks, Tacitus summarises the arguments put forward by those advocating delay. They stress the advantages of their enemies, who have at their disposal strong German troops and fresh Vitellian soldiers from Britain, and then elaborate their own handicaps, such as the fact that they have fewer troops, including some in low spirits after losing the first battle of Bedriacum. They propose that if the Flavians delay, then Mucianus and his troops from the East will arrive, and Vespasian will apply useful pressure from the provinces, 'through which he could set in motion the massive machinery for what was virtually a second war (*per quas velut alterius belli molem cieret*)' (3.1.2). These supporters of delay are not even named, and the impact of their arguments is diminished by being summarised in indirect speech. Moreover, the fact that they advocate doing nothing until Mucianus arrives will hardly boost their audience's self-esteem: Roman soldiers were often competitive and therefore notoriously bad at waiting for reinforcements, even if this was sometimes the most sensible response to a situation (cf. 3.60.1, *Annals* 13.36 and [Caesar] *Bell. Alex.* 27.4).

Antonius Primus next delivers a dynamic address, which starts out in indirect speech, but then switches vividly into direct speech.[26] This change neatly suggests the general's charisma, but other devices also contribute to this impression. Primus shows good instincts by opening his speech with ridicule of the enemy, 'softened by the circus, the theatres and by the pleasures of the city, and exhausted through ill-health' (3.2.2). The previous speakers may have accurately assessed the low morale amongst the Flavian troops, but such negative self-assessment was unlikely to win much support or to improve morale. It was much more rousing for a leader to mock the enemy than to dwell on his own army's weaknesses, and soldiers frequently stirred themselves up by deriding their opponents (cf. [Caesar] *Bell. Alex.* 25.1), which would make them receptive to this strategy. Primus boldly shatters his opponents' stereotypical image of tough German Vitellians and casts these northerners as soft easterners, debilitated by alluring city life, which is a viewpoint already substantiated by the preceding narrative (2.87.1, 2.93, and 2.99.1). Even if the Vitellians will recover somewhat once they leave Rome to face the Flavian challenge, Primus' assessment is accurate at the time of the debate.[27]

Primus shrewdly keeps discussion of strategy to a minimum, dismissing with an impatient trio of questions some tactical points raised by the advocates of delay. Instead, the general keeps his speech on a personal level, building up a polarised contrast between the demoralised enemy and his own heroic men. He appeals to distinct racial groups within the Flavian army as a whole, claiming that the Pannonian legions are eager for revenge, while the armies of Moesia are a 'fresh force' (3.2.3). This rhetorical technique auspiciously recalls the way in which the great general Alexander addressed remarks tailored to each nationality amongst his troops (Justin 11.9.4 and Curtius Rufus 3.10.4-10). In addition, Primus stresses that 'our forces are stronger and untouched by vices' (3.2.3), and that the Flavians, ashamed at their earlier defeat at Bedriacum (when they were fighting for Otho), will actually improve discipline. Caesar uses a similar strategy by appealing to his troops' sense of shame (*pudor*) after a defeat (*BC* 3.73.5). Primus' appealing picture of tough, well-disciplined Flavians as opposed to lax, weak Vitellians can hardly fail to win listeners to his viewpoint, however misleading such images might be in reality. Primus is telling his audience exactly what they want to hear.

The climax comes when the general imaginatively depicts the inevitable result of an encounter between two such ill-matched sides in battle:

> Previously, two regiments from Pannonia and Moesia broke through the Vitellian line. Now, the combined forces of sixteen regiments, with a roar, a thunder and a cloud [of dust], will bury and overwhelm horses and cavalry who have forgotten how to fight.

> duae tunc Pannonicae ac Moesicae alae perrupere hostem: nunc sedecim

alarum coniuncta signa pulsu sonituque et nube ipsa operient ac super-
fundent oblitos proeliorum equites equosque.[28] (3.2.4)

In a clever reversal, Primus shifts the emphasis away from those
(ex-Othonian) Flavians, who took part unsuccessfully in the first battle
of Bedriacum, and about whom the advocates of delay had been so
worried. Instead, the general focuses on two heroic Pannonian and
Moesian cavalry regiments in such a way as to recall Homer's 'cloud of
men' image.[29] Such language momentarily casts these contingents in
terms of an epic army. Indeed, for someone who had not read the earlier
narrative of the battle, it would be understandable to conclude that
these troops did not lose at Bedriacum at all. Primus claims that 'even
then the cavalry was not beaten' (3.2.3): this is true of the skirmish, but
not of the battle as a whole. Primus daringly twists defeat into victory
to finish his speech on a high note. It is striking that Tacitus switches
into direct speech at precisely the point when the general is being the
most misleading. Chilver finds it surprising that these two Pannonian
and Moesian cavalry units are not mentioned by name in the account
of the earlier battle,[30] but this is to ignore Tacitus' interest in Primus'
character. Tacitus had previously highlighted the bravery of the *Vitellian* Italian Legion in stopping the temporary rout caused by these
Othonian units (2.41.2), which conflicts with Primus' version of the
same event. This divergence is surely deliberate: the general's boastful
but inaccurate recollection of this moment suggests his manipulative
nature and rhetorical skills. Primus is re-inventing the past in such a
way as to orchestrate the present.

Yet Primus' ability to accentuate the positive makes him a dynamic
leader. A careful reader, who could recall the earlier narrative of the first
battle of Bedriacum, would learn something about Primus' personality
and methods, but even without that contrast between speech and
narrative, we see that his rhetoric is colourful and effective. His hasty
shift from the past to the future is clearly marked by an antithetical
'then now *(tunc nunc)*', progression (3.2.4; cf. Cicero *Phillipic* 7.5.14).
Moreover, in his description of the imaginary final battle he vividly
evokes the sound of horsemen overwhelming the Vitellians 'with a
thundering din *(pulsu sonituque)*' (3.2.4; cf. Cicero *Marc.* 3.9). Cicero
makes Crassus observe that three elements bring illumination and
decoration to a speech: these are the rare word, the new coinage and the
metaphor *(De Oratore* 3.38.152). So, Primus uses a simple but effective
metaphor to forecast the results of his actions: 'you will soon hear that
the door of Italy is open *(iam reseratam Italiam ... audietis)*' (3.2.4).[31]
The defenders of delay also use a metaphor when referring to provincial
support, 'through which he could set in motion the massive machinery
for what was virtually a second war *(per quas velut alterius belli molem
cieret)*' (3.1.2).[32] Notice the way in which 'virtually *(velut)*' is used to tone

down a phrase which might strike a reader as too bold (cf. 3.59.1). This qualification suggests a more cautious manner of speaking in comparison with Primus' bold language.

Direct and lively metaphor could be a productive way of communicating, particularly for military men. The general Fabius Rullianus, while arguing against Decius Mus for the command in Etruria, observes that it was unfair for one man to plant a tree while another man gathered its fruit (Livy 10.24.5). He does not lessen the force of his language with an 'as it were (*velut*)'. Primus himself later deploys another striking metaphor in a letter to Vespasian, referring to 'a storm of cavalry (*equestri procella*)' (3.53.2; cf. Livy 10.5.7). Elsewhere Quintilian, discussing appropriate styles, had advised that 'simple language best suits soldiers' (11.1.32; cf. *Rhetorica ad Herennium* 4.52.65) and Livy refers to the knight Sextus Tempanius' 'unadorned speech' (4.41.1). Yet a simple and direct style did not mean loss of impact, as Tacitus shows when relaying the 'exact words' of the soldier Subrius Flavus, a participant in the Pisonian conspiracy, who is asked by Nero why he has forgotten his military oath. Subrius Flavus' words are described as 'unadorned and powerful' (*Annals* 15.67.3).[33] In Primus' case it is not just the words but the style of delivery which adds impact: he speaks 'with flashing eyes and savage voice, so that he could be heard over a wide area' (3.3.1). Nevertheless, although the general's infectious rhetoric is impressive, his task is made easier because his arguments coincide with the wishes of the soldiers, who desire swift action (cf. 2.6.2-2.7.1). Once the changing exigencies of civil war require Primus to prompt his soldiers to act against their wishes, then the magnetic general will face a greater challenge.

Primus' speech has some interesting resonances with Suetonius Paulinus' arguments for delay rather than speed, which are voiced at an Othonian council of war before the first battle of Bedriacum (2.32).[34] There are several verbal parallels between the two speeches, which encourage a reader to compare the different ways in which Suetonius Paulinus and Antonius Primus put forward their claims. This in turn sheds light on why the former loses while the latter wins his case. Both speeches open with similar phrases: Paulinus begins by observing, 'speed is useful to the enemy, but delay to the Othonians (*festinationem hostibus, moram ipsis utilem*)' (2.32.1), while Primus asserts that 'speed is useful to the Flavians, but will prove deadly to Vitellius (*festinationem ipsis utilem, Vitellio exitiosam*)' (3.2.1). The choice of adjectives in each case is suggestive. Paulinus locates himself in the realm of rational argument by proposing to consider why speed would be *useful* to the enemy, while delay would serve their own interests. Primus does not totally reject this rational element, but he injects powerful emotions into his analysis by considering why speed will be *deadly* for Vitellius. Notice too that where Paulinus carefully considers both sides of the argument, Primus largely restricts himself to contemplating the advantages of speedy action. Paulinus is more thorough, but does not grasp his audience's attention in the same way as Primus. The passion of Primus as a speaker is encapsulated by the verb 'he poured out these words (*haec ... effudit*)' (3.3), which contrasts with the more restrained description of Paulinus who 'argued (*disseruit*)' (2.32.1).[35] Tacitus later plays with the incongruity of Musonius Rufus, a Stoic philosopher, mingling with the Flavian soldiers and 'discoursing on (*disserens*) the advantages of peace and the perils of war' (3.81.1). Most soldiers find Rufus funny and even more think he is boring, until he eventually stops his ill-timed lecture.[36] Primus' style is distinctly more gripping.

Paulinus' thoroughness and Primus' brevity emerge clearly when each general analyses the enemy's strength around the empire. As we have seen, Primus gives a lightning survey of Vitellian forces:

> Germany, the source of their strength, is not far away, Britain is only separated by the Channel, Gaul and Spain are close at hand, and from both places they can get men, horses and tribute, and then there is Italy itself and the resources of Rome. (3.2.2)

This creates just enough pressure to provoke a healthy desire for action, but it is not so daunting as to be discouraging. So, Onasander notes that fear can be useful in galvanising soldiers, but warns the general not to overstep the mark because excessive fear can simply incapacitate an army (*Strat.* 14.1-2). By contrast Paulinus' thorough analysis is much longer and more methodical:

> The whole of Vitellius' army has now arrived, and there are few reinforcements at his rear, since the Gallic provinces are in turmoil and it would be unwise to abandon the Rhine with such hostile tribes ready to invade. The army in Britain is held back by the enemy and the sea; the Spanish provinces are not exactly overflowing with troops; the Narbonese province, invaded by our fleet and defeated in battle, is trembling; Italy north of the Po is enclosed by the Alps and cannot be reinforced by sea, and in any case it has been devastated by the passage of their army. (2.32.1)

It comes as no surprise that Paulinus' exhaustive arguments are swept away by an emotive plea on the part of Titianus and Proculus, who claim that 'fortune, the gods and Otho's divine power inspired his planning and would inspire its performance' (2.33.1). The failure of Paulinus' earlier speech arguing for delay and the subsequent collapse of the Othonian cause must surely add tension when Primus argues so passionately for speedy action. Emotion previously superseded rational analysis, but the result then was disastrous.

Primus makes a startling claim in one section of his speech. The general pledges his personal commitment to the cause and draws a clear distinction between himself and other less devoted commanders: 'Unless somebody stops me, I will both plan and execute the scheme. You, who have not compromised yourselves, can restrain the legions. Some lightly armed cohorts will be enough for me' (3.2.4).[37] This stance should remind us of other impatient Roman commanders, such as Marius, who claimed that 'if half of the army were entrusted to him, he would have Jugurtha in chains within a few days' (Sallust *Jug.* 64.5). Primus' enthusiasm for immediate action certainly conflicts with Vespasian's cautious plans, but it seems likely that the Flavian soldiers will respond positively to such decisive leadership. There is a fundamental difference between the speech of Primus, the 'keenest instigator of war' (3.2.1) and that of Paulinus, the 'natural delayer' (2.25.2), who seems more typical of the average civil war general in AD 68-9. Primus' active involvement in the situation and his pledge to carry out his plan creates a valuable bond with his men.[38] Paulinus was simply not prepared to stick his neck out in this way, even if his advice was shrewd.

Thus, we learn almost as much about the psychology of the soldiers who are present at the Flavian council as we do about Primus himself. Tacitus carefully stresses that both centurions and soldiers bother to infiltrate this meeting, which suggests that a strong allegiance between Primus and the lower ranks already exists before his speech. Yet Primus' words clearly strengthen the relationship since the common soldiers respond by praising him as 'the one true leader' (3.3). The heterogeneous audience at this council therefore differs crucially from the exclusively senior officers who attended Otho's council before the first battle of Bedriacum. Although Primus' vision of well-disciplined Flavian troops methodically crushing decadent Vitellians plays to the crowd, his bold pledge to execute his plan wins the legionaries' confidence and enthusiasm. Such commitment from a senior officer is something for which they, as well as other soldiers, have yearned for some time. We have already seen how the Othonian troops, deprived of their emperor, ask Verginius Rufus 'now to accept the principate, now to head an embassy to Caecina and Valens' (2.51).[39] Under the circumstances, it is understandable that these defeated troops urgently want a general who will act on their behalf before the victorious Vitellian commanders, but this request is not entirely whimsical. After all, they have already approached Verginius Rufus unsuccessfully on another occasion with a similar offer, which suggests some consistency (cf. Pliny *Epistles* 6.10.4). After Otho's death, Verginius Rufus once again refuses the soldiers' pleas and earns their resentment as a result: 'he still retained the admiration and esteem of the men, but they hated him for disdaining them' (2.68.4). By contrast, Primus indicates his deep commitment to the troops, who therefore respond enthusiastically to him.

Antonius Primus has made a promising start, but how far will he live

up to the expectations of his soldiers? The real test of his powers will
come when Primus must make his men do something which they find
disagreeable. An illuminating example is the mutiny against Tampius
Flavianus (3.10). Various officers try to calm the soldiers, but without
success. Only Primus can get the troops to listen to him, which is
certainly an achievement, but his ploy of throwing Flavianus into
chains in order to remove him from the hostile crowd does not fool the
soldiers for a second: 'the soldiers, realising that this was a farce,
scattered the guards around the platform and prepared to resort to
extreme violence' (3.10.3). Primus underestimates his soldiers in a
manner reminiscent of Germanicus, who manufactures a fake letter
from Tiberius to soothe his mutinous troops, but is shocked when the
men see through this trick (*Annals* 1.37.1). Primus may be *more* acceptable than the other officers, but the general still commands precariously
by consent from below. Only his threat of suicide dampens the mutiny,
but this is a dangerous ploy. When Germanicus tried the same tactic,
one soldier, Calusidius, offered him a sharper sword (*Annals* 1.35.5).[40]
Maintaining one's dignity as a commander in such situations is considered desirable, but both Germanicus and Primus have arguably
compromised their standing as generals by threatening suicide.[41] In
any case, Tacitus carefully points out that the soldiers are 'exhausted
by the work of digging' (3.11.1), which diminishes Primus' credit for
soothing their tempers. Although Primus is the most energetic leader
to have entered the narrative so far, his capacity for maintaining
discipline is still presented as being erratic.

Even Primus' forceful rhetoric does not always impress the troops as
fundamentally as his initial speech did (3.2). After decisively beating
the Vitellians, the Flavian troops want to storm Cremona immediately,
although night has fallen. Primus tries to deter them in a speech which
uses many familiar techniques, namely a series of forceful direct questions to convey his arguments and personal appeals to individual
soldiers (3.20). Tacitus formulates the speech with the same shift from
indirect to direct speech, which reminds us of the general's charisma.
Yet there are also significant differences. No longer does Primus align
his own interests quite so firmly with those of his soldiers: 'It is fitting
that the soldiers should be hungry for battle, but generals more often
do good by foresight, deliberation and delay than by rashness' (3.20.1;
cf. Dio 41.33.4-5). Otho had drawn the same distinction between the
duties of the soldiers and their general (1.84.2). Such sentiments certainly comply with the advice of the military handbooks, which urge the
sensible commander to hold back from taking part in the battle himself,[42] but literary texts often present idealised images of swashbuckling
generals who effortlessly combine the roles of soldier and officer. So
Catiline pledges his spirit and his body to the cause, serving as both a
soldier and general in the final conflict, although the fact that he is

killed shows the risks run by a commander who simultaneously plays two roles.[43] When Antonius Primus addresses his troops (3.20.1), he totally reverses his previous collusive words by re-establishing the traditional boundary between soldiers and general. The speech rapidly dissolves the unique bond of trust, which he worked so hard to establish with his men, and almost causes a mutiny. This is narrowly averted when the Flavian soldiers hear about the imminent arrival of six Vitellian legions: 'This terror opened up stubborn minds to the general's advice' (3.21.1). Already, Primus seems to have fallen from that pedestal of popularity on which he stood so firmly at the start of the book.[44]

In the face of such pressure, Antonius Primus must develop unusual methods of leadership, which increasingly diverge from the commendable techniques of the ideal general. So, Primus harangues his men during the night-battle at Cremona: 'firing up some (*alios*) by shame and threats, many (*multos*) by praise and encouragement, all (*omnes*) by hope and promises' (3.24.1). Tacitus supplements the conventional image of a general using praise and blame to galvanise his troops by adding the detail that Primus inspires all his men by hope and promises. We are not told what exactly these hopes and promises are, but the implication is that plunder or money is involved.[45] Primus' appeal to financial instincts certainly transcends the differences between separate contingents within the army, and is designed to be attractive to all the soldiers: the *alios ... multos ... omnes* succession reflects this.[46] Even if Primus' subsequent words to the Pannonian legions (3.24.1), the Moesian troops (3.24.2), the Third Legion (3.24.2) and the Praetorians (3.24.3) perhaps recall the methods of idealised commanders such as Caesar, who wisely uses different techniques to motivate veterans and rookies ([Caesar] *Bell. Afr.* 81), at the same time Tacitus hints that Primus' effectiveness as a leader depends not just on his rhetoric, but also on the incentives which he can offer. Tacitus thereby suggests to a reader how the dynamics of leadership change under the constraints imposed by civil war. We might usefully compare Catiline's words to his men before battle: 'Remember that you are carrying in your right hands riches, honour and glory, as well as the freedom of your country' (Sallust *Cat.* 58.8). Sallust here makes Catiline subordinate the freedom of the country, which ideally should be the most important motivating factor, to the soldiers' greed (cf. Caesar *BC* 2.39). Primus too exploits the fact that his heterogeneous troops all share a common desire for booty, as is shown when their 'greed for plunder' (3.26.3) outweighs even their desire for safety. The climax comes when Primus, or perhaps one of his colleagues, offers Cremona to the troops as a prize for victory (3.28). This sort of disreputable incentive was usually offered by foreign, not Roman commanders, as when Juba gives the town of Vaga to his men to plunder ([Caesar] *Bell. Afr.* 74.2), or if a Roman commander did make such an offer, it would ideally be in the context of a foreign rather than a civil war. As we have already seen, Primus' gesture is certainly revealing about the collective character of the soldiers, but at the same time, it shows the extremes to which their commander has been driven. Nor are such materialistic appeals any guarantee of permanent loyalty: when Cassius Longinus granted large rewards to his soldiers, only a 'semblance of affection' was the result ([Caesar] *Bell. Alex.* 48.3).

Tacitus' Primus nonetheless understands the importance of maintaining appearances, however questionable his leadership was in reality. So, the general sends auxiliary troops into the territory of Cremona to acquire a taste for plundering citizens, albeit 'under the pretext of acquiring supplies' (3.15.2). Such foraging was generally considered a respectable and necessary part of an army's duties, which made this a convincing façade.[47] Primus' desire to disguise the true purpose of these missions is reflected in the concerns of the Flavian soldiers themselves, who are also sensitive about their image. So, the soldiers veil their private cravings for booty by pretending to want to press on towards Cremona and enforce the surrender of the enemy (3.19.2). Yet there is still a crucial difference between Antonius Primus and the Flavian soldiers. While the soldiers consider it desirable to cloak their violence behind a respectable façade, it is not essential for them to do so because of the anonymity provided by their sheer numbers. Likewise, the ordinary Vitellian soldiers, 'safer in their obscurity' (3.31.2), continue to resist the Flavian forces while their leaders, who are more conspicuous, fear for their own safety.[48] Antonius Primus, because he is in command, is under considerable pressure to answer for both his and the soldiers' actions. His vulnerability is highlighted by the widespread condemnation of his alleged 'vulgar (*vernile*) joke' (3.32.3; cf. 2.88.2). Primus, while in the baths washing off bloodstains after the battle, is supposed to have complained about the luke-warm water, but added that it would soon heat up. His remark is unfortunately overheard and understood to be an order to set fire to Cremona, although the town, as Tacitus explains, is already on fire. Commentators have interpreted this story either as Tacitus' condemnation of Primus or as an attempt to exculpate the general, who was in the baths when the city was set on fire and therefore could not have been involved.[49] Yet both these readings focus too exclusively on Primus alone at the expense of the context. Morgan has argued convincingly that this comment was actually made by somebody other than Primus, and that Tacitus' strategy is not to exculpate Primus, but to highlight the roles played in the disaster by the Flavian soldiers and the citizens of Cremona.[50] Tacitus certainly uses suggestive metaphorical language when describing Primus as 'firing up (*accendens*) all the soldiers by hope and promises' (3.24.1), but this is not the same as giving the order to set fire to the city. The fact that people are prepared to attribute the dubious remark to the general reveals their anxiety to hold one individual responsible for the disaster, however inadequate this may be.

Tacitus dramatically juxtaposes this gossip with the start of the following chapter: 'Forty thousand armed men burst into the town ...' (3.33.1). Tacitus is not always so specific about troop-numbers and the precise figure is meant to have an impact (cf. 2.87.1). Thus, the ineffectual and unsatisfying accusation against one individual is contrasted powerfully with the relentless stampede of the troops.[51] For an observer to say indignantly that it was all the general's fault is a curiously unsatisfying explanation of such mass destruction. If Tacitus had been writing epic, then perhaps it would have been feasible for a heroic Primus to try to block the massive advance, but sometimes even Aeneas cannot control his men successfully once they have been roused.[52] In any case, Tacitus suggests that the Flavian generals, including Primus, tried hard to calm the soldiers and to prevent slaughter. There is a brief reference to the fact that the troops were soothed 'by their generals' pleas' and that Primus 'eulogised his victorious army, promised mercy to the vanquished, but kept quiet about Cremona' (3.32.1). Certainly, he, or somebody else, may have pointed to the city as a victory-prize in the heat of battle, but once victory has been achieved, the offer is not repeated.

Tacitus conspicuously does not report Primus' placatory words to the troops (3.32.1), even in indirect speech. Perhaps this is because the general's speeches already dominate Book 3, but there may be more to this omission than a desire to avoid repetition. Certainly, Tacitus could have presented a valiant Primus making a desperate plea to save Cremona, but this might have been read as an unsubtle attempt to clear the general's name. We have already seen that after the civil war, Primus' exclusion from Vespasian's regime made him a useful scapegoat, which meant that opinions tended to divide sharply for or against the general. Yet for Tacitus, exoneration or accusation of one individual was a less pertinent issue than unravelling the complicated events which preceded the destruction of Cremona. As Henderson remarks, 'History is not *simply* bound to vindicate winners.'[53] If anybody was capable of controlling the Flavian forces, then it was surely Primus, but the point is that even a man of his stature cannot exert his influence against the collective determination of the soldiers. The general is excellent at stirring his troops before or even during a battle, but finds himself powerless to placate them subsequently. In this respect Primus partially resembles Otho, who 'had no authority to prevent crimes: he could only order them' (1.45.2).

The crux of the problem is that Primus commands by consent from below rather than by imposition of authority from above. Although Primus has a better chance than his fellow officers of persuading his men to obey him, there is no guarantee of consistent success. So, the general manages to restrain the Flavian soldiers at Carsulae with a speech (3.60), but fails to curb them before Cremona (3.20) even though he deploys similar arguments in both speeches. Primus' observation that 'he would serve them by calculation and strategy (*ratione et consilio*), the general's proper arts' (3.20.2) is echoed by his subsequent assertion that 'the first steps of civil war must be left to chance: victory is achieved by calculation and strategy (*consiliis et ratione*)' (3.60.2). There is also continuity in the feelings of the Flavian troops, who want hasty action on both occasions. At Cremona they worry that waiting for the city to surrender will enable the commanders to seize all the rewards (3.19). Outside Carsulae they think that waiting for reinforcements will enable the incoming legions to share the profit rather than the dangers. Yet, at Carsulae Primus manages to mollify the soldiers, although this proved impossible at Cremona. To a reader's bemusement, Primus can use the same argument in two different situations and achieve diametrically opposed results. This is revealing about the potential limits of speech and rhetoric in a civil war. However strong a bond exists between a commander and his men, the words of one individual are not always sufficiently powerful to overcome collective desire for a particular course of action.[54]

Primus' ability to control the troops may have been flawed, but he was still perceived as an extremely powerful commander, whose influence with the army was second to none. This inevitably meant problems once the war was in its final stages, because the general's jealous colleagues suspected that his leverage on the soldiers could precipitate fresh trouble and undermine their own power. Thus, the rivalry between Mucianus and Primus becomes an increasingly important theme in the narrative, as readers are presented with a series of tendentious stories generated by this hostile relationship. Indeed, Tacitus' complex portrait of Primus surely reflects these bitter conflicts between men who were supposedly on the same side. Tacitus highlights Primus' resentment of the suave Mucianus 'through whose charges his own perilous exploits had been cheapened' (3.53.1), and each general tries to belittle the other in letters to the emperor (3.53 and 4.80.2). Primus has already been characterised as 'a past master at sowing slander against others' (2.86.2), although in the event Mucianus proves more adept at defamation and astute political action. Mucianus quickly succeeds in undermining Primus' power in Rome (4.11), although the rogue general, who was thought to retain the soldiers' support, 'could not be crushed openly' (4.39.4). Primus' reputation may have saved his life, even if his real influence on the soldiers was unpredictable. So, Mucianus lulls Primus into a false sense of security with public praise in the senate and private offers of lucrative posts, but then swiftly hamstrings the general by dispersing his partisan legions around the empire. Thereafter, the threat posed by Primus was never the same again, although

Mucianus still feels obliged to intervene when (a possibly not so naive) Domitian wants to appoint the general as one of his staff-officers (4.80.1). By contrast, Dio's narrative omits the rivalry between Mucianus and Primus, who quickly fades from the narrative after being rocketed to prominence by his passionate soldiers; Suetonius allocates both men an even smaller role.[55]

Vespasian too had to regard Primus with a deep ambivalence. The emperor knew how much he owed to the general, but found Primus' arrogant talk of the debt deeply embarrassing (4.80.2-3). Besides, there was no room for such an aggressively warmongering figure in the new peacetime regime. In a different era, Machiavelli noted that: 'The first thing one does to evaluate the intelligence of a ruler is to examine the men he has around him; and when they are capable and loyal, he can always be considered wise ... But when they are otherwise, one can always form an unfavourable opinion of him in all other things; because the first mistake he makes, he makes in this choice of ministers' (*Il Principe* 22). Any mud that had stuck to Primus was in danger of being transferred to the emperor, so Vespasian decided to freeze Primus out of power. This ploy succeeded, but Tacitus never allows us to forget that if Primus had not been outmanoeuvred politically by Mucianus and Vespasian, then the civil war could have continued unabated. So, Primus is said to have approached Scribonianus Crassus, the elder brother of Galba's heir, Piso, and urged him to seize power (4.39.3). Galba too had considered Scribonianus for adoption (1.15.2), but preferred the younger brother as a more suitable candidate. If Primus' offer was genuine, it is hardly surprising that Scribonianus refused: after buying back Piso's severed head, which had been held for ransom (1.47.2), Scribonianus must have lost his appetite for imperial power.[56] Perhaps the whole story was exaggerated, or even made up, in order to justify retrospectively Primus' removal from the centre of power, although Tacitus characterises the general as sufficiently angry to have approached Scribonianus in this way. At any rate, this suggestive anecdote appears only in Tacitus' narrative and serves as a gloomy pointer to how the civil war might have developed. Hayden White, discussing the difference between chronicles and historical stories, suggests that the historian arranges the events of a chronicle into a 'hierarchy of significance'.[57] Tacitus includes the Scribonianus anecdote to point the reader towards an alternative outcome, which did not happen, but which dramatises the tensions in the relationship between Vespasian and Primus.

Conclusions

Tacitus' estimate of Antonius Primus does indeed fluctuate, as critics have suggested, but not for the reason which they propose, namely

Tacitus' inability to handle his source material. As Tacitus shows, Primus himself displays continuity in his leadership methods, even if the soldiers are more receptive to the general at some points in the narrative than at others. Tacitus points out how after the second battle of Bedriacum Primus allowed his legions the right to appoint centurions to replace those who had been killed, 'in order to give them a taste (*imbueret*) for insubordination' (3.49.2). The phrasing recalls Tacitus' earlier observation that before Cremona, Primus sent his auxiliaries on a plundering mission 'in order that the soldiers might be given a taste (*imbueretur*) for plundering citizens' (3.15.2). Similar motives are attributed to Primus in both cases, even if the general can afford to be much more open about his tactics in the second instance than in the first.

Nonetheless, the Flavian victory at Bedriacum was still a crucial turning point because it heralded Primus' transition from a wartime to a peacetime general. After the decisive battle Primus conducted himself 'not so blamelessly' (3.49.1), forcing the new Flavian regime to acknowledge his power as an uncomfortable reality, but the end of the fighting called for different techniques. Primus' impulsive, corner-cutting and charismatic brand of military leadership was no longer required once the crisis was over, and in fact such a turbulent personality was a positive liability in peacetime. Even at the best of times, emperors could be jealous of successful generals, as is shown by the difficult relationships between Nero and Domitius Corbulo (Tacitus *Histories* 2.76.3, Dio 62.17 and Ammianus Marcellinus 15.2.5) and between Domitian and Julius Agricola (Tacitus *Agricola* 41-2 and Dio 66.20). After a civil war, tensions were likely to be more acute. Not only could Primus detract from Vespasian's own military reputation, but the general was also perceived as having the power to reactivate the civil war. In addition, Primus exacerbated the situation by his lack of political sensitivity. One of his impulsive dispatches to Vespasian had argued that 'as for the mishap at Cremona, this was the fault of the war: previous rifts between citizens had involved the country in greater loss and in the destruction of several cities' (3.53.2). Such a blunt and dismissive tone both contradicts Primus' original shame about the sack (3.34.2) and complicates Vespasian's effort to heal the wounds of the civil war. Tacitus' portrait of Primus points to a change, to a certain extent in the behaviour of the general himself, but more importantly in the texture of the historical events and in the different requirements of a peacetime principate.

Another general who had offered invaluable service in a civil war to a future emperor is Augustus' right-hand man, Marcus Agrippa, who, unlike Primus, continued to play a role after peace was established. Yet Agrippa was in a far more stable position than Primus. Not only did his friendship with Augustus predate the war, but there was nobody as hostile as Mucianus to challenge his position in the new regime. In addition, the ignoble Agrippa could hardly compete with the distinguished lineage of Octavian, whereas Primus may have felt emboldened to challenge Vespasian, whose family background was not so grand. Moreover, Vespasian, unlike Augustus, had sons to do his fighting for him, which lessened the need for a man like Primus. In any case, Agrippa behaved with some delicacy once the fighting was over by consistently subordinating his own ambitions to Augustus' interests. Even if writers tended to idealise Agrippa's submissive altruism in their literary portraits,[58] the general's survival and eventual marriage to Augustus' daughter indicate his central position in the new regime. Primus and Agrippa may have been equally talented soldiers, but the latter had many advantages on his side, which made integration in the new regime easier.

The precedent of Agrippa shows that a general who had been indispensable in a civil war could continue to play a role during peacetime. However, Tacitus' Antonius Primus lacked the necessary political skills to carve a niche for himself and thus found himself slowly eclipsed: circumstances had changed, but the general could not adapt and so he had to make way for more versatile men. No other surviving account of the civil war explores the shifting fortunes of Antonius Primus so thoroughly. As is the case with so many other individual portraits in the *Histories*, Tacitus portrays the character of the rogue Flavian general with great subtlety, enabling readers to understand both his meteoric rise and his rapid fall from favour. Even if Primus' leadership was in reality erratic, the fact that he was perceived to exert influence on the troops with some measure of success necessitated the end of his career after the war was over. Tacitus uses Antonius Primus as a marker both of the collective character of the troops and of the shifting political situation: his interaction with the soldiers may in the short term have been the most successful model of leadership with which we are presented in the *Histories*, but his long-term failure reveals how threatened by him the Flavian principate felt.[59]

Epilogue

In the *Histories* Tacitus has shown us a complex and variegated picture of each civil war army, which is just as subtle as his presentation of the individual emperors. Tacitus uses his historical narrative to differentiate the civil war armies from one another and to give them distinct collective identities. This is in great contrast with Plutarch's notion of large groups of fighting men caught in the grip of irrational forces, which is dramatic, but which leaves many important questions unanswered. Where did these irrational forces come from? How were they sustained? How could they be prevented from emerging again? These are all questions which Tacitus addresses in the *Histories*, and they are questions which he must have considered crucial. After all, *Histories* 1-3, the books which deal primarily with the civil wars, cover a single year (AD 69), but at the same time they constitute perhaps as much as a quarter of the original work, which seems to have narrated events until the end of Domitian's principate in AD 96 (1.1.4). Tacitus has written a remarkably top-heavy historical narrative, possibly inspired and justified by his experiences of the dangerous years AD 96-98. Over this period the assassination of Domitian, popular with the soldiers, and the succession of Nerva, elderly and without an heir, could so easily have led to a repetition of the earlier struggles for power which followed the death of Nero and the accession of Galba. No wonder Tacitus was drawn to analyse these civil war armies so carefully: their conduct in the year of the four emperors had an enduring relevance. It was therefore worthwhile for Tacitus to embark on the potentially uncomfortable task of writing about relatively recent history in order that his readers could better understand the collective mentality of the soldiers and their place in the empire. Moreover, it seems likely that the final books of the *Histories* foreshadowed some of the military problems which Nerva faced during his brief principate, even if the narrative itself stopped dramatically with the assassination of Domitian. This structural pattern is repeated in the *Annals*: the first book has a top-heavy feel to it with its extensive description of the two mutinies, while the narrative ends with the death of Nero. This was a stopping point which Tacitus had in effect forced on himself previously by starting the *Histories* where he did, but the end of the *Annals* may also have mirrored the closing moments of the *Histories*. The two narratives in a sense could have run in tandem with the dangers of collective violence looming, but not narrated, at the end.

Within the narrative itself, Tacitus offers subtle portraits of each army and shows how patterns of behaviour developed over time. He acknowledges that an army is a complex entity whose individual components could be motivated by different factors at any one moment, despite an illusion of unanimity in their actions. At the same time he shows us that each army was not just a random collocation of smaller groups of soldiers. Tacitus shows how the Othonian and Vitellian armies in particular develop a surprising sense of collective morality which transcends the dubious behaviour of their officers. Where centurions and tribunes on all sides have shown themselves to be treacherous, inconsistent and indecisive, these men gradually emerge from the narrative as loyal, steady and determined, even if the individual emperors themselves do little to deserve such affection. We might well ask whether the destructive Flavian soldiers would have followed this pattern of moral improvement, if they had not won the civil war under Antonius Primus' leadership. Tacitus complicates, and in part reverses, the familiar picture of fickle soldiers who gradually assimilate themselves to the character of their commander, whether he is honourable or defective. In the *Histories* we see troops who actually change for the better as they struggle to overcome the erratic and confused signals being sent out by their immediate superiors, many of whom were simply trying to tread water until the trouble was over by pledging loyalty to whoever was currently in power. Caesar (*BC* 3.99; cf. Appian *BC* 2.82.345) says that at the battle of Pharsalus he lost about thirty centurions, but in AD 68-9 very few of these intermediate officers are prepared to commit themselves to the cause and offer a firm lead to their men. The end result is not so much a chain of command as a web of incoherence.

Thus we see soldiers on all sides gradually develop a mistrust of their immediate commanding officers, which prolongs the war by fragmenting the armies and making them less efficient fighting machines. This element of mistrust means that on campaign soldiers are not driven to impress their generals by engaging in flamboyant military exploits. When the legionary structure was functioning properly, then the soldiers could look on an officer in an almost fraternal way as one of their own number for whom they would do anything.[1] In the absence of such a bond, however, there was no incentive to fight to the best of one's ability and the unprompted pursuit of plunder was not considered the disgrace that it might have been in a healthy army. Once such behaviour patterns had become entrenched, they were difficult to reverse, which meant that even the charismatic Antonius Primus still could not control his men with complete success.

The pervasive mistrust of immediate officers also resulted in the soldiers investing an excessive amount of emotional energy at the highest level of the command structure in the emperors themselves, even if they were unworthy of such affection or not known personally to many of their men. This created an imbalance. If any one of the emperors had participated more directly in the action, rather than leaving the business of war to subordinates, then the civil war might have ended much sooner than it did. Tacitus suggests that Galba, Otho, Vitellius and even Vespasian are each, in their own way, misguided characters who do not themselves fully understand the dynamics at work in the armies under their command. Galba could so easily have stayed alive if he had not idealised his soldiers and thus underestimated the importance of the donative. Otho's decision to stay away from the fighting showed no awareness of his central position in the affections of his soldiers nor of the devastating effect his absence would have on their morale. Vitellius could have galvanised his soldiers and ended the war by acting quickly to confront the Flavian challenge. Even Vespasian's stubborn insistence on a corn-blockade might have ultimately led his soldiers to abandon him, if Antonius Primus had not improvised a more active campaign in the emperor's name.

In each case Tacitus has suggested a mismatch between the emperor as supreme commander-in-chief and the needs of the armies themselves. In itself this was not necessarily a recipe for disaster, but in the absence of committed army officers who could act as a buffer zone, each emperor's unwillingness to participate directly in the action had a detrimental effect on the ability of their armies to perform decisively. Not one of Tacitus' emperors seems to have had the capacity to take control of the flawed military hierarchy and to terminate the war. The fact that the conflict ended when it did was perhaps largely a matter of luck that no other imperial challenger materialised to step into the dead Vitellius' shoes. Tacitus' own explanation of why the civil war happened is, if anything, much more disturbing than Plutarch's formulation. Whereas Plutarch's notion of spontaneous collective madness partly absolves society of blame for such self-destructive behaviour, Tacitus presents us with a much more rational picture of a civil war which gradually gains momentum, but which could have potentially ended much earlier if the right leader had intervened. In AD 98 that role was played by Trajan, but Tacitus has crafted the narratives of the *Histories* and the *Annals* as a pair which, particularly when considered together, show how vulnerable the imperial structure was to self-destructive forces generated by the disastrous combination of flawed emperors and frustrated armies.

Notes

Preface

1. For an introduction to the history of the civil wars, see T.E.J. Wiedemann, 'From Nero to Vespasian', 256-82 in A.K. Bowman, E. Champlin and A.W. Lintott (eds), *Cambridge Ancient History Vol. X* (Cambridge 1996; 2nd edition), K. Wellesley, *The Long Year* AD 69 (Bristol 1989. Second edition) and P.A.L. Greenhalgh, *The Year of the Four Emperors* (London 1975).

2. C.S. Kraus and A.J. Woodman, *Latin Historians* (*Greece and Rome New Surveys in the Classics* 27, 1997) 2.

3. A. Lintott, 'Cassius Dio and the History of the Late Republic', *ANRW* 2.34.3 (1997) 2497-2523 esp. 2498.

4. A.J. Woodman, *Rhetoric in Classical Historiography* (London and Sydney 1988).

5. This uneven focus is changing. E. Keitel and M.G. Morgan have redressed the balance with articles concentrating exclusively on the *Histories*. C. Damon is preparing a new commentary on *Histories* 1 for the Cambridge series.

Introduction

1. Cf. D.A. Russell, 'On Reading Plutarch's Lives', *G&R* 13 (1966) 139-54 esp. 145.

2. See G. Rudé, *The Crowd in History 1730-1848* (London, New York, Sydney 1964) 3. G. Le Bon, *The Crowd: A Study of the Popular Mind* (London 1896) proved a particularly influential work in widening the debate about crowd psychology. M. Harrison, *Crowds and History: Mass Phenomena in English Towns, 1790-1835* (Cambridge 1988) 3-46 offers a useful overview of scholarly debate about the role of the crowd in history.

3. J.T. Johnson, *Ideology, Reason and the Limitations of War: Religious and Secular Concepts 1200-1740* (Princeton 1975) 26, and J.T. Johnson, *Just War Tradition and the Restraint of War: A Moral and Historical Inquiry* (Princeton 1981). C. von Clausewitz, *On War* (Harmondsworth 1982) 101, is more cynical: war is simply 'an act of force to compel our enemy to do our will'. This work was originally published in 1832. On the 'just war' in the ancient world, see P.A. Brunt, *Roman Imperial Themes* (Oxford 1990) 305-8. A. Feldherr, *Spectacle and Society in Livy's History* (Berkeley and Los Angeles 1988) 125-6 discusses the undercutting of the 'just war' theory at Livy 1.23.7.

4. See J. Henderson, 'Lucan / The Word at War', *Ramus* 16 (1987) 150 on the likeness of the civil war opponent.

5. See further P. Vaughn, '*Hostes Rei Publicae*: Images of the Enemy in Republican Literature' Ph.D. thesis (Berkeley 1997). Cf. S. Orwell and I. Angus (eds), *The Collected Essays, Journalism and Letters of George Orwell* (New York

1968) vol. 3, 151-2 for Orwell's view that the bombings of World War II for the first time shattered 'the immunity of civilians, one of the things that have made war possible'. Yet the assumption that civilians had been immune from the horrors of war in the past is not entirely accurate, even if the scale of civilian involvement in World War II was unprecedented.

6. C. Bandera, 'Sacrificial Levels in Virgil's *Aeneid*', *Arethusa* 14 (1981) 217-39 and R.O.A.M. Lyne, 'Vergil and the Politics of War', *CQ* 33 (1983) 188-203 [= S.J. Harrison, *Oxford Readings in Vergil's Aeneid* (Oxford 1990) 316-38].

7. Cf. P.S. Derow, 'Herodotus Readings', *Classics Ireland* 2 (1997) 29-51 esp. 37-8, C.B.R. Pelling, 'East is East and West is West. Or Are They? National Stereotypes in Herodotus', *Histos* 1 (1997) and C. Dewald, 'Wanton Kings, Pickled Heroes and Gnomic Founding Fathers: Strategies of Meaning at the End of Herodotus's *Histories*', 62-82 esp. 79, in D.H. Roberts, F.M. Dunn, and D.P. Fowler, *Classical Closure* (Princeton 1997).

8. See M. Lowrie, *Horace's Narrative Odes* (Oxford 1997) 149 for discussion of the substitution of foreign for civil war in Horace *Odes* 1.37: 'Instead of two rational male aristocrats, the figure of Cleopatra allows a more clear-cut opposition: male versus female, Roman versus Egyptian, rational versus irrational, civilised versus barbarian.' Lowrie rightly draws attention to the disintegration of these comforting dichotomies as *Odes* 1.37 progresses. On Horace's relationship with Augustus see P. White, *Promised Verse: Poets in the Society of Augustan Rome* (Cambridge Mass. and London England 1997) 113-17.

9. M. Walzer, *Just and Unjust Wars: A Moral Argument with Historical Illustrations* (Harmondsworth, England 1980) 96.

1. Images of Leaders and Armies

1. See C. Hammond, 'Narrative Explanation and the Roman Military Character', D. Phil. thesis (Oxford 1993) 100 and J.M. Carter, *Julius Caesar: The Civil War Books I and II* (Warminster 1991) 19. On Caesarian propaganda see K. Barwick, *Caesars Bellum Civile: Tendenz, Abfassungszeit und Stil* (Leipzig 1951), J.H. Collins, 'Propaganda, Ethics and Psychological Assumptions in Caesar's Writings' diss. (Frankfurt a.Maine 1952), A. La Penna, 'Tendenze e Arte del *Bellum Civile* di Cesare', *Maia* 5 (1952) 191-233, J.H. Collins, 'On the Date and Interpretation of the *Bellum Civile*', *AJP* 80 (1959) 113-32, M. Rambaud, *L'art de la déformation historique dans les commentaires de César* (Paris 1966), J.H. Collins, 'Caesar as Political Propagandist', *ANRW* 1.1 (1972) 922-66, and B. Levick, 'The Veneti Revisited: C.E. Stevens and the Tradition on Caesar the Propagandist', in K. Welch and A. Powell (eds), *Julius Caesar as Artful Reporter: The War Commentaries as Political Instruments* (London and Swansea 1998) 61-83.

2. E. Gabba, *Republican Rome, the Army and the Allies* trans. P.J. Cuff (Oxford 1976) 20-69 [= *Athenaeum* 29 (1951) 171-272].

3. For the Placentia mutiny see Dio 41.27-35 and Appian *BC* 2.47.191-2.48.199. J.H. Collins, 'Propaganda, Ethics and Psychological Assumptions in Caesar's Writings' diss. (Frankfurt am Main 1952) 118, raises the possibility that the omission is the result of a lacuna, but this seems unlikely.

4. Cf. E. Fantham, 'Caesar and the Mutiny: Lucan's Reshaping of the Historical Tradition in *De Bello Civili* 5.237-373', *CP* 80 (1985) 119-31 esp.

123-4 on Lucan redeploying Caesar's speech (*BC* 1.7) in his version of the Placentia mutiny.

5. See K. Welch, 'Caesar and his Officers in the Gallic War Commentaries', in K. Welch and A. Powell (eds), *Julius Caesar as Artful Reporter: The War Commentaries as Political Instruments* (London and Swansea 1998) 85-110: 'The occurrence of named officers and the narrative space given to them in the seven Caesarian books of the Gallic Wars varies dramatically' (90). This is also true of the portrayal of officers in the *BC*.

6. M. Foucault, 'The Subject and Power', 222 in H.L. Dreyfuss and P. Rabinow (eds), *Michel Foucault: Beyond Structuralism and Hermeneutics* 2nd edition (Chicago 1983) 208-26.

7. Collective remorse in an army is not always so fruitful. Cf. Tacitus *Annals* 1.49 for the massacre which took place after Germanicus instructs Caecina to punish the ringleaders of the mutiny in Germany. Yet M.F. Williams, 'Four Mutinies: Tacitus *Annals* 1.16-30; 1.31-49 and Ammianus Marcellinus *Res Gestae* 20.4.9-20.5.7; 24.3.1-8', *Phoenix* 51 (1997) 44-74 interprets this incident positively: 'Germanicus achieves what he desires by getting the soldiers to discipline themselves voluntarily and he keeps his hands clean.'

8. A. Powell, 'Julius Caesar and the Presentation of Massacre', 111-37 in K. Welch and A. Powell (eds), *Julius Caesar as Artful Reporter: The War Commentaries as Political Instruments* (London 1998) notes how Caesar treats Curio's failings 'with understanding', partly because Curio was 'Caesar's most spectacular recruit and protégé' (121).

9. See further T.R. Stevenson, 'The Ideal Benefactor and the Father Analogy in Greek and Roman Thought', *CQ* 42 (1992) 421-36. Pliny *HN* 7.25.92 offers an alternative, critical view of Caesar: 'For I would not regard it as glorious that besides his victories in civil war, he killed 1,192,000 people in his battles, which was a great injury to the human race (even if it was unavoidable), as he himself admitted it to be by not publishing the casualties of the civil wars.'

10. Cf. R. Syme, *The Roman Revolution* (Oxford 1939) 70, M. Harmand, *L'armée et le soldat à Rome de 107 à 50 avant notre ère* (Paris 1967) 453, B. Dobson, 'The Significance of the Centurion and Primipilaris in the Roman Army and Administration', *ANRW* 2.1 (1974) 392-434 and Z. Yavetz, *Julius Caesar and his Public Image* (London 1983) 162-3.

11. Cf. Appian *BC* 2.60.249, Valerius Maximus 3.2.23, Plutarch *Caesar* 16.2-3, Suetonius *Divus Iulius* 68.4, Florus 2.13.40 and Lucan *Phar.* 6.140-262. See further M. Leigh, *Lucan: Spectacle and Engagement* (Oxford 1997) 158-90.

12. Puleo is the reading in the *OCT*. J.M. Carter, *Julius Caesar: The Civil War Book III* (Warminster 1993) 191, restores 'Pullienus' as the proper name.

13. Lucan at *Pharsalia* 7.470-3 curses Crastinus for throwing the first lance of the battle. See further M. Leigh, *Lucan: Spectacle and Engagement* (Oxford 1997) 140-42, 192-3, 203-4 and 215-16 on the different versions of the Crastinus story.

14. K. Welch, 'Caesar and his Officers in the Gallic War Commentaries', 85-110 in K. Welch and A. Powell (eds), *Julius Caesar as Artful Reporter: The War Commentaries as Political Instruments* (London and Swansea 1998) notes that in the *BG* most centurions, however brave, remain 'names on a page with little or no personality' (90), and much the same is true in the *BC* apart from cases like Crastinus.

15. Caesar consistently spares his enemies whereas the Pompeians are depicted as exacting punishment: for Caesar's clemency, see *BC* 1.18.4, 1.23.3, 2.22.6, 2.32.8, 3.10.1, 3.11.4, and 3.27.2, and for vindictive Pompeians see

1.76.4, 2.44.2, 3.8.3, 3.14.3 and 3.28.2. Cf. Cicero *Marc.* 1.1, 4.12 and 6.18. For a discussion of Caesar's *clementia*, see J. Masters, *Poetry and Civil War in Lucan's Bellum Civile* (Cambridge 1992) 78-87 and J. Carter, *Julius Caesar: The Civil War Book III* (Warminster 1993) 217-18.

16. A. Lintott, 'Lucan and the History of the Civil War', *CQ* 45 (1971) 488-505 compares the two versions of the reconciliation in Caesar and Lucan on 490-1.

17. Cf. K. Bradley, *Slavery and Rebellion in the Roman World 140-70 BC* (Bloomington and London 1989) 53-5.

18. See L. Rawlings, 'Caesar's Portrayal of Gauls as Warriors', 171-92 in K. Welch and A. Powell (eds), *Julius Caesar as Artful Reporter: The War Commentaries as Political Instruments* (London and Swansea 1998), who notes Caesar's deployment of the Gallic *mobilitas et levitas animi* motif (174). For Gauls changing sides, see *BG* 7.38 and 7.54, and for doubtful Gallic loyalty see *BG* 1.42, 4.13.2 and 7.5.

19. For *nostri* see *BC* 1.64.1, 2.42.2, 3.37.6 and for *Pompeiani* see *BC* 1.15.5, 3.84.2. Cf. 'Afranians' (*BC* 1.54.1). For later deployment of the label *Pompeiani* see P. Grenade, 'Le mythe de Pompée et les Pompéiens sous les Césars', *REA* 52 (1950) 28-63. C. Hammond, review of J.M. Carter, *JRS* 82 (1992) 248-9 observes that Caesar never uses the term 'Caesarians' himself. J. Marincola, *Authority and Tradition in Ancient Historiography* (Cambridge 1997) 287-8 notes that usually *nostri* is 'not used by Roman authors when writing about civil war, where it might seem manifestly inappropriate'.

20. See Cassius Hemina, fragment 34 in *HRR* (Roman defeats in Spain). Cf. E. Rawson, 'The First Latin Annalists', *Latomus* 35 (1976) 689-717 = E. Rawson, *Roman Culture and Society* (Oxford 1991) 245-57.

21. On suggestive names, see A.J. Woodman and R.H. Martin, *The Annals of Tacitus Book 3* (Cambridge 1996) 491-3 and 381 (on another Bibulus).

22. J.M. Carter, *Julius Caesar: The Civil War Book III* (Warminster 1993) 166.

23. On internal and external focalisation, see G. Genette, *Narrative Discourse* trans. J.E. Lewin (Oxford 1980) esp. 189-98 and M. Bal, *Narratology: Introduction to the Theory of Narrative* trans. C. van Boheemen (Toronto 1985) 100-15. For the first sustained application of this theory to a classical text, see I.J.F. de Jong, *Narrators and Focalizers* (Amsterdam 1987).

24. For Shakespeare see see E. Schanzer, *Shakespeare's Appian: A Selection from the Tudor Translation of Appian's Civil Wars* (Liverpool 1956) and K. Muir, *The Sources of Shakespeare's Plays* (London 1977) 224-5, and for Karl Marx see G.E.M. De Ste. Croix, *The Class Struggle in the Ancient World* (London 1981) 24 and 208.

25. Cf. A. Gowing, *The Triumviral Narratives of Appian and Cassius Dio* (Ann Arbor Michigan 1993), reviewed by C.B.R. Pelling, *JRS* 84 (1994) 225-6, K. Brodersen, 'Appian und sein Werk', *ANRW* 2.34.1 (1993) 339-63, and M. Hose (below, n. 27) 142-355, reviewed by J.W. Rich, *CR* 46 (1996) 317-8. K. Brodersen is preparing an *OCT* and J.M. Carter has produced a new translation, *Appian: The Civil Wars* (Harmondsworth 1996), from which extracts in this section will be taken.

26. Appian uses the title *Emphulia* for this section of the work at *Prooimion* 14.

27. On Appian's readership, see A. Gowing, *The Triumviral Narratives of Appian and Cassius Dio* (Michigan 1993) 283-7 and M. Hose, *Erneuerung der Vergangenheit: Die Historiker im Imperium Romanum von Florus bis Cassius Dio* (Stuttgart and Leipzig 1994) 330-4. On the papyrus containing fragments of Herodotus and Appian discovered at Dura-Europus, which is suggestive about Appian's wide appeal, see C.B. Welles, 'Fragments of Herodotus and Appian from Dura', *TAPA* 70 (1939) 203-14 and T.F. Brunner, 'Two Papyri of Appian from Dura-Europus', *GRBS* 25 (1984) 171-5.

28. Fragment 19 in P. Viereck and A.G. Roos, *Appiani Historia Romana* rev. E. Gabba (Leipzig 1962). Cf. A. Gowing, *op. cit.* 14-16, M. Hose, *Erneuerung der Vergangenheit: die Historiker im Imperium Romanum von Florus bis Cassius Dio* (Stuttgart and Leipzig 1994) 142 and J. vanderLeest, 'Appian and the Writing of the Roman History', diss. (Toronto 1989) 10-12.

29. J.M. Carter, *Appian: The Civil Wars* (Harmondsworth 1996) xi.

30. On Polybius and pragmatic history see J. Marincola, *Authority and Tradition in Ancient Historiography* (Cambridge 1997) 24-5.

31. A. Gowing proposes on 78 that in *BC* 5.17 Appian 'fixes the blame squarely on the leaders', but this is difficult to endorse.

32. Cf. M.A. Speidel, 'Roman Army Pay Scales', *JRS* 82 (1992) 87-106. Under Augustus, the annual pay for a common legionary was 900 sestertii. On monetary equivalents, see C.B.R. Pelling, *Plutarch: Life of Antony* (Cambridge 1988) 119.

33. C. Hammond, 'Narrative Explanation and the Roman Military Character', D. Phil. thesis (Oxford 1993), notes that in the *BC* Caesar regularly portrays his *opponents* as winning loyalty by financial rewards to the soldiers (e.g. *BC* 1.56.2, *BC* 3.31.4).

34. J.B. Campbell, *The Emperor and the Roman Army 31 BC–AD 235* (Oxford 1984) 166 notes 'the tradition of exorbitant donatives established in the late Republic'.

35. Beast imagery could be used to suggest vulnerability (e.g. Livy 9.5.7, of Romans or Caesar *BC* 1.84.4, of the Pompeians: cf. A.J. Woodman, *Velleius Paterculus: The Tiberian Narrative (2.94-131)* (Cambridge 1977) 202 for the 'slaughtering like animals' motif) or ferocity (e.g. Dionysius of Halicarnassus *Roman Antiquities* 16.2.3, of Samnites). Gauls and Germans are often described as beasts (Livy 7.10.3, 7.24.5, 8.14.9, 10.10.11, 38.17.15-16, Dionysius of Halicarnassus 14.10.1, Velleius Paterculus 2.95.2 and 2.106.2. See further *TLL* II 1862.42-1863.12 and T.E.J. Wiedemann, 'Between Men and Beasts: Barbarians in Ammianus Marcellinus' in I.S. Moxon, J.D. Smart and A.J. Woodman (eds), *Past Perspectives: Studies in Greek and Roman Historical Writing* (Cambridge 1986) 189-201.)

36. On Appian *BC* 2, see N.I. Barbu, *Les sources et l'originalité d'Appien dans la deuxième livre des Guerres Civiles* (Paris 1934). E. Gabba, *Appiano e la Storia delle Guerre Civili* (Florence 1956) 213 and 219, believed that Appian derived much material from Asinius Pollio's lost *History*. Cf. E. Badian, 'Appian and Asinius Pollio', *CR* 8 (1958) 159-62, who challenged this assertion, A.B. Bosworth, 'Asinius Pollio and Augustus', *Historia* 21 (1972) 441-73, C.B.R. Pelling, 'Plutarch's Method of Work in the Roman Lives' *JRS* 99 (1979) 73-96 esp. 84 on Pollio, and A. Gowing, 'Appian and Cassius' Speech before Philippi (*BC* 4.90-100)', *Phoenix* 44 (1990) 158-81 esp. 159-61. For a recent survey, see M. Hose, *Erneuerung der Vergangenheit: Die Historiker im Imperium Romanum von Florus bis Cassius Dio* (Stuttgart and Leipzig 1994) 259-65.

37. A. Gowing, *The Triumviral Narratives of Appian and Cassius Dio* (Ann Arbor Michigan 1993) 78.

38. For a useful discussion of accounts of Pharsalus, see C. Bannon, *The Brothers of Romulus: Fraternal Pietas in Roman Law, Literature and Society* (Princeton 1997) 152-6.

39. S.P. Oakley, *A Commentary on Livy Books VI-X*, Vol. 2 (Oxford 1998) 435 suggests that Livy may have bent the truth for dramatic effect: 'Given the Roman method of recruiting and filling up a legion, the idea that Romans and Latins served in the same units is most improbable; indeed, even in the second century, Latins did not serve in the Roman legions.'

40. E. Lussu, *Sardinian Brigade: A Memoir of World War I* trans. M. Rawson (New York 1970) 166.

41. Cf. J.G. Gray, *The Warriors: Reflections on Men in Battle* (New York 1967) ch. 5 'Images of the Enemy'.

42. N. Monsarrat, *The Cruel Sea* (Harmondsworth 1951) 237.

43. Yet there is evidence that Pompey did not have equal faith in all his soldiers: cf. Cicero *Att.* 8.12A.3, 8.12C.4 and 8.12D.

44. On Appian's device of 'heaven-sent madness', see B. Goldmann, *Einheitlichkeit und Eigenständigkeit der Historia Romana des Appian* (Hildesheim 1988) 33-44.

45. *Fortuna* also plays a role in Caesar's account of the civil war, but it is less prominent than in Appian and can favour or hamper both sides equally. As J. Carter, *Julius Caesar: The Civil War Book III* (Warminster 1993), argues on 196, 'to make luck responsible for his success would undercut his presentation of himself as omnicompetent'. See further I. Kajanto, 'Fortuna', *ANRW* 2.17.1 (1981) 502-58 especially 537-8.

46. See A. Gowing, *The Triumviral Narratives of Appian and Cassius Dio* (Ann Arbor, Michigan 1993) 34 and M. Hose, *Erneuerung der Vergangenheit: Die Historiker im Imperium Romanum von Florus bis Cassius Dio* (Stuttgart and Leipzig 1994) 363. Cf. M.J. Moscovich, 'Historical Compression in Cassius Dio's Account of the Second Century BC', *Ancient World* 8 (1983) 137-43.

47. L. De Blois, 'Volk und Soldaten bei Cassius Dio', *ANRW* 2.34.3 (1997) 2650-76 especially 2663 stresses the ideological reasons for Dio's negative portrait of the soldiers. Cf. T.D. Barnes, 'The Composition of Cassius Dio's *Roman History*', *Phoenix* 38 (1984) 240-55 especially 244.

48. Cf. V. Fadinger, *Die Begrundung des Principats. Quellenkritische und Staatsrechtliche Untersuchungen zu Cassius Dio und der Parallelüberlieferung* (Berlin 1969) 77 and A.V. von Stekelenburg, 'Lucan and Cassius Dio as Heirs to Livy: The Speech of Julius Caesar at Placentia', *Acta Classica* 19 (1976) 43-57 esp. 54-5.

49. Cf. J.W. Rich, 'Dio on Augustus' 86-110 esp. 95 in A. Cameron (ed.), *History as Text* (London 1989).

50. Cf. B. Manuwald, *Cassius Dio und Augustus* (Wiesbaden 1979) 282, reviewed by C.B.R. Pelling, *Gnomon* 55 (1983) 221-6. Manuwald prefers to attribute this Thucydidean trait to the sources rather than to Dio himself. On Dio's literary style and tastes see F. Millar, *A Study of Cassius Dio* (Oxford 1964) 40ff. On the damage done to public interests by private concerns see Sallust *Jug.* 25.3 and Livy 2.30.2.

51. See A. Feldherr, *Spectacle and Society in Livy's History* (Berkeley, Los Angeles, London 1998) 120 on Livian *exempla* which teach 'the subordination of the smaller unit in the interests of the larger state'.

52. This division of Rome symbolically reverses the fusion of two peoples under Romulus and Titus Tatius. See Livy 1.13.5.

53. M. Walzer, *Just and Unjust Wars: A Moral Argument with Historical Illustrations* (Harmondsworth, England 1980) 169, who supports his generalisation with a reference to E. Skrjabina, *Siege and Survival: The Odyssey of a Leningrader* (Carbonville, Illinois 1971).

54. It is a commonplace in civil conflict for one side to accuse the other of inviting foreigners, slaves or gladiators into the struggle. Cf. Dio 75.2.5 on Septimius Severus recruiting from the edges of the empire, Cicero *Cat.* 2.4.7 and *Cat.* 2.8.17-2.10.23, *Att.* 7.14.2 and 8.2.1 and Julius Caesar *BC* 1.14.4, 1.24.2 and 3.4.

55. A point noted by A.V. van Stekelenburg, 'Lucan and Cassius Dio as Heirs to Livy: The Speech of Julius Caesar at Placentia', *Acta Classica* 19 (1976) 44. Cf. Tacitus' fondness for the Livian Scipio's speech as a model, noted by R. Syme, *Tacitus* (Oxford 1958) 685 and 733. There is less common ground between Dio's version of the speech and Polybius' rendering (11.28-9). On Scipio's mutinous soldiers see S.G. Chrissanthos, 'Scipio and the Mutiny at Sucro, 206 BC', *Historia* 46.2 (1997) 172-84.

56. L. De Blois, 'Volk und Soldaten bei Cassius Dio', *ANRW* 34.3 (1997) 2650-76 on 2663 calls the language of this speech almost Platonic.

57. See F. Millar, 'Some Speeches in Dio', *MH* 18 (1961) 11-22, esp. 14-15 and A. Gowing, *The Triumviral Narratives of Appian and Cassius Dio* (Ann Arbor Michigan 1993) 244.

58. C.B.R. Pelling, 'Biographical History? Cassius Dio on the Early Principate' 117-44 in M.J. Edwards and S. Swain, *Portraits: Biographical Representation in the Greek and Latin Literature of the Roman Empire* (Oxford 1997) praises Dio's characterisation in the Republican books: 'Time and again we see the same thing: a real interest in psychological reconstruction, which surfaces particularly in a tendency to assign motives; and a real intelligence in carrying that through' (137).

2. The Galbians and Othonians

1. Cf. R.E. Ash, 'Severed Heads: Individual Portraits and Irrational Forces in Plutarch's *Galba* and *Otho*', 189-214 in J.M. Mossman (ed.), *Plutarch and his Intellectual World* (London 1997). On Cluvius Rufus as a possible source for this concept of irrational forces, see F.R.B. Godolphin, 'The Source of Plutarch's Thesis in the Lives of *Galba* and *Otho*', *AJP* 56 (1935) 324-8, G.B. Townend, 'Cluvius Rufus and the *Histories* of Tacitus', *AJP* 85 (1964) 337-77 and D. Wardle, 'Cluvius Rufus and Suetonius', *Hermes* 120 (1992) 466-82.

2. Cf. R. Syme, *Tacitus* (Oxford 1958) 10-18 on Nerva's adoption of Trajan on the Capitol (Dio 68.3.3 and Pliny *Pan.* 8.1).

3. Cf. Livy 1.29.3 on the citizens of Alba, forced by the Romans to abandon their city: 'sad silence and quiet grief (*silentium triste ac tacita maestitia*) overwhelmed their spirits'. On Livy's arresting use of silence see P.G. Walsh, 'The Literary Techniques of Livy', *RhM* 97 (1954) 97-114 and R.M. Ogilvie, *A Commentary on Livy Books 1-5* (Oxford 1965) 486. A. Feldherr, *Spectacle and Society in Livy's History* (Berkeley, Los Angeles, London 1998) 124 note 34 notes that this silence (1.29.3) forges a link with Livy's description of the sack of Rome (5.46.1). On silence in Tacitus, see R. Strocchio, *I Significati del Silenzio nell'Opera di Tacito* (Turin 1992).

4. For a general comparison of Plutarch and Suetonius, see L. Braun, 'Galba und Otho bei Plutarch und Sueton', *Hermes* 120 (1992) 90-102.

5. Cf. J.B. Campbell, *The Emperor and the Roman Army, 31 BC–AD 235* (Oxford 1984) 32-59.

6. Tacitus, like Livy, is sensitive to collective silence and its nuances: see *Histories* 1.40.1 (with R.H. Husband, 'Galba's Assassination and the Indifferent Citizen', *CP* 10 (1915) 321-5), 1.55.1 and 3.67.2. Cf. P. Plass, *Wit and the Writing of History* (Madison, Wisconsin 1988) 144-5.

7. Fire language is used elsewhere of civil war. Cf. Augustus *Res Gestae* 34.1: 'When I had extinguished the civil war'.

8. G.E.F. Chilver, *A Historical Commentary on Tacitus' Histories I and II* (Oxford 1979) 86 remarks: 'The normal *sportula*, even in Domitian's time, was 25 *asses*, Martial 1.59 etc.; so 100 HS (= 400 *asses*) was an enormous bribe.' Yet there are parallels. Cf. [Caesar] *Bell. Alex.* 48.2 and 52.1, and *Bell. Afr.* 87.7.

9. Cf. P. Plass, *Wit and the Writing of History* (Madison, Wisconsin 1988) 60 on the *para prosdokian* pattern of this sentence.

10. On the Golden Milestone, see C. Nicolet, *Space, Geography and Politics in the Early Roman Empire* (Ann Arbor, Michigan 1991) 103 and C. Edwards, *Writing Rome* (Cambridge 1996) 98.

11. Sword-waving is a recurrent motif in the climax of Plutarch's narrative: see *Galba* 25.4, 25.8, 26.2, 26.7, 26.10 and 27.9. Cf. Plutarch *Caesar* 67.3.

12. F. Spaltenstein, *Commentaire des Punica de Silius Italicus (Livres 9 à 17)* Vol. 2 (Lausanne 1990) 206 notes that this simile is Silius' invention. Crowds are often compared with water or the sea: cf. Homer *Iliad* 2.144-6, Demosthenes 19.136, Polybius 11.29.9 and 21.31.9, Appian *BC* 3.12.40, Livy 38.10.5 and Virgil *Aeneid* 1.148-53 and 7.528-30.

13. Cf. Ammianus Marcellinus 20.4.1-22, Julian's acclamation by the soldiers. Concerted military action is the keynote from the very first moment when the soldiers function spontaneously as a unit.

14. Plutarch refers simply to the 'many' (*Galba* 27.9), who falsely presented claims before Otho. Cf. Plutarch *Caesar* 67.4 for a clearer distinction between true and false murderers.

15. L.V. Smith, *Between Mutiny and Obedience* (Princeton 1994) 186.

16. Cf. C.A. Powell, '*Deum Ira, Hominum Rabies*', *Latomus* 31 (1972) 833-48.

17. For further bonding with soldiers see Sallust *Jug.* 96.2 on Sulla. Cf. G.E.F. Chilver, *A Historical Commentary on Tacitus' Histories I and II* (Oxford 1979) 85, who proposes that Tacitus mistakes these troops on the march from Spain for the mutinous praetorians.

18. Tacitus says (1.82.1) that Julius Martialis, a tribune, and Vitellius Saturninus, a legionary prefect, are wounded rather than killed.

19. For other dramatic attempts by a commander to stop a mutiny, see Tacitus *Annals* 1.35.4 (with M.F. Williams, 'Four Mutinies: Tacitus *Annals* 1.16-30; 1.31-49 and Ammianus Marcellinus *Res Gestae* 20.4.9-20.5.7; 24.3.1-8', *Phoenix* 51 (1997) 53), Justin *Epitome* 12.11.7-8 and Plutarch *Pomp.* 13.4. Cf. C.B.R. Pelling, 'Tacitus and Germanicus' 59-85 in A.J. Woodman and T.J. Luce (eds), *Tacitus and the Tacitean Tradition* (Princeton 1993) n. 8 (62-3).

20. Cf. G. Rudé, *The Crowd in History: 1730-1848* (London, New York and Sydney 1964) 247: 'a distinction must be made among leaders operating from outside the crowd, those drawn from within the crowd itself, and those acting (or appearing to act) as intermediaries between the two.' Licinius Proculus and Plotius Firmus fall into the second and third categories, while Otho falls into the first category.

21. Antonius Novellus and Suedius Clemens do not appear again, but Aemilius Pacensis, against whom the soldiers' anger is most acute, dies bravely on the Capitol as he resists the Vitellians on behalf of the Flavians (3.73.2).

22. In this respect, his name may be significant. Cf. Julius Clemens, the benign centurion at *Annals* 1.23.4, 1.26.1 and 1.28.3.

23. On this phrase, see R.E. Ash, 'Warped Intertextualities: Naevius and Sallust at Tacitus *Histories* 2.12.2', *Histos* 1 (1997).

24. Cf. Sallust *Histories* fragment 1.14 (B. Maurenbrecher) 'the gates were open, the fields were filled with farmers (*apertae portae, repleta arva cultoribus)'*. E. Dench, *From Barbarians to New Men* (Oxford 1995) notes (113): 'Within Roman ideology of the late Republic and early Empire, small farmers are of particular moral importance: they live staunch lives away from corrupting contemporary influences and make excellent soldiers (Cato *De Agricultura* Preface 2, Horace *Odes* 3.6.37-8, Livy 2.26.9 and Cicero *Off.* 1.150-1 and 2.89).'

25. See A. Vasaly, *Representations: Images of the World in Ciceronian Oratory* (Berkeley and Los Angeles 1993) 212-17.

26. Ancient writers enjoyed the irony of agriculture abandoned for warfare: see Ovid *Fasti* 1.697-700, Lucan *Phar.* 5.403-4, Virgil *Georgics* 1.506-8 and *Aeneid* 7.635-6. See further R.O.A.M. Lyne, ' *"Scilicet et tempus veniet ..."* Virgil *Georgics* 1.463-514', 47-66 in A.J. Woodman and D. West (eds), *Quality and Pleasure in Roman Poetry* (Cambridge 1974).

27. Cf. Dio 64.9.3: 'Even for this behaviour the men received money, since it was assumed that they had acted from loyalty towards Otho.'

28. W. Schuller, 'Soldaten und Befehlshaber in Caesars *Bellum Civile'* 189-99 in I. Malkin and Z.W. Rubinstein (eds), *Leaders and Masses in the Roman World* (Leiden, New York and Cologne 1995), connects this phenomenon to the fact that 'shame *(pudor)'* only functions during daylight. Cf. Caesar *BC* 1.21 and 2.31.7.

29. Both Tacitus and Virgil choose the masculine form of *dies*. E. Fraenkel, 'Das Geschlecht von *Dies*', *Glotta* 8 (1917) 24-68 = *Kleine Beiträge zur Klassischen Philologie* I (Rome 1964) 27-72, argues that in classical prose only the masculine form of *dies* can sharply fix a single day. On the gender of *dies* in Latin historians, see A.J. Woodman and R.H. Martin, *The Annals of Tacitus Book 3* (Cambridge 1996) 128.

30. Dio-Xiphilinus says that Otho sent his troops into battle 'under several generals' (64.10.1), which caused disaster, while Dio-Zonaras explains that 'he was defeated because of the many commanders rather than through weakness' (64.10.1). Yet the problem is presented as logistical rather than as the result of mistrust between ranks. Dio-Zonaras says that the commanders and soldiers actually agree with one another and all despise Otho's decision to withdraw as 'cowardice' (64.10.2).

31. On the usual duties of tribunes and centurions, see B. Dobson, 'The Daily Life of the Soldier under the Principate', *ANRW* 2.1 (1974) 299-338 and A.K. Goldsworthy, *The Roman Army at War 100 BC–AD 200* (Oxford 1996) 13-16 (centurions) and 30 (tribunes).

32. Cf. Frontinus 4.1.17, Xenophon *Anabasis* 2.6.10, Valerius Maximus 2.7 *Ext.* 2 and Livy 8.35.

33. Tacitus also uses the verb *exosculari* at *Annals* 1.34.2, when the mutinous soldiers put Germanicus' hand into their mouths to feel their toothless gums 'on the pretext of kissing him *(per speciem exosculandi)'*. Plutarch notes that when Cato finished his military service, the soldiers kissed his hands, 'which Romans at that time did rarely and only to a few of their commanders' (*Cato Minor* 12.1).

34. See P. Herrmann, *Der römische Kaisereid* (Göttingen 1968) 50-89 and J.B. Campbell, *The Emperor and the Roman Army* (Oxford 1984) 19-32.

35. See A.J. Woodman and R.H. Martin, *The Annals of Tacitus Book 3* (Cambridge 1996) 352, A.J.L. van Hooff, *From Autothanasia to Suicide: Self-Killing in Classical Antiquity* (London 1990) 198 and 281-2, and P. Plass, *The Game of Death in Ancient Rome: Arena Sport and Political Suicide* (Madison, Wisconsin 1995) 145-6.

36. Pliny *Epistle* 3.16.10 portrays Arria, the wife of A. Caecina Paetus, as thinking that her daughter should kill herself in the event of her husband's death. Pliny *Epistle* 6.24 also describes the death of an unnamed woman whose husband is terminally ill: she ties herself to her husband and commits suicide by jumping into a lake. Tacitus *Annals* 15.64.2 preserves popular criticism of Seneca's wife Paulina, who did not in the end commit suicide with her husband.

37. H.S. Versnel, 'Destruction, *Devotio*, and Despair in a Situation of Anomy: The Mourning for Germanicus in Triple Perspective' 541-618 in *Perennitas: Studi in Onore di Angelo Brelich* (Rome 1980), refers to the 'suicidal contagion' amongst Otho's soldiers and compares 'the near ritual suicide of the American "People's Temple Sect" who followed their prophet Jim Jones in his death in November 1978 in Guyana' (573).

38. Cf. Plutarch *Caesar* 68, *Ant.* 14.6-8, *Brutus* 20, Cicero *Att.* 14.10.1, *Phil.* 1.2.5 and 2.36.91, Suetonius *Divus Iulius* 84.3-4, Dio 44.50 and 45.23.4, and Appian *BC* 2.146.607-2.148.618. On Caesar's funeral (which was a yardstick, as at Tacitus *Annals* 1.8.5), see S. Weinstock, *Divus Iulius* (Oxford 1971) 346-55. For a disturbing modern parallel, see C. McGreal, the *Guardian* 27 Nov. 1995, 1, on Colonel Komo, who was responsible for Ken Saro-Wiwa's execution in Nigeria: 'The Colonel says he wants to prevent the bodies being used to whip up unrest. He denies reports that acid was poured on the corpses to dispose of them more quickly.'

39. See J.M. Bourne, *Britain and the Great War 1914-1918* (London 1989) 222.

40. On the tendency for civil war soldiers to fight more for a man than a cause, see P. Jal, 'Le soldat des guerres civiles à Rome à la fin de la république et au debut de l'empire', *Pallas* 2 (1962) 12-23.

3. The Vitellians and Flavians

1. On Julius Vindex, see P.A. Brunt, 'The Revolt of Vindex and the Fall of Nero', *Latomus* 18 (1959) 531-59, J.B. Hainsworth, 'Verginius and Vindex', *Historia* 11 (1962), 86-96 and C.L. Murison, *Galba, Otho and Vitellius: Careers and Controversies* (Hildesheim 1993) 1-26.

2. F. Spaltenstein, *Commentaire des Punica de Silius Italicus (Livres 9 à 17)* Vol. 2 (Lausanne 1990) 375 finds the analogy overwhelming. Cf. Juvenal *Satires* 12.34 with J.E.B. Mayor, *Thirteen Satires of Juvenal* (London 1878) 227.

3. N. Horsfall, 'Numanus Remulus: Ethnography and Propaganda in *Aeneid* 9.598f ', *Latomus* 30 (1971) 1108-16 suggests that an interest in plunder was a common attribute of those constructed as barbarian.

4. Tacitus later uses the phrase 'storming cities (*expugnationes urbium*)' almost exclusively for Roman wars against foreign nations (*Annals* 4.32.1, 12.16.2, 13.39.2 and 15.6.4). *expugnatio* suggests destruction on a grand scale. Cf. Cicero's exaggerated sacking of a most ancient shrine (*illa expugnatio fani antiquissimi*) (*Verr.* 1.19.50).

5. Likewise, Lucan pairs *furor* and *rabies* in a civil war context, referring to Caesar (*Phar.* 7.551 and 10.72). On the Vitellian troops in general see R. Funari, 'Degradazione Morale e *Luxuria* nell'Esercito di Vitellio (Tacito *Hist.* II). Modelli e Sviluppi Narrativi', *Athenaeum* 80 (1992) 133-58.

6. See Plutarch *Camillus* 18.5, Livy 5.37.5-6 and Florus *Epitome* 1.7. Cf. J.F. Gardner, 'The "Gallic Menace" in Caesar's Propaganda', *G&R* 30 (1983) 181-9. B. Kremer, *Das Bild der Kelten bis in augusteische Zeit, Historia Einzelschriften* 88 (Stuttgart 1994) 62-8, traces the psychological repercussions of the original invasion for the Romans and examines the 'fear of Gauls (*metus Gallicus*)', as a literary theme, especially in Livy. On the historical aspects of the invasion see T.J. Cornell, *The Beginnings of Rome: Italy and Rome from the Bronze Age to the Punic Wars (c. 1000-264 BC)* (London and New York 1995) 313-18.

7. Cf. Cicero, who makes the Carthaginian Hannibal the paradigm for the Roman Caesar (*Att.* 7.11.1. Cf. Lucan *Phar.* 1.303-5).

8. Cf. Tacitus *Annals* 2.26 where Tiberius recalls Germanicus from Germany, proposing that they should leave the Cherusci to their internal squabbles. The subsequent internal foreign war (*Annals* 2.44-46) where Inguiomerus and Maroboduus fight with Arminius vindicates Tiberius' decision. See R.H. Martin and A.J. Woodman, *The Annals of Tacitus Book 3* (Cambridge 1996) 323-4, 329, 337 and 340 on barbarian dissension as a literary motif.

9. See M.G. Morgan, 'Two Omens in Tacitus' *Histories* 2.50.2 and 1.62.2-3', *RhM* 136 (1993) 321-9. For similar omens see Tacitus *Annals* 2.17.2 (victory is prefigured by eight eagles) and Silius Italicus *Pun.* 17.52-8 (eagles lead Scipio's fleet across the sea to Carthage). Note Dio 56.42 for the eagle which emerged from Augustus' pyre.

10. Cf. M.P. Speidel, *Eagle Bearer and Trumpeter, Rheinisches Landesmuseum* (Bonn 1967) 138 and J. Peddie, *The Roman War Machine* (Stroud, Gloucs. 1994) 31: 'On occasions, [the eagle] was featured with its neck strongly bent to the left, as if awaiting authority from Jupiter, with whom it was closely associated, to speed ahead of the marching columns to seek out and destroy their enemies and secure their advance.'

11. See G.E.F. Chilver, *A Historical Commentary on Tacitus' Histories I and II* (Oxford 1979) 130. In mentioning the place by periphrasis rather than by name, Tacitus highlights the spa's peaceful atmosphere. See R. Syme, *Tacitus* (Oxford 1958) 987.

12. M.G. Morgan, 'Rogues' March: Caecina and Valens in Tacitus *Histories* 1.61-70', *MH* 51 (1994) 103-25, argues against the view of G. Walser, 'Das Strafgericht über die Helvetier im Jahre 69 n.Chr.', *Schweiz. Zeitschrift für Geschichte* 4 (1954) 269-70 that the attack on the Helvetii was justified. Morgan views Tacitus' characterisation of Caecina and Valens at *Histories* 1.61-70 as being illuminated by evocations of Caesar's *BG*.

13. For the toga as the quintessential mark of peace see R.M. Ogilvie, *A Commentary on Livy Books 1-5* (Oxford 1970) on 4.10.8 and for the proverbial barbarity of trousers see Cicero *Fam.* 9.15.2, Virgil *Aeneid* 11.777, Ovid *Tristia* 4.6.47, Juvenal 2.169 and Suetonius *Divus Julius* 80.2. Gallia Narbonensis was once called Gallia Bracata (Trousered Gaul).

14. Cf. Plutarch *Otho* 6.6, for Caecina allegedly conversing with Roman officials by sign language. Yet Caecina was born at Vicetia near Verona, and Tacitus says that he was 'eloquent (<s>cito sermone)' (1.53.1). E.G. Hardy, *Plutarch's Lives of Galba and Otho* (London 1890) suggests that Plutarch's text is corrupt.

15. Silius Italicus achieves a similar effect when describing the mixed Carthaginian troops who attack the Romans at Lake Trasimene (5.192-7): there are Asturians, Libyans, Macae, Garamantians, Numidians, Cantabrians and Vascones. Cf. Caesar *BC* 3.4 and Appian *BC* 2.49.201-2 (Pompey's mixed troops) and [Caesar] *Bell. Afr.* 19.3-4 (Labienus' mixed troops).

16. See G.E.F. Chilver, *A Historical Commentary on Tacitus' Histories I and II* (Oxford 1979) 133. J.C. Mann, *Legionary Recruitment and Veteran Settlement during the Principate* (London 1983) 25-8 suggests that until AD 69 recruits for the German provinces were drawn from Italy, Gallia Narbonensis and Spain.

17. Cf. C.S. Kraus, ' "No Second Troy". Topoi and Refoundation in Livy Book

V', *TAPA* 124 (1994) 267-89, who argues that Livy describes the Gaulish sack of Rome with Romans playing Trojans and Gauls playing Greeks.

18. See G.E.F. Chilver, *A Historical Commentary on Tacitus' Histories I and II* (Oxford 1979) 179-80, for the possibility that Tacitus has assigned the 'Vitellian' Pannonians to the wrong army. If this ploy was deliberate, it indicates how important it was to the historian to characterise the Vitellian army as a heterogeneous group.

19. See Livy 7.12.11, 10.28.3 and 38.17.7, Tacitus *Germania* 4, Caesar *BG* 3.19.6, Florus *Epitome* 2.4.1, and Silius Italicus *Pun*. 4.311-12, 8.16 and 15.718.

20. This was perceived as habitual amongst barbarians. Cf. Frontinus *Strategemata* 3.17.1 and Livy 21.7.10. On rashness as a barbarian trait, see C.S. Kraus, *Livy Ab Urbe Condita Book VI* (Cambridge 1994) 166.

21. See R.W. Davies, *Service in the Roman Army* (London 1989) 187-206. On mixed and unmixed wine see J. Davidson, *Courtesans and Fishcakes* (London 1997) 158.

22. Cf. Virgil *Aeneid* 9.316-7 (Nisus' and Euryalus' raid on the Rutulian camp): 'They see bodies scattered everywhere over the grass in drunken sleep.' Virgil's graphic description of Rhoetus' death offers a powerful message against combining warfare and wine: 'Rhoetus belches forth his bloody life and as he dies, brings up wine mixed with blood' (*Aeneid* 9.349-50).

23. E. Hall, *Inventing the Barbarian: Greek Self-Definition through Tragedy* (Oxford 1989) 133-4, describes Thracian fondness for neat wine and gathers examples of this ethnic stereotype from tragedy. Cf. Plutarch *Moralia* 207A and *Alcibiades* 23.5.

24. Cf. T. Ashworth, *Trench Warfare 1914-1918. The Live and Let Live System* (London 1980) 24-38 on fraternisation.

25. Note that at Actium Cleopatra was the official enemy, rather than Antony: see R.A. Gurval, *Actium and Augustus* (Ann Arbor Michigan 1995) 32-33 and M. Reinhold, 'The Declaration of War against Cleopatra', *CJ* 77 (1981-82) 97-103. M. Bell, *In Harm's Way* (London 1995) 128, quotes a Bosnian woman who tries to explain the war to her daughter: 'It would have been a hundred times easier if we had been attacked by some foreign power. It is very hard to fight against people with whom you sat to drink coffee only yesterday.'

26. Their noise resembles that traditionally made by the Gauls in battle. Cf. Livy 5.37.8 and 21.28.1, Polybius 2.29.6 and Diodorus Siculus 5.30.3. See B. Kremer, *Das Bild der Kelten bis in augusteische Zeit*, *Historia Einzelschriften* 88 (Stuttgart 1994) 27-8. Yet Romans too could see the advantages of noise in a battle: Caesar *BC* 3.92.4.

27. Servius, commenting on *Aeneid* 7.664, notes two varieties of javelin: the Roman *pilum* (cf. Silius Italicus *Pun*. 4.550-1) and the Gaulish *gaesum* (cf. Virgil *Aeneid* 8.661-2).

28. Cf. Curtius Rufus 3.3.25 and Sallust *Jug*. 44.5. See J. Peddie, *The Roman War Machine* (Stroud, Gloucestershire 1994) 42-58 for baggage trains and J. Roth, 'The Size and Organisation of the Roman Imperial Legion', *Historia* 43 (1994) 346-62 for camp-followers.

29. D. Whitehead, 'Tacitus and the Loaded Alternative', *Latomus* 38 (1979) 474-95, categorises this as an example where 'no discernible emphasis' is placed on either alternative (480).

30. For barbarian hordes see Herodotus 4.172.1, Xenophon *Anabasis* 1.7.4, 3.2.16, Cicero *Arch*. 9.21 and *Marc*. 3.8, Livy 5.34.2 and 6.7.2, Velleius Paterculus 2.106.1, Tacitus *Germania* 35.2-3, *Annals* 2.21.1 and 14.34.2, and Dio

62.12.2. Cf. C.S. Kraus, *Livy Ab Urbe Condita Book VI* (Cambridge 1994) 131 (the 'one Roman as a match for many foreigners' motif).

31. Cf. R.F. Newbold, 'Nonverbal Communication in Tacitus and Ammianus', *AS* 21 (1990) 189-99.

32. Cf. A.J. Woodman, *Rhetoric in Classical Historiography* (London and Sydney 1988) 186-90 (Tacitus' metahistorical portrayal of Tiberius in *Annals* 4-6 as a foreign monarch making war on his own people).

33. Cf. D.G. Weingärtner, *Die Ägyptenreise des Germanicus* (Bonn 1969), E.D. Hunt, 'Travel, Tourism and Piety in the Roman Empire: A Context for the Beginning of Christian Pilgrimage', *EMC* 28 (1984) 391-417 esp. 394-5 and C. Edwards, *Writing Rome* (Cambridge 1996) 96-102.

34. Livy offers two explanations for the name Lacus Curtius (1.13.5 and 7.6). A. Feldherr, *Spectacle and Society in Livy's History* (Berkeley, Los Angeles, London 1998) 224-5 argues that Tacitus' emphasis on the Lacus Curtius deliberately reverses the heroism of M. Curtius, who bravely plunges to his death for the good of the state. See further A. Rouveret, 'Tacite et les Monuments', *ANRW* 2.33.4 (1991) 3070-72 and S.P. Oakley, *A Commentary on Livy Books VI-X* Vol. 2 (Oxford 1998) 96-102.

35. See Tacitus *Annals* 1.21.1, Sallust *Jug.* 44.5. Cf. T. Wiedemann, 'Sallust's *Jugurtha*: Concord, Discord and the Digressions', *G&R* 40 (1993) 48-57.

36. For unwieldy Gauls see Aulus Gellius *NA* 9.13, Caesar *BG* 2.30.4, Livy 7.10.10 and 7.26.1, and Tacitus *Annals* 3.46.3. For unwieldy Germans see Strabo 7.1.2, Caesar *BG* 1.39.1, Tacitus *Histories* 5.18.1 and Velleius Paterculus 2.106.1.

37. In Roman historiography, clothing and weapons often indicate national character. Huge weapons and animal skins are familiar barbarian attributes (Florus *Epitome* 1.4, Tacitus *Germania* 17 and *Annals* 14.35, Silius Italicus *Pun.* 8.570 and 15.685, Virgil *Aeneid* 8.661, Caesar *BG* 1.25.3, 3.28.3, 4.24.1, 4.33 and 5.16, Livy 21.8, Valerius Flaccus 6.162, Statius *Achilleid* 2.132 and Isidore *Etymologiae* 19.23.4). Cf. C.B.R. Pelling, review of G. Zecchini, *Cassio Dione e la Guerra Gallica di Cesare* (Milan 1978), *CR* 32 (1982) 146-8.

38. Cf. E. Hohl, 'Der Prätorianer-aufstand unter Otho', *Klio* 32 (1939) 307-24 n. 1 (323), J.C. Rolfe, 'Seasickness in Greek and Latin Writers', *AJP* 25 (1904) 192-200 and M.G. Morgan, 'Dispositions for Disaster: Tacitus *Histories* 1.31', *Eranos* 90 (1992) 55-62.

39. Rivers could certainly be enervating: Alexander fell ill after diving into the Cydnus to cool down (Curtius Rufus 3.5.1-9, Arrian *Anabasis* 2.4.7-11, Justin 11.8.5 and Valerius Maximus 3.8 *Ext.* 6). Traditionally, Roman troops were trained to swim (Vegetius *Mil.* 1.10), and it was the mark of a tough soldier to train by swimming in the Tiber (Horace *Odes* 3.7.27-8, 3.12.7, Tibullus 1.4.12, Plutarch *Cato Maior* 20.6 and Ovid *Ars Amatoria* 3.386). Failure to swim competently could cause disaster (Tacitus *Annals* 2.8.3 and Appian *BC* 5.104.432), but skilled swimmers were always useful in an army (Tacitus *Agricola* 18.4 and Dio 69.9.6). See M. Hassall, 'Batavians and the Roman Conquest of Britain', *Britannia* 1 (1970) 131-6 and M.P. Speidel, 'Swimming the Danube Under Hadrian's Eyes. A Feat of the Emperor's Batavian Horse Guard', *AS* 22 (1991) 277-82. Julius Caesar was a particularly good swimmer (Suetonius *Divus Julius* 57, Plutarch *Caesar* 49.8, Appian *BC* 2.90.377 and 2.150.628 and Cassius Dio 42.40), but Romans were often eclipsed by barbarians in this respect ([Caesar] *Bell. Alex.* 29.4).

40. Cf. J. Auberger, 'Quand la nage devint natation', *Latomus* 55 (1996) 48-62 and N. Horsfall, 'Numanus Remulus: Ethnography and Propaganda in *Aeneid*

9.598ff', *Latomus* 30 (1971) 1108-16. Cold baths induced toughness (Strabo 3.3.7, Seneca *Suasoriae* 2.5, Plutarch *Alcibiades* 23.3 and Caesar *BG* 6.21.5). Seneca calls himself a 'cold bath enthusiast' (*Epistle* 83.5), but charts his physical decline by his increasing intolerance for cold water.

41. Medical writers focus on varieties in physique and health as dictated by climate: see [Hippocrates] *Airs, Waters, Places* 24.

42. See Vitruvius 1.4.12, Cicero *De Oratore* 2.71.290, Strabo 5.3.4 and Silius Italicus *Pun.* 8.381. Cf. G.E.F. Chilver, *A Historical Commentary on Tacitus' Histories I and II* (Oxford 1979) 254. The Pomptine marshes were not drained until the 1930s despite many attempts (Suetonius *Divus Julius* 44.3, Plutarch *Caesar* 58.9, Dio 44.5.1 and 45.9.1, Cicero *Phil.* 5.3.7, and Tacitus *Annals* 15.42.2).

43. R. Sallares, *The Ecology of the Ancient Greek World* (London 1991) notes that the frequency of resistance to malaria tends to increase from north to south (238). On malaria, see M.D. Grmek, *Diseases in the Ancient Greek World* trans. M. and L. Muellner (Baltimore and London 1991) 275-83.

44. See M. De Ferdinandy, *Der Heilige Kaiser: Otto III und seine Ahnen* (Tübingen 1969) 490-2 and K. Görich, *Otto III. Romanus Saxonicus et Italicus* (Sigmaringen 1993) 134.

45. On ancient plagues see A.J. Woodman, *Rhetoric in Classical Historiography* (London and Sydney 1988) 38 and H. Zinsser, *Rats, Lice and History* (New York 1934) 77-110.

46. For Gaulish intolerance to hot climates see Livy 7.25.3, 10.28.4, 34.47.5, and 35.5.7. See B. Kremer, *Das Bild der Kelten bis in augusteische Zeit*, *Historia Einzelschriften* 88 (Stuttgart 1994) 33-4.

47. Cf. Tacitus *Germania* 4.3 (Germans who cannot bear thirst or heat). *Roman* soldiers are usually much hardier (Livy 5.6.4), although there are exceptions: Sallust *Histories* 3.96A (L.D. Reynolds) and Caesar *BC* 3.87.

48. Cf. Livy 6.1.11 and 22.50.1, Lucan *Phar.* 7.409, Aulus Gellius *NA* 5.17.2, Silius Italicus *Pun.* 2.33, 4.47, 4.150, 4.279, 5.109, 13.79 and esp. 6.555, where the Roman people recall Allia after the Lake Trasimene defeat. Gaius Caesar's death coincided with the anniversary of Allia as was noted on his cenotaph in Pisa (*CIL* 1421). See C.S. Kraus, *Livy Ab Urbe Condita Book VI* (Cambridge 1994) 93-4 and 250: 'Synchronism of notable events was popular.'

49. Cf. Suetonius *Vitellius* 11.2 who treats this as an isolated item, not as part of a sequence of literary echoes elaborating the collective Vitellian character. On the common source for Suetonius *Vitellius* 11.2 and Tacitus *Histories* 2.91.1, see A.J. Coale, *'Dies Alliensis'*, *TAPA* 102 (1971) 49-58. C.L. Murison, 'Some Vitellian Dates: An Exercise in Methodology', *TAPA* 109 (1979) 187-97 is critical of Coale's reconstruction of chronology.

50. See further C. Edwards, *Writing Rome* (Cambridge 1996) 79-82. Cf. O. Skutsch, 'The Fall of the Capitol Again: Tacitus *Annals* 11.23', *JRS* 68 (1978) 93-4 for an alternative tradition.

51. A.J. Woodman, 'Self-Imitation and the Substance of History: Tacitus *Annals* 1.61-5 and *Histories* 2.70, 5.14-15' 143-55 in A.J. Woodman and D. West (eds), *Creative Imitation and Latin Literature* (Cambridge 1979). Cf. S. Hinds, *Allusion and Intertext* (Cambridge 1998) 18-20, who suggests that while we as critics are now particularly sensitive to allusive artistry, we are at the same time susceptible 'to a kind of philological tunnel vision ... locking us more deeply into a poetic which shows little interest in (and some nervousness about) situating clearly defined allusions within broader dynamics of language and discourse' (20). One crucial factor here must be relevance. The level of authorial intention which we can plausibly detect in different segments of text will inevitably vary, but surely the more meaningful an intertext is, the more likely it is that an author intended us to notice that intertext.

52. See P.R. Hardie, *Virgil Aeneid IX* (Cambridge 1994) 154 on the Capitol as a symbol of perpetuity (Horace *Odes* 1.37.6-8 and 3.30.7-9 and Virgil *Aeneid* 9.448-9).

53. For discussion of Vocula's speech see E. Keitel, 'Speech and Narrative in *Histories* 4' 39-58 in T.J. Luce and A.J. Woodman (eds), *Tacitus and the Tacitean Tradition* (Princeton 1993). Cf. Dio, who makes Caesar suggest to his mutinous troops at Placentia that behaviour, not birth, determines whether one is 'Roman', and that invading Italy is the mark of a Celt (Dio 41.30).

54. As Chapman, an officer during World War I, wrote, 'If you start a man killing, you can't turn him off like an engine'. G. Chapman, *A Passionate Prodigality* (New York 1966) 100.

55. S.P. Oakley, 'Single Combat in the Roman Republic', *CQ* 35 (1985) 407. Cf. A.N. Sherwin-White, *Racial Prejudice in Imperial Rome* (Cambridge 1970) 57-8. For tall barbarians see Caesar *BG* 2.30.4, [Caesar] *Bell. Afr.* 40.5, Vegetius *Mil.* 1.1.3, Silius Italicus *Pun.* 5.110-13, Tacitus *Germania* 20.3, *Annals* 1.64.2, Dio 38.35 and Strabo *Geography* 7.1.2. Caligula, needing German prisoners for a triumph, found the tallest Gauls, made them grow their hair, dye it red, and learn German (Suetonius *Caligula* 47).

56. Cf. P. Knightley, *The First Casualty: The War Correspondent as Hero, Propagandist and Myth Maker* (London 1989) 29.

57. In general see M.H. Hansen, 'The Battle Exhortation in Ancient Historiography: Fact or Fiction?', *Historia* 42 (1993) 161-80, E. Keitel, 'Homeric Antecedents to the *Cohortatio* in the Ancient Historians', *CW* 80 (1987) 153-72 and S. Hornblower, *A Commentary on Thucydides Volume II Books IV-V.24* (Oxford 1996) 82-3.

58. The anaphora emphasises the soldiers' indignation. Cf. Tacitus *Histories* 1.38.1 (Otho's speech) and Livy 6.15.8 (Manlius' speech).

59. Traitors are rarely popular figures, even when their actions benefit the Roman cause (Onasander *Strat.* 38). Tacitus observes: 'indeed traitors are hated even by those whom they prefer' (*Annals* 1.58.1). Not resorting to treachery was perceived as a Roman trait (Livy 5.27.5-6, Tacitus *Annals* 2.88, and Ovid *Tristia* 1.5.39).

60. H.G. Seiler, *Die Masse bei Tacitus* (Erlangen 1936) 68-74, emphasises the importance of automatic obedience amongst soldiers in a well-disciplined army.

61. One commentator on World War I points to the boredom which this inflicts on soldiers: 'War is boring. Most of it consists of sitting around waiting for orders over which you have no control and whose purpose you do not understand.' See J.M. Bourne, *Britain and the Great War 1914-1918* (London 1989) 214.

62. Cf. L.V. Smith, *Between Mutiny and Obedience* (Princeton 1994) 17, on French soldiers from World War I, who learned to place their own limits on the violence ordered by their commanders.

63. So far I have used the term 'Vitellian soldiers' without reference to the individual legions within this larger group. Fabius Valens' initial force consisted mainly of the *V Alaudae* and Caecina's was the *XXI Rapax* (1.61). Both legions are seen in action in the first battle of Bedriacum at 2.43. At 2.100 Caecina leads a force to Cremona consisting of units from the *Prima Germanica*, *IV Macedonica*, *XV Primigenia* and *XVI Gallica*, together with the whole of the *V Alaudae* and the *XXII Primigenia*. At the rear followed the *XXI Rapax* and the *Prima Italica* (2.100.1). Tacitus lists the battle order at the second battle of Bedriacum as *IV Macedonica* (right front), *V Alaudae* and *XV Primigenia* with detachments from the *IX Hispana*, *II* and *XX Valeria Victrix* (centre), *XVI Gallica*, *XXII Primigenia* and *Prima Germanica* (left front); men from the *XXI Rapax* and the *Prima Italica* were scattered throughout (3.22.2). Perhaps the most loyal Vitellian legions are the *V Alaudae* and the *XV Primigenia*.

64. For noble soldiers being abandoned by their commanders, see Caesar *BC* 1.20 and Plutarch *Ant.* 68.4-5 (cf. C.B.R. Pelling, *Plutarch: Life of Antony* (Cambridge 1988) 288 for a less romantic interpretation of the soldiers' behaviour).

65. Cf. R.E. Ash, 'Waving the White Flag: Surrender Scenes at Livy 9.5-6 and Tacitus *Histories* 3.31 and 4.62', *G&R* 45 (1998) 27-44 on Tacitus' evocation of Livy's Caudine Forks capitulation, which makes the Vitellians appear highly Roman.

66. H.S. Versnel, *Triumphus: An Inquiry into the Origin, Development and Nature of the Roman Triumph* (Leiden 1970) 95 notes: 'The chained prisoners, the most prominent of whom were as a rule killed in the dungeon before the sacrifice was made to Iuppiter, walked right in front of the triumphal chariot.' Cf. Ovid *Ars Amatoria* 1.215 and *Tristia* 4.2.21-2. There may also be associations with a funeral procession: see Dio 56.34 and Suetonius *Divus Iulius* 84.4.

67. Tacitus uses the image of soldiers drawing their swords as a symbol of collective power, but not at Vespasian's acclamation (*Histories* 1.27.2, 1.41.1, 1.80.2, 2.88.2, 3.85.1, 4.50.1 and 5.22.2, and *Annals* 1.32.1 and 1.44.2).

68. Cf. Tacitus *Histories* 2.19, *Annals* 1.17.6 and 4.2.2, Vegetius *Mil.* 1.3 and Columella 1 *Praef.* 17 for the idea that the troops based in Rome were pampered.

69. C.A. Powell, *'Deum ira, hominum rabies'*, *Latomus* 31 (1972) 833-48, proposes that the prominence given by Tacitus and Plutarch to the theme of turbulent and irrational soldiers in AD 69 derives from a common source who, writing to meet the approval of a Flavian emperor, wanted to show the working of a divine plan in Vespasian's acquisition of imperial power.

70. The verb 'I grumble *(fremo)*' is associated with raging winds and seas (*TLL* 6.1, 1284-5) and with animals (*TLL* 6.1, 1281-2) or humans acting like beasts (*TLL* 6.1, 1282-4). See Virgil *Aeneid* 7.590 and 11.299 for its appearance in raging crowd similes. It also aligns the Flavian troops with the mutinous Othonians (1.80.2) and with the querulous Vitellians in Lower Germany (1.55.2).

71. Cf. Livy 6.41.11, 9.38.2 and 10.2.8. C.S. Kraus, *Livy Ab Urbe Condita Book VI* (Cambridge 1994) 326, notes that 'charm *(dulcedo)*' is restricted to Livy's first decade. See S.P. Oakley, *A Commentary on Livy Books VI-X: Introduction and Book VI* (Oxford 1997) 713 on the derogatory connotations of *dulcedo*.

72. The verb 'I stimulate *(stimulo)*' further suggests the Flavians' bestial nature. Cf. Lucan *Phar.* 7.567-70, Valerius Maximus 3.2.9 and Silius Italicus *Pun.* 4.439 and 16.367. It recalls Sallust *Cat.* 18.4 where poverty and evil character 'drove *(stimulabant)*' Piso to revolt.

73. On imperial portraits, see J.B. Campbell, *The Emperor and the Roman Army 31 BC–AD 235* (Oxford 1984) 96-9 and J.B. Campbell, *The Roman Army 31 BC–AD 337: A Sourcebook* (London 1994) 131-3.

74. On this legion see E.R. Birley, 'A Note on the Title *Gemina*', *JRS* 18 (1928) 56-60.

75. F.R.D. Goodyear, *Tacitus Annals Vol. 1* (Cambridge 1972) on *Annals*

1.64.4. J.N. Adams, 'The Vocabulary of the Speeches in Tacitus' Historical Works', *BICS* 20 (1973) 124-44 argues (135) that in the *Annals* Tacitus prefers the intransitive *imperito* in the narrative and the transitive *impero* in the speeches.

76. Cf. *OLD, adduco* 11b and *TLL* 1.599 (with Ovid *Fasti* 6.586) and *OLD, habena* 2 and *TLL* 6.2.2394.

77. See Suetonius *Divus Julius* 61, Horace *Satires* 2.1.17-20 and *Epistles* 1.10.38-41, Virgil *Aeneid* 1.62-3, 6.784-7 and 7.600, Silius Italicus *Pun.* 1.144, 1.240, 2.292, 3.226, 10.282, and 17.175, and Statius *Silvae* 1.1 and 5.1.37. Cf. F.M. Ahl, 'The Rider and the Horse: Politics and Power in Roman Poetry from Horace to Statius', *ANRW* 2.32.1 (1984) 40-110.

78. On the name see E.A. Thompson, *The Early Germans* (Oxford 1965) 85. On meaningful names see P. Sinclair, *Tacitus the Sententious Historian* (University Park, Pa. 1995) 30-1 and A.J. Woodman and R.H. Martin, *The Annals of Tacitus Book 3* (Cambridge 1996) 491-3, who offer thought-provoking examples and extensive bibliography.

79. K. Wellesley, *Tacitus: The Histories Book 3* (Sydney 1972) 88, renders *artes bonas* as ' "an honourable career", "a good character" (not "literary attainments" with Wodehouse)' and cites as a parallel Sallust *Cat.* 11.2. The phrase recurs in Vitellius' obituary (3.86.1).

80. The short-sighted Cassius, watching the battle of Philippi from a hill, infamously kills himself after mistaking Brutus' horsemen for the enemy (Plutarch *Brutus* 43). Military standards, usually made of silver rather than gold in order to be more visible (Pliny *HN* 33.19.58), could help. However, in a civil war the Roman legionary uniform alone was no longer enough to differentiate the two sides, though shields could indicate allegiance. Cf. Tacitus *Histories* 3.23.2, Dio 64.14.2 (Flavians taking shields from dead Vitellians), Virgil *Aeneid* 2.391-401, Dio 42.15.5, [Caesar] *Bell. Alex.* 58.3 and 59.1 (civil-war shields bearing Pompey's name), Vegetius *Mil.* 2.18.1-2 (painted shield-designs to prevent soldiers straying from their comrades in battle), and Silius Italicus *Pun.* 15.479. See R. Grigg, 'Inconsistency and Lassitude: The Shield Emblems of the *Notitia Dignitatum*', *JRS* 73 (1983) 132-42.

81. There are no details about how the two men were related. Tampius Flavianus was proconsul of Africa (Pliny *HN* 9.8.26) and consular legate of Pannonia early in the civil war (*ILS* 985). See R. Syme, *Tacitus* (Oxford 1958) 593. On naming practices see B. Salway, 'What's in a Name? A Survey of Roman Onomastic Practice from *c.* 700 BC–AD 700', *JRS* 84 (1994) 124-45.

82. Cf. Pliny *HN* 19.19.50 for gardens (*horti*) being used to denote a villa. In general see P. Grimal, *Les jardins romains* (Paris 1943) and A.G. McKay, *Houses, Villas and Palaces in the Roman World* (London 1975).

83. 'Insolence (*procacitas*)' appears only here in Tacitus' extant works.

84. Cf. Sallust *Cat.* 36.5 (the metaphorical 'plague (*tabes*)', which afflicted the Catilinarian conspirators), Livy 42.5.7 (civil war in Greece spreading 'like a plague (*velut tabes*)'), and Silius Italicus *Pun.* 11.12-13 (the 'dire contagion of a foul disease (*dira ... foedi contagia morbi*)', which prompts people to join Hannibal).

85. In Tacitus' *Histories* people are rarely imbued with anything good: 1.83.4 ('a centurion's and tribune's blood'), 3.49.2 ('licence'), 4.42.4 ('carnage of nobles'), 4.72.2 ('licence and savagery') and 5.5.2 ('despising gods, abandoning patriotism, and regarding parents, children and brothers as expendable'). Elsewhere, people are imbued with more positive qualities: Tacitus *Dialogus* 31.7 ('grammar, music and geometry') and 34.4 ('virtuous eloquence').

86. See K. Wellesley, *Tacitus: The Histories Book 3* (Sydney 1972) Appendix 2 'The Site of Cremona II' 198-204.

87. Cf. Sallust *Jug.* 57.4 'each according to his character (*pro ingenio quisque*)', *Jug.* 58.2 'each according to his character (*quisque pro moribus*)' and Livy 9.3.1 'each according to his character (*pro ingenio quisque*)'. All these examples are in a military context.

88. Onasander says that only the general should control prisoners-of-war after a battle (*Strat.* 35.2). Primus tries to prevent his soldiers from selling their Cremonese prisoners, but in any case nobody will buy them (3.34.2). Cf. I. Shatzman, 'The Roman General's Authority over Booty', *Historia* 21 (1972) 177-205.

89. For impressive heaps of bodies after a battle see Lucan *Phar.* 7.789-91 and Livy 10.29.19. The Flavian march would have been difficult if the battlefield resembled that after the first battle of Bedriacum: one pile of corpses was the same height as a temple roof (Plutarch *Otho* 14.2-3).

90. Cf. M. Fox, *Roman Historical Myths* (Oxford 1996) 132-4.

91. R. Syme, *Tacitus* (Oxford 1958) 118 says that 'Of the books of the *Historiae* a portion at least became known in AD 105'. Silius Italicus died in AD 101 aged 75 after starving himself to death to shorten an incurable ailment (Pliny *Epistles* 3.7).

92. J.M.C. Toynbee, *Death and Burial in the Ancient World* (London 1971) 55, notes: 'Soldiers killed on the battlefield were collectively cremated ...or buried. The funeral expenses were paid by their comrades'. Cf. Virgil *Aeneid* 11.22-3 and Tacitus *Annals* 15.28.2.

93. On the motif of close relatives killing each other as synecdoche for self-destructive civil war, see A.J. Woodman, 'From Hannibal to Hitler: The Literature of War, *University of Leeds Review* 26 (1983) 107-24, esp. 116-19, and P.R. Hardie, 'Tales of Unity and Division in Imperial Latin Epic', 57-71 in J.H. Molyneux (ed.) *Literary Responses to Civil Discord*, *Nottingham Classical Literature Studies* 1 (1992). Cf. [Caesar] *Bell. Hisp.* 27.6, Silius Italicus *Pun.* 9.66-177 and Tacitus *Histories* 3.51 for other family killings in a civil war context.

94. On the ancient punishment for parricide see Cicero, *Pro Roscio Amerino* 25.70. Under later legislation the penalty varied according to the gravity of the act, but the death-penalty remained usual.

95. P. Plass, *Wit and the Writing of History* (Madison, Wisconsin 1988) 31 and 35, cites a parallel epigram: 'Otho did not yet have the authority to prevent wickedness: he could only command it to happen (*sed Othoni nondum auctoritas inerat ad prohibendum scelus: iubere iam poterat*)' (*Histories* 1.45).

96. See Livy 25.26.11, Silius Italicus *Pun.* 14.611-15 and Plutarch *Ant.* 50.1.

97. See Livy 22.52.6, and 27.28.1, Silius Italicus *Pun.* 10.524-77 and 15.387-96, Valerius Maximus 5.1 *Ext.* 6, Plutarch *Marcellus* 30.2, and Cicero *Sen.* 20.75 for Hannibal burying the dead, and see Plutarch *Ant.* 22.6-7, *Pyrrhus* 34.9 and *Alex.* 43.5, and Justin *Epitome* 11.15.15 for a victorious general's gracious burial of a dead enemy.

98. On Suetonius' and Tacitus' different attitudes to smell, see M.G. Morgan, 'The Smell of Victory: Vitellius at Bedriacum (Tacitus *Histories* 2.70)', *CP* 87 (1992) 14-29.

99. Both phrases evoke the Sallustian 'ground polluted with blood (*humus infecta sanguine*)' (Sallust *Jug.* 101.11), which marks one of Marius' victories against Jugurtha. It is pointed that Tacitus in a civil war context twice evokes a phrase from Sallust's description of a foreign war.

100. Cf. S.H. Braund, *Lucan: Civil War* (Oxford 1992) xl-xliv on burial. H.N. Parker, 'The Fertile Fields of Umbria: Propertius 1.22.10', *Mnemosyne* 45 (1992) 88-92, notes the gruesome theme whereby former battlefields often become fertile (Plutarch *Marius* 21.7, Virgil *Georgics* 1.491-7, Ovid *Heroides* 1.53-56, Horace *Odes* 2.1.29-31, Lucan *Phar.* 7.851-2 and Silius Italicus *Pun.* 14.130). Cf. Shakespeare *Richard II* IV.1.137-8: 'The blood of England shall manure the ground / And future ages groan for this foul act.'

101. The only building which the Flavian looters leave intact after sacking Cremona is the Temple of Mefitis, goddess of sulphurous vapours (3.33.2. Cf. Servius *Ad Virg. Aen.* 7.84: ' "mefitis" is a stench from the ground which originates in sulphurous waters'). This might simply be a historiographical motif: see C.S. Kraus, *Livy Ab Urbe Condita Book VI* (Cambridge 1994) 265-6, on Livy 6.33.4. Yet Tacitus' explicit mention of Mefitis can perhaps be linked with the motif of burial: after the battle and the sack of Cremona, the goddess will need all of her purificatory powers to ward off the smell of the rotting corpses and disease. See further on Mefitis G. Radke, *Die Götter Altitaliens* (Münster 1965) 211-12 and R.E.A. Palmer, *Roman Religion and Roman Empire: Five Essays* (Pennsylvania 1974) 138-9. There were temples of Mefitis at Ampsanctus (Pliny *HN* 2.95.208) and on the Esquiline in Rome (Varro *Ling.* 5.49).

102. On darkness enhancing military violence, see Julius Caesar *BC* 1.23 and 2.31.7 and Tacitus *Histories* 1.80.2. Cf. J. Lucas, *Les Obsessions de Tacite* (Leiden 1974) 94-102.

103. R. Syme, *Tacitus* (Oxford 1958) 715 notes that *grandaevus* appears only in the *Histories*. It is mostly poetic (Virgil *Aeneid* 1.121 and Ovid *Met.* 8.520). For the anaphora of *non*, see Tacitus *Annals* 1.51.1, 6.19.3.

104. Cf. G.M. Paul, '*Urbs Capta*: Sketch of an Ancient Literary Motif', *Phoenix* 36 (1982) 144-55, A. Ziolkowski, '*Urbs Direpta*, or How the Romans Sacked Cities' 69-91 in J. Rich and G. Shipley (eds), *War and Society in the Roman World* (London 1993), N. Purcell, 'On the Sacking of Carthage and Corinth' 133-48 in D. Innes, H. Hine and C.B.R. Pelling (eds), *Ethics and Rhetoric: Classical Essays for Donald Russell on his Seventy-Fifth Birthday* (Oxford 1995) and A. Erskine, 'Money-Loving Romans', *PLLS* 9 (1996) 1-11.

105. Cf. Euripides *Hecuba* 23 and Seneca *Troades* 44-56. Cf. E. Fantham, *Seneca's Troades: A Literary Introduction with Text, Translation and Commentary* (Princeton 1982) 214-17.

106. E. Hall, *Inventing the Barbarian: Greek Self-Definition through Tragedy* (Oxford 1989) 19-21, characterises these extracts as 'isolated touches of realism penetrating the stylized literary milieu'. However, national character is an important theme in the *Iliad*, and the two passages are more integrated with the surrounding narrative than this remark allows. Cf. H. Mackie, *Talking Trojan: Speech and Community in the Iliad* (Lanham, Boulder, New York and London 1996) 16-21.

107. Certainly, ancient writers were sensitive to the practical problems of communication within linguistically diverse armies, particularly if large numbers of allies or auxiliaries were present. So, Onasander recommends that, for the allies' sake, the response to the watchword should not be by voice but by gesture (*Strat.* 26). Vegetius divides military signals into three categories, voiced, a watchword, semi-voiced, a trumpet blast, and mute, smoke signals, which may reflect efforts to solve communication problems (*Mil.* 3.5).

108. Cf. 3.18.1 (two Vitellian legions fail to carry out proper military manoeuvres at Bedriacum), 3.22.1 (the Vitellians fail to eat and sleep before attacking the Flavians), 3.54.1 (Vitellius still has prospects even after the Bedriacum defeat, if he will only admit the problem), and 3.59.2 (Vitellius' retreat allows the Flavians to cross the Appennines easily).

109. Cf. F. Ahl, *Lucan: An Introduction* (Ithaca and London 1976) 103-12.

110. Livy's anaphora on *non* exactly mirrors Polybius' triple οὐ.

111. K. Wellesley, *Cornelius Tacitus: The Histories Book 3* (Sydney 1972) 16-18, discusses responsibility for the burning of the Capitol.

112. R.G. Collingwood, *The Idea of History* (Oxford 1961) 40.

113. D. Mankin, *Horace Epodes* (Cambridge 1995) 247, makes the interesting suggestion that Tacitus is here echoing Horace *Epode* 16.3-10, a list of deadly foreign enemies (including Porsenna) who failed to destroy Rome, which is now being torn apart by her own citizens.

4. Galba and Otho

1. Hand-amputation is a marker of imperial cruelty (Suetonius *Claudius* 15.2 and *Domitian* 10.5). Plutarch largely avoids such anecdotal material in his *Galba* and *Otho*. See further R. Ash, 'Severed Heads: Individual Portraits and Irrational Forces in Plutarch's *Galba* and *Otho*', esp. 189-90 in J. Mossman (ed), *Plutarch and his Intellectual World* (London 1997).

2. Tacitus only names two sources explicitly, Pliny the Elder, who was a great admirer of Vespasian, and Vipstanus Messalla, who fought for the Flavians (3.28), but there must have been others (cf. 2.37.1, 3.22.2, 3.29.2, 3.51.1, and 3.59.3). See further K. Wellesley, *Cornelius Tacitus: The Histories Book 3* (Sydney 1972) 6-10. For the theme that war distorts language, see Thucydides 3.82.4 (with the useful note of S. Hornblower, *A Commentary on Thucydides Volume 1 Books I-III* (Oxford 1991) 483), Sallust *Cat.* 52.11, Lucan *Phar.* 1.667-8, Tacitus *Agricola* 30.4 and *Histories* 1.37.4. On Tacitus' frequent allusions to ambivalent language, see P. Plass, *Wit and the Writing of History* (Madison, Wisconsin 1988) 41-5 (esp. n. 33).

3. On Flavian propaganda in general see A. Briessmann, *Tacitus und das Flavische Geschichtsbild, Hermes Einzelschriften* 10 (Wiesbaden 1955), A. Ferrill, 'Otho, Vitellius and the Propaganda of Vespasian', *CJ* 60 (1964-5) 267-9, J. Nicols, *Vespasian and the Partes Flavianae, Historia Einzelschriften* 28 (Stuttgart 1978), and E.S. Ramage, 'Denigration of Predecessor under Claudius, Galba and Vespasian', *Historia* 32 (1983) 201-14.

4. See H. Mattingly (ed), *Coins of the Roman Empire in the British Museum*, Vol. I (London 1923) Galba nos. 24, 65-67, 142, and 197-98. Mattingly notes that the *libertas* variety was 'Perhaps the most popular of all Galba's types' (ccv).

5. See further A. Ferrill, 'Otho, Vitellius and the Propaganda of Vespasian', *CJ* 60 (1964-5) 267-9. Ferrill argues that after the war, Otho and Vitellius were superseded by Nero as a focus for denigration, so Galba's ideology was especially useful. E.S. Ramage, 'Denigration of Predecessor under Claudius, Galba and Vespasian', *Historia* 32 (1983) 201-14, dates the Pseudo-Senecan *Octavia* to early in Vespasian's reign and suggests that it shows the feelings on which Vespasian was trading in promoting his propaganda.

6. See H. Mattingly, *Coins of the Roman Empire in the British Museum* Vol. 2 (London 1930) Vespasian no. 781 for the *sestertius*. See M. Hammond, '*Res olim dissociabiles: Principatus ac Libertas*', *HSCP* 67 (1963) 93-113, A. Watson, 'Vespasian: *adsertor libertatis publicae*', *CR* 23 (1973) 127-8, B. Baldwin, 'Vespasian and Freedom', *RFIC* 103 (1975) 306-8, and C.L. Murison, *Galba, Otho and Vitellius: Careers and Controversies* (Hildesheim 1993) 54-5. C.H.V.

Sutherland, 'The Concepts *Adsertor* and *Salus* as used by Vindex and Galba', *NC* 144 (1984) 29-32 notes that the phrase *adsertor* does not actually appear on Galba's coins: 'Galba could well have supposed that the semantic link between the concept *adsertor* and the personal name of Vindex was uncomfortably close' (31).

7. R.M. Ogilvie, *A Commentary on Livy Books 1-5* (Oxford 1965) 484 comments: 'The noun is first found here (3.45.3) but is presumably much older. *adserere* (commonly with *manu*) is the technical term already in Plautus'. See further *TLL* 2.870-1.

8. See M.G. Morgan, 'The Three Minor Pretenders in Tacitus *Histories* Book 2', *Latomus* 52 (1993) 769-96.

9. See H. Mattingly (ed), *Coins of the Roman Empire in the British Museum*, Vol. I (London 1923) Galba nos. 7 and 8. Cf. M. Hammond, '*Res olim dissociabiles: Principatus ac Libertas*', *HSCP* 67 (1963) 99-100. For a general survey of the iconography, see E. Fabbricotti, *Galba* (Roma 1976).

10. C. Howgego, *Ancient History and Coins* (London 1995) 73 (with figures 107 and 120 for the two coins). Cf. Dio 47.25.3. See M. Crawford, *Roman Republican Coinage* (Cambridge 1974) 508/3 for the Ides of March coin.

11. In addition, Galba sought to recall his republican antecedents through the imagery on his signet ring: see H. Jucker, 'Der Ring des Kaisers Galba', *Chiron* 5 (1975) 349-64. H. Flower, *Ancestor Masks and Aristocratic Power in Roman Culture* (Oxford 1996) 260-3 notes that Galba used ancestral *imagines* as a powerful means of propaganda. P. Kragelund, 'Galba's *pietas*, Nero's Victims and the Mausoleum of Augustus', *Historia* 47.2 (1998) 152-73 discusses Galba's rehabilitation of the victims of Nero's tyranny and the impact of this rehabilitation on the literature of the period.

12. Y. Shochat, 'Tacitus' Attitude to Galba', *Athenaeum* 59 (1981) 199-204. On Tacitus' starting-point, see J.B. Hainsworth, 'The Starting-Point of Tacitus' *Histories* – Fear or Favour by Omission?', *G&R* 11 (1964) 128-36 and T. Cole, '*Initium mihi operis Servius Galba iterum T. Vinius consules ...*', *YCS* 29 (1992) 231-45.

13. See R.H. Martin and A.J. Woodman, *Tacitus Annals 4* (Cambridge 1989) 161. Cf. *Annals* 15.57 (the ex-slave Epicharis commits suicide nobly, while cowardly citizens betray their associates in the Pisonian conspiracy).

14. See especially Plutarch *Galba* 10.2 and Juvenal 8.223. J-P. Rubiés, 'Nero in Tacitus and Nero in Tacitism: The Historian's Craft' 29-47 in J. Elsner and J. Masters (eds), *Reflections of Nero* (London 1994) discusses Tacitus' subsequent treatment of Nero as a tyrant in the *Annals*.

15. Cf. M.S. Smith, *Cena Trimalchionis* (Oxford 1975) 93: 'as well as manumitted slaves, the soldiers of a triumphant general, certain priests and ordinary citizens at a *Saturnalia* might all have been found wearing a *pilleus*.'

16. Cf. D.C.A. Shotter, 'The Starting Points of Tacitus' Historical Works', *CQ* 17 (1967) 158-63: 'To introduce the *Historiae* and the *Annales* with full-length expositions of Galba and Tiberius respectively would to Tacitus' mind, it seems, have taken tidiness of composition to a point where it obscured what was essential' (162-3). E. Keitel, 'Plutarch's Tragedy Tyrants: Galba and Otho', *PLLS* 8 (1995) 275-88, argues that Plutarch has added the image of the tragedy tyrant to the account of the common source to give his own version coherence.

17. See Tacitus *Histories* 1.5.2, Plutarch *Galba* 18.4, Suetonius *Galba* 16.1 and Dio 64.3.3 for the aphorism and *Histories* 1.18.2, 1.23.2, and 1.35.2, Plutarch *Galba* 26.2, Suetonius *Galba* 19.2 and Dio 64.6.2 for the theme of Galba as a disciplinarian.

18. For the expectation that Roman Emperors should be competent military commanders, see M.P. Charlesworth, 'The Virtues of a Roman Emperor and the Creation of Belief', *PBA* 23 (1937) 105-33, A. Wallace-Hadrill, 'The Emperor and his Virtues', *Historia* 30 (1981) 298-323, and M. Griffin, *Nero: The End of a Dynasty* (London 1984) 221-34.

19. Cf. D.C.A. Shotter, *Suetonius, Lives of Galba, Otho and Vitellius* (Warminster 1993) 116.

20. Plutarch names the pair as Cingonius Varro and Mithridates of Pontus and comments that their execution was illegal and despotic, even if it was justified (*Galba* 15.1). For Cingonius Varro's earlier career see Tacitus *Annals* 14.45.2 and for Petronius Turpilianus see Tacitus *Annals* 14.29.1, 14.39 and 15.72.1, *Agricola* 16.3, Frontinus *Aq*. 102.10-11, and Dio 63.1.

21. G.E.F. Chilver, *A Historical Commentary on Tacitus' Histories I and II* (Oxford 1979) suggests (53) that when Tacitus called them *inermes*, he may have meant 'without defensive armour' as at 1.79.4.

22. On the prevalence of superlatives in speeches, see J.N. Adams, 'The Vocabulary of the Speeches in Tacitus' Historical Works', *BICS* 20 (1973) 124-44 esp. 134.

23. When Tacitus makes Otho say that 'Trembling comes over my heart (*horror animum subit*)' whenever he remembers Galba entering the city, there may be an echo of Silius Italicus *Pun*. 6.151. When the old man Marus recalls a giant serpent, which killed several comrades, he says 'The trembling returns when I think of it (*horror mente redit*)'. Otho's reaction to Galba is like Marus' reaction to the monster, which may encourage us to identify the two.

24. Cf. A. Wallace-Hadrill, '*Civilis Princeps*: Between Citizen and King', *JRS* 72 (1982) 32-48: 'To save himself from contempt a monarch must grow a protective shell. Since the first function of a ruler is the possession of power, he must conceal his actual human frailty, blow himself up into a being larger than life, above the common run of humanity' (33).

25. See Cicero *Off*. 1.28.97, *Pro Sestio* 48.102 and *Phil*. 1.14.34, Seneca *De Ira* 1.20.4 and *De Clementia* 1.12.4 and 2.2.2, Suetonius *Caligula* 30.1. Tiberius recast the famous epigram as 'let them hate me, as long as they respect me (*oderint dum probent*)' (Suetonius *Tiberius* 59.2). Stereotypical tyrants were usually portrayed as being afraid (Tacitus *Annals* 6.6, Euripides *Ion* 621-8 and Xenophon *Hieron* 2.8-10). On fear in Tacitus see W.-R. Heinz, *Die Furcht als politisches Phänomenon bei Tacitus* (Amsterdam 1975).

26. Every fifth day, Scipio Africanus made his men do a *decursio* of four miles (Livy 26.51), and there were special marching techniques taught to recruits to enable them to achieve this (Vegetius *Mil*. 1.9). Legionaries needed all their energy to excel at such manoeuvres: Tacitus criticises Plancina's distracting presence at the *decursiones* in Germany (*Annals* 2.55.6). On training in general see R.W. Davies, *Service in the Roman Army* (London 1989) 106-15.

27. Cf. D.T. Benidiktson, 'Structure and Fate in Suetonius' *Life of Galba*', *CJ* 92.2 (1997) 167-73 on Galba's unfortunate characteristics and untimely end as 'a product of his genetic make-up and his Julio-Claudian upbringing' (172).

28. On the adoption of Piso, see C.L. Murison, *Galba, Otho and Vitellius: Careers and Controversies* (Hildesheim 1993) 62-74, and J. Sancery, *Galba ou L'armée face au pouvoir* (Paris 1983) 147-55. The echoes between Tacitus *Histories* 1.15-16 and Pliny *Pan*. 7-8 suggest that we should compare Nerva's adoption of Trajan. See R.T. Bruère, 'Tacitus and Pliny's *Panegyricus*', *CP* 49 (1954) 161-79, K. Büchner, 'Tacitus und Plinius über Adoption des römischen Kaisers (Des Verhältnis von Tacitus *Hist*. 1.15-16 zu Plinius *Panegyricus* 7-8',

RhM 98 (1955) 289-312, P. Fedeli, 'Il "Panegyrico" di Plinio nella Critica Moderna', *ANRW* 2.33.1 (1989) 387-514, esp. 426-32, and K-W. Welwei, 'Verdeckte Systemkritik in der Galbarede des Tacitus', *Gymnasium* 102 (1995) 353-63.

29. *thorax* appears only here in Tacitus' works. Cf. Plutarch *Galba* 27.1 *'tethorakismenon'*: the word may derive from the common source. Suetonius *Galba* 19.1 has the more conventional 'corselet (*lorica*)'.

30. Cf. H.W. Benario, 'Priam and Galba', *CW* 65 (1972) 146-7. For other parallels between Virgil and Tacitus, see N.P. Miller, 'Virgil and Tacitus Again', *PVS* 18 (1986) 87-106, R.T.S. Baxter, 'Virgil's Influence on Tacitus in Book 3 of the *Histories*', *CP* 66 (1971) 93-107 and R.T.S. Baxter, 'Virgil's Influence on Tacitus in *Annals* 1 and 2', *CP* 67 (1972) 246-69. See in general S. Frangoulidis, 'Tacitus (*Histories* 1.40-43), Plutarch (*Galba* 26-27) and Suetonius (*Galba* 18-20) on the Death of Galba', *Favonius* 3 (1991) 1-10.

31. Cf. P. Hardie, *The Epic Successors of Virgil* (Cambridge 1993) 30.

32. H. Heubner, *P. Cornelius Tacitus: Die Historien* Vol. 1 (Heidelberg 1963) *ad loc.* cites Livy 10.34.12 and 25.25.9 as precedents for Tacitus' 'once the doors of the Palace were broken open (*refractis Palatii foribus*)' (1.35.1). Cf. Ennius on the opening of the gates of war: 'Discord broke open the posts and gates (*Discordia ... postis portasque refregit*)' (Horace *Satire* 1.4.60-1). R.M. Ogilvie, *Commentary on Livy Books 1-5* (Oxford 1965) 120, notes that Virgil owed much of *Aeneid* 2 to Ennius' *Annales*. Cf. E.J. Kenney, 'Iudicium Transferendi: Virgil *Aeneid* 2.469-505 and its Antecedents' 103-20 in A.J. Woodman and D. West (eds), *Creative Imitation and Latin Literature* (Cambridge 1979).

33. This scene appealed to other authors (Juvenal 10.267-70 and Ovid *Tristia* 4.1.73-6). Cf. K. Preston, 'An Author in Exile', *CJ* 13 (1917-1918) 411-19 esp. 413 and B.R. Nagle, *The Poetics of Exile. Program and Polemic in the Tristia and Epistulae ex Ponto of Ovid*, Collection Latomus 170 (Brussels 1980) 158.

34. On this chapter, see M.G. Morgan, 'A Lugubrious Prospect: Tacitus *Histories* 1.40', *CQ* 44 (1994) 236-44.

35. Tacitus *Histories* 1.40.1 (also Plutarch *Galba* 26.5) and Virgil *Aeneid* 2.496-9 both use water imagery to describe the surging crowd.

36. See Caesar *BC* 3.104, Cicero *De Divinatione* 2.9.22, Livy *Per.* 112, Florus 2.13.52, Velleius Paterculus 2.53.1-3, Lucan *Phar.* 8.589-822, Plutarch *Pomp.* 77-9, Appian *BC* 2.84.352-2.86.363, Cassius Dio 42.4, Juvenal 10.285-8, Manilius *Astronomica* 4.50-6, Eutropius *Brev.* 6.21.3, Orosius 6.15.28-9, and Ammianus Marcellinus 14.11.32. Cf. A.A. Bell Jr., 'Fact and *Exemplum* in Accounts of the Deaths of Pompey and Caesar', *Latomus* 53 (1994) 824-36 and M. Leigh, *Lucan: Spectacle and Engagement* (Oxford 1997) 118-25.

37. See E. Narducci, 'Il Tronco di Pompeio (Troia e Roma nella Pharsalia)', *Maia* 25 (1973) 317-25, F.M. Ahl, *Lucan: An Introduction* (Ithaca and London 1976) 183-9, J. Moles, 'Virgil, Pompeius and the *Histories* of Asinius Pollio', *CW* 76 (1983) 287-8 and A.M. Bowie, 'The Death of Priam: Allegory and History in the *Aeneid*', *CQ* 40 (1990) 470-81.

38. On Lucan using Pollio as a source, perhaps through the intermediary of Livy, see H.P. Syndikus, *Lucans Gedicht vom Bürgerkrieg* (Munich 1958) 1-12, F.M. Ahl, *Lucan: An Introduction* (Ithaca and London 1976) 23 and 82-4, and P. Grimal, 'Le Poète et l'Histoire' in *Entretiens de la Fondation Hardt* 15, *Lucain* (Geneva 1973) 51-117 esp. 62 and 66. On Pollio's style see A.J. Woodman, *Rhetoric in Classical Historiography* (London 1988) 127-8.

39. Domitian's speech about restoring Galba's memory reveals nothing about his burial (4.40.1). Vespasian vetoed a senatorial decree to honour the spot where Galba had died (Suetonius *Galba* 23). Cf. M. Zimmerman, 'Die *restitutio honorum* Galbas', *Historia* 44 (1995) 56-82.

40. D.T. McGuire, 'History Compressed: The Roman Names of Silius' Cannae Episode', *Latomus* 54 (1995) 110-18: 'Galba and Pompey — two aging defenders of the senatorial order, meet similar ends — murder followed by decapitation – and their deaths stand as stark and powerful images of the two periods of Roman civil war' (116). Cf. D.C. Feeney, *'Stat Magni Nominis Umbra*: Lucan on the Greatness of Pompeius Magnus', *CQ* 36 (1986) 239-43.

41. See Plutarch *Caesar* 39.8, *Pomp.* 65.8, Appian *BC* 2.62.260, and Suetonius *Divus Iulius* 36.

42. R.F. Thomas, 'Virgil's *Georgics* and the Art of Reference', *HSCP* 90 (1986) 171-98 describes the practice whereby an author refers to a number of antecedents as 'multiple reference'.

43. Cf. J. Ginsburg, *'In maiores certamina*: Past and Present in the *Annals'* 86-103 in T.J. Luce and A.J. Woodman (eds), *Tacitus and the Tacitean Tradition* (Princeton 1993): 'While the past is often invoked in the *Annals* as a standard against which to measure the present, it is not an absolute standard; nor is the view that the past was better than the present the only perspective we are given' (87).

44. Cf. G. Williams, *Change and Decline: Roman Literature in the Early Empire* (Berkeley, Los Angeles and London 1978) 239.

45. Cf. G. Williams, *Change and Decline: Roman Literature in the Early Empire* (Berkeley, Los Angeles and London 1978) 6-51 on the nuances of this motif.

46. Cf. Appian *BC* 2.36.145 and 2.41.163, Horace *Epode* 16.1-2, and Dio 41.5, 41.8 and 41.16 for continuity between civil wars. Lucan *Phar.* 2.67-232 initially suggests continuity between past and present, but raises the possibility that the civil war between Caesar and Pompey will be even worse. Cf. E. O'Gorman, 'Shifting Ground: Lucan, Tacitus and the Landscape of Civil War', *Hermathena* 158 (1995) 117-31 esp. 118-19 on the relationship between present and past civil wars in Tacitus.

47. See Varro *Ling.* 5.148-50, and Livy 1.12.10, 1.13.5 and 7.6.1-6. C. Edwards, *Writing Rome* (Cambridge 1996) 77 notes that the Lacus Curtius has a plurality of associations, which may further enhance the moral complexity of Galba's death. Some versions of the legend present Curtius as a Roman hero, others as a Sabine enemy.

48. On Otho's literary portrayal, see H. Drexler, 'Zur Geschichte Kaiser Othos bei Tacitus und Plutarch', *Klio* 37 (1959) 153-78, B.F. Harris, 'Tacitus on the Death of Otho', *CJ* 58 (1962) 73-7, P. Schunk, 'Studien zur Darstellung des Endes von Galba, Otho und Vitellius in den Historien des Tacitus', *SO* 39 (1964) 38-82, B.H. Stolte, 'Tacitus on Nero and Otho', *AS* 4 (1973) 177-90, Y. Shochat, 'Tacitus' Attitude to Otho', *Latomus* 40 (1981) 365-77, G.O. Hutchinson, *Latin Literature from Seneca to Juvenal* (Oxford 1993) 257-61, C.L. Murison, *Galba, Otho and Vitellius: Careers and Controversies* (Hildesheim 1993) 131-42, and C.A. Perkins, 'Tacitus on Otho', *Latomus* 52 (1993) 848-55.

49. C.L. Murison, *Galba, Otho and Vitellius: Careers and Controversies* (Hildesheim 1993) 131-2.

50. Y. Shochat, 'Tacitus' Attitude to Otho', *Latomus* 40 (1981) 365.

51. For the treatment of Galba's severed head, see Tacitus *Histories* 1.49.1, Plutarch *Galba* 27.4 and 28.3, Suetonius *Galba* 20.2 and Dio 64.6.3.

52. See E. Keitel, 'Otho's Exhortations in Tacitus' *Histories'*, *G&R* 34 (1987) 73-82 esp. 79 and A.J. Woodman, *Velleius Paterculus: The Caesarian and*

Augustan Narrative (2.41-93) (Cambridge 1983) 234. Cf. Seneca *Tranq.* 16.1 on good men dying bad deaths.

53. There is a fine example of this type in the figure of Plutarch's Demetrius (*Demetrius* 2.3). See J. Griffin, 'Propertius and Antony', *JRS* 67 (1977) 17-26, reprinted in *Latin Poets and Roman Life* (London 1985) 32-47.

54. A.J. Woodman, '*praecipuum munus annalium*: The Construction, Convention And Context of Tacitus *Annals* 3.65.1', *MH* 52 (1995) 111-26 questions whether this formulation is definitive. On *exempla* see H. Litchfield, 'National *Exempla Virtutis* in Roman Literature', *HSCP* 25 (1914) 1-71, G. Maslakov, 'Valerius Maximus and Roman Historiography: A Study of the *Exempla* Tradition', *ANRW* 2.32.1 (1984) 437-96, W.M. Bloomer, *Valerius Maximus and the Rhetoric of the New Nobility* (London 1992) and J.D. Chaplin, 'Livy's Use of *Exempla* and the Lessons of the Past', Ph.D thesis (Princeton 1993) = *Livy's Exemplary History* forthcoming (Oxford 2000).

55. Cf. M. Leigh, *Lucan: Spectacle and Engagement* (Oxford 1997) 292-306 on the tyrant's gaze.

56. Cf. Tacitus *Annals* 14.59.3. P. Plass, 'An Aspect of Epigrammatic Wit in Martial and Tacitus', *Arethusa* 18 (1985) 187-210, refers (208) to 'Talking Dog' jokes in which the astonishing fact is ignored by someone who concentrates on a triviality such as correcting the dog's pronunciation.

57. Some editions refer to a body rather than to a head here. M.G. Morgan, 'The Three Minor Pretenders in Tacitus *Histories* 2', *Latomus* 52 (1993) 769-96, revives Wurm's suggestion (1853) that 'head (*caput*)' is the correct reading here and not 'body (*corpus*)'.

58. Cf. A.J. Woodman, 'Tacitus' Obituary of Tiberius', *CQ* 39 (1989) 197-205 and C. Gill, 'The Question of Character Development: Plutarch and Tacitus', *CQ* 33 (1983) 469-87.

59. See further J. Geiger, 'Munatius Rufus and Thrasea Paetus on Cato the Younger', *Athenaeum* 57 (1979) 48-72, Y. Grisé, *Le suicide dans la Rome antique* (Paris 1982) 34-53, M. Griffin, 'Philosophy, Cato and Roman Suicide: I', *G&R* 33 (1986) 64-77 and 'Philosophy, Cato and Roman Suicide: II', *G&R* 33 (1986) 192-202 and A.J.L. Van Hooff, *From Autothanasia to Suicide: Self-Killing in Classical Antiquity* (London 1990).

60. See *Otho* 15-17 and *Cato Minor* 68-71. Cf. Cassius Dio 43.10-11 and Appian *BC* 2.98.406-2.99.414.

61. Cf. M.G. Morgan, 'The Unity of Tacitus, *Histories* 1.12-20', *Athenaeum* 81 (1993) 567-86, esp. 567-77.

62. J. Ginsburg, *Tradition and Theme in the Annals of Tacitus* (Berkeley 1981) 37.

63. An unwillingness to explore the deeper nuances of the 'foiling' technique has marked many analyses of Tacitus' characterisation, particularly of Tiberius and Germanicus in the *Annals*, as noted (60) by C.B.R. Pelling, 'Tacitus and Germanicus' 59-85 in T.J. Luce and A.J. Woodman (eds), *Tacitus and the Tacitean Tradition* (Princeton 1993).

64. A. Ferrill, 'Otho, Vitellius and the Propaganda of Vespasian', *CJ* 60 (1964-5) 267-9. Cf. R. Syme, *Tacitus* (Oxford 1958) 205: 'Otho by contrast [with Galba] — affable, pliant, and corrupt — belonged to his own epoch, a choice luxury product of the Neronian court.'

65. Cf. P. Veyne, *Bread and Circuses*, trans. B. Pearce (London 1992), 406, P.A. Gallivan, 'The False Neros: A Re-evaluation', *Historia* 22 (1973) 364-5, M.T. Griffin, *Nero: The End of a Dynasty* (London 1984) 89-90, and C.J. Tuplin, 'The

False Neros of the First Century AD', 364-404 in C. Deroux (ed.), *Studies in Latin Literature and Roman History V* (Brussels 1989).

66. Otho was not alone: the young Titus was also compared with Nero (Suetonius *Titus* 7.1 and [Aurelius Victor] *Epit.* 10.5).

67. See Appian *BC* 3.11.37, Dio 46.48.1, 47.22.4 and 48.3.2, Suetonius *Augustus* 10.1 and 29.2, and Ovid *Fasti* 5.573-80.

68. (a) The First *Adiutrix* Legion remembers Otho fondly and hates Vitellius (3.44) (b) When Flavian troops destroy Cremona, they want to avenge previous Cremonese support for the Vitellians in the war against Otho (3.32.2) (c) Mucianus pinpoints the 'desire for revenge' amongst the defeated Othonians (2.77.3) (d) Vitellius alienates the Illyrian armies when he executes leading Othonian centurions (2.60.1) (e) Vespasian's letter urges his western armies and legates to recruit Praetorians hostile to Vitellius (2.82.3) (f) These Praetorians become the 'main strength of the Flavian party' (2.67.1) (g) Valerius Paulinus recruits all those dismissed from the Praetorian Guard by Vitellius (3.43.1).

69. On death literature see R.H. Martin and A.J. Woodman, *Tacitus Annals IV* (Cambridge 1989) 128. Cf. H. MacL.Currie, 'An Obituary Formula in the Historians (With a Platonic Connection?)', *Latomus* 48 (1989) 346-53.

70. See C. Bertrand-Dagenbach, 'La mort de Pétrone et l'art de Tacite', *Latomus* 51 (1992) 601-5.

71. The verb *voluto* often suggests quiet, measured contemplation: so Virgil uses this verb to depict Aeneas as deep in thought (*Aeneid* 6.157, 6.185, and 10.159). C.M. Bowra, 'Aeneas and the Stoic Ideal', *G&R* 3 (1933-4) 8-21 has compared such moments to the thoughtfulness of the philosophical sage. Perhaps less propitiously, Tacitus associates this verb with Sejanus, Tiberius and Nero (*Annals* 4.12.2, 4.40.7 and 13.15.1).

72. For other dubious instruments see Dio 65.16.4 (razor), *HA Elagabalus* 33 (golden swords), Tacitus *Annals* 5.8 (pen-knife), *Annals* 6.14.1 (chain) and *Annals* 6.49.1 (jumping from a height).

73. See Suetonius *Galba* 11 and Tacitus *Histories* 3.68.2. Y. Grisé, *Le suicide dans la Rome antique* (Paris 1982) classifies suicide by the sword as 'suicide viril par excellence', while opening the veins is a 'mode plus discret et moins brutal s'accordant aux moeurs plus raffinées de la vie urbaine' (96). Cf. Tacitus *Annals* 16.17 and Martial 1.78.7.

74. C.S. Kraus and A.J. Woodman, *Latin Historians, Greece and Rome New Surveys in the Classics* 27 (1997) 35. Cf. I.S. Ryberg, 'Tacitus' Art of Innuendo', *TAPA* 73 (1942) 383-404, R. Develin, 'Tacitus and Techniques of Insidious Suggestion', *Antichthon* 17 (1983) 64-95, esp. 88 for examples about Otho, and P. Sinclair, 'Rhetorical Generalisations in *Annales* 1-6', *ANRW* 2.33.4 (1991) 2795-831.

75. C.A. Perkins, 'Tacitus on Otho', *Latomus* 52 (1993) 848-55, suggests (854-5) that when Tacitus describes Otho's mixed reputation (2.50.1), his good side is 'nearly lost' within its clause so that the sentence ends emphatically with the bad side. Yet it is surely misleading to suggest that Otho's good side emerges from Tacitus' narrative despite his best attempts.

76. P. Plass, *The Game of Death in Ancient Rome* (Madison, Wisconsin 1995) 82, argues that aspects of Otho's suicide, such as frugal distribution of money (*Histories* 2.48.1), deliberately negate many of his faults during life, such as notorious profligacy.

77. Cf. *Histories* 1.13.4 where Otho governs Lusitania *comiter*. On the usefulness of *comitas* in a ruler, see A. Wallace-Hadrill, '*Civilis Princeps*:

Between Citizen and King', *JRS* 72 (1982) 32-48, who defines it as 'the friendly treatment of inferiors'. C.S. Kraus, *Livy Ab Urbe Condita Book VI* (Cambridge 1994) 275 cites Cicero *Pro Caelio* 6.13 on *comitas* as helpful for those dealing with young people.

78. Cf. C.B.R. Pelling, 'Tacitus and Germanicus' 59-85 in T.J. Luce and A.J. Woodman (eds), *Tacitus and the Tacitean Tradition* (Princeton 1993), who argues that Germanicus' *comitas* is consistent, but causes varying results depending on the situation to which it is applied.

79. See B.H. Stolte, 'Tacitus on Nero and Otho', *AS* 4 (1973) 177-90 and M.G. Morgan, 'The Unity of Tacitus *Histories* 1.12-20', *Athenaeum* 81 (1993) 567-86.

80. R.G.M. Nisbet, review of W.V. Clausen, *JRS* 52 (1962) 227-38, esp. 233-4, R. Syme, 'Juvenal, Pliny, Tacitus', *AJP* 100 (1979) 250-78 = 1135-57 in A.R. Birley (ed.), *Roman Papers III* (Oxford 1984), esp. 1143-4, E.S. Ramage, 'Juvenal and the Establishment: Denigration of Predecessor in the Satires', *ANRW* 2.33.1 (1989) 640-707, esp. 679, and S.M. Braund, *Juvenal Satires Book 1* (Cambridge 1996) 149-52 discuss the passage.

81. On the *pathicus* see J.N. Adams, *The Latin Sexual Vocabulary* (London 1982) 123, 133, 190 and 228, M. Foucault, *The Use of Pleasure: The History of Sexuality* Vol. 2, transl. by R. Hurley (London 1992) 220-2 and A. Richlin, *The Garden of Priapus: Sexuality and Aggression in Roman Humour* (Oxford 1992) 12, 92, 122, 146, 202 and 250 n.6.

82. To compare someone with Paris was a familiar insult: Virgil *Aeneid* 4.215 and 7.321, Plutarch *Ant. / Demetrius: Comparatio* 3.4 and Cicero *Att.* 1.18.3.

83. Cf. P.J. Lelièvre, 'Juvenal: Two Possible Examples of Word-Play', *CP* 53 (1958) 241-2.

84. On the background to ancient notions of Asian effeminacy, see E. Hall, 'Asia Unmanned: Images of Victory in Classical Athens', 108-33 in J. Rich and G. Shipley (eds), *War and Society in the Greek World* (London 1993).

85. There is disagreement over the relative dates of Juvenal and Tacitus, but R. Syme, 'Juvenal, Pliny, Tacitus', *AJP* 100 (1979) 250-78 = 1135-57 in A.R. Birley (ed.), *Roman Papers III* (Oxford 1984) argues (1144) that Juvenal is alluding to the *Histories* in the phrase *novis annalibus atque recenti historia* (2.102-3).

86. Cf. C. Edwards, *The Politics of Immorality in Ancient Rome* (Cambridge 1993) 63-97, V.A. Tracy, 'Roman Dandies and Transvestites', *EMC* 20 (1976) 60-3 and A. Corbeill, 'Dining Deviants in Roman Political Invective' 99-128 (esp. 112-23) in J.P. Hallett and M.B. Skinner (eds), *Roman Sexualities* (Princeton 1997).

87. For a comparison of Piso's and Otho's speeches, see E. Keitel, 'The Structure and Function of Speeches in Tacitus' *Histories* I-III', *ANRW* 2.33.4 (1991) 2772-94, esp. 2776-80.

88. Cf. V.H.G. Galbraith, 'Good Kings and Bad Kings in Medieval English History', *History* 30 (1945) 119-32, reprinted in *Kings and Chroniclers* (London 1982), for a relevant discussion of such misleadingly polarised moral categories in another era.

5. Vitellius

1. Cf. P.A. Brunt, '*Lex de Imperio Vespasiani*', *JRS* 67 (1977) 95-116.

2. See J.R. Dunkle, 'The Greek Tyrant and Roman Political Invective of the Late Republic', *TAPA* 98 (1967) 151-71, J.R. Dunkle, 'The Rhetorical Tyrant in Roman Historiography: Sallust, Livy and Tacitus', *CW* 65 (1971) 12-20, A.

Ferrill, 'Herodotus on Tyranny', *Historia* 27 (1978) 386-98, V. Farenga, 'The Paradigmatic Tyrant: Greek Tyranny and the Ideology of the Proper', *Helios* 8 (1981) 1-31, D. Lateiner, *The Historical Method of Herodotus* (Toronto 1989) 172-9, G.J.P. O'Daly, *The Poetry of Boethius* (London 1991) 75-82, P. Veyne, *Bread and Circuses* transl. B. Pearce (London 1992) 404-6, P. Barceló, *Basileia, Monarchia, Tyrannis* (Stuttgart 1993), and J.F. McGlew, *Tyranny and Political Culture in Ancient Greece* (Ithaca 1993) 24-35.

3. See H.J. Tschiedel, *Caesars Anticato: Eine Untersuchung der Testimonien und Fragmente* (Darmstadt 1981). Cf. Seneca *Tranq.* 17.9, Pliny *Epistle* 3.12.2-3 and Lucan *Phar.* 1.128.

4. See A.J. Woodman, *Velleius Paterculus: The Caesarian and Augustan Narrative* (2.41-93) (Cambridge 1983) 53. Cf. Tacitus *Annals* 2.73 (Alexander's double-edged reputation), Livy 9.18.5 (Alexander's temper and love of wine), Sallust *Histories* 3.88 (L.D. Reynolds), Plutarch *Pomp.* 2.3 and Lucan *Phar.* 10.20-52 (Romans hoping to be associated with Alexander positively, but activating negative parallels).

5. On the frugal diet of ideal generals see Livy 21.4.6, Justin 32.4.10, Sallust *Jug.* 89.8, Plutarch *Marius* 7.4, *Cato Minor* 9.9, *Ant.* 4.4, and *Caesar* 17.3, Pliny *Pan.* 13.1, Tacitus *Histories* 2.5.1, Lucan *Phar.* 2.384, Velleius Paterculus 2.114.3, Suetonius *Tiberius* 18.2, Diodorus Siculus 33.1.1 and 33.7.2, Ammianus Marcellinus 16.5.3 and 25.4.4, and *HA Hadrian* 10.2.

6. Cf. Seneca *Thyestes* 778-88, Herodotus *Histories* 1.119.3-5, Suetonius *Tiberius* 62.2 and Claudian *De Bello Gildonico* 174-81, with E.M. Olechowska, *Claudii Claudiani: De Bello Gildonico* (Leiden 1978) 164.

7. See S. Bartsch, *Actors in the Audience: Theatricality and Doublespeak from Nero to Hadrian* (Cambridge Mass. 1994) 148-87 and E.S. Ramage, 'Juvenal and the Establishment: Denigration of Predecessor in the Satires', *ANRW* 2.33.1 (1989) 640-707, esp. 640-4.

8. Cf. Dio Chrysostom 40.12 and 50.8 (Domitian as tyrant). Some emperors even outdid Pliny's tyrannical Domitian: *HA Elagabalus* 25.9 (wax, wood and ivory food), *HA Elagabalus* 26.5 (paintings of food) and Suetonius *Caligula* 37.1 (golden bread and meat).

9. P. Veyne, *Bread and Circuses* transl. B. Pearce (London 1992) 220-1 notes that in republican times, funerals were followed by public feasting (Livy 38.55 and 39.46). Domitian appears to be reversing this pattern by making a feast the prelude to funerals.

10. This may have been a particularly appropriate trick. M. Vickers, 'Artful Crafts: The Influence of Metalwork on Athenian Painted Pottery', *JHS* 105 (1985) 108-28, argues that black pottery is the poor man's silver and that the various colours in pottery represented valuable materials (black = silver, orange-red = gold, purple = copper, white = ivory).

11. E. Gowers, *The Loaded Table: Representations of Food in Roman Culture* (Oxford 1993) 38, notes: 'This meal seems to have been restaged in 18th century France by the gourmet Grimot de la Reynière, a complicated act of revenge on his parents.'

12. On Josephus' portrait of Vitellius see B. Richter, *Ein Zerrbild der Geschichtsschreibung* (Frankfurt-am-Main 1992).

13. Cf. Cicero *Pro Sestio* 9.20, Suetonius *Nero* 27.2, Tacitus *Annals* 14.2, Silius Italicus *Pun.* 11.41, Cassius Dio 69.7.3, Horace *Epistle* 1.19.5, Juvenal 1.49 and Martial 1.28.

14. Cf. Cicero *Pro Rege Deiotaro* 7.21, *Att.* 13.52.1, Cassius Dio 68.1.3 and

Athenaeus *Deipnosophistae* 11.484b. On vomiting, see E. Gowers, *The Loaded Table: Representations of Food in Roman Literature* (Oxford 1993) 19.

15. Cf. Livy 2.27 (temple), Pliny *HN* 7.158 (theatre), Suetonius *Claudius* 21.1 (theatre) and Suetonius *Titus* 7.3 (amphitheatre).

16. Cf. Pliny *HN* 2.112.242-4, Juvenal 10.1, Seneca *NQ* 1 *Pr.* 13, Ovid *Met.* 4.21, Silius Italicus *Pun.* 1.141, 3.3, 3.325, 3.399, 5.272, 7.108, 9.185, 14.8 and 17.637, Velleius Paterculus 1.2.3, Pindar *Nem.* 4.69, Statius *Thebaid* 1.686 and Lucan *Phar.* 3.229-334.

17. D.C.A. Shotter, *Suetonius, Lives of Galba, Otho and Vitellius* (Warminster 1993) 182.

18. Cf. Xenophon *Agesilaos* 9.3, Macrobius *Sat.* 7.5.32, Sallust *Histories* 2.70 (L.D. Reynolds), Seneca *Helv.* 10.4 and Tacitus *Annals* 15.37. See further A.J. Woodman, 'Nero's Alien Capital. Tacitus as a Paradoxographer: *Annals* 15.36-37', 173-88 in A.J. Woodman and J. Powell (eds), *Author and Audience in Latin Literature* (Cambridge 1992) and J. Goddard, 'The Tyrant at Table', 67-82 in J. Elsner and J. Masters (eds), *Reflections of Nero: Culture, History and Representation* (London 1994). On the Roman Empire equated with the *orbis terrarum* see C. Nicolet, *Space, Geography and Politics in the Early Roman Empire* trans. H. Leclerc (Michigan 1991).

19. Vitellius did not restrict himself to luxurious food: allegedly he would grab flesh from the sacrificial altars, or guzzle down smoking meat from roadside snackbars, or else he would happily wolf down yesterday's half-eaten scraps (Suetonius *Vitellius* 13.3).

20. For a later instance of food being used to denigrate see B. Bryson, *Made in America* (London 1994) 223-4: 'The patrician New Yorker Martin Van Buren was ousted from the Presidency in 1840 in large part because one of his Whig opponents made a celebrated speech attacking Van Buren for serving such unmanly fare in the White House as strawberries, cauliflower and celery.'

21. A. Corbeill, 'Dining Deviants in Political Invective' 100 in J.P. Hallett and M.B. Skinner (eds), *Roman Sexualities* (Princeton 1997).

22. Fragment 101.11-13 (= Athenaeus *Deipnosophistae* 2.36a) in R. Kassel and C. Austin, *Poetae Comici Graeci Vol. VIII* (Berlin and New York 1995) 35, claims that drinking wine mixed with an even portion of water leads to madness, but that drinking unmixed wine causes paralysis. On mixed and unmixed wine see J. Davidson, *Courtesans and Fishcakes* (London 1997) 158.

23. Cf. R.G.M. Nisbet, *Cicero: In Pisonem* (Oxford 1961) 192-7 and R. Syme, *Roman Revolution* (Oxford 1939) 149-61: 'In the allegation of disgusting immorality, degrading pursuits and ignoble origin, the Roman politician knew no compunction or limit' (149).

24. Mud continues to stick. Cf. E.M. Jellinek, 'Drinkers and Alcoholics in Ancient Rome', *Journal of Studies on Alcohol* 37 (1976) 1718-41: 'Antony's alcoholism was so notorious that many authors made reference to it' (1734). Jellinek seems unaware of the cumulative invective about Antony's drinking.

25. Cf. A.F. Stewart, 'To Entertain an Emperor: Sperlonga, Laokoon and Tiberius at the Dinner-Table', *JRS* 67 (1977) 76-90.

26. Cf. M. Leigh, 'Varius Rufus, *Thyestes* and the Appetites of Antony', *PCPS* 42 (1996) 171-97.

27. Cf. M.P.O. Morford, 'The Distortion of the *Domus Aurea* Tradition', *Eranos* 66 (1968) 158-79 and G. Zander, 'La Domus Aurea: Nuovi Problemi Architettonici', *Bollettino del Centro di Studi per la Storia dell'Architettura* 12 (1958) 47-64 (on post-Neronian changes to the *Domus Aurea*, perhaps made by Otho, who may have wanted to take up residence).

28. B. Baldwin, *Suetonius* (Amsterdam 1983) 283 characterises Suetonius' description of Vitellius' role here as 'the playing of Hess to Nero's Hitler', which seems overly dramatic.

29. See Suetonius *Vespasian* 4.4, Tacitus *Annals* 16.5.3, and Dio 66.11. Cf. Philostratus *Vita Apollonii* 5.29, where Vespasian cries at seeing Nero demean himself. Cf. S. Bartsch, *Actors in the Audience: Theatricality and Doublespeak from Nero to Hadrian* (Cambridge Mass. 1994) 6-7.

30. See Dio 62.18, Tacitus *Annals* 15.39.3, Suetonius *Nero* 38 and Juvenal *Satire* 8.221. There is also a lost work by Lucan called *De Incendio Urbis* (cf. Statius *Silvae* 2.7.60-61). See M.J. McGann, 'Lucan's *De Incendio Urbis*: The Evidence of Statius and Vacca', *TAPA* 106 (1975) 213-17.

31. R. Engel, 'Das Characterbild des Kaisers Vitellius bei Tacitus und sein historischer Kern', *Athenaeum* 55 (1977) 345-68, tries to rehabilitate what he sees as being the thoroughly negative picture of Vitellius in Tacitus and other sources.

32. I. Bruns, *Die Persönlichkeit in der Geschichtsschreibung der Alten* (Berlin 1898) distinguishes between direct and indirect characterisation in ancient historiography. Cf. E. Aubrion, *Rhétorique et histoire chez Tacite* (Metz 1985) 386-7 and C.S. Kraus and A.J. Woodman, *Latin Historians, Greece and Rome New Surveys in the Classics* 27 (1997) 33-4.

33. On the distinction between internal audience and external reader, see A. Sharrock, *Seduction and Repetition in Ovid's Ara Amatoria 2* (Oxford 1994) 10. On reader response criticism, see J.P. Tomkins (ed.), *Reader Response Criticism: From Formalism to Post-Structuralism* (Baltimore 1980) and E. Freund, *The Return of the Reader: Reader-Response Criticism* (London and New York 1987).

34. Heubner's text excises this phrase, but otherwise there are two possible readings, 'eagerness to get their wishes (*aviditate impetrandi*)' or 'eagerness for power (*aviditate imperandi*)'. Both readings cast the soldiers in a bad light and marginalise Vitellius.

35. Z. Rubin, *Civil-War Propaganda and Historiography*, Collection Latomus 173 (Brussels 1980) 75, observes that Dio, in his introduction to the declaration between Severus and Albinus in a later civil war (76.4.1), gives the impression that Severus (like Vespasian) did not enter the war with great enthusiasm and that Albinus (like Vitellius) was the aggressor.

36. R. MacMullen, 'Personal Power in the Roman Empire', *AJP* 107 (1986) 512-24 esp. 518.

37. On Publius Vitellius, see Suetonius *Vitellius* 2.3, Ovid *Pont.* 4.7.27, Pliny *HN* 11.71.187, and Tacitus *Annals* 1.70, 2.6.1, 2.74.2, 3.10.1, 3.13.2, 3.17.2, 3.19.1 and 5.8.

38. For Vitellius' *ignavia* see 1.50.1 (with Otho), 2.94.2 and 3.36.1. Cf. *Annals* 16.18, where *ignavia* is Petronius' chief characteristic.

39. See [Caesar] *Bell. Alex.* 57.1, Appian *BC* 5.16.65, Tacitus *Annals* 1.32.2, and Dio 48.9.1-2 and 78.32.3.

40. Cf. P. Plass, *Wit and the Writing of History* (Madison, Wisconsin 1988) 47 on the 'double take forced on the ear'.

41. For the metaphor of drinking blood see Cicero *Phil.* 11.5.10, *Pro Sestio* 24.54, Livy 26.13.13, Plato *Republic* 579d-e, Valerius Maximus 2.8.7 and 9.2.1, and Plutarch *Marius* 43.7. Cf. [Caesar] *Bell. Afr.* 46.2.

42. Cf. D.C. Earl, *The Moral and Political Tradition of Rome* (London 1967) 60 and P. Jal, *La guerre civile à Rome: étude littéraire et morale* (Paris 1963) 464-72 on warped clemency in civil war.

43. *Bonitas* (appearing only here in Tacitus' works) is not typically used to describe a good general. *comitas* is the special quality of Germanicus, but his competence as an officer is questionable (*Annals* 1.33.2, 2.13.1 and 2.72.2). After his victory, Vitellius gave his son the name 'Germanicus' (2.59.3). Cf. J. Keenan and J. Thomas, 'Vitellius Germanicus: On Tacitus *Histories* 2.70', *AHB* 2 (1988) 113-17.

44. Cf. E. Keitel, 'The Structure and Function of Speeches in Tacitus' *Histories* I-III', *ANRW* 2.33.4 (1991) 2772-94: 'Tacitus expresses his scorn for Vitellius as a leader by according him no oration at all in the *Histories*' (2786). On the parade at Lugdunum, see M.G. Morgan, 'An Heir of Tragedy: Tacitus *Histories* 2.59.3', *CP* 86 (1991) 138-43.

45. G.E.F. Chilver, *A Historical Commentary on Tacitus' Histories I and II* (Oxford 1979) 224.

46. See Livy 1.24-5, 21.42, [Caesar] *Bell. Hisp.* 25, and Appian *BC* 1.50.219-20. Cf. S.P. Oakley, 'Single Combat in the Roman Republic', *CQ* 35 (1985) 392-410 and S.P. Oakley, *A Commentary on Livy Books VI-X. Vol. II Books VII-VIII* (Oxford 1998) 113-48.

47. S.P. Oakley, *A Commentary on Livy Books VI-X. Vol. II Books VII-VIII* (Oxford 1998) notes that *praesulto* is a 'rare (and perhaps newly coined) word' (132).

48. On wrestling see M.B. Poliakoff, *Combat Sports in the Ancient World: Competition, Violence, and Culture* (Yale 1987) 23-53.

49. Although the verb *conlaudavit* appears only here in Tacitus' extant works, it would be rash to suggest that Tacitus himself was deliberately echoing this passage of Livy, since so much of both historians is lost. The verb is reasonably common in the surviving books of Livy, featuring twenty-nine times.

50. See Sallust *Jug.* 100.3, Caesar *BC* 1.3, [Caesar] *Bell. Alex.* 10.5, Plutarch *Ant.* 44.3, Onasander *Strat.* 33.6 and Dio 69.9.3.

51. Cf. F. Kraner and W. Dittenberger, *Julius Caesar: Commentarii de Bello Gallico* (Berlin 1960) 5: 'Caesar wußte sehr gut, welche Wirkung ein *zu rechter Zeit* ausgesprochenes anerkennendes Wort auf Untergebene ausübt'.

52. Cf. Tacitus *Agricola* 21.1, where urban delights wear down the fighting spirit of the Britons.

53. Cf. Florus *Epitome* 1.47.7 (the east as a source for corruption), Sallust *Cat.* 37.5 and Tacitus *Annals* 15.44 (all vice travels to Rome), and Juvenal 3.62 (the Syrian river Orontes casts its 'muck' into the Tiber). There are of course some exceptions to this idealised geographical pattern of corruption, particularly the degeneration of the Carthaginian troops at Capua narrated at Livy 23.18.10-16 and 23.45.1-4, but Capua had been Hannibal's ally and thus an enemy of Rome. See further A. Lintott, 'Imperial Expansion and Moral Decline in the Roman Republic', *Historia* 21 (1972) 626-38, D.F. Conley, 'The Stages of Rome's Decline in Sallust's Historical Theory', *Hermes* 109 (1981) 379-82 and B. Levick, 'Morals, Politics and the Fall of the Roman Republic', *G&R* 29 (1982) 53-62.

54. Cf. R.F. Thomas, *Lands and Peoples in Roman Poetry: The Ethnographical Tradition*, *Cambridge Philological Society Suppl.* Vol. 7 (Cambridge 1982) 111.

55. Cf. D.S. Levene, 'Pity, Fear, and the Historical Audience: Tacitus on the Fall of Vitellius', 128-49 in S. Braund and C. Gill (eds), *The Passions in Roman Thought and Literature* (Cambridge 1997).

56. On the 'king of the grove', see T.F.C. Blagg, 'Le mobilier archéologique du sanctaire de Diane *nemorensis*', 103-9 in O. de Cazanove and J. Scheid (eds),

Les Bois Sacrés (Naples 1993) and T.F.C. Blagg, *Mysteries of Diana: The Antiquities from Nemi* (Nottingham 1983).

57. M.G. Morgan, 'The Three Minor Pretenders in Tacitus *Histories* 2', *Latomus* 52 (1993) 769-96 suggests that the juxtaposition of Geta and Vitellius (2.72) is arranged 'in such a way as to accentuate the latter's folly'.

58. See N.P. Miller and P.V. Jones, 'Critical Appreciations III: Tacitus *Histories* 3.38-9', *G&R* 25 (1978) 70-80.

59. C. Bannon, *The Brothers of Romulus* (Princeton 1997) 135 notes: 'The general acceptance of fraternal devotion as a factor in politics left room for abuse: an appeal to fraternal devotion could be merely a pretext concealing less worthy interests.'

60. Cf. Machiavelli *The Discourses* 3.4: 'The death of Tarquinius Priscus at the hands of the sons of Ancus, and the death of Servius Tullius at the hands of Tarquin the Proud, show how difficult and dangerous it is to deprive anyone of his kingdom and to leave him alive even though one might try to win him over with benefits.'

61. Cf. K. Wellesley, *Cornelius Tacitus: The Histories Book 3* (Sydney 1972) 164. For the application of funeral motifs to doomed living mortals in tragedy, see R.A.S. Seaford, 'The Last Bath of Agamemnon', *CQ* 34 (1984) 247-54.

62. On this motif, see K.M.D. Dunbabin, '*Sic erimus cuncti* ... The Skeleton in Graeco-Roman Art', *JDAI* 101 (1986) 185-255, discussing the display of skeletons at banquets as an epicurean *memento mori*.

63. The presence of children does not always rouse enough pity to change the situation: see Tacitus *Annals* 12.47.4 where Mithridates' wife and children are still executed and Dio 66.16.2 where Peponila uses her children to try to soften Vespasian's heart.

64. D.S. Levene, 'Pity, Fear and the Historical Audience: Tacitus on the Fall of Vitellius', 128-49 in S. Braund and C. Gill (eds), *The Passions in Roman Literature and Thought* (Cambridge 1997) notes (143) that the Tacitean Vitellius loves his family, which is his most attractive trait (1.75.2, 2.59.3, and 3.38), but Suetonius portrays him as cruel to his family (*Vitellius* 6, 7, and 14).

65. The vivid Latin here is characterised by a string of historic presents. In general, see J.P. Chausserie-Laprée, *L'expression narrative chez les historiens latins* (Paris 1969) 369-410, H. Pinkster, 'Tempus, Aspect und Aktionsart in Latin', *ANRW* 2.29.1 (1983) 270-319, and G. Serbat, 'Les Temps du Verbe en Latin I', *REL* 53 (1975) 367-405 and 'Les temps du verbe en latin II', *REL* 54 (1976) 308-52. Note the qualifications of M. Leigh, *Lucan: Spectacle and Engagement* (Oxford 1997) 311-24.

66. See E. Keitel, '*Foedum Spectaculum* and Related Motifs in Tacitus *Histories* II-III', *RhM* 135 (1992) 342-51, esp. 349-51.

67. K. Wellesley, *Cornelius Tacitus: The Histories Book 3* (Sydney 1972) 186 disagrees: 'The diminutive is descriptive, not pathetic as at 67.2.' That seems somewhat arbitrary, especially since Suetonius uses a genuinely descriptive phrase, 'carrying-chair (*gestatoria sella*)' (*Vitellius* 16).

68. The phrase is Sallustian. Cf. Sallust *Jug.* 88.6, where the fickle Bocchus is described in this way.

69. J. Burke, 'Emblematic Scenes in Suetonius' *Vitellius*', *Histos* 2 (1998) suggests that, according to Suetonius, at the scene of the emperor's death, 'at last Vitellius' character and circumstances achieve a gruesome but fitting harmony'. See further E. Cizek, 'La mort de Vitellius dans les vies des douze Césars de Suétone', *REA* 77 (1975) 125-30.

70. Cf. *CIL* VI 31293 = 97 in M. McCrum and A.G. Woodhead, *Documents of the Flavian Empire* (Cambridge 1961).

6. Vespasian, Domitian and Titus

1. On Tacitus' career, see R. Syme, *Tacitus* (Oxford 1958) 59-74 and G. Alföldy, 'Bricht der Schweigsame sein Schweigen? Eine Grabinschrift aus Rom', *MDAI(R)* 102 (1995) 251-68.

2. See R. Syme, *Tacitus* (Oxford 1958) 180. Cf. Sallust *Histories* 1.6 (L.D. Reynolds), who bluntly states his position: 'Nor has the fact that I fought on a different side in a civil war diverted me from the truth.'

3. On this motif, see A.J. Woodman, 'Theory and Practice in Ancient Historiography', *Bull. Council University Classics Depts.* 7 (1978) 6-8, T.P. Wiseman, 'Practice and Theory in Ancient Historiography', *History* 66 (1981) 375-93 and M.J. Wheeldon, 'True Stories: The Reception of Historiography in Antiquity', 33-63 in A. Cameron, *History as Text: The Writing of Ancient History* (London 1989).

4. See P.T. Eden, *Seneca Apocolocyntosis* (Cambridge 1984) 63 on protestations of impartiality.

5. Cf. Cicero *Marc.* 5.13-15. The language of coercion is also used to try to justify collaboration with foreign invaders. In France after World War II, Marshal Pétain pleaded before the High Court of Justice: 'Every day, a dagger at my throat, I struggled against the enemy's demands.' See further R.O. Paxton, *Vichy France: Old Guard and New Order 1940-1944* (New York 1972) 358, who observes: 'It is tempting to identify with Resistance and to say, "That is what I would have done." Alas, we are far more likely to act, in parallel situations, like the Vichy majority' (383).

6. See B.W. Jones, *The Emperor Titus* (London 1984) 91-3 on the conspiracy. Cf. Dio 66.16.3-4, Suetonius *Titus* 6.2, and [Aurelius Victor] *Epit.* 10.4 for Caecina's execution. R. Syme, *Tacitus* (Oxford 1958) 101, finds it hard to reconcile the allegation of conspiracy with Eprius Marcellus' previous loyalty to the regime.

7. For Vespasian's *fortuna* see 1.10.3, 2.1.1, 2.76.1, 2.80.1, 2.84.2, 3.43.1, 3.49.1, 3.59.2, 3.64.1, 3.82.3, 4.81.3 and 5.10.1. Cf. C.B.R. Pelling, *Plutarch: Life of Antony* (Cambridge 1988) 1: 'Actium was one of those battles which mattered ... Antony might well have won it. If he had, he would have been remembered very differently: great Antonian poets would have ensured that, with epics perhaps of Hercules and Anton, not Aeneas and Iulus.'

8. Suetonius notes that the study of language and literature was unknown in early Rome, since the state was 'devoted to warfare' (*De Grammaticis et Rhetoribus* 1.1; cf. R. Kaster (ed.), *C. Suetonius Tranquillus De Grammaticis et Rhetoribus* (Oxford 1995) 46-7). Portraits of ideal generals, who devote more energy to warfare than to clever speeches, implicitly hark back to this idealised past.

9. Cf. Curtius Rufus on Alexander, who was 'mentally not unaffected by superstition (*non intactae a superstitione mentis*)' (4.6.12; cf. Plutarch *Alex.* 25.4 and Arrian *Anabasis* 2.27.1). For the debate about whether Curtius Rufus predates Tacitus, see H. Bödefeld, 'Untersuchungen zur Datierung der Alexandergeschichte des Q. Curtius Rufus', diss. (Düsseldorf 1982) and J. Fugmann, 'Zum Problem der "Historiae Alexandri Magni" des Curtius Rufus', *Hermes* 123 (1995) 233-43.

10. Cf. Diodorus Siculus 13.12.6 and Plutarch *Nicias* 23.

11. Cf. Curtius Rufus 4.10.1-7, Livy 44.37, Cicero *Sen.* 14.49, Valerius Maximus 8.11.1, Onasander *Strat.* 10.25-8 and Frontinus *Strategemata* 1.12.8 (advice on 'taming fear, which soldiers develop from bad omens'). N. Machiavelli, *Discourses* 3.33, stresses the importance of making troops believe that the gods are on their side.

12. On the changing role of prodigies between republic and empire, see D.S. Levene, *Religion in Livy* (Leiden 1993) 4-5.

13. The senate repeatedly banished these astrologers from Italy (Tacitus *Annals* 2.32.3 and 12.52.3). See Dio 66.9 for the inconsistency of Vespasian banishing the astrologers, despite habitually consulting them himself.

14. Cf. A. Wallace-Hadrill, *Suetonius: The Scholar and his Caesars* (London 1983) 189-97 on Suetonius' fascination with omens.

15. So, Clytemnestra dreams of the dead Agamemnon, who plants a sceptre which turns into a tree (Sophocles *Electra* 417-23), Silvia dreams of two palm trees (Ovid *Fasti* 3.31-8), Scipio throws a spear which turns into an oak tree (Silius Italicus *Pun.* 16.584-91), Caesar, in the year before his death, notices a palm-tree with a new shoot (Dio 43.41), which is ironic given that palms were associated with victory (cf. Caesar *BC* 3.105.6 and Suetonius *Aug.* 92.1 and 94.11), and there is the fig-tree, which withers and revives before the murder of Agrippina (Tacitus *Annals* 13.58). Cf. S.K. Dickison and M. Plympton, 'The Prodigy of the Fig-Tree: Tacitus *Annals* 13.58', *RSC* 25 (1977) 183-6. For old testament parallels too, see Genesis 40.9-13, Ezekiel 17 and the later Daniel 4. Cf. E.L. Ehrlich, *Der Traum im Alten Testament, Beihefte zur Zeitschrift für die Alttestamentliche Wissenschaft* 73 (Berlin 1953) 65-73 and 113-22.

16. G.E.F. Chilver, *A Historical Commentary on Tacitus' Histories I and II* (Oxford 1979) 237 and R. Syme, *Tacitus* (Oxford 1958) 522. Livy was selective in dealing with portents: see D.S. Levene, *Religion in Livy* (Leiden 1993) 34-7.

17. See Ennius *Annales* 223-4 (Skutsch), Horace *Odes* 4.6.10, Horace *Epodes* 5.18, Virgil *Aeneid* 3.64 and 6.216, Catullus 64.291, Ovid *Met.* 10.141-2 and *Tristia* 3.13.21, Silius Italicus *Pun.* 10.534, and Statius *Silvae* 5.1.136. Cf. C. Connors, 'Seeing Cypresses in Virgil', *CJ* 88 (1992-3) 1-17.

18. Cf. M.G. Morgan, 'Vespasian and the Omens in Tacitus *Histories* 2.78', *Phoenix* 50 (1996) 41-55, who suggests (47) that the two omens would have set up an antithesis between 'the young Vespasian and the not-so-young Domitian'.

19. Cf. M.G. Morgan, 'Vespasian and the Omens in Tacitus *Histories* 2.78', *Phoenix* 50 (1996) 41-55 esp. 49.

20. On Sallust's portrayal of Marius' transformation, see D.S. Levene, 'Sallust's *Jugurtha*: An "Historical Fragment"?', *JRS* 82 (1992) 53-70. The soothsayer urges Marius to rely on luck, but Sallust's preface (*Jug.* 1.3) had attacked those who relied on *fortuna*.

21. On Vespasian's panic, see M.G. Morgan, 'Vespasian's Fears of Assassination: Tacitus *Histories* 2.74-75', *Philologus* 138 (1994) 118-28.

22. Cf. V.L. Ehrenberg, *Alexander and the Greeks* (1938) 52-61 and R. Syme, *Tacitus* (Oxford 1958) 770-1 on Alexander the Great's 'yearning (*pothos*)', and I. Borzsak, 'Zum Verständnis der Darstellungskunst des Tacitus: Die Veränderungen des Germanicus-Bildes', *Acta Antiqua Academiae Scientarum Hungricae* 18 (1970) 272-92 on Germanicus. Marius also feels this sort of 'desire (*cupido*)' at Sallust *Jug.* 89.6 and 93.3. Desire to see things can be contrasted with desire to conquer or found cities (cf. Livy 1.6.63), although the two are not mutually exclusive in the literary tradition.

23. Cf. K. Scott, 'The Role of Basilides in the Events of AD 69', *JRS* 34 (1934) 138-40.

24. Cf. Tacitus' account of the miraculous Egyptian Phoenix (*Annals* 6.28), on the dating of which see H. Jacobson, 'Tacitus and the Phoenix', *Phoenix* 35 (1981) 260-1.

25. On curing eye-disease with spit, see R. Muth, *Träger der Lebenskraft: Ausscheidungen des Organismus im Volksglauben der Antike* (Vienna 1954) 84-5 and 103-4. On the hazards of eye-disease, see R. Jackson, *Doctors and Diseases in the Roman Empire* (London 1988) 82-5 and 121-3.

26. Cf. A.D. Nock, 'Deification and Julian', *JRS* 47 (1957) 115-23 esp. 118 n. 28, who proposes '[the new] Sar[apis]' as a reading in a papyrus describing Vespasian and his acclamation in Alexandria in AD 69.

27. Cf. Pyrrhus, famously hostile to Rome, who could allegedly cure diseases of the spleen by rubbing the affected area with his big toe (Plutarch *Pyrrhus* 3.9. Cf. Pliny *HN* 7.2.20).

28. The philosopher David Hume was subsequently outraged by this scene, which he discusses in his tract *De Miraculis*. Weighing up 'the probity of so great an emperor', 'the historian noted for candour and veracity', and 'the persons, from whose authority he related the miracle, of established character for judgement and veracity', Hume still cannot bring himself to believe in Vespasian's curing of the two invalids: 'No evidence can well be supposed stronger for so gross and palpable a falsehood.' See D. Hume, *Of Miracles* (La Salle Illinois 1985) with an introduction by A. Flew, 41-2.

29. On the tendency of audiences in the east to be impressed by such scenes see D. Potter, *Prophets and Emperors: Human and Divine Authority from Augustus to Theodosius* (Cambridge Ma. 1994) 173.

30. This may have been a Flavian political catchword after the war. Tacitus associates the phrase with the abortive Pisonian conspiracy of AD 65 (*Annals* 15.50.1) and Pliny uses it of Trajan (*Pan.* 8.3). There is a also a literary precedent (Virgil *Aeneid* 11.335. Cf. *Georgics* 1.500).

31. See F. Magi, *I Rilievi Flavi del Palazzo della Cancelleria* (Rome 1945), H. Last, 'On the Flavian Reliefs from the Palazzo della Cancelleria', *JRS* 38 (1948) 9-14, J.C.M. Toynbee, *The Flavian Reliefs from the Palazzo della Cancelleria* (London 1957), E. Simon, *Zu der Flavische Reliefs von der Cancelleria, JDAI* 75 (1960) 134-56, E. Keller, *Studien zu den Cancelleria-Reliefs, Klio* 49 (1967) 193-215, I.A. Richmond, 'Two Flavian Monuments' 218-28 in P. Salway (ed.), *Roman Archaeology and Art: Essays and Studies* (London 1969), A.M. McCann, *A Re-dating of the Reliefs from the Palazzo della Cancelleria, MDAI(R)* 79 (1972) 249-76, F. Ghedini, *Riflessi della politica domiziana nei rilievi flavi di Palazzo della Cancelleria, BCAR* 91 (1986) 291-309 and R. Darwall-Smith, *Emperors and Architecture: A Study of Flavian Rome, Collection Latomus* 231 (Brussels 1996).

32. See B.M. Levick, *Tiberius the Politician* (London and Sydney 1976) 29, B.M. Levick, 'Drusus Caesar and the Adoptions of AD 4', *Latomus* 25 (1966) 227-44 esp. 229-31 and 'Tiberius' Retirement to Rhodes in 6 BC', *Latomus* 31 (1972) 779-813 esp. 782-4.

33. On Vitellius' marriages and children, see C.L. Murison, *Galba, Otho, Vitellius: Careers and Controversies* (Hildesheim 1993) 150-5.

34. C.H.V. Sutherland and R.A.G. Carson, *The Roman Imperial Coinage* (London 1984) vol. 1, plate 31, number 101 (= *BMC* 28).

35. The boy was probably blind, but the phrase does not exclude the possibility that he had actually lost an eye, which is a physical disfigurement traditionally associated with tough generals. Cf. Sertorius (Plutarch *Sertorius*

1.8) and Antigonus 'Monophthalmus', whose nickname took a turn for the worse when people started to call him 'Cyclops' (Aelian *VH* 12.43).

36. R. Garland, *The Eye of the Beholder: Deformity and Disability in the Greco-Roman World* (London 1995) 5-6.

37. Ancient writers perceived a difference between congenital problems and afflictions which struck during a person's life. So, R. Garland, *The Eye of the Beholder: Deformity and Disability in the Greco-Roman World* (London 1995) 5-6, comments that 'Congenital blindness is conventionally interpreted as a deformity as well as a disability, whereas the onset of blindness in later life is usually regarded merely as a disability'. Aristotle proposed that 'deformed children come from deformed parents, lame from lame, and blind from blind' (*Historia Animalium* 585b29). Plutarch notes that 'if a city is a single and continuous whole, surely a family is too, attached as it is to a single origin which reproduces in its members a certain force and common quality pervading them all' (*Moralia* 559D). Cf. Homer *Odyssey* 8.311-12, [Hippocrates] *Gon.* 7.8, Lucretius *De Rerum Natura* 4.1218-26, Censorinus 6.5 and 6.8, and Lactantius *De Opificio Dei* 12. See further W.W. Fortenbaugh, 'Plato: Temperament and Eugenic Policy', *Arethusa* 8 (1975) 283-305, G.E.R. Lloyd, *Science, Folklore and Ideology* (Cambridge 1983) 86-91 and R. Garland, *The Greek Way of Life* (Ithaca 1990) 33-5.

38. Cf. E.F. Leon, 'The *Imbecillitas* of the Emperor Claudius', *TAPA* 79 (1948) 79-86 and B.M. Levick, *Claudius* (London 1990) 13-17.

39. G.E.F. Chilver and G.B. Townend, *A Historical Commentary on Tacitus' Histories IV and V* (Oxford 1985) note that there is no information about Tacitus' source for this confidential talk between Titus and Vespasian, which is recorded nowhere else (62).

40. See further C.J. Bannon, *The Brothers of Romulus* (Princeton 1997) 141-45.

41. See further C.J. Bannon, *The Brothers of Romulus* (Princeton 1997) 149. Cf. Livy *Per.* 79, Tacitus *Histories* 3.51, and Lucan *Phar.* 1.376 and 2.151.

42. It was traditional that tyrants could not tolerate members of their family as partners (cf. Herodotus 1.92.4, 3.30 and 3.39, Justin 11.2.3 and Nicolaus of Damascus *FGH* 90 F61). Also, fraternal discord is recurrent in the 'commonplace about the times' set-piece (Virgil *Georgics* 2.510, Lucretius 3.70-3, Catullus 64.399, Ovid *Met.* 1.143-9 and Seneca *Phaedra* 555-8). Cf. T. Wiedemann, 'Sallust's *Jugurtha*: Concord and the Digressions', *G&R* 40 (1993) 48-57 and P. Hardie, *The Epic Successors of Virgil* (Cambridge 1993) 10.

43. Cerialis had a reputation as a rash commander, who tended not to think ahead. He was a friend and relative by marriage of Vespasian, but is not heard of after his second consulship in AD 74. Cf. G.B. Townend, 'Some Flavian Connections', *JRS* 51 (1961) 54-61.

44. E. Schäfer, 'Domitians Antizipationen in *Histories* 4', *Hermes* 105 (1977) 455-77, notes that Tacitus diminishes Vespasian's importance by this episode, and prefigures the later tyrannical Domitian.

45. See R. Syme, *Tacitus* (Oxford 1958) 267, J. Ginsburg, *Tradition and Theme in the Annals of Tacitus* (Berkeley 1981) 110n5, 111n14 and 129, and R.H. Martin and A.J. Woodman, *Tacitus Annals Book IV* (Cambridge 1989) 262-3. On infratextual closure in general, see D.P. Fowler, 'First Thoughts on Closure: Problems and Prospects', *MD* 22 (1989) 75-122 esp. 86-97 and D.P. Fowler, 'Second Thoughts on Closure', 3-22 esp. 13, in D.H. Roberts, F.M. Dunn, and D.P. Fowler (eds), *Classical Closure* (Princeton 1997).

46. Cf. H. Heubner, *P. Cornelius Tacitus: Die Historien* Vol. 4 (Heidelberg

1976) 210 and G.E.F. Chilver and G.B. Townend, *A Historical Commentary on Tacitus' Histories IV and V* (Oxford 1985) 87.

47. D.S. Levene, 'Sallust's *Jugurtha*: An "Historical Fragment" ', *JRS* 82 (1992) 53-70 esp. 53.

48. The escape was subsequently praised (Statius *Thebaid* 1.21-2, Silius Italicus *Pun.* 3.609-10, Martial 9.101-14 and Josephus *BJ* 4.649). Tacitus *Histories* 3.74.1 deflates the heroic status of the incident. Cf. K. Wellesley, 'Three Historical Puzzles in *Histories* 3', *CQ* 49 (1956) 207-14 esp. 211-14 and P. Southern, *Domitian Tragic Tyrant* (London and New York 1997) 17-18.

49. Cf. Tacitus *Agricola* 45.2, Pliny *Pan.* 48.4, Suetonius *Domitian* 18.1 and Philostratus *Vita Apollonii* 7.28. Cf. R.O.A.M. Lyne, 'Lavinia's Blush: Virgil *Aeneid* 12.64-70', *G&R* 30 (1983) 55-64 and A. La Penna, '*Rubor* e *Inpudentia* da Pompeo a Domiziano (Nota a Tacito *Agr.* 45.2)', *Maia* 27 (1975) 117-19.

50. Sulla's dictatorship is thematically linked with blood by Lucan: the orgy of killing in Rome creates a river of blood that bursts the banks of the Tiber and forces its way to the sea (*Phar.* 2.209-20). Cf. E. Fantham, *Lucan: De Bello Civili II* (Cambridge 1992) 117-20.

51. Eubulus 97.2 in R. Kassel and C. Austin, *Poetae Comici Graeci* Vol. V (Berlin and New York 1986) 246, and Philippides 19.1 in R. Kassel and C. Austin, *Poetae Comici Graeci* Vol. VII (Berlin and New York 1989) 344, both refer to women using mulberry juice as a facial wash. Dioscorides *De Materia Medica* 4.87 says that flour was used as a poultice. If these were widely used as beauty products to promote a healthy skin and clear complexion, then the quip works on another level as well.

52. Cf. Plutarch *Moralia* 567B, Plato *Gorgias* 524a8-525a7, Lucian *Cataplus* 24-6, Philo of Alexandria *De Specialibus Legibus* 1.103, Epictetus *Discourses* 2.18.11, Themistius *Orationes* 20.234 and Tacitus *Annals* 6.6.

53. Cf. G. Zanker, '*Enargeia* in the Ancient Criticism of Poetry', *RhM* 124 (1981) 297-311 and A.D. Walker, '*Enargeia* and the Spectator in Greek Historiography', *TAPA* 123 (1993) 353-77.

54. On Serapis (Latin form of the Greek name), see U. Wilcken, *Urkunden der Ptolemäerzeit I* (Berlin and Leipzig 1922) 7-37, C.B. Welles, 'The Discovery of Sarapis and the Foundation of Alexandria', *Historia* 11 (1962) 271-98, P.M. Fraser, *Ptolemaic Alexandria I* (Oxford 1972) 246-76 and S.A. Takács, *Isis and Sarapis in the Roman World* (Leiden 1995) 94-8 on Vespasian and Serapis. The Alexander romance explicitly associates Alexander with the early history of Serapis' cult ([Callisthenes] 1.33).

55. A. Henrichs, 'Vespasian's Visit to Alexandria', *ZPE* 3 (1968) 51-80 has proposed that Vespasian's visit to the Temple of Serapis was carefully modelled on Alexander's visit to the Siwah oasis in the Libyan desert: so, Alexander alone went into the temple while his attendants had to stay outside (Strabo 17.1.43). Readers may therefore already have been thinking in terms of Alexander through such coincidence of detail. Cf. A.B. Bosworth, *Conquest and Empire: The Reign of Alexander the Great* (Cambridge 1988) 71-4.

56. Cf. K. Büchner, 'Die Reise des Titus', *Studien zur römischen Literatur* 4 (Wiesbaden 1964) 83-98.

57. Cf. J-.P. Nerandeau, *La jeunesse dans la littérature et les institutions de la Rome Républicaine* (1979) 249-58 on the structural polarisation between youth (associated with 'frenzy (*furor*)') and old age (associated with 'discipline (*disciplina*)') and E. Eyben, *Restless Youth in Ancient Rome* (London 1992), trans. P. Daly, 44-52. B.W. Jones, 'The Reckless Titus' 408-20 in C. Deroux (ed.),

Studies in Latin Literature and Roman History VI (Brussels 1992) is critical of Titus.

58. Cf. Livy 26.18.11, Justin 7.6.3, Diodorus Siculus 17.2.1-2, Plutarch *Alex.* 11.6 and Tacitus *Annals* 1.46.1 and 13.6.2.

59. W.H. Fyfe (trans.) and D.S. Levene (rev. and ed.), *Tacitus: The Histories* (Oxford 1997) 291.

60. Cf. G.H. MacCurdy, 'Julia Berenice', *AJP* 56 (1935) 246-53, J.A. Crook, 'Titus and Berenice', *AJP* 72 (1951) 162-75, R. Jordan, *Berenice* (New York 1974), P.M. Rogers, 'Titus, Berenice and Mucianus', *Historia* 29 (1980) 86-95, D.C. Braund, 'Berenice in Rome', *Historia* 33 (1984) 120-3 and B.W. Jones, *The Emperor Titus* (London 1984) 59-76.

61. See L. Davis, *The Course of Honour* (London 1997) for an entertaining novel which reconstructs the passionate relationship between Vespasian and the freedwoman Caenis.

62. D.C. Braund, 'Berenice in Rome', *Historia* 33 (1984) 120-3 emphasises a history of Roman hostility towards relationships between Roman men and foreign queens, especially Cleopatra. Nor was reaction in the east likely to have been much more enthusiastic. As Miriam Griffin has pointed out to me, Titus would have had to convert to Judaism and marry Berenice for opinion in Judaea to be favourable.

7. Antonius Primus

1. On Antonius Primus, see M. Treu, 'M. Antonius Primus in der taciteischen Darstellung', *WJA* 3 (1948) 241-62, T.A. Dorey, 'Tacitus' Treatment of Antonius Primus', *CP* 53 (1958) 244 and D.C.A. Shotter, 'Tacitus and Antonius Primus', *LCM* 2 (1977) 23-7.

2. That one man rarely possessed both decent political skill and military flair is a familiar motif. Cf. Homer *Iliad* 18.251-2, Livy 1.53.1, 2.43.10 and 9.1.2, Sallust *Cat.* 2.1, Dionysius of Halicarnassus 2.4, [Caesar] *Bell. Afr.* 54.5, Polybius 16.21 and 23.5.

3. M. Meulder, 'Bons et mauvais généraux chez Tacite', *Revue Belge de Philologie et d'Histoire* 73 (1995) 75-89 esp. 81.

4. See 1.35.1 (Galba), 2.11.3 (Otho), and 2.89.1 (Vitellius). The unwarlike Vitellius 'in a general's cloak' is especially inappropriate. Cf. Livy 31.14.1, 41.10.5-7 and 42.49.1, Cicero *Verr.* 5.13.34, and Dio 39.6. See J. Rüpke, *Domi Militiae* (Stuttgart 1990) 125. Descriptions of Caligula in triumphal military garb are meant to seem similarly incongruous (Dio 59.17.3 and Suetonius *Caligula* 19.2).

5. See 2.7.1 (with M.G. Morgan, 'Tacitus *Histories* 2.7.1', *Hermes* 123 (1995) 335-40), 2.25.2, 2.30.1, 3.40.2 and 5.14.2.

6. H. Strasburger, 'Der Einzelne und die Gemeinschaft im Denken der Griechen', *HZ* 177 (1954) 227-48, refers to the idealised Greek concept of 'eine höchste Entfaltung der individuellen Initiative im Dienste des Staates' (245). Primus' initiative as an individual is indisputable, but the status of his service to Rome is more ambiguous.

7. In another era the Prussian Chief-of-Staff, General von Moltke, observed: 'The greatest kindness in war is to bring it to a speedy conclusion'. M. Walzer, *Just and Unjust Wars: A Moral Argument with Historical Illustrations* (Harmondsworth, England 1980) 47.

8. On the dating of Martial's epigrams, see M. Citroni, 'Marziale e la Letteratura per i Saturnali', *ICS* 14 (1989) 201-26. Book 10 was originally written before Domitian's murder on 18 Sept. AD 96, but Martial produced a revised anthology of Books 10 and 11 for Nerva.

9. G.E.F Chilver, *A Historical Commentary on Tacitus' Histories I and II* (Oxford 1979) 247. Cf. K. Wellesley *Cornelius Tacitus: The Histories Book 3* (Sydney 1972) 15, M. Treu, 'M. Antonius Primus in der taciteischen Darstellung', *WJA* 3 (1948) 241-62 esp. 241, J. Nicols, *Vespasian and the Partes Flavianae, Historia Einzelschriften* 28 (Stuttgart 1978) 141-2 and A. Briessman, *Tacitus und das flavische Geschichtsbild, Hermes Einzelschriften* (Wiesbaden 1955) 49.

10. One text which has benefited from increasing critical subtlety is Ovid's *Ars Amatoria*, which was often condemned as ineffectually repetitive. See now A. Sharrock, *Seduction and Repetition in Ovid's Ars Amatoria II* (Oxford 1994) 1-20. For a survey of the impact of various critical theories on classical literature, see D. and P. Fowler in S. Hornblower and A. Spawforth (eds), *The Oxford Classical Dictionary* (Oxford 1996) 871-5.

11. Such contrasts remained popular. Machiavelli compares the impulsive Decius Mus and the cautious Fabius Rullianus, who fought on the same side at the battle of Sentinum in 295 BC, and concludes that 'Fabius' plan was much better than that of Decius' (*Discourses* 3.45).

12. Cf. O. Skutsch, *The Annals of Quintus Ennius* (Oxford 1985) 531, on the possibility that 'delayer (*cunctator*)', the label so often attached to Fabius, might originally have been a gibe, even if it had a laudatory sense when Ennius wrote. T.P. Wiseman, *Remus: A Roman Myth* (Cambridge 1995) 7, makes the interesting observation that the name Remus is derived from 'to delay (*remorari*)'.

13. This suggestion is made by C.S. Kraus, *Livy Ab Urbe Condita Book VI* (Cambridge 1994) 223. Cf. S.P. Oakley, *A Commentary on Livy Books VI-X. Vol. II Books VII-VIII* (Oxford 1998) 579-604.

14. C.G. Starr, *The Influence of Sea-Power on Ancient History* (Oxford 1989) 75, refers to a Vespasianic coin inscribed with 'Naval Victory (*Victoria Navalis*)' and associates this with the role of sea power in winning the principate for Vespasian. Cf. H. Mattingly, *Coins of the Roman Empire in the British Museum* (London 1926) vol. 2, plate 2, number 32 (= *BMC* 481).

15. Cf. G.E.F. Chilver, *A Historical Commentary on Tacitus' Histories IV and V*, completed and revised by G.B. Townend (Oxford 1985) 63, on possible exaggeration of the crisis by Flavian propagandists, and G. Rickman, *The Corn Supply of Ancient Rome* (Oxford 1980) 68 and 231-5 on Africa and Egypt.

16. Cf. M.G. Morgan, 'Tacitus *Histories* 2.83-84: Content and Positioning', *CP* 89 (1994) 166-75, who argues that Tacitus provocatively highlights Mucianus' plan of attacking southern Italy (2.83.2) to characterise him as a commander who was prepared (like Primus) to resort to violence.

17. See Suetonius *Augustus* 16.1, Velleius Paterculus 2.77.1 and Dio 48.36.

18. On food riots see A.W. Lintott, *Violence in Republican Rome* (Oxford 1968) 212-14, C. Virlouvet, *Famines et Émeutes à Rome des origines de la République à la mort de Néron* (Rome 1985) 63-80, P.J.J. Vanderbroeck, *Popular Leadership and Collective Behaviour in the Late Roman Republic (c.80-50 BC)* (Amsterdam 1987) 148, D. Cherry, 'Hunger at Rome in the Late Republic', *EMC* 37 (1993) 433-50 and F. Millar, *The Crowd in Rome in the Late Republic* (Ann Arbor Michigan 1998) 44, 60 and 155.

19. Bell deconstructs the image of the humane embargo in a discussion of fighting techniques in the former Yugoslavia: 'It wasn't war in the enclaves: it was murder. People there were being killed by the Serb blockades through malnutrition, starvation and medical neglect, as surely and deliberately as if they had been singled out and shot by the firing squad. It just took longer.' See M. Bell, *In Harm's Way* (London 1995) 194. Cf. M. Walzer, *Just and Unjust Wars: A Moral Argument with Historical Illustrations* (Harmondsworth, England 1980) 172-5 on the British blockade of Germany in World War I.

20. Williams highlights the complexities of avoiding war in the twentieth century, which he argues can be motivated by selfish concerns: 'We say, understandably, that we must avoid war at all costs, but what we commonly mean is that we will avoid war at any cost but our own.' See R. Williams, *Modern Tragedy* (London 1966) 82.

21. See W.K. Pritchett, *The Greek State at War* Vol. 2 (Berkeley 1974) 155 on soldiers forcing unwilling commanders to fight. Cf. Thucydides 5.65.6 and 8.78.1, Appian *BC* 2.67.276, Lucan *Phar.* 7.45-61, Plutarch *Pomp.* 66.1-4 and *Marius* 16.7-10, [Caesar] *Bell. Afr.* 82 and *Bell. Alex.* 61.4.

22. On Calvia Crispinilla, Nero's 'sinister wardrobe-mistress' (cf. Dio 63.12.4), see M. Griffin, *Nero: The End of a Dynasty* (London 1984) 180-1.

23. (i) **Moesia:** K. Wellesley, *Cornelius Tacitus: The Histories Book 3* (Sydney 1972) 209-15 and R. Syme, 'The March of Mucianus', *Antichthon* 11 (1977) 78-92 (= A.R. Birley (ed.), *Roman Papers III* (Oxford 1984) 998-1013) (ii) **Cremona:** M.G. Morgan, 'Cremona in AD 69. Two Notes on Tacitus' Narrative Techniques', *Athenaeum* 84 (1996) 381-403 (iii) **The Capitol:** T.P. Wiseman, 'Flavians on the Capitol', *AJAH* 3 (1978) 163-78 and K. Wellesley, 'What Happened on the Capitol in December AD 69?', *AJAH* 6 (1981) 166-90. (iv) **Civilis:** P.A. Brunt, 'Tacitus on the Batavian Revolt', *Latomus* 19 (1960) 494-517 (= *Roman Imperial Themes* (Oxford 1990) 33-52) and R. Urban, *Der Bataveraufstand und die Erhebung des Iulius Classicus* (Trier 1985).

24. K. Wellesley, *Cornelius Tacitus: The Histories Book 3* (Sydney 1972) 98, criticises Tacitus' exaggerated phrasing, because the historian thereby defends Primus' decision to act quickly. Tacitus only uses 'calamity (*lues*)', on one other occasion in his extant works (*Annals* 2.47.2) to describe a destructive earthquake in Asia. The word is associated with natural forces running out of control. Cf. Seneca *Phaedra* 1017, of a storm. See *TLL* 7.2.1794-97.

25. Cf. Caesar *BG* 5.28-30 (another council of war where the advocates of speed prevail with disastrous results), Livy 22.14.4-15 (Marcus Minucius, frustrated at Fabius Maximus' delays, hastily attacks Hannibal, which nearly causes disaster) and Appian *BC* 2.103.428 (Pompey the younger plans to engage Caesar immediately, although the older men advocate delay and are proved right after defeat at Munda).

26. E. Paratore, *Tacito, Nuovi Saggi* 34 (Rome 1962) 73, notes that Tacitus also uses this shift in Primus' two other speeches (3.20.1 and 3.24.1), which suggests his dashing and audacious character. Conversely, J.M. Scott, 'The Rhetoric of Suppressed Speech: Tacitus' Omission of Direct Discourse in his *Annales* as a Technique in Character Denigration', *AHB* 12.1-2 (1998) 8-18, discusses Tacitus' technique of denigrating characters (particularly Nero) by suppressing direct speech. N.P. Miller, 'Dramatic Speech in the Roman Historians', *G&R* 22 (1975) 45-57 is generally useful, but does not discuss the transition from *oratio obliqua* to *oratio recta* within a single speech.

27. Cf. Sallust *Jug.* 45.2 and Seneca *Epistle* 56.9 for the notion that action tended to toughen undisciplined troops.

28. Cf. 3.18.2, the second battle of Bedriacum: 'Primus did not follow up his advantage, realising that although the outcome was successful, the battle had long been doubtful and had cost the cavalry and horses (*equites equosque*) many wounds and much hard fighting.' The configuration *equites equosque* is unusual and may contrast Primus' earlier idealised picture of the battle with a less glorious reality. The *Flavian* cavalry and horses suffer, rather than the Vitellians, as anticipated in the speech.

29. See *Iliad* 4.274, 16.66, 17.755 and 23.133. Cf. Herodotus 8.109.2, Livy 35.49.5, and Virgil *Aeneid* 9.33.

30. G.E.F. Chilver, *A Historical Commentary on Tacitus' Histories I and II* (Oxford 1979) 205-6.

31. For the metaphor of unlocking, see Cicero *Phil.* 7.1.2 (Italy), Silius Italicus *Pun.* 4.196 (road) and 17.501 (Alps), and Lucan *Phar.* 2.682 (ocean). Cf. E. Fantham, *Lucan De Bello Civili II* (Cambridge 1992) 214 and C.S. Kraus, *Livy Ab Urbe Condita Book VI* (Cambridge 1994) 140. Tacitus elsewhere uses the same metaphor in connection with the corn-blockade and refers to the decision that Vespasian should 'secure the bolts of Egypt (*obtinere claustra Aegypti*)' (2.82.3). Cf. 3.8.2, Suetonius *Vespasian* 7.1 and Livy 45.11.5. See further *TLL* III 1321-2.

32. Cf. 1.61.2. See further *TLL* VIII 1345-6.

33. Brevity as well as simplicity tended to characterise military speakers. Livy describes the speeches of Fabius Rullianus and Decius Mus as being short, 'which was appropriate for soldiers and men who relied more on deeds than words' (10.24.4). Cf. Vespasian, who addressed his men 'in soldierly fashion (*militariter*)' (2.80.2), although Tacitus does not report his words in detail. Vespasian's speeches in the *Histories* are conspicuous by their absence.

34. See E. Keitel, 'The Structure and Function of Speeches in Tacitus' *Histories* I-III', *ANRW* 2.33.4 (1991) 2772-94, esp. 2790-4 on councils, E. Aubrion, *Rhétorique et histoire chez Tacite* (Metz 1985) 646-53 and especially P.H. Herzog, *Die Funktion des militärischen Planens bei Tacitus* (Frankfurt-am-Main 1996) 98-191.

35. The verb *dissero* appears elsewhere in the *Histories* at 1.83.1 (Otho), 1.90.2 (Otho), 2.2.2 (Tacitus), 2.53.1 (Eprius Marcellus), 2.96.2 (Vitellius), 3.2.1 (Antonius Primus), 3.3 (*non ... disseruit*, Antonius Primus), 3.52.2 (Mucianus), 3.81.1 (Musonius Rufus), 4.40.1 (Domitian) 4.57.3 (Vocula), 4.73.1 (Cerialis) and 4.81.2 (doctors). *effundo* in the sense of pouring out words is much more unusual, but see 4.68.5 (the Treviran Julius Valentinus). Cf. *TLL* 5.2.224. Quintilian 11.2.39 notes the kind of speeches which seem to be *effusa*, but have been learned carefully beforehand.

36. Musonius Rufus can also be found giving advice at *Annals* 14.59.1. Tacitus notes his banishment in AD 65 after the Pisonian conspiracy (*Annals* 15.71.4). Dio claims that he was the only philosopher spared when Vespasian expelled the philosophers from Rome (66.13). Pliny says that he 'valued and admired' Musonius Rufus (*Epistle* 3.11.5).

37. A parallel can be drawn between Primus and another general, Ulysses S. Grant, to whom a grateful President Lincoln said at their first private meeting: 'All I had wanted and had ever wanted was someone who would take the responsibility and act ....' See J. Keegan, *The Mask of Command* (London 1987) 232.

38. P.A. Brunt, 'The Army and the Land in the Roman Revolution', *JRS* 52 (1962) 69-86 notes the importance of individual generals in motivating soldiers (76). Cf. N. Machiavelli, *Discourses* 1.43.

39. Cf. Plutarch *Otho* 18.5-7. On Verginius Rufus, see D.C.A. Shotter, 'Verginius Rufus and Tacitus', *CQ* 17 (1967) 370-81, B.M. Levick, 'L. Verginius

Rufus and the Four Emperors', *RhM* 128 (1985) 319-46 and C.L. Murison, *Galba, Otho and Vitellius: Careers and Controversies* (Hildesheim 1993) 15-20.

40. Cf. C.B.R. Pelling, 'Tacitus and Germanicus' 59-85 esp. 62 n. 8 in T.J. Luce and A.J. Woodman (eds), *Tacitus and the Tacitean Tradition* (Princeton 1993). M.F. Williams, 'Four Mutinies: Tacitus *Annals* 1.16-30; 1.31-49 and Ammianus Marcellinus *Res Gestae* 20.4.9-20.5.7; 24.3.1-8', *Phoenix* 51 (1997) 53 questions how far we should criticise Germanicus' gesture here.

41. So, in a dignified manner Alcibiades succeeds in controlling the mob who want to sail against the Piraeus in 411 BC (Thucydides 8.86.5). Cf. Machiavelli *Discourses* 1.54: 'A person who has command of an army or who finds himself in a city where a tumult has arisen should present himself before those involved with as much grace and dignity as he can muster, wearing the insignia of whatever rank he holds in order to impress them.'

42. See Onasander *Strat.* 33.4. Cf. Plutarch *Pelopidas / Marcellus Comp.* 3 and Ovid *Met.* 13.365-8.

43. Sallust *Cat.* 20.16 and 60.4. Cf. Caesar *BG* 5.33.2, Suetonius *Augustus* 10.4, Lucan *Phar.* 7.87-8, Appian *BC* 2.51.209 and [Caesar] *Bell. Alex.* 21.1, Curtius Rufus 3.11.7 and Tacitus *Histories* 4.66.2.

44. Cf. E. Keitel, 'The Structure and Function of Speeches in Tacitus' *Histories* I-III', *ANRW* 2.33.4 (1991) 2772-94: 'Tacitus gives Antonius more speeches than anyone else in Book 3 (3.2, 10, 20, 24, 60) to chart the vicissitudes of his relations with his troops' (2793).

45. Promises in the *Histories* are often financial in nature: see 1.25.1, 2.8.1, 3.58.3 and 4.30.2.

46. Cf. K. Wellesley, *Cornelius Tacitus: The Histories Book 3* (Sydney 1972) 109.

47. See Caesar *BC* 1.16, [Caesar] *Bell. Afr.* 11.3 and 67.2. See further A.K. Goldsworthy, *The Roman Army at War 100 BC-AD 200* (Oxford 1996) 290-2.

48. Cf. M. Walzer, *Just and Unjust Wars: A Moral Argument with Historical Illustrations* (Harmondsworth, England 1980) 310-11, on the infamous My Lai massacre of civilians in Vietnam: Lieutenant Calley, who led the unit into the village, was called to account, but the enlisted men, who carried out the murders, were never charged.

49. K. Wellesley, *Cornelius Tacitus: The Histories Book 3* (Sydney 1972) 122 (condemnation), and F. Ritter, *Cornelii Taciti Historiae* (Cambridge and London 1848) 226 (exculpation). See H. Heubner, *P. Cornelius Tacitus: Die Historien* Vol. 3 (Heidelberg 1972) 87-8 for further discussion.

50. M.G. Morgan, 'Cremona in AD 69: Two Notes on Tacitus' Narrative Technique', *Athenaeum* 84 (1996) 381-403.

51. Cf. Titus, blamed for the destruction of the temple in Jerusalem (Valerius Flaccus 1.13 and Sulpicius Severus 2.30), although Josephus incriminates the soldiers instead (*BJ* 6.228, 232, 252-3 and 256-66). See G. Alon, *Jews, Judaism and the Classical World* trans. I. Abrahams (Jerusalem 1976) 252-68. Likewise, Velleius Paterculus 2.74.4 blames the soldiers rather than Octavian for the brutal sack of Perusia. See R.A. Gurval, *Actium and Augustus* (Ann Arbor Michigan 1995) 176-7 for the more ambiguous connection between Perusia and Octavian in Propertius 2.1.

52. See Virgil *Aeneid* 12.311-23. Cf. [Caesar] *Bell. Afr.* 82. On the theme of the one and the many in epic, see P. Hardie, *The Epic Successors of Virgil* (Cambridge 1993) 3-10. For one commander, Caecina, who successfully stops his frightened men from breaking out of their camp by throwing himself in their path, see Tacitus *Annals* 1.66.2.

53. J. Henderson, 'Tacitus: The World in Pieces' in *Fighting for Rome: Poets and Caesars, History and Civil War* (Cambridge 1998) 260.

54. Cf. Curtius Rufus 9.2.12-34, where Alexander fails to persuade his army to cross the Hyphasis and march further eastwards, for a dramatic presentation of the failure of one charismatic individual's rhetoric in the face of collective determination.

55. See Dio 65.9-11, 65.14, 65.17-18 and Suetonius *Vitellius* 18 (Primus) and Dio 65.8-9, 65.14, 65.18, 65.22, 66.2, 66.9, 66.13 and Suetonius *Vespasian* 6.4 and 13 (Mucianus).

56. The family had suffered under the later Julio-Claudians. Claudius executed Scribonianus' eldest brother, Cn. Pompeius Magnus, in c. AD 46 (Suetonius *Claudius* 27.2, 29.1-2, Tacitus *Histories* 1.48.1, Seneca *Apocolocyntosis* 11.2 and 11.5, Dio 60.29.6a, 60.30.6a) and Nero had eliminated his other brother, M. Licinius Crassus Frugi (Pliny *Epistles* 1.5.3, Tacitus *Histories* 1.48.1 and 4.42.1). See further D. McAlindon, 'Senatorial Opposition to Claudius and Nero', *AJP* 77 (1956) 113-32, esp. 126-8.

57. H. White, *Metahistory* (Baltimore 1973) 7.

58. Cf. A.J. Woodman, *Velleius Paterculus: The Caesarian and Augustan Narrative (2.41-93)* (Cambridge 1983) 199, J.W. Rich, *Cassius Dio: The Augustan Settlement* (London 1990) 18, M. Reinhold, *Marcus Agrippa: A Biography* (Geneva, New York 1933) 149-66 and J.-M. Roddaz, *Marcus Agrippa* (Rome 1984) 496-533. See Suetonius *Augustus* 66.3 and *Tiberius* 10 for some alleged turbulence in the relationship between Agrippa and Augustus.

59. There is a parallel between Primus and the following character sketch of Colonel Bob Stewart, former commander of the Cheshire Regiment in Bosnia: 'He hated to delegate. He was impatient with detail and paperwork, and famous for walking out of negotiating sessions which he felt were getting nowhere .... He was not at all times a model of tact and temperance. He paid more attention to the soldiers serving under him than those above him, and did not seek to win the favour of the generals. But the faults were the downside of his virtues. Even his critics conceded his courage .... Bob Stewart was the right man in the right place at the right time. It made no difference. Within two years of leaving Bosnia he received his notice of redundancy ...' (M. Bell, *In Harm's Way* (London 1995) 158). Antonius Primus and Colonel Stewart are both presented as falling from grace as a result of their unconventional leadership techniques.

Epilogue

1. Cf. Caesar *BC* 1.7, [Caesar] *Bell. Afr.* 10.3-4 and *Bell. Alex.* 39.

Abbreviations

AHB	*Ancient History Bulletin*
AJAH	*American Journal of Ancient History*
AJP	*American Journal of Philology*
ANRW	*Aufstieg und Niedergang der Römischen Welt*
AS	*Ancient Society*
BCAR	*Bullettino della Commissione Archeologica Communale in Roma*
BICS	*Bulletin of the Institute of Classical Studies*
BMC	*Coins of the Roman Empire in the British Museum* ed. H. Mattingly (London 1923-).
CIL	*Corpus Inscriptionum Latinarum* (Berlin 1863–)
CJ	*Classical Journal*
CP	*Classical Philology*
CQ	*Classical Quarterly*
CR	*Classical Review*
CW	*Classical World*
EMC	*Echos du Monde Classique*
FGH	*Die Fragmente der Griechischen Historiker* ed. F. Jacoby (Berlin and Leiden 1923-58)
G&R	*Greece and Rome*
GRBS	*Greek, Roman and Byzantine Studies*
HSCP	*Harvard Studies in Classical Philology*
HRR	*Historicorum Romanorum Reliquiae* ed. H. Peter (Leipzig 1914)
HZ	*Historische Zeitschrift*
ICS	*Illinois Classical Studies*
ILS	*Inscriptiones Latinae Selectae* ed. H. Dessau (Berlin 1892-1916)
JDAI	*Jahrbuch des Deutschen Archäologischen Instituts*
JHS	*Journal of Hellenic Studies*
JRS	*Journal of Roman Studies*
JWI	*Journal of the Warburg Institute*
LCM	*Liverpool Classical Monthly*
MAAR	*Memoirs of the American Academy in Rome*
MD	*Materiali e Discussioni per l'Analisi dei Testi Classici*
MDAI(R)	*Mitteilungen des Deutschen Archäologischen Instituts* (Röm. Abt.)
MH	*Museum Helveticum*
NC	*Numismatic Chronicle*
OCT	*Oxford Classical Text*
PBA	*Proceedings of the British Academy*
PCPS	*Proceedings of the Cambridge Philological Society*

PLLS	Papers of the Leeds Latin Seminar
PVS	Proceedings of the Virgil Society
REA	Revue des Études Anciennes
REL	Revue des Études Latines
RhM	Rheinisches Museum
RFIC	Rivista di Filologia e di Istruzione Classica
RSC	Rivista di Studi Classici
SO	Symbolae Osloenses
TAPA	Transactions and Proceedings of the American Philological Association
TLL	Thesaurus Linguae Latinae
WJA	Würzburger Jahrbücher für die Altertumswissenschaft
YCS	Yale Classical Studies
ZPE	Zeitschrift für Papyrologie und Epigraphik

Ancient Works

Alex.	Plutarch Alexander
Ant.	Plutarch Antony
Ant. Rom.	Dionysius of Halicarnassus Antiquitates Romanae
Aq.	Frontinus De Aquaeductibus
Arch.	Cicero Pro Archia
Att.	Cicero Epistulae ad Atticum
BC	Appian Bella Civilia
BC	Caesar De Bello Civili
Bell. Afr.	[Caesar] Bellum Africum
Bell. Alex.	[Caesar] Bellum Alexandrinum
Bell. Hisp.	[Caesar] Bellum Hispaniense
BG	Caesar De Bello Gallico
BJ	Josephus Bellum Judaicum
Brev.	Eutropius Breviarium
Cat.	Sallust Bellum Catilinae
Epit.	Aurelius Victor Epitome de Caesaribus
Fam.	Cicero Epistulae ad Familiares
Gon.	[Hippocrates] Peri Gones
HA	Historia Augusta
Helv.	Seneca Ad Helviam
HN	Pliny the Elder Historia Naturalis
Imp. Pomp.	Cicero De Imperio Gn. Pompeii
Jug.	Sallust Bellum Jugurthinum
Ling.	Varro De Lingua Latina
Marc.	Cicero Pro Marcello
Met.	Ovid Metamorphoses
Mil.	Vegetius De Re Militari
NA	Aulus Gellius Noctes Atticae
Nem.	Pindar Nemean Odes
NQ	Seneca Quaestiones Naturales
Off.	Cicero De Officiis
Pan.	Pliny Panegyricus
Per.	Livy Periochae
Phar.	Lucan Pharsalia
Phil.	Cicero Orationes Philippicae

Pomp.	Plutarch *Pompey*
Pont.	Ovid *Epistulae ex Ponto*
Praef.	*Praefatio*
Pun.	Silius Italicus *Punica*
Sat.	Macrobius *Saturnalia*
Sen.	Cicero *De Senectute*
Strat.	Onasander *Strategikos*
Tranq.	Seneca *De Tranquillitate Animi*
Tusc.	Cicero *Tusculanae Disputationes*
Verr.	Cicero *In Verrem*
VH	Aelian *Varia Historia*

Bibliography

Adams, J.N., 'The Vocabulary of the Speeches in Tacitus' Historical Works', *BICS* 20 (1973) 124-44.

Adams, J.N., *The Latin Sexual Vocabulary* (London 1982).

Ahl, F.M., *Lucan: An Introduction* (Ithaca and London 1976).

Ahl, F.M., 'The Rider and the Horse: Politics and Power in Roman Poetry from Horace to Statius', *ANRW* 2.32.1 (1984) 40-110.

Alföldy, G., 'Bricht der Schweigsame sein Schweigen? Eine Grabinschrift aus Rom', *MDAI(R)* 102 (1995) 251-68.

Alon, G., *Jews, Judaism and the Classical World* trans. by I. Abrahams (Jerusalem 1976).

Ash, R.E., 'Severed Heads: Individual Portraits and Irrational Forces in Plutarch's *Galba* and *Otho*', 189-214 in Mossman, J.M. (ed.), *Plutarch and his Intellectual World* (London 1997).

Ash, R.E., 'Warped Intertextualities: Naevius and Sallust at Tacitus *Histories* 2.12.2', *Histos* 1 (1997).

Ash, R.E., 'Waving the White Flag: Surrender Scenes at Livy 9.5-6 and Tacitus *Histories* 3.31 and 4.62', *G&R* 45 (1998) 27-44.

Ashworth, T., *Trench Warfare 1914-1918. The Live and Let Live System* (London 1980).

Auberger, J., 'Quand la nage devint natation', *Latomus* 55 (1996) 48-62.

Aubrion, E., *Rhétorique et histoire chez Tacite* (Metz 1985).

Badian, E., 'Appian and Asinius Pollio', *CR* 8 (1958) 159-62.

Bal, M., *Narratology: Introduction to the Theory of Narrative* trans. by C. van Boheemen (Toronto 1985).

Baldwin, B., 'Vespasian and Freedom', *RFIC* 103 (1975) 306-8.

Baldwin, B., *Suetonius* (Amsterdam 1983).

Bandera, C., 'Sacrificial Levels in Virgil's *Aeneid*', *Arethusa* 14 (1981) 217-39.

Bannon, C.J., *The Brothers of Romulus: Fraternal Pietas in Roman Law, Literature and Society* (Princeton 1997).

Barbu, N.I., *Les sources et l'originalité d'Appien dans la deuxième livre des Guerres Civiles* (Paris 1934).

Barceló, P., *Basileia, Monarchia, Tyrannis* (Stuttgart 1993).

Barnes, T.D., 'The Composition of Cassius Dio's *Roman History*', *Phoenix* 38 (1984) 240-55.

Bartsch, S., *Actors in the Audience: Theatricality and Doublespeak from Nero to Hadrian* (Cambridge Mass. 1994).

Barwick, K., *Caesars Bellum Civile: Tendenz, Abfassungszeit und Stil* (Leipzig 1951).

Baxter, R.T.S., 'Virgil's Influence on Tacitus in Book 3 of the *Histories*', *CP* 66 (1971) 93-107.

Baxter, R.T.S., 'Virgil's Influence on Tacitus in *Annals* 1 and 2', *CP* 67 (1972) 246-69.

Bell, A.A., 'Fact and *Exemplum* in the Accounts of the Deaths of Pompey and Caesar', *Latomus* 53 (1994) 824-36.

Bell, M., *In Harm's Way* (London 1995).

Benario, H.W., 'Priam and Galba', *CW* 65 (1972) 146-7.

Benediktson, D.T., 'Structure and Fate in Suetonius' *Life of Galba*', *CJ* 92 (1997) 167-73.

Bertrand-Dagenbach, C., 'La mort de Pétrone et l'art de Tacite', *Latomus* 51 (1992) 601-5.

Birley, E.R., 'A Note on the Title "Gemina" ', *JRS* 18 (1928) 56-60.

Blagg T.F.C, *Mysteries of Diana: The Antiquities from Nemi* (Nottingham 1983).

Blagg T.F.C, 'Le mobiler archéologique du sanctuaire de Diane *Nemorensis*' 103-9 in de Cazanove, O., and Scheid, J., (eds), *Les bois sacrés* (Naples 1993).

De Blois, L., *The Roman Army and Politics in the First Century* BC (Amsterdam 1987).

De Blois, L., 'Volk und Soldaten bei Cassius Dio', *ANRW* 2.34.3 (1997) 2650-76.

Bloomer, W.M., *Valerius Maximus and the Rhetoric of the New Nobility* (London 1992).

Bödefeld, H., 'Untersuchungen zur Datierung der Alexandergeschichte des Q. Curtius Rufus', diss. (Düsseldorf 1982).

Borzsak, I., 'Zum Verständnis der Darstellungskunst des Tacitus: Die Veränderungen des Germanicus-Bildes', *Acta Antiqua Academiae Scientarum Hungricae* 18 (1970) 272-92.

Bosworth, A.B., 'Asinius Pollio and Augustus', *Historia* 21 (1972) 441-73.

Bosworth, A.B., *Conquest and Empire: The Reign of Alexander the Great* (Cambridge 1988).

Bourne, J.M., *Britain and the Great War 1914-1918* (London 1989).

Bowie, A.M., 'The Death of Priam: Allegory and History in the *Aeneid*', *CQ* 40 (1990) 470-81.

Bowra, C.M., 'Aeneas and the Stoic Ideal', *G&R* 3 (1933-4) 8-21.

Bradley, K., *Slavery and Rebellion in the Roman World 140 BC-70 BC* (Bloomington and London 1989).

Braun, L., 'Galba und Otho bei Plutarch und Sueton', *Hermes* 120 (1992) 90-102.

Braund, D.C., 'Berenice in Rome', *Historia* 33 (1984) 120-123.

Braund, S.H., *Lucan: Civil War* (Oxford 1992).

Braund, S.M., *Juvenal Satires Book 1* (Cambridge 1996).

Briessmann, A., *Tacitus und das Flavische Geschichtsbild*, *Hermes Einzelschriften* 10 (Wiesbaden 1955).

Brodersen, K., 'Appian und sein Werk', *ANRW* 2.34.1 (1993) 339-63.

Bruère, R.T., 'Tacitus and Pliny's *Panegyricus*', *CP* 49 (1954) 161-79.

Brunner, T.F., 'Two Papyri of Appian from Dura-Europus', *GRBS* 25 (1984) 171-5.

Bruns, I., *Die Persönlichkeit in der Geschichtsschreibung der Alten* (Berlin 1898).

Brunt, P.A., 'The Revolt of Vindex and the Fall of Nero', *Latomus* 18 (1959) 531-59.

Brunt, P.A., 'Tacitus on the Batavian Revolt', *Latomus* 19 (1960) 494-517.

Brunt, P.A., 'The Army and the Land in the Roman Revolution', *JRS* 52 (1962) 69-86.

Brunt, P.A., '*Lex de Imperio Vespasiani*', *JRS* 67 (1977) 95-116.

Brunt, P.A., 'Roman Imperial Illusions', 433-88 in *Roman Imperial Themes* (Oxford 1990).

Bryson, B., *Made in America* (London 1994).

Büchner, K., 'Tacitus und Plinius über Adoption des römischen Kaisers (Des Verhältnis von Tacitus *Hist*. 1.15-16 zu Plinius *Panegyricus* 7-8', *Rheinisches Museum* 98 (1955) 289-312.

Büchner, K., 'Die Reise des Titus', *Studien zur römischen Literatur* 4 (Wiesbaden 1964) 83-98.

Burke, J.W., 'Emblematic Scenes in Suetonius' *Vitellius*', *Histos* 2 (1998).

Campbell, J.B., *The Emperor and the Roman Army, 31 BC–AD 235* (Oxford 1984).

Campbell, J.B., *The Roman Army 31 BC–AD 337: A Sourcebook* (London 1994).

Carter, J.M., *Julius Caesar: The Civil War Books I and II* (Warminster 1991); *Book III* (Warminster 1993).

Carter, J.M., *Appian: The Civil Wars* (Harmondsworth 1996).

Chaplin, J.D., 'Livy's Use of *Exempla* and the Lessons of the Past', Ph.D thesis (Princeton 1993) = *Livy's Exemplary History* forthcoming (Oxford 2000).

Chapman, G., *A Passionate Prodigality* (New York 1966).

Charlesworth, M.P., 'The Virtues of a Roman Emperor and the Creation of Belief', *PBA* 23 (1937) 105-33.

Chausserie-Laprée, J.P., *L'Expression narrative chez les historiens latins* (Paris 1969).

Cherry, D., 'Hunger at Rome in the Late Republic', *Echos du Monde Classique* 37 (1993) 433-50.

Chilver, G.E.F., *A Historical Commentary on Tacitus' Histories I and II* (Oxford 1979).

Chilver, G.E.F., *A Historical Commentary on Tacitus' Histories IV and V* completed and revised by G.B. Townend (Oxford 1985).

Chrissanthos, S.G., 'Scipio and the Mutiny at Sucro, 206 BC', *Historia* 46.2 (1997) 172-84.

Citroni, M., 'Marziale e la Letteratura per i Saturnali', *Illinois Classical Studies* 14 (1989) 201-26.

Cizek, E., 'La mort de Vitellius dans les *Vies des douze Césars* de Suétone', *REA* 77 (1975) 125-30.

Clausewitz, C. von, *On War* (Harmondsworth 1982).

Coale, A.J., *'Dies Alliensis'*, *TAPA* 102 (1971) 49-58.

Cole, T., *'Initium mihi operis Servius Galba iterum T. Vinius consules ...'*, *YCS* 29 (1992) 231-45.

Collingwood, R.G., *The Idea of History* (Oxford 1961).

Collins, J.H., 'Propaganda, Ethics and Psychological Assumptions in Caesar's Writings', diss. (Frankfurt am Main 1952).

Collins, J.H., 'On the Date and Interpretation of the *Bellum Civile*', *AJP* 80 (1959) 113-32.

Collins, J.H., 'Caesar as Political Propagandist', *ANRW* 1.1 (1972) 922-66.

Conley, D.F., 'The Stages of Rome's Decline in Sallust's Historical Theory', *Hermes* 109 (1981) 379-82.

Connors, C., 'Seeing Cypresses in Virgil', *CJ* 88 (1992-3) 1-17.

Corbeill, A., 'Dining Deviants in Roman Political Invective', 99-128 in Hallett, J.P, and Skinner, M.B., (eds), *Roman Sexualities* (Princeton 1997).

Cornell, T.J., *The Beginnings of Rome: Italy and Rome from the Bronze Age to the Punic Wars (c. 1000-264 BC)* (London and New York 1995).

Crawford, M., *Roman Republican Coinage* (Cambridge 1974).

Crook, I.A., 'Titus and Berenice', *AJP* 72 (1951) 162-75.

Darwall-Smith, R., *Emperors and Architecture: A Study of Flavian Rome*, Collection *Latomus* 231 (Brussels 1996).

Davidson, J., *Courtesans and Fishcakes* (London 1997).

Davies, R.W., *Service in the Roman Army* (London 1989).

Davis, L., *The Course of Honour* (London 1997).

Dench, E., *From Barbarians to New Men* (Oxford 1995).

Derow, P.S., 'Herodotus Readings', *Classics Ireland* 2 (1997) 29-51.

Develin, R., 'Tacitus and Techniques of Insidious Suggestion', *Antichthon* 17 (1983) 64-95.

Dewald, C., 'Wanton Kings, Pickled Heroes and Gnomic Founding Fathers: Strategies of Meaning at the End of Herodotus's *Histories*', 62-82 in Roberts, D.H., Dunn, F.M., and Fowler, D.P., (eds), *Classical Closure* (Princeton 1997).

Dickison, S.K. and Plympton, M., 'The Prodigy of the Fig-Tree: Tacitus *Annals* 13.58', *RSC* 25 (1977) 183-6.

Dobson, B., 'The Daily Life of the Soldier under the Principate', *ANRW* 2.1 (1974) 299-338.

Dobson, B., 'The Significance of the Centurion and Primipilaris in the Roman Army and Administration', *ANRW* 2.1 (1974) 392-434.

Dorey, T.A., 'Tacitus' Treatment of Antonius Primus', *CP* 53 (1958) 244.

Drexler, H., 'Zur Geschichte Kaiser Othos bei Tacitus und Plutarch', *Klio* 37 (1959) 153-78.

Dunbabin, K.M.D., *'Sic erimus cuncti ... The Skeleton in Graeco-Roman Art'*, *JDAI* 101 (1986) 185-255.

Dunkle, J.R., 'The Greek Tyrant and Roman Political Invective of the Late Republic', *TAPA* 98 (1967) 151-71.
Dunkle, J.R., 'The Rhetorical Tyrant in Roman Historiography: Sallust, Livy and Tacitus', *CW* 65 (1971) 12-20.
Earl, D.C., *The Moral and Political Tradition of Rome* (London 1967).
Eden, P.T., *Seneca Apocolocyntosis* (Cambridge 1984).
Edwards, C., *The Politics of Immorality in Ancient Rome* (Cambridge 1993).
Edwards, C., *Writing Rome* (Cambridge 1996).
Ehrlich, E.L., *Der Traum im Alten Testament, Beihefte zur Zeitschrift für die Alttestamentliche Wissenschaft* 73 (Berlin 1953).
Ehrenberg, V.L., *Alexander and the Greeks* (1938).
Elsner J., and Masters J., (eds), *Reflections of Nero: Culture, History and Representation* (London 1994).
Engel R., 'Das Characterbild des Kaisers Vitellius bei Tacitus und sein historischer Kern', *Athenaeum* 55 (1977) 345-68.
Erskine, A., 'Money-Loving Romans', *PLLS* 9 (1996) 1-11.
Eyben, E., *Restless Youth in Ancient Rome* (London 1992).
Fabbricotti, E., *Galba* (Roma 1976).
Fabia, P., *Les sources de Tacite dans les histoires et les Annales* (Paris 1893).
Fadinger, V., *Die Begrundung des Principats. Quellenkritische und Staatsrechtliche Untersuchungen zu Cassius Dio und der Parallelüberlieferung* (Berlin 1969).
Fantham, E., *Seneca's Troades: A Literary Introduction with Text, Translation and Commentary* (Princeton 1982).
Fantham, E., 'Caesar and the Mutiny: Lucan's Reshaping of the Historical Tradition in *De Bello Civili* 5.237-373', *CP* 80 (1985) 119-31
Fantham, E., *Lucan De Bello Civili II* (Cambridge 1992).
Farenga, V., 'The Paradigmatic Tyrant: Greek Tyranny and the Ideology of the Proper', *Helios* 8 (1981) 1-31.
Fedeli, P., 'Il "Panegyrico" di Plinio nella Critica Moderna', *ANRW* 2.33.1 (1989) 387-514.
Feeney, D.C., '*Stat Magni Nominis Umbri*: Lucan on the Greatness of Pompeius Magnus', *CQ* 36 (1986) 239-43.
Feldherr, A., *Spectacle and Society in Livy's History* (Berkeley and Los Angeles 1998).
De Ferdinandy, M., *Der Heilige Kaiser: Otto III und seine Ahnen* (Tübingen 1969).
Ferrill, A., 'Otho, Vitellius and the Propaganda of Vespasian', *CJ* 60 (1964-5) 267-9.
Ferrill, A., 'Herodotus on Tyranny', *Historia* 27 (1978) 386-98.
Flower, H., *Ancestor Masks and Aristocratic Power in Roman Culture* (Oxford 1996).
Fortenbaugh, W.W., 'Plato: Temperament and Eugenic Policy', *Arethusa* 8 (1975) 283-305.
Foucault, M., 'The Subject and Power', in Dreyfuss, H.L., and Rabinow, P., (eds), *Michel Foucault: Beyond Structuralism and Hermeneutics* 2nd edition (Chicago 1983) 208-26.
Foucault, M., *The Use of Pleasure: The History of Sexuality* Vol. 2 trans. by R. Hurley (London 1992).
Fowler, D.P., 'First Thoughts on Closure: Problems and Prospects', *MD* 22 (1989) 75-122.
Fowler, D.P., 'Second Thoughts on Closure', 3-22 in Roberts, D.H., Dunn, F.M., and Fowler, D.P., (eds), *Classical Closure* (Princeton 1997).
Fox, M., *Roman Historical Myths* (Oxford 1996).
Fraenkel, E., 'Das Geschlecht von *Dies*', *Glotta* 8 (1917) 24-68 = *Kleine Beiträge zur Klassischen Philologie I* (Rome 1964) 27-72.
Frangoulidis, S., 'Tacitus (*Histories* 1.40-43), Plutarch (*Galba* 26-27) and Suetonius (*Galba* 18-20) on the Death of Galba', *Favonius* 3 (1991) 1-10.
Fraser, P.M., *Ptolemaic Alexandria I* (Oxford 1972).
Freund, E., *The Return of the Reader: Reader-Response Criticism* (London and New York 1987).
Fugmann, J., 'Zum Problem der "Historiae Alexandri Magni" des Curtius Rufus', *Hermes* 123 (1995) 233-43.

Funari, R., 'Degradazione Morale e *Luxuria* nell'Esercito di Vitellio (Tacito *Hist.* II). Modelli e Sviluppi Narrativi', *Athenaeum* 80.1 (1992) 133-58.

Fyfe, W.H. (trans.) and Levene, D.S. (rev. and ed.), *Tacitus: The Histories* (Oxford 1997).

Gabba, E., *Appiano e la Storia delle Guerre Civili* (Florence 1956).

Gabba, E., *Republican Rome, the Army and the Allies* trans. P.J. Cuff (Oxford 1976) 20-69 = *Athenaeum* 29 (1951) 171-272.

Gagé, J., 'Vespasien et la mémoire de Galba', *REA* 54 (1952) 290-315.

Galbraith, V.H.G., 'Good Kings and Bad Kings in Medieval English History', *History* 30 (1945) 119-32, reprinted in *Kings and Chroniclers* (London 1982).

Gallivan, P.A., 'The False Neros: A Re-evaluation', *Historia* 22 (1973) 364-5.

Gardner, J.F., 'The "Gallic Menace" in Caesar's Propaganda', *G&R* 30 (1983) 181-9.

Garland, R., *The Greek Way of Life* (London and Ithaca 1990).

Garland, R., *The Eye of the Beholder: Deformity and Disability in the Greco-Roman World* (London and Ithaca 1995).

Geiger, J., 'Zum Bild Julius Caesars in der römischen Kaiserzeit', *Historia* 24 (1975) 444-53.

Geiger, J., 'Munatius Rufus and Thrasea Paetus on Cato the Younger', *Athenaeum* 57 (1979) 48-72.

Genette, G., *Narrative Discourse* trans. by J.E. Lewin (Oxford 1980).

Ghedini, F., *Riflessi della politica domiziana nei rilievi flavi di Palazzo della Cancelleria*, *BCAR* 91 (1986) 291-309.

Gill, C., 'The Question of Character Development: Tacitus and Plutarch', *CQ* 33 (1983) 469-87.

Ginsburg, J., *Tradition and Theme in the Annals of Tacitus* (Berkeley 1981).

Ginsburg, J., '*In maiores certamina*: Past and Present in the *Annals*', 86-103 in Luce, T.J., and Woodman, A.J., (eds), *Tacitus and the Tacitean Tradition* (Princeton 1993).

Girard, R., *Violence and the Sacred* trans. P. Gregory (Baltimore and London 1977).

Goddard, J., 'The Tyrant at Table', 67-82 in Elsner, J., and Masters, J., (eds), *Reflections of Nero: Culture, History and Representation* (London 1994).

Godolphin, F.R.B., 'The Source of Plutarch's Thesis in the Lives of *Galba* and *Otho*', *AJP* 56 (1935) 324-8.

Goldmann, B., *Einheitlichkeit und Eigenständigkeit der Historia Romana des Appian* (Hildesheim 1988).

Goldsworthy, A.K., *The Roman Army at War 100 BC – AD 200* (Oxford 1984).

Goodyear, F.R.D., *Tacitus Annals* Volume 1 (Cambridge 1972).

Görich, K., *Otto III. Romanus Saxonicus et Italicus* (Sigmaringen 1993).

Gowers, E., *The Loaded Table: Representations of Food in Roman Literature* (Oxford 1993).

Gowing, A., 'Appian and Cassius' Speech before Philippi (*BC* 4.90-100)', *Phoenix* 44 (1990) 158-81.

Gowing, A., *The Triumviral Narratives of Appian and Cassius Dio* (Ann Arbor 1993).

Grafton, A.T. and Swerdlow, N.M., 'Calendar Dates and Ominous Days in Ancient Historiography', *Journal of the Warburg Institute* 51 (1988) 14-42.

Gray, J.G. *The Warriors: Reflections on Men in Battle* (New York 1967).

Greenhalgh, P.A.L., *The Year of the Four Emperors* (London 1975).

Grenade, P., 'Le mythe de Pompée et les pompéiens sous les Césars', *REA* 52 (1950) 28-63.

Griffin, J., 'Propertius and Antony', *JRS* 67 (1977) 17-26, reprinted in *Latin Poets and Roman Life* (London 1985) 32-47.

Griffin, M., *Nero: The End of a Dynasty* (London 1984).

Griffin, M., 'Philosophy, Cato and Roman Suicide: I', *G&R* 33 (1986) 64-77.

Griffin, M., 'Philosophy, Cato and Roman Suicide: II', *G&R* 33 (1986) 192-202.

Grigg, R., 'Inconsistency and Lassitude: the Shield Emblems of the *Notitia Dignitatum*', *JRS* 73 (1983) 132-42.

Grimal, P., *Les jardins romains* (Paris 1943).

Grimal, P., 'Le poète et l'histoire' in *Entretiens de la Fondation Hardt* 15, *Lucain* (Geneva 1973) 51-117.

Grisé, Y., *Le suicide dans la Rome antique* (Paris 1982).

Grmek, M.D., *Diseases in the Ancient Greek World* trans. M. and L. Muellner (Baltimore and London 1991).

Gurval, R.A., *Actium and Augustus: The Politics and Emotions of Civil War* (Ann Arbor Michigan 1995).

Hainsworth, J.B., 'Verginius and Vindex', *Historia* 11 (1962) 86-96.

Hainsworth, J.B., 'The Starting-Point of Tacitus' *Histories* – Fear or Favour by Omission?', *G&R* 11 (1964) 128-36.

Hall, E., *Inventing the Barbarian: Greek Self-Definition through Tragedy* (Oxford 1989).

Hall, E., 'Asia Unmanned: Images of Victory in Classical Athens', 108-33 in Rich, J., and Shipley, G., (eds), *War and Society in the Greek World* (London 1993).

Hammond, C., review of Carter, J.M., *JRS* 82 (1992) 248-9.

Hammond, C., 'Narrative Explanation and the Roman Military Character', D. phil. thesis (Oxford 1993).

Hammond, M., '*Res olim dissociabiles: Principatus ac Libertas*', *HSCP* 67 (1963) 93-113.

Hansen, M.H., 'The Battle Exhortation in Ancient Historiography: Fact or Fiction?', *Historia* 42 (1993) 161-80.

Hanson, J.A., 'The Glorious Military' 51-85 in Dorey, T.A., and Dudley, D.R., (eds), *Roman Drama* (London 1965).

Hardie, P.R., 'Tales of Unity and Division in Imperial Latin Epic' 57-71 in Molyneux, J.H., (ed.), *Literary Responses to Civil Discord*, *Nottingham Classical Literature Studies* 1 (1992).

Hardie, P.R., *The Epic Successors of Virgil* (Cambridge 1993).

Hardie, P.R., *Virgil Aeneid IX* (Cambridge 1994).

Hardy, E.G., *Plutarch's Lives of Galba and Otho* (London 1890).

Harmand, J., *L'armée et le soldat à Rome de 107 à 50 avant notre ère* (Paris 1967).

Harris, B.F., 'Tacitus on the Death of Otho', *CJ* 58 (1962) 73-7.

Harrison, M., *Crowds and History: Mass Phenomena in English Towns, 1790-1835* (Cambridge 1988).

Hassall, M., 'Batavians and the Roman Conquest of Britain', *Britannia* 1 (1970) 131-6.

Heinz, W-R., *Die Furcht als politisches Phänomen bei Tacitus* (Amsterdam 1975).

Henderson, J., *Fighting for Rome: Poets and Caesars, History and Civil War* (Cambridge 1998).

Henrichs, A., 'Vespasian's Visit to Alexandria', *ZPE* 3 (1968) 51-80.

Herrmann, P., *Der römische Kaisereid* (Göttingen 1968).

Herzog, P.H., *Die Funktion des militärischen Planens bei Tacitus* (Frankfurt am Main 1996).

Heubner, H., *P. Cornelius Tacitus: Die Historien* Vol. 1 (Heidelberg 1963); Vol. 2 (Heidelberg 1968); Vol. 3 (Heidelberg 1972); Vol. 4 (Heidelberg 1976); Vol. 5 (Heidelberg 1982).

Hohl, E., 'Der Prätorianer-aufstand unter Otho', *Klio* 32 (1939) 307-24.

Hornblower, S., *A Commentary on Thucydides* Vol. I *Books I-III* (Oxford 1991); Vol. II *Books IV-V.24* (Oxford 1996).

Hornblower, S., and Spawforth, A., (eds), *The Oxford Classical Dictionary* (Oxford 1996).

Horsfall, N., 'Numanus Remulus: Ethnography and Propaganda in *Aeneid* 9.598f ', *Latomus* 30 (1971) 1108-16.

Hose, M., *Erneuerung der Vergangenheit: Die Historiker im Imperium Romanum von Florus bis Cassius Dio* (Stuttgart and Leipzig 1994).

Howgego, C., *Ancient History and Coins* (London 1995).

Hume, D., *Of Miracles* (La Salle Illinois 1985) with an introduction by A. Flew.

Hunt, E.D., 'Travel, Tourism and Piety in the Roman Empire: A Context for the

Beginning of Christian Pilgrimage', *Echos du Monde Classique* 28 (1984) 391-417.

Husband, R.H., 'Galba's Assassination and the Indifferent Citizen', *CP* 10 (1915) 321-5.

Hutchinson, G.O., *Latin Literature from Seneca to Juvenal* (Oxford 1993).

Immerwahr, H.R., *Form and Thought in Herodotus* (Cleveland 1966).

Jackson, R., *Doctors and Diseases in the Roman Empire* (London 1988).

Jacobson, H., 'Tacitus and the Phoenix', *Phoenix* 35 (1981) 260-1.

Jal, P., 'Le soldat des guerres civiles à Rome à la fin de la république et au debut de l'empire', *Pallas* 2 (1962) 12-23.

Jal, P., *La guerre civile à Rome: étude littéraire et morale* (Paris 1963).

Jellinek, E.M., 'Drinkers and Alcoholics in Ancient Rome', *Journal of Studies on Alcohol* 37 (1976) 1718-41.

Johnson, J.T., *Ideology, Reason and the Limitations of War: Religious and Secular Concepts 1200-1740* (Princeton 1975).

Johnson, J.T., *Just War Tradition and the Restraint of War: A Moral and Historical Inquiry* (Princeton 1981).

Jones, B.W., *The Emperor Titus* (London 1984).

Jones, B.W., 'The Reckless Titus' 408-20 in Deroux, C., (ed.), *Studies in Latin Literature and Roman History VI* (Brussels 1992).

de Jong, I.J.F., *Narrators and Focalizers* (Amsterdam 1987).

Jordan, R., *Berenice* (New York 1974).

Jucker, H., 'Der Ring des Kaisers Galba', *Chiron* 5 (1975) 349-64.

Kajanto, I., '*Fortuna*', *ANRW* 2.17.1 (1981) 502-58.

Kassel, R., and Austin, C., *Poetae Comici Graeci* Vol. V (Berlin and New York 1986); Vol. VII (Berlin and New York 1989); Vol. VIII (Berlin and New York 1995).

Kaster, R., *C. Suetonius Tranquillus De Grammaticis et Rhetoribus* (Oxford 1995).

Keegan, J., *The Mask of Command* (London 1987).

Keenan, J. and Thomas, J., 'Vitellius Germanicus: On Tacitus *Histories* 2.70', *AHB* 2 (1988) 113-17.

Keitel, E., 'Otho's Exhortations in Tacitus' *Histories*', *G&R* 34 (1987) 73-82.

Keitel, E., 'Homeric Antecedents to the *Cohortatio* in the Ancient Historians', *CW* 80 (1987) 153-72.

Keitel, E., 'The Structure and Function of Speeches in Tacitus' *Histories* I-III', *ANRW* 2.33.4 (1991) 2772-94.

Keitel, E., '*Foedum Spectaculum* and Related Motifs in Tacitus *Histories* 2-3', *Rheinisches Museum* 135 (1992) 342-51.

Keitel, E., 'Speech and Narrative in *Histories* 4' 39-58 in Luce, T.J., and Woodman, A.J., (eds), *Tacitus and the Tacitean Tradition* (Princeton 1993).

Keitel, E., 'Plutarch's Tragedy Tyrants: Galba and Otho', *PLLS* 8 (1995) 275-88.

Keller, E., *Studien zu den Cancelleria-Reliefs*, *Klio* 49 (1967) 193-215.

Kenney, E.J., '*Iudicium Transferendi*: Virgil *Aeneid* 2.469-505 and its Antecedents' 103-20 in Woodman, A.J. and West, D., (eds), *Creative Imitation and Latin Literature* (Cambridge 1979).

Knightley, P., *The First Casualty: The War Correspondent as Hero, Propagandist and Myth Maker* (London 1989).

Kragelund, P., 'Galba's *Pietas*, Nero's Victims and the Mausoleum of Augustus', *Historia* 47 (1998) 152-73.

Kraner, F. and Dittenberger, W., *Julius Caesar: Commentarii de Bello Gallico* (Berlin 1960).

Kraus, C.S., *Livy Ab Urbe Condita Book VI* (Cambridge 1994).

Kraus, C.S., ' "No Second Troy". Topoi and Refoundation in Livy Book V', *TAPA* 124 (1994) 267-89.

Kraus, C.S. and Woodman, A.J., *Latin Historians*, Greece and Rome New Surveys in the Classics 27 (1997).

Kremer, B., *Das Bild der Kelten bis in augusteische Zeit*, Historia Einzelschriften 88 (Stuttgart 1994).

Last, H., 'On the Flavian Reliefs from the Palazzo della Cancelleria', *JRS* 38 (1948) 9-14.

Lateiner, D., *The Historical Method of Herodotus* (Toronto 1989).

Leach, E.W., 'The Soldier and Society: Plautus' *Miles Gloriosus* as Popular Drama', *RSC* 27 (1979) 185-209.

Le Bon, G., *The Crowd: A Study of the Popular Mind* (London 1896).

vanderLeest, J., 'Appian and the Writing of the Roman History', Diss. (Toronto 1989).

Leigh, M., 'Varius Rufus, *Thyestes* and the Appetites of Antony', *PCPS* 42 (1996) 171-97.

Leigh, M., *Lucan: Spectacle and Engagement* (Oxford 1997).

Lelièvre, P.J., 'Juvenal: Two Possible Examples of Word-Play', *CP* 53 (1958) 241-2.

Leon, E.F., 'The *Imbecillitas* of the Emperor Claudius', *TAPA* 79 (1948) 79-86.

Levene, D.S., 'Sallust's *Jugurtha*: An "Historical Fragment" ', *JRS* 82 (1992) 53-70.

Levene, D.S., *Religion in Livy* (Leiden 1993).

Levene, D.S., 'Pity, Fear, and the Historical Audience: Tacitus on the Fall of Vitellius', 128-49 in Braund, S., and Gill, C., (eds), *The Passions in Roman Thought and Literature* (Cambridge 1997).

Levick, B.M., 'Drusus Caesar and the Adoptions of AD 4', *Latomus* 25 (1966) 227-44.

Levick, B.M., 'Tiberius' Retirement to Rhodes in 6 BC', *Latomus* 31 (1972) 779-813.

Levick, B.M., *Tiberius the Politician* (London and Sydney 1976).

Levick, B.M., 'Sulla's March on Rome in 88 BC', *Historia* 31 (1982) 503-8.

Levick, B.M., 'Morals, Politics and the Fall of the Roman Republic', *G&R* 29 (1982) 53-62.

Levick, B.M., 'L. Verginius Rufus and the Four Emperors', *RhM* 128 (1985) 319-46.

Levick, B.M., *Claudius* (London 1990).

Levick, B.M, 'The Veneti Revisited: C.E. Stevens and the Tradition on Caesar the Propagandist' 61-83 in Welch, K., and Powell, A., (eds), *Julius Caesar as Artful Reporter: The War Commentaries as Political Instruments* (London and Swansea 1998).

Lintott, A.W., *Violence in Republican Rome* (Oxford 1968).

Lintott, A.W., 'Lucan and the History of the Civil War', *CQ* 45 (1971) 488-505.

Lintott, A.W., 'Imperial Expansion and Moral Decline in the Roman Republic', *Historia* 21 (1972) 626-38.

Lintott, A.W., 'Cassius Dio and the History of the Late Republic', *ANRW* 2.34.3 (1997) 2497-523.

Litchfield, H., 'National *Exempla Virtutis* in Roman Literature', *HSCP* 25 (1914) 1-71.

Lloyd, G.E.R., *Science, Folklore and Ideology* (Cambridge 1983).

Lowrie, M., *Horace's Narrative Odes* (Oxford 1997).

Lucas, J., *Les obsessions de Tacite* (Leiden 1974).

Luce, T.J., 'Design and Structure in Livy 5.32-55', *TAPA* 102 (1971) 265-302.

Lussu, E., *Sardinian Brigade: A Memoir of World War I* trans. M. Rawson (New York 1970).

Lyne, R.O.A.M., ' "Scilicet et tempus veniet ..." Virgil *Georgics* 1.463-514', 47-66 in Woodman, A.J., and West, D., (eds), *Quality and Pleasure in Roman Poetry* (Cambridge 1974).

Lyne, R.O.A.M., 'Lavinia's Blush: Virgil *Aeneid* 12.64-70', *G&R* 30 (1983) 55-64.

Lyne, R.O.A.M., 'Vergil and the Politics of War', *CQ* 33 (1983) 188-203 = S.J. Harrison, *Oxford Readings in Vergil's Aeneid* (Oxford 1990) 316-38.

Machiavelli, N., in Musa, N. (trans. and ed.), *The Prince: A Bilingual Edition* (New York 1964).

Mackie, H., *Talking Trojan: Speech and Community in the Iliad* (Lanham Maryland 1996).

MacL.Currie, H., 'An Obituary Formula in the Historians (With a Platonic Connection?)', *Latomus* 48 (1989) 346-53.

Magi, F., *I Rilievi Flavi del Palazzo della Cancelleria* (Rome 1945).

Mankin, D., *Horace Epodes* (Cambridge 1995).

Mann, J.C., *Legionary Recruitment and Veteran Settlement during the Principate* (London 1983).
Manuwald, B., *Cassius Dio und Augustus* (Wiesbaden 1979).
Marincola, J., *Authority and Tradition in Ancient Historiography* (Cambridge 1997).
Martin, R.H., 'Tacitus and the Death of Augustus', *CQ* 5 (1955) 123-8.
Martin, R.H. and Woodman, A.J., *Tacitus Annals 4* (Cambridge 1989).
Maslakov, G., 'Valerius Maximus and Roman Historiography: A Study of the *Exempla* Tradition', *ANRW* 2.32.1 (1984) 437-96.
Masters, J., *Poetry and Civil War in Lucan's Bellum Civile* (Cambridge 1992).
Mattingly, H., *Coins of the Roman Empire in the British Museum* Vol. 1 (London 1923); Vol. 2 (London 1930).
Maurenbrecher, B. (ed.), *C. Sallusti Crispi Historiarum Reliquiae* (Stuttgart 1893).
Mayor, J.E.B., *Thirteen Satires of Juvenal* (London 1878).
McAlindon, D., 'Senatorial Opposition to Claudius and Nero', *AJP* 77 (1956) 113-32.
McCann, A.M., *A Re-dating of the Reliefs from the Palazzo della Cancelleria, MDAI(R)* 79 (1972) 249-76.
McClelland, J.S., *The Crowd and the Mob from Plato to Canetti* (London 1989).
McCrum, M. and Woodhead, A.G., *Documents of the Flavian Empire* (Cambridge 1961).
MacCurdy, G.H., 'Julia Berenice', *AJP* 72 (1951) 162-75.
McGann, M.J., 'Lucan's *De Incendio Urbis*: The Evidence of Statius and Vacca', *TAPA* 106 (1975) 213-17.
McGlew, J.F., *Tyranny and Political Culture in Ancient Greece* (Ithaca 1993).
McGuire, D.T., 'History Compressed: The Roman Names of Silius' Cannae Episode', *Latomus* 54 (1995) 110-18.
McKay, A.G., *Houses, Villas and Palaces in the Roman World* (London 1975).
MacMullen, R., 'Personal Power in the Roman Empire', *AJP* 107 (1986) 512-24.
Meulder, M., 'Bons et mauvais généraux chez Tacite', *Revue Belge de Philologie et d'Histoire* 73 (1995) 75-89.
Millar, F., 'Some Speeches in Dio', *MH* 18 (1961) 11-22.
Millar, F., *A Study of Cassius Dio* (Oxford 1964).
Millar, F., *The Crowd in Rome in the Late Republic* (Ann Arbor Michigan 1998).
Miller, N.P., and Jones, P.V., 'Critical Appreciations III: Tacitus *Histories* 3.38-9', *G&R* 25 (1978) 70-80.
Miller, N.P., 'Virgil and Tacitus Again', *PVS* 18 (1986) 87-106.
Miller, N.P., 'Dramatic Speech in the Roman Historians', *G&R* 22 (1975) 45-57.
Moles, J., 'Virgil, Pompeius and the *Histories* of Asinius Pollio', *CW* 76 (1983) 286-7.
Monsarrat, N., *The Cruel Sea* (Harmondsworth 1951).
Morford, M.P.O., 'The Distortion of the *Domus Aurea* Tradition', *Eranos* 66 (1968) 158-79.
Morgan, M.G., 'An Heir of Tragedy: Tacitus *Histories* 2.59.3', *CP* 86 (1991) 138-43.
Morgan, M.G., 'Dispositions for Disaster: Tacitus *Histories* 1.31', *Eranos* 90 (1992) 55-62.
Morgan, M.G., 'The Smell of Victory: Vitellius at Bedriacum, Tacitus *Histories* 2.70', *CP* 87 (1992) 14-29.
Morgan, M.G., 'The Three Minor Pretenders in Tacitus *Histories* 2', *Latomus* 52 (1993) 769-96.
Morgan, M.G., 'Two Omens in Tacitus' *Histories* 2.50.2 and 1.62.2-3', *Rheinisches Museum* 136 (1993) 321-9.
Morgan, M.G., 'The Unity of Tacitus, *Histories* 1.12-20', *Athenaeum* 81 (1993) 567-86.
Morgan, M.G., 'Rogues' March: Caecina and Valens in Tacitus *Histories* 1.61-70', *MH* 51 (1994) 103-25.
Morgan, M.G., 'Tacitus *Histories* 2.83-84: Content and Positioning', *CP* 89 (1994) 166-75.
Morgan, M.G., 'A Lugubrious Prospect: Tacitus *Histories* 1.40', *CQ* 44 (1994) 236-44.
Morgan, M.G., 'Vespasian's Fears of Assassination: Tacitus *Histories* 2.74-75', *Philologus* 138 (1994) 118-28.
Morgan, M.G., 'Tacitus *Histories* 2.7.1', *Hermes* 123 (1995) 335-40.

Morgan, M.G., 'Vespasian and the Omens in Tacitus *Histories* 2.78', *Phoenix* 50 (1996) 41-55.

Morgan, M.G., 'Cremona in AD 69. Two Notes on Tacitus' Narrative Technique', *Athenaeum* 84 (1996) 381-403.

Moscovich, M.J., 'Historical Compression in Cassius Dio's Account of the Second Century BC', *Ancient World* 8 (1983) 137-43.

Muir, K., *The Sources of Shakespeare's Plays* (London 1977).

Murison, C.L., 'Some Vitellian Dates: An Exercise in Methodology', *TAPA* 109 (1979) 187-97.

Murison, C.L., *Galba, Otho and Vitellius: Careers and Controversies* (Hildesheim 1993).

Muth, R., *Träger der Lebenskraft: Ausscheidungen des Organismus im Volksglauben der Antike* (Vienna 1954).

Nagle, B.R., *The Poetics of Exile. Program and Polemic in the Tristia and Epistulae ex Ponto of Ovid*, *Collection Latomus* 170 (Brussels 1980)

Narducci, E., 'Il Tronco di Pompeio (Troia e Roma nella Pharsalia)', *Maia* 25 (1973) 317-25.

Nerandeau, J-.P., *La jeunesse dans la littérature et les institutions de la Rome républicaine* (Paris 1979).

Newbold, R.F., 'Nonverbal Communication in Tacitus and Ammianus', *AS* 21 (1990) 189-99.

Nicolet, C., *Space, Geography and Politics in the Early Roman Empire* trans. by Leclerc, H. (Ann Arbor, Michigan 1991).

Nicols, J., *Vespasian and the Partes Flavianae*, *Historia Einzelschriften* 28 (Stuttgart 1978).

Nisbet, R.G.M., *Cicero: In Pisonem* (Oxford 1961).

Nisbet, R.G.M., review of W.V. Clausen, *JRS* 52 (1962) 227-38.

Nock, A.D., 'Deification and Julian', *JRS* 47 (1957) 115-23.

Oakley, S.P., 'Single Combat in the Roman Republic', *CQ* 35 (1985) 392-410.

Oakley, S.P., *A Commentary on Livy VI-X Vol. I Introduction and Book VI* (Oxford 1997); Vol. II *Books VII-VIII* (Oxford 1998).

O'Daly, G.J.P., *The Poetry of Boethius* (London 1991).

O'Gorman, E., 'Shifting Ground: Lucan, Tacitus and the Landscape of Civil War', *Hermathena* 158 (1995) 117-31.

Ogilvie, R.M., *Commentary on Livy Books 1-5* (Oxford 1965).

Olechowska, E.M., *Claudii Claudiani: De Bello Gildonico* (Leiden 1978).

Orwell, S., and Angus, I., (eds), *The Collected Essays, Journalism and Letters of George Orwell* (New York 1968).

Palmer, R.E.A., *Roman Religion and Roman Empire: Five Essays* (Pennsylvania 1974).

Paratore, E., *Tacito, Nuovi Saggi* 34 (Rome 1962).

Parker, H.N., 'The Fertile Fields of Umbria: Propertius 1.22.10', *Mnemosyne* 45 (1992) 88-92.

Paxton, R.O., *Vichy France: Old Guard and New Order 1940-1944* (New York 1972).

Paul, G.M., '*Urbs Capta*: Sketch of an Ancient Literary Motif', *Phoenix* 36 (1982) 144-55.

Pease, A.S., *M. Tulli Ciceronis De Divinatione Liber Primus* (Illinois 1920).

Peddie, J., *The Roman War Machine* (Stroud, Gloucestershire, 1994).

Pelling, C.B.R., 'Plutarch's Method of Work in the Roman Lives', *JRS* 99 (1979) 73-96.

Pelling, C.B.R., review of Zecchini, G., *Cassio Dione e la Guerra Gallica di Cesare* (Milan 1978), *CR* 32 (1982) 146-8.

Pelling, C.B.R., review of Manuwald, B., *Cassius Dio und Augustus* (Wiesbaden 1979), *Gnomon* 55 (1983) 221-6.

Pelling, C.B.R., *Plutarch: Life of Antony* (Cambridge 1988).

Pelling, C.B.R., 'Tacitus and Germanicus' 59-85 in Woodman, A.J., and Luce, T.J., (eds), *Tacitus and the Tacitean Tradition* (Princeton 1993).

Pelling, C.B.R., review of Gowing, A., *JRS* 84 (1994) 225-6.

Pelling, C.B.R., 'East is East and West is West. Or Are They? National Stereotypes in Herodotus', *Histos* 1 (1997).

Pelling, C.B.R., 'Biographical History? Cassius Dio on the Early Principate' 117-44 in Edwards, M.J., and Swain, S.C.R., (eds), *Portraits: Biographical Representation in the Greek and Latin Literature of the Roman Empire* (Oxford 1997).

La Penna, A., 'Tendenze e Arte del *Bellum Civile* di Cesare', *Maia* 5 (1952) 191-233.

La Penna, A., '*Rubor* e *Inpudentia* da Pompeio a Domiziano', *Maia* 27 (1975) 117-19.

Perkins, C.A., 'Tacitus on Otho', *Latomus* 52 (1993) 848-55.

Pinkster, H., 'Tempus, Aspect und Aktionsart in Latin', *ANRW* 2.29.1 (1983) 270-319.

Plass, P., 'An Aspect of Epigrammatic Wit in Martial and Tacitus', *Arethusa* 18 (1985) 187-210.

Plass, P., *Wit and the Writing of History* (Madison, Wisconsin 1988).

Plass, P., *The Game of Death in Ancient Rome* (Madison, Wisconsin 1995).

Poliakoff, M.B., *Combat Sports in the Ancient World: Competition, Violence, and Culture* (Yale 1987).

Potter, D., *Prophets and Emperors: Human and Divine Authority from Augustus to Theodosius* (Cambridge Ma. 1994).

Powell, C.A., '*Deum Ira, Hominum Rabies*', *Latomus* 31 (1972) 833-48.

Powell, A., 'Julius Caesar and the Presentation of Massacre' 11-37 in Welch, K., and Powell, A., (eds), *Julius Caesar as Artful Reporter: The War Commentaries as Political Instruments* (London and Swansea 1998).

Preston, K., 'An Author in Exile', *CJ* 13 (1917-18) 411-19.

Price, S., 'The Future of Dreams: From Freud to Artemidorus' 365-87 in Halperin, D.M., Winkler, J.J., and Zeitlin, F.I., (eds), *Before Sexuality* (Princeton 1990).

Pritchett, W.K., *The Greek State at War* Vol. 2 (Berkeley 1974).

Purcell, N., 'On the Sacking of Carthage and Corinth' 133-48 in Innes, D., Hine, H. and Pelling, C.B.R., (eds), *Ethics and Rhetoric: Classical Essays for Donald Russell on his Seventy-Fifth Birthday* (Oxford 1995).

Quint, D., *Epic and Empire* (Princeton 1993).

Radke, G., *Die Götter Altitaliens* (Münster 1965).

Ramage, E.S., 'Denigration of Predecessor under Claudius, Galba and Vespasian', *Historia* 32 (1983) 201-14.

Ramage, E.S., 'Augustus' Treatment of Julius Caesar', *Historia* 34 (1985) 223-45.

Ramage, E.S., 'Juvenal and the Establishment: Denigration of Predecessor in the Satires', *ANRW* 2.33.1 (1989) 640-707.

Rambaud, M., *L'art de la déformation historique dans les commentaires de César* (Paris 1966).

Rawlings, L., 'Caesar's Portrayal of Gauls as Warriors' 171-92 in Welch, K., and Powell, A., (eds), *Julius Caesar as Artful Reporter: The War Commentaries as Political Instruments* (London and Swansea 1998).

Rawson, E., 'The First Latin Annalists', *Latomus* 35 (1976) 689-717.

Rawson, E., *Roman Culture and Society* (Oxford 1991).

Reinhold, M., *Marcus Agrippa: A Biography* (Geneva, New York 1933).

Reynolds, L.D., (ed.), *C. Sallusti Crispi Catilina, Iugurtha, Historiarum Fragmenta Selecta Appendix Sallustiana* (Oxford 1991).

Rich, J.W., 'Dio on Augustus' 86-110 in Cameron, A., (ed.), *History as Text* (London 1989).

Rich, J.W., *Cassius Dio: The Augustan Settlement* (London 1990).

Rich, J.W., review of Hose, M., *CR* 46 (1996) 317-18.

Richlin, A., *The Garden of Priapus: Sexuality and Aggression in Roman Humour* (Oxford 1992).

Richmond, I.A., 'Two Flavian Monuments' 216-28 in P. Salway (ed.), *Roman Archaeology and Art: Essays and Studies* (London 1969).

Richter, B., *Ein Zerrbild des Geschichtsschreibung* (Frankfurt-am-Main 1992).

Rickman, G., *The Corn Supply of Ancient Rome* (Oxford 1980).

Ritter, F., *Cornelii Taciti Historiae* (Cambridge and London 1948).

Roddaz, J.-M., *Marcus Agrippa* (Rome 1984).

Rogers, P.M., 'Titus, Berenice and Mucianus', *Historia* 29 (1980) 86-95.

Rolfe, J.C., 'Seasickness in Greek and Latin Writers', *AJP* 25 (1904) 192-200.

Roth, J., 'The Size and Organisation of the Roman Imperial Legion', *Historia* 43 (1994) 346-62.

Rouveret, A., 'Tacite et les Monuments', *ANRW* 2.33.4 (1991) 3051-99.

Rubiés, J-P., 'Nero in Tacitus and Nero in Tacitism: the Historian's Craft' 29-47 in Elsner, J., and Masters, J., (eds), *Reflections of Nero: Culture, History and Representation* (London 1994).

Rubin, Z., *Civil-War Propaganda and Historiography*, Collection Latomus 173 (Brussels 1980).

Rudé, G., *The Crowd in History: 1730-1848* (London, New York and Sydney 1964).

Rüpke, J., *Domi Militiae* (Stuttgart 1990).

Russell, D., 'On Reading Plutarch's Lives', *G&R* 13 (1966) 139-54.

Ryberg, I.S., 'Tacitus' Art of Innuendo', *TAPA* 73 (1942) 383-404.

Sallares, R., *The Ecology of the Ancient Greek World* (London 1991).

Salway, B., 'What's in a Name? A Survey of Roman Onomastic Practice from *c.* 700 BC–AD 700', *JRS* 84 (1994) 124-45.

Sancery, J., *Galba ou L'armée face au pouvoir* (Paris 1983).

Schäfer, E., 'Domitians Antizipationen in *Histories* 4', *Hermes* 105 (1977) 455-77.

Schanzer, E., *Shakespeare's Appian: a Selection from the Tudor Translation of Appian's Civil Wars* (Liverpool 1956).

Schuller, W., 'Soldaten und Befehlshaber in Caesars *Bellum Civile*', 189-99 in Malkin, I., and Rubinstein, Z.W., (eds), *Leaders and Masses in the Roman World* (Leiden, New York and Cologne 1995).

Schunk, P., 'Studien zur Darstellung des Endes von Galba, Otho und Vitellius in den Historien des Tacitus', *SO* 39 (1964) 38-82.

Scott, J.M., 'The Rhetoric of Suppressed Speech: Tacitus' Omission of Direct Discourse in his *Annales* as a Technique in Character Denigration', *AHB* 12.1-2 (1998) 8-18.

Scott, K., 'Octavian's Propaganda and Antony's *De Sua Ebrietate*', *CP* 24 (1929) 133-41.

Scott, K., 'The Political Propaganda of 44-30 BC', *MAAR* 11 (1933) 7-49.

Scott, K., 'The Role of Basilides in the Events of AD 69', *JRS* 34 (1934) 138-40.

Seaford, R.A.S., 'The Last Bath of Agamemnon', *CQ* 34 (1984) 247-54.

Seiler, H.G., *Die Masse bei Tacitus* (Erlangen 1936).

Serbat, G., 'Les Temps du Verbe en Latin I', *REL* 53 (1975) 367-405.

Serbat, G., 'Les Temps du Verbe en Latin II', *REL* 54 (1976) 308-52.

Shatzman, I., 'The Roman General's Authority over Booty', *Historia* 21 (1972) 177-205.

Sharrock, A., *Seduction and Repetition in Ovid's Ara Amatoria 2* (Oxford 1994).

Sherwin-White, A.N., *Racial Prejudice in Imperial Rome* (Cambridge 1970).

Shochat, Y., 'Tacitus' Attitude to Galba', *Athenaeum* 59 (1981) 199-204.

Shochat, Y., 'Tacitus' Attitude to Otho', *Latomus* 40 (1981) 365-77.

Shotter, D.C.A., 'The Starting Points of Tacitus' Historical Works', *CQ* 17 (1967) 158-63.

Shotter, D.C.A., 'Verginius Rufus and Tacitus', *CQ* 17 (1967) 370-81.

Shotter, D.C.A., 'Tacitus and Antonius Primus', *LCM* 2 (1977) 23-7.

Shotter, D.C.A., *Suetonius, Lives of Galba, Otho and Vitellius* (Warminster 1993).

Simon, E., *Zu der Flavische Reliefs von der Cancelleria*, *JDAI* 75 (1960) 134-56.

Sinclair, P., 'Rhetorical Generalisations in *Annales* 1-6', *ANRW* 2.33.4 (1991) 2795-831.

Sinclair, P., *Tacitus the Sententious Historian* (University Park, Pa. 1995).

Skrjabina, E., *Siege and Survival: The Odyssey of a Leningrader* (Carbonville, Illinois 1971).

Skutsch, O., 'The Fall of the Capitol Again: Tacitus *Annals* 11.23', *JRS* 68 (1978) 93-4.

Skutsch, O., *The Annals of Quintus Ennius* (Oxford 1985).

Smith, L.V., *Between Mutiny and Obedience* (Princeton 1994).

Smith, M.S., *Cena Trimalchionis* (Oxford 1975).

Southern, P., *Domitian Tragic Tyrant* (London and New York 1997).

Spaltenstein, F., *Commentaire des Punica de Silius Italicus (livres 9 à 17)* Vol. 2 (Lausanne 1990).

Speidel, M.A. 'Roman Army Pay Scales', *JRS* 82 (1992) 87-106.

Speidel, M.P., *Eagle Bearer and Trumpeter, Rheinisches Landesmuseum* (Bonn 1967).

Speidel, M.P., 'Swimming the Danube under Hadrian's Eyes. A Feat of the Emperor's Batavian Horse Guard', *AS* 22 (1991) 277-82.

Starr, C.G., *The Influence of Sea-Power on Ancient History* (Oxford 1989).

de Ste. Croix, G.E.M., *The Class Struggle in the Ancient Greek World* (London and Ithaca 1983).

von Stekelenburg, A.V., 'Lucan and Cassius Dio as Heirs to Livy: The Speech of Julius Caesar at Placentia', *Acta Classica* 19 (1976) 43-57.

Stevenson, T.R., 'The Ideal Benefactor and the Father Analogy in Greek and Roman Thought', *CQ* 42 (1992) 421-36.

Stewart, A.F., 'To Entertain an Emperor: Sperlonga, Laokoon and Tiberius at the Dinner-Table', *JRS* 67 (1977) 76-90.

Stolte, B.H., 'Tacitus on Nero and Otho', *AS* 4 (1973) 177-90.

Strasburger, H., 'Der Einzelne und die Gemeinschaft im Denken der Griechen', *HZ* 177 (1954) 227-48.

Strocchio, R., *I Significati del Silenzio nell'Opera di Tacito* (Turin 1992).

Sullivan, D., 'Innuendo and the "Weighted Alternative" in Tacitus', *CJ* 71 (1975/6) 312-36.

Sutherland, C.H.V. 'The Concepts *Adsertor* and *Salus* as used by Vindex and Galba', *NC* 144 (1984) 29-32.

Sutherland, C.H.V., and Carson, R.A.G., (eds), *The Roman Imperial Coinage* Vol. 1 (London 1984).

Syme, R., *Roman Revolution* (Oxford 1939).

Syme, R., *Tacitus* (Oxford 1958).

Syme, R., 'The March of Mucianus', *Antichthon* 11 (1977) 78-92 = 998-1013 in Birley, A.R., (ed.), *Roman Papers III* (Oxford 1984).

Syme, R., 'Juvenal, Pliny, Tacitus', *AJP* 100 (1979) 250-78 = 1135-1157 in Birley, A.R., (ed.), *Roman Papers III* (Oxford 1984).

Syme, R., 'Biographers of the Caesars', *MH* 37 (1980) 104-28 = 1251-75 in Birley, A.R., (ed.), *Roman Papers III* (Oxford 1984).

Syndikus, H.P., *Lucans Gedicht vom Bürgerkrieg* (Munich 1958).

Takács, S.A., *Isis and Sarapis in the Roman World* (Leiden 1995).

Thomas, R.F., *Lands and Peoples in Roman Poetry: The Ethnographical Tradition, Cambridge Philological Society* Suppl. Vol. 7 (Cambridge 1982).

Thomas, R.F., 'Virgil's *Georgics* and the Art of Reference', *HSCP* 90 (1986) 171-98.

Thompson, E.A., *The Early Germans* (Oxford 1965).

Tomkins, J.P., (ed.), *Reader Response Criticism: From Formalism to Post-Structuralism* (Baltimore 1980).

Townend, G.B., 'Some Flavian Connections', *JRS* 51 (1961) 54-61.

Townend, G.B., 'Cluvius Rufus and the *Histories* of Tacitus', *AJP* 85 (1964) 337-77.

Townend, G.B., 'The Restoration of the Capitol in AD 70', *Historia* 36 (1987) 243-8.

Toynbee, J.C.M., *The Flavian Reliefs from the Palazzo della Cancelleria* (London 1957).

Toynbee, J.M.C., *Death and Burial in the Ancient World* (London 1971).

Tracy, V.A., 'Roman Dandies and Transvestites', *EMC* 20 (1976) 60-3.

Treu, M., 'M. Antonius Primus in der taciteischen Darstellung', *WJA* 3 (1948) 241-62.

Tschiedel, H.J., *Caesars Anticato: Eine Untersuchung der Testimonien und Fragmente* (Darmstadt 1981).

Tuplin, C.J., 'The False Neros of the First Century AD' 364-404 in Deroux, C., (ed.), *Studies in Latin Literature and Roman History V* (Brussels 1989).

Urban, R., *Der Bataveraufstand und die Erhebung des Iulius Classicus* (Trier 1985).

Vanderbroeck, P.J.J., *Popular Leadership and Collective Behaviour in the Late Roman Republic, 80-50 BC* (Amsterdam 1987).

Van Hooff, A.J.L., *From Autothanasia to Suicide: Self-Killing in Classical Antiquity* (London 1990).

Vasaly, A., *Representations: Images of the World in Ciceronian Oratory* (Berkeley and Los Angeles 1993).

Vaughn, P., '*Hostes Rei Publicae*: Images of the Enemy in Republican Literature', Ph.D thesis (Berkeley 1998).

Venini, P., *Vite di Galba, Otone, Vitellio* (Turin 1977).

Versnel, H.S., *Triumphus: An Inquiry into the Origin, Development and Nature of the Roman Triumph* (Leiden 1970).

Versnel, H.S., 'Destruction, *Devotio*, and Despair in a Situation of Anomy: The Mourning for Germanicus in Triple Perspective' 541-618 in *Perennitas: Studi in Onore di Angelo Brelich* (Rome 1980).

Veyne, P., *Bread and Circuses* trans. Pearce, B., (London 1992).

Vickers, M., 'Artful Crafts: The Influence of Metalwork on Athenian Painted Pottery', *JHS* 105 (1985) 108-28.

Viereck, P., and Roos, A.G., *Appiani Historia Romana* rev. Gabba, E., (Leipzig 1962).

Virlouvet, C., *Famines et émeutes à Rome des origines de la république à la mort de Néron* (Rome 1985).

Walbank, F.W., *A Historical Commentary on Polybius* Vol. 1 (Oxford 1957).

Walker, A.D., '*Enargeia* and the Spectator in Greek Historiography', *TAPA* 123 (1993) 353-77.

Wallace-Hadrill, A., 'The Emperor and his Virtues', *Historia* 30 (1981) 298-323.

Wallace-Hadrill, A., 'Galba's *Aequitas*', *NC* 141 (1981) 20-39.

Wallace-Hadrill, A., '*Civilis Princeps*: Between Citizen and King', *JRS* 72 (1982) 32-48.

Wallace-Hadrill, A., *Suetonius* (London 1983).

Walser, G., 'Das Strafgericht über die Helvetier im Jahre 69 n.Chr.', *Schweiz. Zeitschrift für Geschichte* 4 (1954) 260-70.

Walsh, P.G., 'The Literary Techniques of Livy', *RhM* 97 (1954) 97-114.

Walzer, M., *Just and Unjust Wars: A Moral Argument with Historical Illustrations* (Harmondsworth, England 1980).

Wardle, D., 'Cluvius Rufus and Suetonius', *Hermes* 120 (1992) 466-82.

Watson, A., 'Vespasian: *adsertor libertatis publicae*', *CR* 23 (1973) 127-8.

Weingärtner, D.G., *Die Ägyptenreise des Germanicus* (Bonn 1969).

Weinstock, S., *Divus Iulius* (Oxford 1971).

Welch, K., 'Caesar and his Officers in the Gallic War Commentaries' 85-110 in Welch, K., and Powell, A., (eds), *Julius Caesar as Artful Reporter: The War Commentaries as Political Instruments* (London and Swansea 1998).

Welch, K., and Powell, A., (eds), *Julius Caesar as Artful Reporter: The War Commentaries as Political Instruments* (London and Swansea 1998).

Welles, C.B., 'Fragments of Herodotus and Appian from Dura', *TAPA* 70 (1939) 203-14.

Welles, C.B., 'The Discovery of Sarapis and the Foundation of Alexandria', *Historia* 11 (1962) 271-98.

Wellesley, K., 'Three Historical Puzzles in Histories 3', *CQ* 49 (1956) 207-14.

Wellesley, K., *Tacitus: The Histories Book 3* (Sydney 1972).

Wellesley, K., 'What Happened on the Capitol in December AD 69?', *AJAH* 6 (1981) 166-90.

Wellesley, K., *The Long Year AD 69* (Bristol 1989, 2nd edition).

Welwei, K-W., 'Verdeckte Systemkritik in der Galbarede des Tacitus', *Gymnasium* 102 (1995) 353-63.

Wheeldon, M.J., 'True Stories: The Reception of Historiography in Antiquity', 33-63 in Cameron, A., (ed.), *History as Text: The Writing of Ancient History* (London 1989).

White, H., *Metahistory* (Baltimore 1973).

White, P., 'Julius Caesar in Augustan Rome', *Phoenix* 42 (1988) 334-56.

White, P., *Promised Verse: Poets in the Society of Augustan Rome* (Cambridge Mass. and London 1997).

Whitehead, D., 'Tacitus and the Loaded Alternative', *Latomus* 38 (1979) 474-95.
Wiedemann, T., 'Between Men and Beasts: Barbarians in Amminaus Marcellinus' in Moxon, I.S., Smart, J.D., and Woodman, A.J., (eds), *Past Perspectives: Studies in Greek and Roman Historical Writing* (Cambridge 1986) 189-201.
Wiedemann, T., *Emperors and Gladiators* (London 1992).
Wiedemann, T., 'Sallust's *Jugurtha*: Concord, Discord and the Digressions', *G&R* 40 (1993) 48-57.
Wilcken, U., *Urkunden der Ptolemäerzeit I* (Berlin and Leipzig 1922).
Williams, G., *Change and Decline: Roman Literature in the Early Empire* (Berkeley, Los Angeles and London 1978).
Williams, G., *Banished Voices: Readings in Ovid's Exile Poetry* (Cambridge 1994).
Williams, M.F., 'Four Mutinies: Tacitus *Annals* 1.16-30; 1.31-49 and Ammianus Marcellinus *Res Gestae* 20.4.9-20.5.7; 24.3.1-8', *Phoenix* 51 (1997) 44-74.
Williams, R., *Modern Tragedy* (London 1966).
Winterbottom, M., 'On Impulse' 313-22 in Innes, D., Hine, H., and Pelling, C.B.R., (eds), *Ethics and Rhetoric: Classical Essays for Donald Russell on his Seventy-Fifth Birthday* (Oxford 1995).
Wiseman, T.P., 'Flavians on the Capitol', *AJAH* 3 (1978) 163-78.
Wiseman, T.P., 'Practice and Theory in Ancient Historiography', *History* 66 (1981) 375-93.
Wiseman, T.P., 'Democracy and Myth: the Life and Death of Remus', *LCM* 16 (1991) 115-24.
Wiseman, T.P., *Remus: A Roman Myth* (Cambridge 1995).
Woodman, A.J., 'Theory and Practice in Ancient Historiography', *Bull. Council University Classics Depts.* 7 (1978) 6-8.
Woodman, A.J., 'Self-Imitation and the Substance of History: Tacitus *Annals* 1.61-5 and *Histories* 2.70, 5.14-15' 143-55 in Woodman, A.J., and West, D., (eds), *Creative Imitation and Latin Literature* (Cambridge 1979) = 70-85 in Woodman, A.J., *Tacitus Revisited* (Oxford 1998).
Woodman, A.J., 'From Hannibal to Hitler: The Literature of War, *University of Leeds Review* 26 (1983) 107-24 = 1-20 in Woodman, A.J., *Tacitus Revisited* (Oxford 1998).
Woodman, A.J., *Velleius Paterculus: The Caesarian and Augustan Narrative (2.94-131)* (Cambridge 1977).
Woodman, A.J., *Velleius Paterculus: The Caesarian and Augustan Narrative (2.41-93)* (Cambridge 1983).
Woodman, A.J., *Rhetoric in Classical Historiography* (London and Sydney 1988).
Woodman, A.J., 'Tacitus' Obituary of Tiberius', *CQ* 39 (1989) 197-205 = 155-67 in Woodman, A.J., *Tacitus Revisited* (Oxford 1998).
Woodman, A.J., 'Nero's Alien Capital. Tacitus as a Paradoxographer: *Annals* 15.36-37' 173-88 in Woodman, A.J., and Powell, J., (eds), *Author and Audience in Latin Literature* (Cambridge 1992) = 168-89 in Woodman, A.J., *Tacitus Revisited* (Oxford 1998).
Woodman, A.J., '*praecipuum munus annalium*: The Construction, Convention and Context of Tacitus *Annals* 3.65.1', *MH* 52 (1995) 111-26 = 86-103 in Woodman, A.J., *Tacitus Revisited* (Oxford 1998).
Woodman, A.J., and Martin, R.H., *The Annals of Tacitus Book 3* (Cambridge 1996).
Woodman, A.J., *Tacitus Revisited* (Oxford 1998).
Yavetz, Z., *Julius Caesar and his Public Image* (London 1983).
Zander, G., 'La Domus Aurea: Nuovi Problemi Architettonici', *Bollettino del Centro di Studi per la Storia dell'Architettura* 12 (1958) 47-64.
Zanker, G., '*Enargeia* in the Ancient Criticism of Poetry', *Rh. Mus.* 124 (1981) 297-311.
Zimmerman, M., 'Die *restitutio honorum* Galbas', *Historia* 44 (1995) 56-82.
Zinsser, H., *Rats, Lice and History* (New York 1934) 77-110.
Ziolkowski, A., '*Urbs Direpta*, or How the Romans Sacked Cities' 69-91 in Rich, J., and Shipley, G., (eds), *War and Society in the Roman World* (London 1993).

Glossary of Place Names

In most cases, the original Latin form of a place name is preserved, except where the modern English name is so familiar that to retain the Latin would seem alienating: e.g. Carthage rather than Carthago, Anglesey rather than Mona, and Caudine Forks rather than Furculae Caudinae.

The following places have not been conclusively identified, or have no modern equivalent: Actium, Aquileia, Bedriacum, Bovillae, Castores, Pharsalus, Philippi, Sinuessa Spa, Trasimene, Vada.

Latin / English

Albintimilium	Ventimiglia, Italy
Allia	river, 11 miles north of Rome, near Crustumerium
Ampsanctus	Le Mufite, Italy
Aricia	Ariccia, Italy
Ariminum	Rimini, Italy
Aventicum	Avenches, Switzerland
Bauli	Bacolo (near Baiae), Italy
Brundisium	Brindisi, Italy
Cannae	Canne (village in Apulia, north of Canusium), Italy
Carsulae	Casigliano, Italy
Carthago Nova	Cartagena, Spain
Clarus	Zillah, Libya
Clusium	Chiusi, Italy
Colonia Agrippinensis	Cologne, Germany
Colonia Trevirorum	Trier, Germany
Corfinium	Pelino, Italy
Cremera	River La Varca, Italy
Cremona	Cremona, Italy
Divodurum	Metz, France
Dura-Europus	Town on the Euphrates
Dyrrachium	Durazzo, Albania
Gades	Cadiz, Spain
Ganges	Ganges, India
Gomphi	Kalabaka, Greece
Hadrumentum	Sousse, Tunisia
Hispalis	Seville, Spain
Ister	River, lower part of the Danube
Lugdunum	Lyon, France
Massilia	Marseille, France
Mevania	Bevagna, Italy
Misenum	Miseno, Italy
Munda	Monda, Spain
Mytilene	Mytilini, Greece
Narnia	Narni, Italy
Numantia	Garray, near Soria, Spain

Orontes	River Asi, Syria
Paphos	Kouklia, Cyprus, Greece
Perusia	Perugia, Italy
Placentia	Piacenza, Italy
Praeneste	Palestrina, Italy
Puteoli	Pozzuoli, Italy
Sentinum	near Sassoferrato, Italy
Sinope	Sinop, Turkey
Spelunca	Sperlonga, Italy
Ticinum	Pavia, Italy
Trebia	Trebbia, river flowing north into the Po.
Urvinum	Urbino, Italy (but Wellesley proposes Collemancio, Italy)
Vergellus	Branch of the River Ofanto, Italy
Vetera	Xanten, Germany
Vicetia	Vicenza, Italy
Vocetius	Botzberg, Germany

English / Latin

Antioch	Antiochia
Appennines	Appennini
Carmel	Carmelus
Caudine Forks	Furculae Caudinae
Pomptine Marshes	Paludes Pomptinae
Sicily	Sicilia

Index Locorum

Numbers in bold refer to the pages and notes of this book.

General Index

120, 125, 127-9, 143, 147-9, 161, 163-5,
190n2, 203n1, 206n39
Tiberius, emperor 103, 104, 105, 119,
122, 136, 140, 143, 158, 181n8,
183n32, 192n25, 195n63, 196n71
Titus, emperor 102, 128, 130, 133-4,
136-46, 149, 151
Trajan, emperor 11, 97, 129, 169
treachery 30, 49, 52, 53, 60, 73, 87, 119,
120, 127, 128, 131, 139, 168, 185n59,
203n6
trees 44, 118, 131-2, 155, 204n15
tyrants 10, 19, 56, 74, 76, 96-8, 101, 102,
103, 105, 108, 111, 112, 122, 123, 132,
140, 141, 191n14, 191n16, 192n25,
195n55, 197n2, 198n8, 206n42

Verginius Rufus, Lucius 116, 157
Vespasian, emperor 35, 49, 50, 51, 52, 55,
56, 57, 58, 59, 60, 69, 71, 85-7, 95, 102,
104, 105, 107, 109, 115, 119, 122,
127-46, 147, 149, 150, 151, 152, 155,

157, 161, 163, 164, 165, 169
Virgil 2, 33, 37, 38, 54-5, 63, 67, 68, 69,
79, 81, 84, 92, 123-4, 196n71, 197n82
Vitellius, emperor 23, 35, 37, 39, 40, 41,
43, 44, 45, 46, 47, 48, 49, 51, 52, 53, 55,
56, 57, 58, 60, 65, 67, 68, 70, 82, 87,
95-125, 145, 147, 149, 150, 152, 155,
156, 169
vomiting 99, 101-3

Walter of Châtillon 68
war (just) 1, 2, 87, 95, 171n3
weapons 21, 27-8, 33, 43-4, 46, 56, 62, 63,
67, 68, 69, 77, 78, 79, 80, 88, 92, 111,
121, 178n11, 182n27, 183n37, 186n67,
187n80, 196n72
wine, *see* alcohol
women 35, 52, 55, 63, 66, 67, 81, 85, 88,
91, 92, 93, 104, 118, 136, 140, 144, 151,
179n36, 207n51, 208n62, 210n22
wrestling 50, 115, 201n48